D1582740

Efficient Organizational Design

Efficient Organizational Design

Balancing Incentives and Power

Marco Weiss

First published 2007 by
PALGRAVE MACMILLAN
Houndmills, Basingstoke, Hampshire RG21 6XS and
175 Fifth Avenue, New York, N.Y. 10010
Companies and representatives throughout the world.

PALGRAVE MACMILLAN is the global academic imprint of the Palgrave
Macmillan division of St. Martin's Press, LLC and of Palgrave Macmillan Ltd.
Macmillan® is a registered trademark in the United States, United Kingdom
and other countries. Palgrave is a registered trademark in the European
Union and other countries.

ISBN-13: 978–0–230–51552–9
ISBN-10: 0–230–51552–5

This book is printed on paper suitable for recycling and made from fully
managed and sustained forest sources.

A catalogue record for this book is available from the British Library.

Library of Congress Cataloging-in-Publication Data
Weiss, Marco, 1972–
     Efficient organizational design : balancing incentives and
power/Marco Weiss.
        p.cm.
     Originally presented as the author's thesis (doctoral) – Universität Frankfurt
am Main.
     Includes bibliographical references and index.
     ISBN-13: 978–0–230–51552–9 (cloth)
     ISBN-10: 0–230–51552–5 (cloth)
     1. Organizational effectiveness. 2. Organizational sociology. 3. Strategic
planning. 4. Organization – Case studies. I. Title.
HD58.9. W455 2007
302.3'5—dc22   2006047186

10 9 8 7 6 5 4 3 2 1
16 15 14 13 12 11 10 09 08 07

Printed and bound in Great Britain by
Antony Rowe Ltd, Chippenham and Eastbourne

Contents

List of Figures   ix

List of Tables   x

Foreword by Reinhard H. Schmidt   xi

Preface   xv

1 **Introduction**   1
  1.1 Motivation   1
  1.2 Objectives   5
  1.3 Methodology   7
  1.4 Outline   11

PART I THEORY OF ORGANIZATIONAL DESIGN

2 **Foundations of Organizational Design**   17
  2.1 Theories of the firm   17
      The history of firms   18
      The existence of firms   20
      The boundaries of firms – transaction
      cost theory   22
      The structure of firms – agency theory   25
      The governance of firms – incomplete
      contract theory   27
      The firm as a knowledge-creating entity   30
      The firm as a system   33
  2.2 Configuration of systems   36
      Elements and systems   37
      Path dependencies   42
      Consistent configurations – application
      of the theory   46
  2.3 Value creation of organizational design   48
      Defining value   48
      Measuring value   50

2.4 Changes in the business environment 53
Technological progress 53
Regulation and liberalization 56
Standard setting 58
The financial system 61
2.5 The inadequacy of traditional theories of the firm 63

3 **Building Blocks of Organizational Design** 72
3.1 The strategy of the organization 72
The purpose of the organization 74
The market-based perspective 76
The resource-based perspective 80
The accounting-based perspective 85
Construction and deconstruction of the value chain 86
3.2 The boundaries of the organization 89
Setting the boundaries 90
Shifting the boundaries 95
Blurring the boundaries 99
3.3 The internal structure of the organization 103
Information and knowledge 105
Power and authority 110
Incentives and motivation 118
Co-ordination and co-operation 127
3.4 The governance of the organization 134
Specific investments, stakeholders and ownership 136
The different constituencies 139
Governance mechanisms 145
Organizational forms 151

4 **Designing Efficient Organizations** 164
4.1 Synthesis of the building blocks – designing for fit 164
Taking stock 165
Complementarities between the building blocks 167
Configuration of business models 174
4.2 Adaption to the environment – designing for change 178
Constant change as a design feature 179
Staying at the peak – continuous adjustments 182
Switching peaks – radical adjustments 187
4.3 Efficient organizational design 192

PART II   PRACTICE OF ORGANIZATIONAL DESIGN

5   **The European Securities Transaction Industry**   **197**
   5.1   Introduction   197
   5.2   Three concepts for evaluation   202
   5.3   The securities transaction industry   204
       Economies of the securities transaction
       value chain   204
       Vertical interdependencies in the value chain   207
       Regulation   208
   5.4   Strategic conduct – the provider's action set   209
       Boundary decisions   210
       Communication standards and accessibility   211
       Ownership structure and governance   214
       Interdependencies in the action set   215
   5.5   Proposals for an efficient organizational design   218
       System 1 – Regulated monopoly   218
       System 2 – Competitive fragmentation   220
       System 3 – Contestable monopolies   222
   5.6   Comparative organizational analysis   224

6   **The German Co-operative Banking Group**   **233**
   6.1   Introduction   233
   6.2   Strategy and internal structure   238
       Deutsche Bank   238
       The co-operative banking group   240
   6.3   Corporate governance   243
       Deutsche Bank   243
       The co-operative banking group   244
   6.4   Comparative organizational analysis   246
       The narrow view of efficiency   246
       Differences in the designs   247
       Complementarities between the
       building blocks   249
       The broader view of efficiency   250

7   **Open-source Projects**   **254**
   7.1   Introduction   254

7.2	The software industry	261
	The economics and technology of software production	262
	What is open-source software?	264
	Paradigms of innovation	265
7.3	The system of proprietary software	267
	Organizational design of proprietary source firms	267
	Consistency and shortcomings	270
7.4	The system of open-source software	272
	Organizational design of open-source projects	273
	Consistency and the open-source ecosystem	278
7.5	Comparative organizational analysis	282
	Comparison of the organizational designs	282
	Efficient organizational design	287
8	**Conclusion**	**293**
Bibliography		296
Index		317

List of Figures

2.1	Lattice with join and meet	39
2.2	Supermodular function leading to bimodal 'landscape'	40
2.3	Rugged landscape	44
3.1	The four main themes of internal organization	104
4.1	Consistency as the capstone of organizational design	167
5.1	Regulated monopoly	219
5.2	Competitive fragmentation	221
5.3	Contestable monopolies	223
7.1	The web of open source	280

List of Tables

4.1	Important organizational design parameters	166
5.1	Comparison of the three idealized TCS systems	228
6.1	Key facts and figures for the banking groups	236
6.2	Systemic features of the two banking groups	251
7.1	Market share of different web browsers	256
7.2	Synopsis of the designs of open and proprietary sources	283

Foreword

From its beginnings, academic research in economics, and even more so that in management or business administration, has aspired to be two things at the same time: academically respectable and practically relevant for managers or economic policy-makers. But one should not overlook the difficulty of aspiring towards two goals at the same time. There can be a dilemma. Academic rigour can prevail at the expense of practical relevance, and vice versa. For academics, there has been increasing pressure in recent years to produce academically respectable work, and therefore many of them give a higher priority to the requirements of the academic world over the practical one.

How serious is this dilemma, and where is it relevant? In almost any subfield of economics and business administration, tremendous progress has been achieved in recent decades. However, it is not always balanced. In some, only academic rigour and the depth of insight have increased, and in others research output has become more useful for practitioners but is not very interesting from an intellectual standpoint. Fortunately, there are also some areas where the dilemma simply does not exist. Finance, the field with which I am most familiar, is one example. All those areas where advances have occurred along both dimensions at the same time share two features. First, formalism and mathematics are important and appropriate not only from an academic perspective but also for practitioners. Second, the managers for whom this kind of academic research is relevant typically have a functional specialization; they may be chief financial officers (CFOs) or chief controllers, but not general managers.

General management functions have for a long time not benefited from academic research. Strategy, organizational design and general business policy are among areas long neglected by serious scholars. Here the dilemma described above is seen clearly. This statement presupposes that there is a considerable number of highly interesting academic developments. They exist, and they are also relevant for general managers. But, so far, the diverse intellectual contributions are not only largely unrelated to each other, but also, more importantly, relatively little has been done to synthesize them in a way that demonstrates their relevance for general managers. This is where this book by Dr Marco Weiss makes a much needed and highly innovative contribution to the literature.

What do general managers do? Their most important function is to make fundamental decisions that shape the future of the corporations for which they are responsible. They decide on strategies; they detect and then foster the relative strengths or core competencies of their corporations; they design the organizational architecture; they determine which lines of business to expand, contract, and even spin off; in short, they determine and alter the boundaries of their firms. And finally, to the extent that they are able, they shape the governance structures to which they and the other managers are subject. If they are aware of Dr Weiss's argument in this book, they understand that strategy, organizational design, the firm's boundaries and its governance structures are not four unrelated areas of concern. They are closely related to each other or, to use the terminology of this book, they are a single system – composed of elements that mutually support each other and should be shaped accordingly. They should be parts of a consistent system.

How do general managers make fundamental decisions that they hope will turn corporations into consistent systems and successful actors in a number of relevant markets? It would be naïve to assume that they ask their own strategy or corporate development department or outside consultants to write a blueprint for their corporation's development, look at the blueprint, and finally adopt it. Instead, fundamental decisions are the outcome of a complicated process of creative thinking and debate. Real business leaders take time to think on their own, and then spend time discussing the issues with others – their advisers, their own staff and, most importantly, their peers in top management groups – before making their decision. But what concepts are required and useful in thinking, communicating and arguing with others? Dr Weiss's book presents these concepts and, much to the pleasure of academic economists, demonstrates convincingly how much they owe to recent academic developments in economics.

General managers need concepts for their most important tasks, but because of the complexity of the real-life problems they have to solve, they need more than one concept – such as the narrowly defined concept one typically finds in a single academic article. They need to be eclectic; and that is why this book is also eclectic. It presents, discusses and evaluates different concepts from the literature on strategy, theories of the firm, organizational design and governance. But these different concepts are not merely arrayed in the sense of a box of tools, but rather as a set of concepts that can be synthesized for thinking, arguing and deciding, so the second feature of Dr Weiss's book is that it is synthetic: it shows how different economic concepts can be used together to build good, successful organizations.

Much like an architect, a general manager has to be creative, using different building blocks and different kinds of materials, and making sure that what he or she constructs forms a consistent whole. A building in which the elements are not compatible with each other cannot be a good building, and, of course, what makes a good building depends to a large extent on the function the building is supposed to fulfil. The same considerations apply to those who want to build a successful corporation.

By writing a book that does not conform to the dominant academic style, Dr Weiss has put himself into the shoes of his potential readers. The book is eclectic, as general managers need to be, and it is not analytical (which means, in a literal sense, aiming at cutting a whole into separate parts), but rather focuses on synthesis, as general managers need to do in their work. That makes this book not only fascinating but also very useful.

For academically orientated readers, and particularly those with a background and an interest in economics, the book also provides important positive messages. One is that it demonstrates clearly the strength and relevance of recent economic theories. The second message is that, in the field of strategy and management as a research area, an eclectic-synthetic approach is both appropriate and promising. Academics also need to understand that concepts are more than just theory: they are ways of thinking and building blocks in reality as well as merely theoretical constructions. They can learn from his book that synthesis or construction is also a task worth the effort and useful not only to guide their actions but also for understanding real-world phenomena such as complex organizations. Finally, professional academic economists will be pleased to learn that, even if they address 'soft' topics such as strategy and organizational design in a practically relevant manner, they need not leave the terrain entirely to psychologists, social scientists and practitioners. They have a contribution to make.

So there are quite a number of claims in this book; mainly claims regarding the intellectual and practical relevance of certain economic theories, and of a specific way of using these theories. How can such claims be supported? Evidently, it is impossible to provide a mathematical proof of relevance. The proof of the proverbial pudding is in its eating. This is why the book is divided into two parts. The first part presents the building blocks and the notion of complementarity and consistency – or, to use another term, a systemic view of organizations – and in the second part, Dr Weiss presents three case studies showing how the concepts can fruitfully be applied. The case studies analyse specific organizational forms of economic activity that are puzzles to conventional economic analysis in the sense that it is not easy to understand why they exist, how they function, and why they are surprisingly successful. In answering these questions in the three case studies, Dr Weiss performs an operation that is in a certain sense the reverse of construction: it is a reconstruction of unconventional business models.

I am sure that this book's outstanding contribution to economic and organizational studies will find a large number of readers for whom it is as much of an eye-opener as it was for me.

REINHARD H. SCHMIDT

Professor Reinhard H. Schmidt holds the Wilhelm Merton Chair for International Banking and Finance at Johann Wolfgang Goethe-University in Frankfurt. He is one of the leading researchers in the field of comparative analysis of financial systems and has published together with some colleagues from Frankfurt University a book on the German financial system. In addition, Professor Schmidt has published extensively in the areas of corporate governance and microfinance. He is a member of the European Shadow Financial Regulatory Committee.

Preface

Designing organizations for efficiency is a challenging task. It involves combining the different building blocks such as strategy and structure, and the boundaries and governance of organizations in a consistent manner. This book provides comprehensive guidelines on how organizations should be designed to maximize the value they create, and explores the building blocks and numerous parameters of organizational design in detail. Two of the most important parameters in any organizational design are the way that incentives are set and the way that power is distributed in organizations. Constituencies of organizations invest to generate value. However, they will do so only if they can be sure that they also hold the power to appropriate that value in the future. Otherwise, incentives for value creation are weakened, and the efficiency of the organizational design is impaired. Balancing incentives for and the power of all constituencies involved in organizations therefore becomes mandatory to achieve efficiency.

Combining the ideas of systems theory with the methodology of comparative organizational analysis, this book first develops a theoretical framework for designing organizations for efficiency, then subsequently applies this framework in three case studies of innovative organizational designs. A case study of the European securities transaction industry reveals how imbalances in the provision of incentives and the assignment of power can lead to inefficiencies in a whole industry. A case study of the German co-operative banking group shows how the deliberate weakening of power at the top of an organization can improve incentives for all constituencies throughout the organization. A case study of open source communities provides insights into the way that an innovative design can take on huge and successful firms entrenched by network effects or economies of scale and scope. In all three settings, power and incentives, as well as other important parameters of organizational design, have to be configured consistently for value creation.

This book has been accepted as a Ph.D. thesis at the Faculty of Economics and Business Administration of the Johann Wolfgang Goethe-University in Frankfurt. My most sincere thanks are due to Reinhard H. Schmidt for his support and professional advice while I was writing the book. I am grateful to him for providing ample freedom for research and encouragement. I also thank Uwe Walz for co-assessing the dissertation.

Furthermore, I would like to thank all my colleagues and students at the Wilhelm Merton Chair and the Department of Finance at the Goethe-University Frankfurt for providing an inspiring research environment. I am especially indebted to Frank Greifenstein, Christian Laux, Samuel Lee, Jens Massmann, Marion Schnellrieder, Baris Serifsoy, and Marcel Tyrell for listening to my opinions and sharing their ideas. In addition, I thank Jacob de Smit for discussions during our time at the European Business School.

The application of the theoretical ideas about organizational design in the form of case studies in the second part of this book has benefited from the comments and advice of numerous people:

• The comparative analysis of the European securities transaction industry is based on joint work with Baris Serifsoy (see Serifsoy and Weiss, 2007). I am grateful to him for sharing the work as well as the fun we had at several conferences. I appreciate discussions with Stefan Mai and Andreas Wolf of the Deutsche Börse Group. Comments from Dirk Baur, Charles M. Kahn, Alistair Milne and Ingo Walter, as well as from participants at the conference on 'Clearing and Settlement of Financial Markets: Europe and Beyond' at the Cass Business School in London, are gratefully acknowledged.
• The ideas behind the case study of co-operative banking have been presented at the xvth International Conference of Co-operative Economy at the Westfälische Wilhelms-University Münster. The comments of the participants at this forum and discussions with Mathias Beers and Valentin Marinov are greatly appreciated. I also thank Theresia Theurl and Eric C. Meyer for including the presentation in the conference proceedings (see Weiss, 2005).
• For discussions of the phenomenon of open source I am indebted to Justin P. Johnson, Josh Lerner, Jens Prüfer, Urs Schweizer, and participants of the 4th GEABA Symposium on the Economic Analysis of the Firm, at the Goethe-University Frankfurt. Sincere thanks are due in particular to Samuel Lee and Nina Moisa for co-authoring a paper on open source.

Valuable comments on the manuscript by Nicolai J. Foss and Nandish Patel are gratefully acknowledged. I would like to express my thanks also to Sigrid Dexheimer and Philomena Whelan for proof-reading, and to Mirabelle Boateng, Jacky Kippenberger, and the staff of Palgrave Macmillan for editing and publishing the book. Keith Povey and Elaine Towns did an excellent job editing and improving the final typescript.

Finally, I reserve my greatest thanks to Anne Hofer for her enduring patience, to my grandmother Lucia, and to my parents, Lieselotte and Heinz-Werner, for always having faith in me. It is to them that I dedicate this book.

MARCO WEISS

1
Introduction

1.1 Motivation

Organizational design

This book is about organizational design. How economic activities are designed has deep implications for the efficiency with which organizations operate and the amount of value they create. The 'wrong' organizational design leads to dysfunctional decisions made by the constituencies within the organizations that carry out the economic activity. Value is either destroyed or the potential for the creation of value is not fully exploited. The goal of this book is to show how 'good' organizational design is the basis for the full realization of potential for creating and distributing value.

One of the most widely studied organizational arrangements in economics is the firm. Firms need a consistent organizational design to be successful and profitable.[1] The main building blocks of any organizational design are the firm's strategy that establishes the purpose of the firm; the firm's boundaries that reflect the scope of its business opportunities; the firm's internal structures that determine how the strategy translates into success or failure; and the firm's governance that ultimately distributes any success or failure to the firm's constituencies. These building blocks and the relevant economies within and between them need also to be taken into account by organizational arrangements other than the firm.

How good the organizational design is can be evaluated by its efficiency: in the case of a firm – which is probably the best-understood organizational design because it has been the subject of many years of research – the predominant way to measure efficiency prescribed by economists is through the maximization of shareholder value measured by market capitalization. However, many firms do not adhere to the basics of good organizational design and, instead, pursue a strategy that is not supported by the internal structure, the available technology or the size and scope of the firm. Inefficiencies and the creation of value below potential – or even an outright destruction of value – are the result. Corrections for such a misalignment in the organizational design occur eventually – albeit often through the dismantling of firms that cannot survive when in competition with better-designed organizations. In the meantime, either value is destroyed or the potential for value creation is not fully exploited. One of the most visible and spectacular corrections occurred during the 1980s hostile takeover wave in the USA. With such redesigns, efficiency is usually enhanced via many changes in the organizational design. During the restructuring of the 1980s this meant a lot of downsizing or splitting up of former corporate empires, such as RJR Nabisco.[2] By focusing the strategy on the core competencies of the firm, by adjusting the boundaries through the sale of many unrelated businesses, and by high-powering the incentive structure through the use of financial instruments such as debt and private equity, efficiency was tremendously enhanced, and value and profit generated.

In other organizational designs, the profit motive is not that dominant: much of the economic activity at the time of writing is carried out not by firms but by organizations that are not primarily interested in the maximization of market capitalization. Non-profit organizations or co-operatives do not share such a narrow focus on shareholder value but are interested in the broad maximization of their members' interests or the welfare of their beneficiaries. Regulatory agencies or rules set up by governments, as a second example, have a direct effect on the possibilities of other firms creating value. The right boundaries of regulation and the incentive structure of people making regulatory decisions directly affect the well-being and growth opportunities of both firms and society alike. The wrong regulatory regime, or too much of it, stifles innovation and does not allow for the full exploitation of value creation and efficiency. Private or public universities, as another example, are interested in the discovery of new knowledge, and their objective is often to provide a challenging work and study place for their various constituencies to advance the scientific frontier. In such environments, incentives are not provided through the use of extrinsic elements, such as direct monetary rewards, although they can be the result of the basic research, especially in the science of nature. Also, if the researchers' decision-making power in these organizational arrangements is too limited this will not allow them to exploit fully the potential for value creation: once again, efficiency is impaired if the wrong organizational design is implemented.

This book analyses parameters of organizational design and synthesizes these elements into distinct patterns of successful configurations that make up an organizational design. It is shown that only certain distinct patterns of configurations of key elements of organizational design lead to success for the whole organizational system. Firms and non-profit organizations alike have to choose through their strategy which of these distinct configurations to adopt. They have to take into account their established organizational and governance structures as well as their positions and resources. And, finally, they have to complement these existing design elements with new structures, positions and resources where necessary to exploit the full value generation potential.

Incentives and power

The two major themes of this book are incentives and power: power that the constituencies in the organizational design can and will wield to their advantage. Such power manifests itself in incentives to make decisions that affect oneself, other related parties within the organization, and the welfare of the whole society in which any organization is embedded. Using power and shaping incentives frequently alters the rent or the utility accruing to a particular person or group. Power and economic rents are the flipside of the same coin: economic rents can be gained from a position of power and, if economic rents exist, the distribution of power matters.

In economics, especially in the theory of the firm, the firm is a repository of power and a means of achieving rents above the market rate. For example, the firm's boundaries are defined by the power and authority relationship that is different from the simple exit mechanism of competitive markets. But power does not only rest in firms. Depending on their structure, markets also convey power, as the literature on industrial organization points out. In oligopolistic or monopolistic market settings, economic rents can be earned by the firm. The distribution of these rents among the multiple stakeholders of the firm, however, is usually not of interest in this literature.

Two scenarios of how power affects the distribution of economic rents are possible. First, by using power, the own share of economic rents can be increased, to the detriment of the share of others. In this zero-sum case, a redistribution of rents does not alter overall welfare and efficiency, provided both parties – the one that gains and the other that loses – value that share equally. Second, by using the power, additional rents can be generated that can be distributed among the agents taking part in the venture, thereby increasing total welfare and efficiency. But it could also be the case that the sum of all economic rents is diminished by the use of power, leaving all agents worse off.

The expectation of how power will be used in the future as uncertainty unfolds, and of how the expected share of the total value that is generated will be changed, affects decisions today. Investment decisions are subject to the expected share of the value generated in the future. This value is, however, subject to the decisions of many agents. The wise use of this decision-making power and the consideration of possible externalities on the other parties, and on the welfare in general, determine the relative efficiency of the organizational design. Clearly, any organizational arrangement that would lead to an outcome where these investment decisions generate the value that equals the social maximum would be preferable to any other. But this is not always possible, because of the complicated web of expectations about the expected value of one's own share of the total.

The interesting questions that arise are how such power can consciously be gained by, or assigned to, a particular agent or constituency, and how this power can be used to the advantage or the detriment of the individual agent, other constituencies in the organization or society at large: power has different sources and shapes. It can arise from a unique resource or market position that gives its owner incentives from a monopoly position. It can also be assigned by means of a hierarchical structure based on contractual arrangements. The building of coalitions composed of many individual agents can alter the balance of power and affect incentives as well as technological advances often do – to mention just a few factors affecting incentives and power of individuals. The interplay of markets on the outside and, possibly, on the inside of the organization is a crucial determinant of the structure of incentives and power of any organization. How this interplay works will be shown in the course of this book.

Balancing incentives and power in organizations

The balancing of the two themes of incentives and power in an efficient organizational design is the motivation behind this book. The way in which incentives and power are woven into the nexus of specific investments in the organizational design determines how efficiently, and how smoothly, the organization will work. Successful and efficient organizational designs create economic rents for the constituencies participating in them. The incentives for rent generation, however, cannot be seen as independent of the distribution of these economic rents: the incentives to generate the total wealth that leads to maximum social efficiency and welfare for the organization are determined by the private benefits every stakeholder can extract from this pool. This distribution in turn is determined by the relative power every stakeholder has *vis-à-vis* the other parties.[3] Strategic interaction among stakeholders[4] and the use of the surrounding markets help to influence the distribution of power between different stakeholders, thereby also affecting indirectly the distribution of economic rents and the division of total welfare.

Example 1.1 With the beginning of industrialization, it was the so-called Luddites who engaged in a struggle against technological progress as the spinning and weaving industry was transformed by the use of mechanical spinning wheels. In this process of automatization, people working in the industry lost their jobs and often their livelihood, but overall welfare was enhanced through the innovation. The reaction of the Luddites – outright demolition of the new factories, for example – is not usually seen in its radical form today, where many industries have been transformed by globalization and competition from abroad. At the start of the twenty-first century creative destruction is still functioning, and thousands of workers lose their jobs and suffer a steep depreciation in the value of their skills as opportunities for value creation shift.

In a more dynamic perspective, with the environment often changing rapidly, financial capital is increasingly being replaced by human capital as the single most important resource for many organizations. Human capital that is specific to a particular relationship or organization becomes more important, and ultimately – as financial capital becomes more and more abundant[5] – becomes the major source of real and sustainable competitive advantage. This movement demands changes: changes in the way that organizations are structured, changes in the strategies they follow and that industries exhibit, and changes that cut deeply into the way society functions.

Good organizational design can help with this transition in a dynamic setting requiring design changes. Design changes that have to be supported by the various constituencies through incentives stimulating their investment decisions and through the distribution of the rewards, thereby changing the relative power each person can hold.

1.2 Objectives

Organizational design is a complex system. If design matters, there is more to the efficient performance of an economic activity than the neoclassical recipe of taking some inputs, manipulating them in some way, and getting the output.[6] When design matters, institutions matter.[7] And when design matters, the economics between the various design parameters also matter. Institutions and the economics between them shape the relative power that the constituencies in the organization are able to acquire and use. The expectation of the use of power, through many investment decisions, affects the overall economic efficiency of the whole organizational arrangement.

Although the organizational form primarily under investigation throughout this book is the firm in the traditional sense of economics, the development of a general framework enabling an analysis of new organizational arrangements that do not look like a 'firm' any longer is the main objective of this book. Such a general framework can be used to give meaningful advice about designing organizations, and the book is devoted to this task, looking in detail at the various building blocks any theory of organizational design has to take into consideration. In this sense, the theory presented here is prescriptive in nature: anyone taking part in any organization can use the insights from the book to create organizations that are designed more efficiently.

Taking the theme of power as a starting point, it can be noted that power in organizational design:

- can be conveyed on a macro basis through the governance of the organization and its surrounding markets;
- can be acquired through settings on a micro basis in the internal structure;
- can be influenced by the boundary decisions and the scope of the organization; and
- can be the basis for sustainable economic rents identified by the strategic direction the organization has chosen.

These four building blocks are interconnected, and any value-creating organizational design has to take these interdependencies into account. The economics within and between these building blocks, as well as their fit, is the subject of this book. Of special concern here is the relationship between power, investment incentives and the efficiency of the resulting organizational design.

Within these four building blocks of organizational design lie other, more pronounced, questions:

- Where does the value-creating potential for the organizational arrangement come from? What is the source of the competitive advantage? Why is the organization in business at all; what is its *raison d'être?*

- What are the critical resources and economics for a sustainable competitive advantage? What is the role of the markets in which the organization operates?
- What is the optimal scope of the organization? Which tasks should it perform and which should it abstain from?
- How distinct should the boundary of the organization be? How open should it remain for new arrangements?
- Which internal structures, and which organizational processes, support the resources and positions responsible for the creation of value?
- Who should have decision rights, on which parameters and in what circumstances?
- How detailed should the measurement of success be? How complex should *ex-ante* distribution rules for value be?
- Which legal structure fits the purpose of the organization best? What is the stance of the organization regarding other organizations performing related activities? What is the stance of the organization *vis-à-vis* its own constituencies?

This book answers these questions by considering the overall issue of what constitutes good organizational design. A dynamic perspective considers how changes in business conditions affect the best design out of many organizational blueprints, and whether some designs perform better than others in the circumstances of the surrounding environment.

1.3 Methodology

There are four crucial aspects to the methodology used in this book describing and evaluating different organizational arrangements. The book relies on the thoughts generated by systems theory and by comparative organizational analysis. It is eclectic in nature, combining different strands of literature in distinct research areas, and makes extensive use of longer case studies in the part on the practice of organizational design, with shorter examples in the theoretical part where appropriate.

Systems theory

Without going into too much detail – a description of the rationale behind systems theory is presented in Section 2.2 – any organizational design can be described as a complex system of various distinct parameters and subsystems that are configured in a certain way. This book departs from the well-established path that is applied in most of the natural and social sciences. In these academic fields, investigation into certain natural phenomena is analytical. *Ana-lysis* – that is, the dissolving of the phenomenon under investigation into ever smaller, and therefore more manageable, pieces – is the primary method applied in these sciences. It allows for deeper insights whenever discrete and largely independent modules exist.

The main methodology in engineering science is not analytical in nature but focuses on the assembly of many smaller parts into a new phenomenon with its own characteristics. Whenever design and architecture matter, then *syn-thesis* – that is, the putting together of various pieces – is needed to understand the coherent whole. Instead of focusing on one small aspect, this approach takes into account the different constituting elements only in so far as they are part of the bigger picture.[8]

Economic theory often takes the first route of dissecting a piece of evidence analytically into smaller problems that can be 'solved'. Elaborate models by themselves explain only a small portion of the whole, and the notion of '*ceteris paribus*' is often applied to such an analysis. The second route, that of synthesis, is largely disregarded. This bias in the methodological approach can, for example, be seen in the work of one of the most distinguished writers on the nature of the firm – Nobel Laureate Ronald H. Coase – whose aim was 'to construct a theory which will enable us to *analyze* the determinants of the institutional structure of production … [and] how the functions which are performed by firms are divided up among them'.[9]

Most scholars in economics follow Coase by modelling only certain aspects of the overall phenomenon – for example, by focusing on the relationship of a principal and an agent to describe small details based on asymmetries in information distribution to explain a specific organizational outcome. Such models concentrate on few aspects, and the solutions proposed by these models might not hold up when faced with the complexity seen in practice.[10] Adding more and different models to describe other aspects might illuminate the research object from different angles. The analytical approach does not seem feasible whenever the danger exists that crucial aspects of the whole will be neglected by the assumption that all other things remain equal.

This book, departing from the mainly analytical methodology of economics, investigates organizational design not by modelling a certain aspect or facet in the finest possible detail, but rather by using existing models and frameworks where appropriate in order to better understand how organizational design is synthesized from different building blocks.

The focus of the book is on the design of the whole system and how this design fares when evaluated against the purpose for which it was set up.

Comparative organizational analysis

A further question arises: what do we do with such systems synthesized from various elements? Or, put differently; if there is a choice among design modules that can be combined in many ways, is there a superior combination leading to an overall design that is 'better' than all other possible combinations? By comparing different designs with each other, this question can be answered. One of the first researchers to use the methodology of comparative organizational analysis for different institutions was Masahiko Aoki. Aoki (1995) analyses, in the context of trade theory, the emergence of different organizational conventions in different economies and how these differences can be of value. Aoki (2001) extends this approach using game theory to show 'the complexity and diversity of overall institutional arrangements across the economies as an instance of multiple equilibria'.[11] He employs a dynamic perspective to understand 'the mechanism of institutional evolution/change in a framework consistent with an equilibrium view of institutions'.[12] These 'multiple equilibria' that form endogenously can then be compared and evaluated for their relative efficiency.

The comparison usually begins with an analysis of the design under investigation and a description of its individual components. Which combinations of these components are feasible for the synthesis of the overall design is the next step of the investigation.[13] Very often these investigations lead to two or more distinct patterns and configurations for the overall design, with a specific combination of a subset of components usually observed together. In economics and business, such distinct patterns of configurations lead to consistent organizational designs or feasible and success-promising business models.

Example 1.2 The method labelled in economics as comparative organizational analysis is not specific to economics. Use is also made of this method in the technical world. Using a process of reverse engineering, a competitor's product, such as a car or a household appliance, is disassembled into its various components and a careful investigation of the materials used or the functioning of the item can then be undertaken. The aim of this procedure is to understand how the individual components work together, and thereby to learn how the designed product achieves its performance. By comparing two different designs it becomes possible to discern which one is better.

The third step undertaken in a comparative organizational analysis is the comparison of the distinct overall designs. Here, the way in which whole systems achieve their performance is under investigation. If no absolute benchmark exists against which this performance can be measured, the use of relative measurement – the direct comparison of two or more distinct design patterns – is a good way to evaluate which design is better.

Eclecticism and redundancy

Another methodology uncommon to the way mainstream economics usually argues, is a presentation of the argument that is, first, eclectic in so far as it chooses selectively among many models and frameworks and, second, is redundant in so far as some themes occur repeatedly throughout the book.

By sacrificing the clarity of a specific and narrowly focused analytical model for the fog of the complex setting that makes up organizational design, the investigation has necessarily to be eclectic in nature. The building blocks of organizational design can be explained through a myriad of competing, and sometimes contradicting, models. Not all aspects can be explained here, and the temptation to advance ever further with analytical methodology can be great. This book must be eclectic in nature to avoid losing the whole wood while focusing on a single tree. By being eclectic, valuable insights can be gained that otherwise would be lost because of the highly modularized perspective following the activity of 'ana-lyzing'.[14]

Example 1.3   A phenomenon from reality can be described by many different models. In geography, maps with different scales and different objects shown on them allow the user to get a pretty good view of how the earth looks in reality. Choosing the right model or map, however, is a necessity, since a map in too large a scale will cause a person hiking in the mountains to get lost, and a map with too small a scale will not take a person driving from one city to another via the best route. An eclectic approach – choosing from potentially overlapping models which one best serves the purpose – is necessary.

At the same time as some aspects are left out by this eclecticism, redundancies will occur. When analysing a certain organizational design it might be necessary to repeat a certain feature frequently, since it serves many purposes in the overall system. A traditional book has to present items sequentially, one building block after another. This is not a problem as long as enough modularity exists between them. If interdependencies between elements of different modules exist, the repetition of the main characteristics of this complementary relationship must be appropriate even if it leads to redundancy in the presentation.

The use of case studies and examples

To accomplish both objectives in this book – a careful analysis of the different features as well as a good synthesis of these findings to a consistent organizational design – case studies and broad frameworks are the appropriate methodology rather than the modelling of ever-finer details.[15] Short examples are used throughout the text to highlight the practical relevance of the theoretical aspects analysed. The importance of models and frameworks, and the relationship between them, can be highlighted with these examples.

The second part of the book presents three case studies to show how the reasoning explained in the first part can be used to gain meaningful insights into unconventional organizational designs. Again, the methodology of making extensive use of case studies is at odds with mainstream economics. As Michael Porter explains: 'Academic journals have traditionally not accepted or encouraged the deep examination of case studies, but the nature of strategy requires it. The greater use of case studies in both books and articles will be necessary for real progress at this stage.'[16] This argument holds not only for the field of strategic management, which is only one of several building blocks, but is even more necessary when explaining a still more complex phenomenon – the organizational design as a whole.

1.4 Outline

This book follows the structured approach prescribed by the method of comparative organizational analysis. In the first part of the book, the theory of organizational design and the various building blocks are described. Section 2.1 briefly recounts the different branches of the economic theory of the firm. How the characteristics of different modules lead to the emergence of consistent systems is the subject of Section 2.2. An eclectic description of the development of some exogenous factors in today's business environment that have a direct effect on the feasibility and success of these systems is given in Section 2.4.

The different building blocks of organizational design, such as the strategy, the boundary decision, the internal structure, and the governance of organizations, are investigated in Chapter 3. Important insights from the different strands of literature on economics and business (for example, strategic management, industrial organization and organizational economics) are used where appropriate to understand the functioning of the individual modules. Chapter 4 synthesizes these modules by making use of the insights from the system perspective into feasible and success-promising organizational designs. The evaluation of organizational designs in different environments and over different time frames closes the comparative organizational analysis.

The second part of the book uses this methodology and investigates organizational designs in practice. It presents three case studies to show differences in organizational systems and to investigate three 'firms'. The first deals with the securities transaction market in the European Union (EU), the second with the network of the German co-operative banking group, and the third with the community working on open-source projects.

The first case study in particular may at first sight seem a little far-fetched: no single firm operates the European securities transaction industry, but a multitude of exchanges and settlement institutions prevail there. Businessmen, politicians and academics alike describe this setting as highly inefficient. If one looks at the USA, where one firm, the Depository Trust & Clearing Corporation (DTCC), acts as the sole provider of post-trade services, the quest for a potentially better design becomes evident. Like the DTCC in the USA, a single regulated firm might be the best design. Other systems, however, also have their merits and might improve on efficiency.

The second case study deals with the German co-operative banking group. A comparison is undertaken with a bank operating a more traditional business model that is more in line with standard economic theory. The German co-operative banking group, or *Genossenschaftsverbund*, is made up of several autonomous banks that concentrate on their respective markets and leave everything for which a single bank is too small to their central bank or other production banks. It appears that such a group of many autonomous banks of different sizes can be an efficient organizational design.

The third case study looks at ways in which open-source software projects achieve their success. Open-source software is available without charge on the internet, and with many of its products it is even the market leader – for example the Apache web server. This case study deals with the question of how such a 'firm' that expects never to make any profit is nevertheless an efficient organizational design that can compete with companies such as Microsoft that fit the standard economic model of a firm more closely. Chapter 8 concludes.

Notes

1. Putting the notion of consistency between the different building blocks of an organization into the centre of any theory of organization design follows the argument proposed by Jay Galbraith, who has similarly defined organization design as 'the search for coherence'; see Galbraith (1977, p. 5).
2. See the study of this hostile takeover by Burrough and Helyar (1990).
3. See Coff (1999).
4. Game theory formalizes with the bargaining theory the strategic interaction of different stakeholders who have different possibilities and powers to obtain a certain amount of the economic rent. Such a formalization is not dealt with in this book.
5. For evidence of this 'financial revolution', see Rajan and Zingales (2001b).
6. See Leijonhufvud (1986, p. 203).
7. See North (1990, p. 3).
8. See also Romme (2003) for a synopsis of the science and the design perspective of organizations.
9. Coase (1993, p. 73, emphasis added).
10. As an aside, note that the firm itself is structured along these complexity-reducing lines of thought by setting up departments. It is, however, not clear whether this is the cause or the effect of the analytical approach largely used in economics.
11. Aoki (2001, p. 2).
12. Aoki (2001, p. 3).
13. See Burton and Obel (1984, p. 14) for the use of this methodology.
14. Similarly, evaluating Dunning's 'Eclectic Paradigm' (see Dunning, 1992), Schmidt (1995, p. 82) emphasizes the fact that by combining three distinct elements a better logical sense is achieved.
15. See Porter (1994, pp. 427–9) for a distinction between models and frameworks, and their best use in economics and business studies.
16. Porter (1994, p. 431).

Part I
Theory of Organizational Design

2
Foundations of Organizational Design

2.1 Theories of the firm

The firm is a prime example in the economic literature of an organizational design. Since Smith ([1776] 1937) explained, with his well-known example of the pin factory, the merits of specialization in increasing efficiency and welfare, the profit-orientated firm as a fundamentally different way to arrange economic activities compared to markets has led many researchers to investigate the phenomenon of the firm and the different organizational forms it can take. Often, these investigations were analytical in nature, modelling the existence and functioning of firms, and assuming certain shortcomings and failures that do not allow markets to perform properly. Often, these investigations were also narrow in so far as the basic assumptions as to why firms exist – such as the purpose of a firm being to make a profit for its owners – have been made implicitly.

This has ruled out a broader view of firms as only one example of a successful organizational design, and led many researchers to conclude that firms are only second-best to the ideal of a perfect market solution. Applying a systems perspective of organizational design, however, urges one to take many more parameters into account to describe the complexities of efficient economic performance. Markets and firms then become – together with other institutional arrangements – complementary elements in achieving the optimum efficiency for the whole system. Firms are embedded in markets, and firms need these markets for their proper functioning; markets find many firms exchanging resources in them, and markets need these firms to perform efficiently – for example, by aggregating the information that resides in firms.

It is the purpose of this section to introduce the reader to the various strands that have developed in the economic literature of the theory of the firm, and to build a foundation on which further investigations into organizational design can rest. For good overviews on the theory of the firm and a classification similar to the one applied here, see also Holmström and Tirole (1989) and Foss *et al.* (2000).

The history of firms

The modern industrial firm, which led to the managerial capitalism that is so widespread in today's major economies, came into existence after the Industrial Revolution, in the second half of the nineteenth century. Exogenous changes of a general nature, such as the invention of railways, the steamship and the telegraph, and the subsequent building of the respective networks was one driving force that changed the dynamics of business. Combined with industry-specific innovations, such as new processes for refining and processing raw materials or intermediate goods, these changes of a general nature started the transformation of capital-intensive industries. A new business model became feasible.[1]

New sources for competitive advantage

This new business model relied on scale, benefiting firms that were the first to reach a critical mass in their industry through making investments in production facilities, distribution channels, and the sophistication of management. No longer was economic activity characterized by the small, labour-intensive craft system. The new process and product innovations specific to a certain industry allowed and demanded a new organization of production activities: firms built huge, capital-intensive plants to reap economies of scale and scope. The small, one-man craft shops that relied on skilled labour were thus forced to adapt or to go out of business. Scale economies resulted from the fact that the unit cost of making various products declined tremendously as the total amount produced increased, while scope economies resulted from producing many goods simultaneously. Very often these two effects worked together.

With inventions such as railways and the telegraph, the scheduling of inputs and outputs became much easier. That was a necessary condition, since the new production technology was vulnerable to deviations from the minimum efficient scale at which the cost reductions were greatest. To keep production at that level demanded the management of the 'throughput', as Chandler (1990, p. 26) calls it.

Why did firms grow?

To insure themselves against the risk of deviations, firms integrated forward into distribution and backwards into purchasing or exploration. By investing in the extraction facilities for raw materials, the production site for intermediate goods, and even the means of transport between the various sites, the modern industrial firm could make sure that the necessary inputs were to hand when needed to achieve the economies of scale and scope possible in the new production process.[2]

The same logic holds true for the downward activities in the value chain. Firms that followed the new model of production had the capacity to displace intermediaries who had distributed these goods previously. The cost advantage obtained by bundling the orders of different suppliers together was no longer enough to permit the continued existence of these intermediaries. The firms that had made big investments into production facilities in order to reap these economies of scale and scope were large enough also to undertake distribution efficiently themselves. This allowed them to make sure that the finished goods in fact left the plant and did not sit idle – a feature that guaranteed the necessary throughput.

The third investment, besides those in production and distribution facilities that Chandler (1990) considers necessary for the success of the modern industrial firm, was management know-how and capabilities. This allowed for the administration of these new industrial giants, especially the good co-ordination that became necessary between different stages of the value chain. The integration of research and development (R&D) activities into the firm was desirable to continuously improve production processes and to undertake market research in pursuit of new business opportunities abroad or in related markets.

Example 2.1 In the system of mass production, people were no longer the scarce factor that, by use of their labour, created the most value-added in the production of goods. Instead, the new production processes relied on capital to achieve economies of scale and scope. The fact that the new methods of production were different from the craft system devalued the human capital of many highly skilled people in this time of transition. With all those machines in place, lesser skills were needed among the people working with them, and many workers became redundant in the process. The simplicity with which the machines could be handled did not require training as intensive as in the craft system. After a relatively short period of training, all workers were able to perform the tasks that had previously been reserved for those who had progressed from apprentice to master. Human capital was destroyed, and the new processes did not require as much of it as before. A different set of skills was now needed: the ability to manage and to organize on this vastly increased scale that these huge factories brought with them. With the possibility of replacing workers almost at will, power was shifted from workers to capitalists in the organization of economic activity.

Continued

> The simple fact of relative scarcity of financial capital and the consequently high valuation put a premium on capital. During the 1920s and the time of the great Depression, pictures showed crowds of people waiting at the gates of large firms in, for example, the steel or automotive industries. Employees were hired and fired as the capitalists pleased, and labour was essentially a standardized commodity not at all able to command an economic rent or premium.

Once the production processes, the distribution channels, and the management and administrative procedures were in place, it was profitable for firms to use the generated surplus to diversify into related industries and to leverage the capabilities and resources into new markets and products. This is also emphasized by Penrose (1959) in a theme taken up by the resource-based view of strategic management (see also Section 3.1): learning processes – especially at the management level – allow activities to become routine. This in turn leads to free capacities over time, as more and more tasks become routine. The resulting slack allows for the growth of the firm into related fields.

The impact on the market structure

The minimum scale of efficiency did not allow more than a few companies to compete in these industries. The big investments needed created valuable barriers of entry into these oligopolistic industries. The generation of economic rents was possible,[3] and these rents were appropriated by the owners of the scarce resource – the providers of financial capital. The firms in these oligopolies also had a strategic interest. Firms competed on market share: the larger one's own share, the better could one use the new scale-intensive technologies. And, as a flipside, the larger one's own market share, the smaller the share of the competitors and the worse their position regarding the optimum production scale, which resulted in a less profitable position. Therefore, firms started to market their products actively and to build brand names.

Market size, a crucial parameter in determining the optimal plant size, was variable. Markets developed and demand increased as new and better products were manufactured and sold at steadily declining prices. In a co-evolutionary process, both firms and markets grew as the old business model of the craft system was replaced by the then new and superior system of mass production, which had been made possible by changes in the business environment.

The existence of firms

The emergence of the modern industrial firm prominent in the system of mass production led economic writers to theorize about the nature of the firm and why firms existed at all. What exactly was the advantage that the institution 'firm' brought over the institution 'market' with its sophisticated price mechanism? Why could the technological progress not be handled in the craft system, where market transactions at arm's length play a more prominent role? Stylized facts and characteristics commonly associated with firms are:

- the long-term nature and ongoing relationship in contrast to the arm's length transactions;
- the notion that firms allocate authority to some partners over others – power that is different from the simple exit mechanism in markets; and
- the team production that takes place within the firm.

Authority in relationships

The first two facts listed were identified and described by Coase (1937), who neglected the aspect of joint production. As Coase (1937, p. 390) wrote in his seminal article on the nature of the firm: 'The main reason why it is profitable to establish a firm would seem to be that there is a cost of using the price mechanism. The most obvious cost of "organizing" production through the price mechanism is that of discovering what the relevant prices are.' Transaction costs lead to the introduction of the institutional arrangement 'firm' to increase the efficiency of the organization of economic activity: by substituting a series of contracts that would govern market transactions through one long-term contract that 'only state[s] the limits to the power of the entrepreneur',[4] rationally acting people can economize on transaction costs. The existence of firms is thus, under certain circumstances, a more efficient organizational design than reliance on the market.

Coase's further reasoning sheds more light on the authority relationship within firms: in long-term contracts, too many details must be left out initially:

> [T]he service which is being provided is expressed in general terms, the exact details being left until a later date ... The details of what the supplier is expected to do is not stated in the contract but is decided later by the purchaser. When the direction of resources (within the limits of the contract) becomes dependent on the buyer in this way, that relationship which I term a 'firm' may be obtained.[5]

Team production

The third stylized fact – that firms are an efficient means for team production – was advanced by Alchian and Demsetz (1972). In their view, however, only the aspect of team production and neither the long-term relationship nor the allocation of power leads to the existence of firms: 'Team production ... is production in which (1) several types of resources are used and (2) the product is not a sum of separable outputs of each cooperating resource. An additional factor creates a team organization problem – (3) not all resources used in team production belong to one person.'[6] In such a setting, the providers of the necessary resources can rely too much on each other to produce the joint output when the inputs cannot be measured accurately. A problem of free-riding arises. How can an efficient amount of effort and investment be stimulated in this setting? Alchian and Demsetz (1972) propose to introduce a monitor who measures the input, and rewards the providers accordingly. To induce the monitor to fulfil this role, s/he is made residual claimant.

Evaluation

All three arguments listed above for the existence of firms feature prominently in later theories of the firm, and all three reasons have led to separate strands of literature that are described in more detail later in this section, when discussing transaction cost theory, incomplete contract theory, and agency theory. The firm is hence an efficient arrangement for organizing economic transactions whenever either the use of the market mechanism involves higher costs because of the long-term relationship or the necessity of joint production in a team. Of concern in the course of this book is the problem that arises if the assumptions of both Coase (1937) and Alchian and Demsetz (1972) hold simultaneously: what can economic theory and business models reveal in practice about the nature of the firm in particular, or organizational design in general, if team production is necessary *and* the long-term relationships allocate power in this institutional arrangement different from that existing in markets?

The boundaries of firms – transaction cost theory

Building on the ideas emphasized by Coase (1937), Oliver Williamson further develops the theme of transaction costs. By introducing the behavioural assumptions that decision-makers act opportunistically[7] and are bounded rationally,[8] Williamson (1985) argues that, in such a setting, the necessity of relationship-specific investments might lead to an underinvestment problem.

Specific investments

Specific investments, if worthwhile to undertake, increase efficiency and are thus value-enhancing. By investing resources in a way that is specific to the relationship, an economic rent or quasi-rent is generated above the return that can be gained in a competitive market setting.[9] The source of this economic rent is the asset-specificity: the economic process affected by the specific investment is performed more efficiently. Specific intermediate products can be assembled more easily into the finished good than could intermediate products sourced at arm's length in the marketplace. But specific investments not only generate economic rents; they also incur up-front investment costs that are sunk and can be only partially recouped after the 'fundamental transformation'[10] has occurred. This fundamental transformation replaces *ex ante* competition with *ex post* bargaining between the two parties forming the relationship. Klein *et al.* (1978, p. 298) clarify this link between asset-specificity and appropriable quasi-rents: 'After a specific investment is made and such quasi-rents are created, the possibility of opportunistic behaviour is very real.'

Anticipating the possibility of opportunistic behaviour in the course of the relationship, potential business partners are reluctant to incur such sunk costs. The danger that all or a part of the economic rent may be expropriated in a hold-up situation, where 'each party to the contract may engage in inefficient behavior in an attempt to ... obtain a larger share of the available quasi-rents'[11] leads to investment decisions that do not generate the full possible value of economic rent in the first place – a rather inefficient outcome.

Possible solutions

One solution proposed by Williamson (1985) to circumvent this under-investment problem is to bundle the decision-making into a unified governance structure by adjusting the boundaries of the firm. Decision-making and investment behaviour can be made more efficient by integrating different activities vertically along the value chain, thereby eliminating the possibility for hold-up and mitigating market imperfections. Thus, whenever the problems of relationship-specific investments are serious, the adjustment of the boundaries of the firm can lead to a better organizational design. This idea is pursued further in Section 3.2.

Example 2.2 The classical example for vertical integration related to the specific nature of investments involves the long-term contractual agreement between Fisher Body and General Motors in 1919 to provide closed auto bodies. When demand conditions changed, Fisher Body took advantage of the imperfect cost-plus, exclusive dealing contract that was designed to prevent

---

Continued

the parties from expropriating rents from one another. Fisher Body adopted an extremely labour-intensive production process and located plants far away from the General Motors assembly plant. The result was inefficiently produced automobile bodies that were highly profitable for Fisher to supply but very costly for General Motors to obtain. Clearly, the bilateral governance did not work and, as predicted in such cases by transaction cost theory, the two companies consequently merged in 1926.[a]

---

[a] See Klein *et al.* (1978, pp. 308–10) and Williamson (1985, pp. 114ff.) for this example.

But vertical integration does not come without costs in terms of increased complexity and weakened incentives to make the right decisions. Agency theory, described in the next section, concentrates on the latter aspect. Intermediate solutions that allow for better investment decisions by integrating some aspects but stop short of full integration can therefore be a more efficient organizational arrangement. The provision of 'hostages'[12] can offer such hybrid solutions. In many franchising contracts, for example, the franchisee rents the building in which the services are provided, on a short-term basis from the franchisor. This assures the franchisee that the franchisor cannot hold him/her up to extract an undue share of rents. The franchisor paid for much of the initial investment – thereby offering a hostage. But such an arrangement also reminds the franchisor that the franchisee still has the right incentives as the 'owner' of the franchise. Because of the short-term lease contract, the franchisee can be 'fired' by the franchisor if misbehaviour should occur.[13] Such unilateral or bilateral exchange of hostages leads to self-enforcing contracts; that is, contracts that both parties will fulfil, since the future rents that can be earned in a well-functioning relationship are greater than the immediate gain one party could achieve by holding up the other. Whenever the detection of non-adherence to an initial contract results in the termination of the relationship and thereby in a loss of future economic rents from this relationship, this threat acts as a means to adhere to the terms made in advance and the contract becomes self-fulfilling.[14]

Evaluation

In transaction cost theory, the firm emerges when the markets that economic agents have to operate in are failing because of peculiarities in the exchange relationship such as specificity of assets. Such specificity of assets is the underlying source of economic rents. The existence of economic rents and the desire to appropriate them leads to the failure of organizational designs relying solely on contracts and markets. If markets are not functioning properly, integrating the activities that rely on specific investments is the standard solution. But the solution of integrating any specific assets under a unified governance encounters problems if human assets have to invest specifically in the relationship.[15] Human capital is inalienable from its owner, the human being behind it. Other remedies are needed: hybrids such as franchising might be better organizational designs in this case when investments in both physical and human capital are important. In the course of this book, other solutions will be explored that rest on more parameters than only the boundary decision.

The structure of firms – agency theory

As mentioned above, one reason for the existence of firms can be team production. As outlined above, Alchian and Demsetz (1972) argue that the firm is distinct from a market solution because of the nature of production. Whenever teams are necessary to produce certain goods or services, the individual team member has an incentive to free-ride on the efforts of the others when his/her behaviour is difficult or costly to observe – that is, there is private information about the exerted effort. In such instances it might pay to assign the monitoring role to a particular agent, who thus ensures that production takes place at an efficient level. This agent 'employs' the others, and the resulting 'firm' can be characterized as a 'nexus for contracting relationships', to use the phrase coined by Jensen and Meckling (1976, p. 311).[16] It is this idea that is taken up in agency theory.

Asymmetric information

The main assumption in agency theoretical models is the existence of private or asymmetrically distributed information. Two important ramifications can be distinguished in agency theoretic models. In the case of *ex-ante* information asymmetry, the principal does not know the characteristics of the potential agent. In the classical example by Akerlof (1970), the buyer of a used car does not know the characteristics of the car that the seller offers. If the buyer adjusts the price s/he is willing to pay to the average quality in the market, potential sellers who know the high quality of their vehicles withdraw from the market. This adverse selection leads to a market failure with only the worst types still trading – an inefficient design. Solutions to this type of information asymmetry are the careful screening of the characteristics of the agent by the principal, the acquisition of a credible signal by the agent,[17] or the design of different contracts leading agents to self-select, given their characteristics. All three solutions are, however, not without cost, and the most efficient outcome, the 'first-best' in the terminology of agency theory, cannot be achieved.

In the case of *ex-post* information asymmetry, the principal does not know how the agent behaves after a contract has been signed. The moral hazard that arises in such situations is modelled in the classical paper by Holmström (1979). If the principal can neither observe the effort of the agent directly nor infer the behaviour of the agent from the outcome, s/he cannot distinguish between cases in which low performance is either a result of little effort by the agent or simply the result of adverse circumstances. The agent has suboptimal incentives to perform in this case – again an inefficient design. Solutions to this type of information asymmetry are monitoring by the principal or the provision of higher-powered incentives by making the reward of the agent contingent on the outcome. Both solutions are, however, not costless: besides the direct monitoring costs in the first case, it is the suboptimal risk-sharing between a risk-neutral principal and a risk-averse agent that inevitably occurs in the second case. As Holmström (1979) has shown, only the second-best can be achieved in this setting unless other mechanisms – such as, for example, longer-term contracts – allow for other outcomes. In both variants of asymmetric and private information, agency costs play an important role, and a residual loss remains.[18]

The separation of ownership and control

The theory of the firm proposed by Jensen and Meckling (1976) rests on the argument that a separation of ownership and control gives rise to agency costs.[19] By defining an agency relationship as 'a contract under which one or more persons (the principal(s)) engage another person (the agent) to perform some service on their behalf which involves delegating some decision making authority to the agent',[20] they rejoin the notion of authority emphasized by Coase (1937) with that of private information in the thinking of Alchian and Demsetz (1972).

The balancing of the agency costs involved with debt and equity financing, and the share of the agent's equity, leads to an optimal capital structure (and by this the existence of the firm) that minimizes the agency costs: the debt induces agents to expend greater effort and make better decisions,[21] whereas the outside equity does not only allow the agents to diversify and obtain a better risk position but also allows outside equity holders to act as budget-balance breakers, so that better incentives can be given to the individual agents in the team production process.[22]

The theory of the firm based on an agency theoretical analysis is further developed by Fama and Jensen (1983b). By examining closely the relationship between residual claims and the decision process, they suggest a separation of the management of decisions (initiation and implementation) from the control of decisions (ratification and monitoring). This separation allows for better incentives for the agents, thereby increasing the efficiency of the overall design.[23] Furthermore, by separating decision management and decision control, the multi-tasking problem described by Holmström and Milgrom (1991) is alleviated.[24]

Evaluation

The main issue in agency theory is the correct setting and alignment of incentives *ex ante*, i.e. before the contract is signed and before any nexus of contracts is developed. There is no *ex post* dimension to agency theory, hence there is no need to allocate residual control rights along with the residual claims. Everything, including the distribution of the economic rents in the case of success, is stated in the initial contract. Thus agency theoretical models make the implicit assumption that all contracts in this nexus for contracting relationships are complete, which is the starting point for the critique of the incomplete contracting theory described in the next section.

The agency approach is not a complete theory of the firm. It states how incentives can be given, but remains silent on the issue of what is or should be within the boundaries of the firm, and which contracts remain on the outside. In principle, the reward structure for an independent supplier can be completely the same as the one offered to an employee. Newer agency models – for example, Bolton and Rajan (2003) – use the principal–agent setting to analyse the boundaries and internal hierarchy of firms to counter these shortcomings in a formal model.

Agency theory, however, adds and emphasizes an important dimension that should not be neglected in a comprehensive theory of organizational design: the way economic agents deal with risk, and to whom risk is assigned in any organizational design, is important. The ideas of the agency theory are taken up in later chapters of the book.

The governance of firms – incomplete contract theory

A useful way of thinking when describing the governance of firms is the property rights or incomplete contract approach developed by Grossman and Hart (1986), Hart and Moore (1990), and Hart (1995) that builds on the transaction cost theory described above.

Incompleteness of contracts

Because of either bounded rationality or the transaction costs associated with writing and enforcing contracts, the proponents of the property rights approach state that contracts must necessarily remain incomplete. The correct future decisions cannot be prescribed in a complete contract primarily because unforeseen contingencies might arise in the future that are not *ex- ante* specifiable. A second reason is the problem that even if an *ex ante* complete contract would be feasible, the *ex post* enforcement would be a challenge. The actions undertaken and decisions made by the contract partners can be observable for each of them but not be verifiable to a third party that enforces such a contract. If contracts are incomplete in such a way, residual control rights matter. A residual control right is the right to make decisions whenever the contract does not state otherwise. Such residual control rights give authority or power. The assignment of property rights in the form of residual rights of control is referred to as ownership. According to Hart (1995), the control rights over assets determine the boundaries of the firm. All those assets jointly owned are within the domain of the firm.

Unlike the agency theory, where everything including the distribution of economic rents is spelt out initially, the incomplete contract theory realizes that this *ex-post* dimension is important. To whom the *ex-post* power of residual control rights is assigned *ex ante* in the initial contract has very serious consequences for the efficiency of the organizational design: 'Ex ante efficient contracts implement ex post inefficiencies for incentive reasons that the contract parties are tempted to renegotiate.'[25]

Ownership and power

The property rights theory emphasizes the residual rights of control and the power that goes with it. The issue of the most efficient assignment of power in any organizational design recurs throughout this book. It therefore makes sense to understand where such power originates.

How best to resolve the trade-off between *ex ante* and *ex post* inefficiency is the centrepiece in the incomplete contracts literature. Similar to transaction cost theory, the adjustment of firm boundaries allows economic activity to be structured more efficiently. Unlike transaction cost theory, however, the incomplete contracts approach provides an answer to the question of who should be in charge of the unified governance: ownership is allocated to the party most affected in its investment incentives. The residual rights of control associated with ownership should be allocated to the party that makes the most important asset-specific investment. In this case, the incentive to make good decisions and to undertake the correct actions are aligned in a way that comes closest to reaching the most efficient outcome.

Power and authority arise out of the ownership of assets and the control rights that are associated with these assets. The willingness of agents to undertake non-contractible investments specific to a particular asset depends on the ownership of the asset. Whoever owns the asset can be sure that a hold-up situation against him/her is not possible, and that the economic rent generated by specific investments in the asset is surely his/hers.

The dark side of ownership

Ownership is a powerful incentive for the owner. But the ownership of assets and the power that comes with it also has a downside. It enhances the investment incentives of the owner but at the same time reduces the incentives of other constituencies to invest specifically. By threatening to withdraw the assets or to make decisions to the detriment of the other parties involved, power and authority can be wielded by the owner. If other parties to the firm also need to make specific investments, the allocation of all residual control rights to a particular party gives too strong a power. Since the return on investments cannot be allocated *ex ante* for all contingencies that may arise, the contractual incompleteness and the powerful position of the owner deters the other parties. They will not invest for fear of being expropriated by the one with the residual decision rights. The result is economic inefficiency. How can organizations be designed to overcome this inefficiency?

The set of residual control rights is not closed. Investing the agent's resources in a specific way (that is, specialized to the other assets under joint ownership) makes the agent vulnerable to hold-up, as explained in the previous paragraph. The specific investment, however, creates new residual control rights that also generate power. New power is created because the threat of withdrawal will diminish the economic rents that could otherwise be obtained by having the two co-specialized assets working together. A complex nexus of power emerges that determines the possibilities of safeguarding economic rents and affects other, potentially efficiency-enhancing, investment decisions.[26]

In the case of physical assets, this power can be bundled with the power conveyed from the existing assets through the integration of the new, specialized asset in a single firm. Power struggles within this nexus of power and the inefficiencies related to these struggles can thus be avoided. This possibility is not provided for specific human assets: because of the inalienability of human capital the integration option does not exist.

Evaluation

We can summarize that the allocation of ownership to a particular party provides incentives to make the right decisions and undertake the right actions when contracts are incomplete and time inconsistencies exist: the incompleteness of information to write or enforce contracts leads to *ex-post* renegotiation possibilities which in turn affect *ex-ante* investment incentives. Ownership is the incentive device with which to mitigate this problem. The correct assignment of property rights ensures the efficiency of economic transactions. Ownership, however, can also lead to a consequent loss in economic efficiency whenever there is more than one party affected by the trade-off between *ex-ante* and *ex-post* efficiency, since that party's incentives are weakened.

Since complete contracts cannot be written, good organizational design relies on self-enforcement or relational contracts. In such a situation, the threat of withdrawal from the relationship might be sufficient. The loss of potential future rents provides the parties with incentives to perform.

The incomplete contract theory falls short of being a full theory of the firm: the employment relationship is not explained by it, because employees cannot be owned. So human assets cannot be under joint ownership, which in the case of physical assets determines the boundaries of the firm. The importance of specific human capital, however, is increasing in many industries and many activities. Simultaneously, the nexus of specific investments determines, and is determined by, the nexus of power within the organizational design. The investigation of this complementary relationship is the essence of this book.

The firm as a knowledge-creating entity

Foss (1996a) states that the incompleteness of contracts does not only create incentive problems and inconsistencies over time but also allows for organizational learning. Firms emerge as an efficient institutional arrangement: within these institutions it is possible to create knowledge in a co-specialized and co-ordinated manner as such investments would not be undertaken in a pure market environment.[27]

Communication and co-ordination

The main themes emphasized by this theoretical approach are the various tasks that an organizational design has to perform to gather and process information about its environment and the changes that occur. An important aspect involves the co-ordination between these tasks and the agents performing them. Incentive conflicts that were the driving force in the theories of the firm described so far are usually disregarded, or are assumed to have been solved – that is, all members of the organization share the same goals and opportunism does not prevail. The focus of the knowledge- or competence-based perspective is on the bounded rationality of the constituents of the firm, and often the information acquisition and processing capabilities are modelled as the scarce resource in the organization. The firm in this sense is an efficient organizational design, since it allows its members to specialize in the collection and processing of different types of information and to share their information with other people in this communication network.[28] The boundaries of the organization are explained by the trade-off between the benefits of specialization and the costs of communication. The organizational structure takes on the classic form of a hierarchy – a pyramid in which duplicated communication is avoided.

The same theme of economizing on communication costs can be found in Demsetz (1993). The reason for the existence of the firm is the fact that the better-informed can direct the less well-informed – that is, '[d]irection substitutes for education (that is, for the transfer of the knowledge itself)'.[29] The boundaries of the firm are shaped by the difference in knowledge necessary for producing and using certain goods or services. '[E]ncapsulating this knowledge into products or services that can be transferred between firms cheaply because the instructions needed to use them do not require in-depth knowledge about how they are produced'[30] is then the most efficient organizational design.

Similarly, Conner and Prahalad (1996) explain the existence of the firm depending on the resources it has to use rather than opportunistic behaviour. If the best decision about how to deploy some resources can be derived more efficiently from the direction of another agent than by acquiring the necessary information itself, a decision-maker with cognitive limitations substitutes the direction and the embedded knowledge of this other agent for the decision s/he would otherwise have made: 'If the employee cannot absorb the manager's wisdom before the employee profitably can apply it, the employee may opt to be directed by the manager and hence to be employed in a firm.'[31]

Note that, besides hierarchical direction, a common set of shared knowledge and information can also allow for the co-ordination of local decisions. Such a set of shared knowledge can be interpreted as an organizational culture with the codes of conduct, standards and routines the firm has acquired over time.[32]

Austrian economics and rent protection

It might be easier to collect information when specializing in a certain field, and to communicate information in a context where either the value can be rapidly understood because of shared codes, or used efficiently because of direction that is not questioned by the subordinate. But why is it worthwhile at all to collect such information, and why should it be done in firms? The answer to the first question can be found in Austrian economics.[33] The most important problem economic agents face, according to Austrian economics, is how to co-ordinate their plans and actions with those of others. Perfect competition in a neoclassical sense does not occur, since the discovery of the relative prices is an ongoing process[34] and the economy is therefore always out of equilibrium. With superior knowledge or better discovery capabilities, an advantage can be gained – an advantage that manifests itself in an economic rent.

The answer to the second question – why this innovation process must be done in firms – is provided by Liebeskind (1996). The advantage of firms over markets is their ability to protect economic rents arising from information gathering and discovery activities in such a dynamic setting: 'By protecting knowledge, firms may serve to induce investment in strategic innovation, because incentives to innovate depend on the degree to which the innovator can appropriate future rent streams.'[35] The economic rent gained from the knowledge cannot be protected as well in the market, since property rights for new knowledge are difficult and costly to obtain in the form of patents or copyrights. Furthermore, such titles can be circumvented and are not easy to enforce: it is difficult to detect the illegal use of knowledge because of the public-good nature of information. Firms or other organizational arrangements can use parameters such as adjustments in the remuneration structure of employees through the use of seniority pay. This increases the cost of terminating the relationship to appropriate the economic rent for the employee since s/he forgoes the economic rent created by the seniority pay structure.[36] By setting many such parameters correctly, a firm is the superior organizational design compared to a market.

Evaluation

Why do we need and how do we use the knowledge-based perspective of the theory of the firm? Although the knowledge-based theory frequently uses the insights of Coase (1937), it is derived from a much larger set of ideas from different disciplines. By taking into account insights from the literature on strategic management, Austrian economics, sociology and evolutionary biology, this branch of viewing the firm is more process-orientated. It takes a more dynamic perspective than the other theories of the firm based on organizational economics described so far, where everything that 'is worth discovering is assumed to have been discovered already'.[37]

The knowledge-based theory of the firm, while often criticizing the assumptions made in mainstream organizational economics, is not without its own critics. Williamson (1999), for example, denounces the weaknesses in the competence perspective that arise from the lack of formalization and from the bias that is caused by finding only 'ex post rationalizations for success'[38] rather than giving some predictive guidelines. However, he also detects advantages in the knowledge-based theory of the firm and concludes: 'I see the relation between competence and governance as both rival and complementary – more of the latter than the former, since some of the differences turn out to be more apparent than real.'[39]

This critique is accepted and the complementary relationship between the governance and competence perspectives has been recognized: a theory of the firm explaining its existence and boundaries on the basis of knowledge alone is not sufficient. Concepts such as opportunism and moral hazard, as applied in organizational economics, are needed.[40]

This complementary relationship between the two approaches to organizations fits perfectly with the objectives of this book and the methodology applied here, since the objectives of this book are to compare the relative merits of different organizational designs in their entirety. Certainly, the ability of any such design to cope with change is of great importance. The aspect of change in particular is emphasized in knowledge-based theory which, together with the insights from organizational economics, provides a promising ground for research when comparing different organizational systems and the way in which their elements work together.[41] This view is described briefly in the next section.

The firm as a system

To view the firm as a system is not really a full theory of the firm on its own. It builds on the insights of the other perspectives described so far, and makes use of the tools and methodologies developed in these, thereby to some degree integrating the various ways of thinking. The first and arguably the most important contribution that describes the firm explicitly as a system is by Holmström and Milgrom (1994). The main theme of their paper is described below.

A balance of incentives

The main theme behind this approach to the theory of the firm is the observation that certain patterns of organizational design parameters occur together and co-vary in a specific way. In the opinion of Holmström and Milgrom (1994) it is therefore misleading to focus only on a single aspect of the whole, as previous theories of the firm have done: Coase (1937) focused on the authority relationship between employer and employee; transaction cost economics and the incomplete contracting approach both emphasized the importance of ownership; and agency theory spelt out the importance of monitoring and the correct compensation scheme. Decisions and recommendations made in the light of each of these theories, however, do not take into account how these choices are intertwined – the systemic nature is neglected.[42]

By extending the model developed in a previous article,[43] Holmström and Milgrom (1994) analyse three different incentive instruments and 'whether a coordinated use of the instruments explains their typical covariation'.[44] These incentive instruments are:

- payment for measured performance of the agent;
- allocation of ownership of assets; and
- job design and the degree of freedom for the agent.

The important insight of Holmströom and Milgrom (1991), and especially Holmström and Milgrom (1994), is that, whenever different tasks compete for the attention of the agent in charge of them, it is necessary to balance the incentives to provide effort for these tasks. If this condition – the 'equal compensation principle'[45] – is violated, too much effort will go into the task that offers the most compensation. A worker paid solely for the quantity produced must be held accountable for the care of the machines s/he uses in the production process. Otherwise, the care of these machines will be neglected. It is therefore necessary either to design the job in such a way that the operation can only use a specific machine or to require him/her to own the machine. In the first case, it is the restriction that the worker has to work with the machine over a long period and might lose output – for which s/he is paid – when the machine breaks down because of the worker's negligence. In the second case, it is the incentives arising out of ownership and the potential resale value that leads the worker to be concerned not only with the highest output but also about the machines and tools used.

Holmström and Milgrom (1994) thus establish two distinct organizational designs. The combination of the employee not owning the assets s/he works with, the employee being subject to a low-powered incentive scheme, and the employee taking orders from his/her superiors in the hierarchy, characterizes the firm. A mixture of these three parameters is unlikely to be observed. If the configuration of one parameter changes, changes in the configuration of the other parameters are likely, and the resulting organizational design is that of a market-based solution: the agent owns the assets s/he works with, is free to work on whichever project s/he likes, and faces the high-powered incentives that markets provide.

Evaluation

Summarizing the insights provided by Holmström and Milgrom (1994), note that the view of the firm as a system postulates that the ownership of assets and the power relationship between the worker and the firm depends on the intensity of the incentive system provided by the design of the job, which is dependent in turn on how the other two incentive instruments are configured. Two ideal organizational designs can be distinguished: a firm and a market. Both organizational designs have in common balanced incentives provided within each.

Example 2.3   The idea of a firm as an incentive system can be illustrated using the example of sales agents. Two distinct forms of organization can be observed: some companies employ their own sales force, while others rely on independent agents to market their products. Holmström and Milgrom (1994) attribute this choice in organizational design to the tasks that sales agents have to perform. Whenever it makes sense that these agents do not only sell the products but also provide intensive feedback about customer needs and work closely together with other sales agents, the company will integrate the sales force and employ the agents, paying them a fixed salary and only modest commission. Furthermore, the products to be sold, the territory and the customers are allocated to the employee. Independent agents earn output-based commissions and cannot be restricted in their choice to also sell products of competitors. In the case of any problems with the products of one company, they would adjust their product portfolio and switch easily to competing products without providing the company with an early warning that some customers have encountered problems with the product. This information-gathering and learning function could also be enhanced by job rotation – the periodic switching of territories in which the different sales agents work. Such a measure, however, would be fiercely rejected by independent sales people, who 'own' their customers and usually have closer ties with them than with the companies from whom they obtain their wares. See also the original empirical studies of Anderson and Schmittlein (1984) and Anderson (1985).

Two shortcomings of the approach described here should be noted. The first critique is that many more elements than the three identified by Holmström and Milgrom (1994) are intertwined, and the relationship between these incentive instruments is more complex: asset ownership not only provides incentives to perform but can also be used as a bargaining device to obtain more of the economic rents provided in a firm. Thus, not only do incentives need to be balanced, but a balance of power within the organizational design must also be devised. The second main 'shortcoming' of this perspective is the lack of good papers applying this approach that incorporate more aspects of a firm. The next section looks more deeply into systems theory to provide a solid basis for the arguments developed in this book.

2.2 Configuration of systems

This book is about organizational design. A design is an intentional arrangement of various elements to make use of certain features of these elements.[46] An architect, drawing up the blueprints for a new building, has to understand both the intention of the client and the purpose of the building. S/he has to take into account the location and the characteristics of the ground it is to be built on, such as whether it is likely to be flooded from time to time, or whether it is earthquake-prone. After planning for a solid foundation, careful calculations must be made that take into account the different materials and their respective characteristics. The electrical wiring and plumbing system has to be planned and co-ordinated so that the new building can be occupied safely by its potential users. Restrictions of the planning authority – for example, a maximum height – have to be met. An architect has to take into account all these details to design a consistent building constructed from his/her blueprint, which is only then of value to those who will use it.

Designing organizations is akin to this process of planning a building: an organization's intention in business has to be formulated, necessary investments have to be made, a decision has to be taken as to which resources and processes are to be used to produce whatever kind of products or services are needed, regulatory demands have sometimes to be met, and, by no means least, any resulting economic rents have to be distributed at a certain point in time to whomever they belong. Like an architect, the designer of an organization has to take into account the characteristics (or in economic terms the relative prices and costs) of these elements: the firm has to buy raw materials and intermediate goods in the market and has to sell any products or services produced in the market. The technology of production has to be selected, given the cost of the necessary investments for plants and machinery. Like an architect, the designer of an organization also has to take into account any interdependencies between these elements: a financial budget for a specific division, for example, could be diverted from its most efficient use by the division's managers if no adequate monitoring system is applied at the same time.

Systems theory is applied in economics as well as in other disciplines to take these interdependencies into consideration when analysing the elements and evaluating the synthesis. The term was first used in the papers of Milgrom and Roberts (1990b), Holmström and Milgrom (1994) and Milgrom and Roberts (1995a), who have formalized the traditional notion of the firm as a system, described in Section 2.1. Here the basic ideas of system theory are sketched and important concepts are described. The focus is on applications from economics, especially the design of organizations like firms. For a rigorous mathematical treatment refer to Topkis (1998).

Elements and systems

Elements and modularity

Large structures often consist of elements that may or may not be intertwined with each other in varying degrees. The notion 'element' is used here to characterize the smallest unit of such larger structures. If these structures are broken up, dissolved or 'analysed', such elements are found to be the building blocks of the total structure. In the context of organizational design, these elements can be thought of as the underlying resources and processes that make up the whole organization. In the example of the sales agents described in the previous section, such basic elements have been the incentive instruments of ownership and pay-for-performance.

If such elements do not interfere with each other, and if the exact relationship between such elements is not important, distinct substructures or 'modules' can be identified. Each module consists of a set of elements that are interconnected with other elements within the same module, but have little in common with elements that are part of other modules: 'A module is a unit whose structural elements are powerfully connected among themselves and relatively weakly connected to elements in other units. ... Modules are units in a larger system that are structurally independent of one another, but work together'.[47] The separation of elements into distinct subunits and the resulting modularization can run along many lines because of technical necessities, geographical distances or customer segmentation. Modularity along technical and product lines is an important feature in the software industry – for example, in the process of writing a software code for complex programs such as operating systems. See Chapter 7 for the application of modularity in the context of open-source processes.

The process of modularization is good news for those analysing the characteristics of the larger structure. The complexity of the overall system is reduced: not every connection between all the elements of the system has to be investigated, but only the connections between elements of the same module. The relationship between modules and all the elements they contain can then be managed through suitable interfaces.[48]

Example 2.4   Modularization in business and economics is quite apparent: an interface exists through which many modules are assembled. The modules in this case are firms procuring raw materials and other inputs, and offering their output to other firms or consumers on the market interface. The founding of different firms frees managers from having to understand the complexity of the overall economy. Instead, they 'just' have to focus on their module and the interrelationships between the elements in their firm. By relying on markets for the necessary exchange of goods and services between these firms, an interface between the distinct modules is utilized. Firms themselves often take the process of modularization a step further by setting up departments or holding structures.

Supermodularity and complementarity

This process of modularization reduces the complexity of the overall system. However, such modularization might not always be feasible: dissolving – or analysing – the larger structure into distinct modules might lead to the negligence of relationships between and across these modules that can only be captured when the modules are put together – or synthesized – with the whole system. In such a case, modularization is not possible because of a characteristic that is labelled 'supermodularity' in mathematics. Supermodularity formalizes the idea of synergy – that the whole is more than the sum of its parts. In well-behaved mathematical settings this amounts to a positive cross-derivative of the objective function with respect to the two variables in question, which requires such a function to be continuous and twice differentiable. It is often necessary to further restrict the setting to a concave objective function and constraints that are convex to obtain a meaningful result. These restrictions, however, often cannot be applied to business settings: certain inputs are not divisible and thus lead to inconsistencies with convexity. And increasing returns to scale or learning effects are inconsistent with the requirement of concavity of the objective function.[49]

Whenever such convenient assumptions do not make sense – for example, in the case of a binary decision whether or not to integrate a business into the firm – the use of a positive cross-derivative to detect such supermodular characteristics is not possible. In this case, however, the mathematics of lattice theory can be used. A supermodular function can be defined according to Topkis (1998, p. 43) thus: 'Suppose that $f(x)$ is a real-valued function on a lattice X. If

$$f(x') + f(x'') \leq f(x' \vee x'') + f(x' \wedge x'')$$

for all x' and x'' in X, then $f(x)$ is supermodular on X.' A lattice is a partially ordered set that contains the join and the meet of each pair of its elements x' and x''. The join of x' and x'' is denoted by $x' \vee x''$ and defined as the component-wise maximum of the vectors x' and x''. Similarly, the meet is denoted by $x' \wedge x''$ and defined as the component-wise minimum of these two vectors. The join and meet as well as the lattice X are shown in Figure 2.1.

A supermodular function on this lattice has the property that the sum of the values for join and meet are higher than the sum of the values for the original vectors; see the sketch in Figure 2.2. In other words, when starting from the coordinate-wise minimum $x' \wedge x''$ any change in only one dimension to the point x' or x'' results in a lower functional value than changing both dimensions simultaneously, to the respective component-wise maximum $x' \vee x''$: raising one of the variables increases the return to raising the other.[50]

To clarify the concept of supermodularity further, note that the definition of a supermodular function is akin to that of economies of scope. If the revenue r of producing two goods x' and x'' in one firm is higher than if the goods were produced in two separate firms, the inequality

$$r(x') + r(x'') \leq r(x' + x'')$$

must hold. In this case, superadditivity leads to synergies. The difference between supermodularity and superadditivity is that the latter makes use of the sum rather than of the component-wise maximum and minimum of the underlying vectors.[51]

Whenever the objective function exhibits such supermodular features, complementarities between the elements represented by the vectors are present. Complementarity is a characteristic between two or more elements

Figure 2.1   Lattice with join and meet

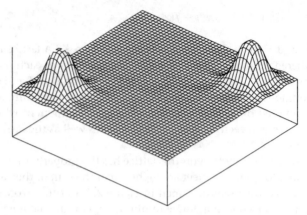

Figure 2.2   Supermodular function leading to bimodal 'landscape'

in a system or module. In the presence of complementarity between these two elements, the efficiency of the total system is increased by moving the configuration of these elements in a co-ordinated way in the same direction: increasing (or introducing) one element increases the returns to also increasing (or introducing) the other element.

Complementarities in business and economics, in other scientific disciplines, and everyday life often prevail:

- Investments in research capabilities for product and process innovations and flexibility are complementary in firms.[52]
- In the case of co-specialized assets,[53] having one such asset is of little use without having the other as well.
- When setting up a computer, any investment in hardware must be accompanied by an investment in the necessary software, and vice versa.
- Technological innovations are accompanied in a co-evolutionary way by the rise of new institutions.[54]
- Economic agents act on the values and information they have, but these values and information may be dependent on the networks and institutions in which the agents are embedded.[55]

Systems and consistency

If large structures are composed of various elements and many modules that have such complementarity relationships between them, we speak of them as a *system*. In such a system, no single element can be adjusted without considering the effects on other, complementary elements in the system. The way the elements in a system are configured matters: the right configuration – that is, the one that exploits complementarities between the elements of the system – leads to consistency within it. In this way the system is configured efficiently.

Consistency has two aspects. The first is that no small adjustment in the configuration of any element can further improve the efficiency of the overall system – that is, the system is at a (local) optimum. The second aspect to consistency is that no change in one element alone, however large it might be, can improve the efficiency of the system. To change a consistent system without impairing its efficiency requires a co-ordinated change in all elements, or all modules.

Where do we find systems?[56] In many areas of social science, systems theory is used to describe and investigate complex interactions. For example:

- The way people form their values and beliefs depends on the social system in which they are embedded, and with whom they interact frequently and build friendships. However, in a feedback process, the same people also shape the norms and beliefs as participants in such a social network. The result can be that two communities, albeit with an initially identical distribution of individuals, evolve in separate directions and exhibit significant differences in their wealth level, school quality and crime rates.[57]
- The efficacy of the political system depends on a carefully adjusted system of checks and balances of the various powers in politics. If the distribution of power is tilted towards a specific party and ideology (as in communism) or towards a specific person (as in a dictatorship), a political, economic and cultural decline is often the result.
- In economics and finance, a lot of research is undertaken on financial systems, a distinction between the different configurations, and the relative efficiency of a market-based or bank-based financial system.[58]
- Any organization forms a business system. The configuration of the various organizational design instruments and the assignment of power to economic agents involved in the organization determines the efficiency with which the objectives of the organization, themselves subject to a feedback process, can be met.

Note here that another important feature of systems is that their complexity leads to ambiguity. It is often not clear in exactly which way different elements interact, or how strong any existing complementarities between such elements are. The difference between cause and effect is difficult to detect. Such ambiguity can be exploited strategically, especially if, over time, different resources and routines are bundled in the firm. In this case, a simple 'copy and paste' of best practices is not possible.

Path dependencies

Complementarities do not only exist at a certain point in time, but can also be present over the course of time. This being the case, decisions made today will not only influence the set of decisions that can be made in the future, but today's decisions and investments will also alter the relative advantage of these future decisions. Stated differently, a decision that has to be made today is often influenced by past decisions. Whenever complementarities between two elements exist over time, a feeling of 'If only I had ...' is often present. Such complementarities over time are usually referred to as path dependent processes, or as feedback loops in systems theory.

Feedback and path dependencies

Positive feedback loops lead to 'the tendency for that which is ahead to get further ahead, for that which loses advantage to lose further advantage'.[59] This becomes important, sometimes even a self-fulfilling prophecy, in more and more industries: increasing returns lead to a winner-takes-all competition – for example, in the securities transactions industry or the software industry for many programs. Whenever economies of scale[60] exist, size matters – and decisions and investments, once made, have a strong influence on the current size of any organization. Whenever network effects[61] prevail, scope matters – and again, past investment decisions effect the current scope of the network.

Example 2.5   A well-known example that led to the prevalence of Microsoft in the software industry is the decision in 1980 by IBM – then the dominant supplier of computer hardware – to use DOS as the operating system for its computers. A growing base of users with an IBM- or IBM-compatible computer and DOS as the operating system encouraged other software companies to write applications for this combination, thereby contributing to the winning role that DOS achieved as the standard operating system. Microsoft later successfully leveraged its dominant position by offering product upgrades from text-based DOS to the graphical user interface Windows. It also penetrated adjacent markets with its Office Suite and Internet Explorer. Exploiting complementarities between its operating system and its web browser, Microsoft was able to shatter the dominance of Netscape in the browser war of the mid-1990s.[a]

---

[a]   See Chapter 7 for more details on this browser war. See also the well-known example of the persistence of the QWERTY keyboard in David (1985).

Products that emerge from winner-takes-all competition become de facto standards, and the lock-in effects of such standards lead to high switching costs, which in turn reinforce the dominant position of the quasi-monopolist. This makes the position of the winner of such a competition relatively stable and unique. The same position cannot be reached again but is the result, over time, of a path-dependent process and positive feedback loops. Decisions, once made, carry their results into the future, changing the action space and the relative advantage of decisions and actions for oneself and for other agents or organizations.

It is no coincidence that those industries that do not belong to the world of diminishing returns and the resulting concave objective function emphasized in microeconomic textbooks are also the industries that rely most heavily on knowledge: knowledge, in so far as it can be codified, is duplicated almost without cost. And the knowledge becomes even more valuable when shared or combined with the knowledge of other agents. Only the combination of knowledge creates value: in the case of financial markets, liquidity and the desire not to fall prey to superior knowledge in a tight market lead to strong network effects when trading in securities. The combining of the knowledge and the capabilities of different programmers in the software industry (see Chapter 7) leads to superior programming. The themes of knowledge and the power that results from it are taken up again in later sections of this book.

Rugged landscapes

The concept of path dependencies is easily understood by those who hike in mountainous terrain. Set to climb the highest mountain, it is often not possible simply to walk uphill. If such a course is followed, a minor peak with a less spectacular view might be reached, from which the only way onwards is downhill. Instead, it is often necessary to make a long detour as the direct path is barred by steep cliffs, deep valleys or torrents that are impossible to cross. Only after a long search for the right path, especially if one cannot rely on the luxury of a map and the knowledge that is codified within, the summit might finally be conquered. An illustration of such a rugged landscape is given in Figure 2.3.

The analogy of hill-walking is also used in the literature on economic systems. In a special issue of *Organization Science* on complexity and rugged landscapes, such non-linear phenomena are explored. Some ideas

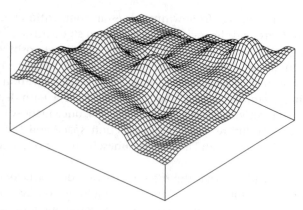

Figure 2.3   Rugged landscape

from these and related papers are illustrated here to clarify the notion of designing complex systems.

- If no interdependencies exist in a system between different elements or agents, the resulting landscape has a single peak. Rational decision-making, as modelled in traditional microeconomic theory, will hence lead to the efficient outcome of the ascent to the highest point. If no single optimum exists, a search for the overall optimum is necessary and good organizational design might even require an increase in the interdependencies between the elements in the system to induce the search for the highest peak. This can be achieved by structuring the organization to increase interaction between its agents; for example, by setting up cross-functional teams. Levinthal and Warglien (1999) model this by designing fitness landscapes to which economic agents adapt. By altering these fitness landscapes, managers can influence how agents operate locally. By establishing and modifying such environments, improvised and self-organized solutions occur. The whole system evolves through the local searches of the agents, who are encouraged to find the overall optimum through a suitable landscape design.[62]
- Path dependencies and positive feedback loops can magnify small initial differences between two configurations when external change occurs that is responded to by internal adaptation.[63] Sterman and Wittenberg (1999) model the rise and fall in scientific paradigms that depend on the quality of the theory, which is reinforced by the researchers believing in it and working on it. They also apply this thinking to management fads that are fashionable for only a few

years, to be replaced by other much-hyped management concepts that equally fail to live up to their promises. In the example of hill-walking in rugged landscapes, such a situation of nearly identical configurations that lead nevertheless to very different configurations over time because of path dependencies and positive feedback loops translates into two hikers faced with deteriorating weather conditions. Searching for shelter, they might end up in places far apart although they might initially have been very close to one other – for example, separated only by a small torrent.

- Lane and Maxfield (1997) draw attention to the foresight horizon and link this to strategy. With complex foresight horizons, the environment of the system changes rapidly and the agents operating in the system are faced with the task of estimating the best future strategy in light of the uncertainty created by such complex, rugged landscapes. If the terrain is not plain but littered with small hills or obstacles, the complexity and ambiguity of the system matters. In such a terrain it is advisable for a group of hikers to rely on scouts to explore the situation beyond the horizon. In the context of organizations, that translates into the fostering of relationships within and across the organizations' boundaries to absorb new information and to remain flexible.
- Milgrom and Roberts (1995b) show that, in the case of such a complex foresight horizon, the search problem can be simplified when the complementarity relationship between the elements of the system is known. In this case, the qualitative direction of the optimal response to an environmental challenge is clear: '[T]he complementarity structure gives the decision maker lots of information about the form of a "good" (but not necessarily optimal) decision and allows her to focus attention on that limited set.'[64] Furthermore, Milgrom and Roberts (1995b) concentrate in their paper on the path that leads from a local peak to the highest peak. In a rugged landscape of many hills and valleys, with many local peaks, the non-convexities imply that adjustments may need to be made in the form of big leaps rather than a series of small steps. Only large-scale changes in the configuration of many of the complementary elements thus allow for a jump from one peak to the next; a series of small steps might not lead to any change. In the analogy of hill-walking, this translates to the possibility that the group of hikers, clearly seeing the higher peak while on top of a minor peak, could easily make a big leap by flying by helicopter from one sunny peak to the other. However, when making small steps searching for the right path, the walk towards the higher peak involves the risk of getting lost in fog below when descending through the valley between the two peaks.

Consistent configurations – application of the theory

Modern manufacturing

The first authors to use the mathematical approach to systems theory in the realm of economics were Milgrom and Roberts (1990b). They showed how the modern manufacturing system applied by the motor vehicle manufacturer, Toyota, was indeed a system, with the main parameters configured in a consistent way. They list sixteen elements, from production and marketing to strategy and structure, that are complementary to each other and form two distinct systems – the business model of mass production introduced at the beginning of the twentieth century by Henry Ford, as described by Chandler (1990); and the business model of modern manufacturing championed by Toyota.

By introducing flexible machines, Toyota was able to use short production runs and supply a large variety of different models. The flexibility allowed for a reduction in inventories and the specific targeting of different consumer segments. It was worthwhile for Toyota to introduce such a flexible production line alongside the practices of a high-performance work system. This system puts a premium on the skills and initiative of employees, and allows the use of cross-functional teams that in turn reinforce the returns to the whole system by shortening development cycles for new models. Such process improvements along the production line allow the use of even shorter production runs.

Although ultimately inadequate mathematically,[65] Milgrom and Roberts (1990b) showed that systems theory can be of use for a rigorous treatment of the systemic nature of many economic phenomena.

The airline industry

In the context of the airline industry, the framework of systems theory was applied by Porter (1996), and Greifenstein and Weiss (2004). Two distinct business models resting on fundamentally different configurations of key parameters compete with each other. The business model of full-service carriers rests on a hub-and-spoke structure, where smaller aircraft, operating on legs with less generic traffic, feed larger aircraft that operate between the few hubs of an airline company or on intercontinental routes. One of the main target groups is business travellers. A high-quality service is provided in the form of the check-through of luggage, special lounges at airports, frequent flyer programmes, and on-board service during the flight. The cost position for airlines operating along this business model is high, because of the need for different aircraft and the resulting need for a range of operating and maintenance work groups. The reliance on travel agents to bundle together different parts of a journey and the necessary commissions incurred further adds to prices that are already high compared to those of low-cost airlines.

In their business model, low-cost airlines configure many of these parameters with their opposite: they concentrate on routes that are of similar length and fly point-to-point, usually from secondary airports that are more cost effective. Doing this allows them to operate only one type of aircraft, so that only one pool of staff is necessary for operation and maintenance. The complex logistics of baggage handling and on-board meals is eliminated, thus saving time in the turnaround time of aircraft – an aspect that is further reinforced by the use of less crowded secondary airports. The easily understood pricing scheme allows for a direct ticket sale to customers considering flying with the company. The whole configuration of the system supports cheap fares and thereby entices people to fly who would otherwise not have considered it, or would have chosen another destination. The appeal to people of visiting their friends and relatives easily complements the system of low-cost airlines.

The way in which the configuration of co-ordination and control mechanisms affects cost and quality outcomes in the departure process of flights is considered in more detail in a field study by Gittell (1998). She also concludes that 'particularly for coordination and control, two of the critical backbones of organization design, the messages communicated through the design must be clear and consistent'.[66] A more detailed exploration of these two distinct business systems can be found in Greifenstein and Weiss (2004).

Corporate governance institutions

In the case of corporate ownership and governance structures, Bebchuk and Roe (2004) show that past positions matter for their evolution over time because of sunk costs, network externalities and complementarities. Path dependencies explain the prevalence of the current distinct governance systems that can be observed in both America and continental Europe. The ownership patterns that emerged previously led to some dominant interest groups. Rent-seeking behaviour by those controlling the system leads to the persistence of this – even when a more efficient design could be obtained. The fear of a potential loss of private benefits of control for those powerful interest groups entrenches the current system, since these groups protect their economic rents by their decisions not to change the configuration of the governance system.

This argument is developed further by Schmidt and Spindler (2002). By using the analogy of hill-walking, they reason that any deviation from a local peak, and the consistent system it constitutes, is, by definition, enough to make the whole system inconsistent. By changing the configuration of only one element, a small step downhill is made and efficiency is hampered. When policy-makers want to restore efficiency to the governance system, they generally face two options – either to adjust other elements as well, or to restore the one element that has led to the inconsistent configuration. Schmidt and Spindler (2002) argue that, even in the case of a severe crisis, the option to restore the original system has its merits, since the immediate benefits are greatest. The group of hikers in the rugged landscape of systems theory is best advised to go back to the sunshine on top of the local peak rather than continue to search for the highest peak and risk getting lost in the fog lying in the valley.

Both papers thus show that the persistence effects of consistent systems can be great. Change or convergence to one equilibrium system of best practices is not easy if complementarities and path dependencies prevail.

2.3   Value creation of organizational design

Systems theory formalizes the idea that elements of any organizational design need to be configured in a consistent way if complementarities exist between them. Only the right fit between the various parameters of system design leads to value creation. But what exactly is meant by 'value'? What really is success in an organizational design, and what leads to its efficiency? And, furthermore, how can we measure such value creation? The purpose of this section is to clarify the notion of value and efficiency, and of profit and success.

Defining value

A 'good' organizational design creates value for those taking part in that organization, and for those using the products and services of that organization. Such value manifests itself in economic rents generated by the design and distributed to its various organizational constituencies.

Economic rents

An economic rent is the surplus generated by a resource or a bundle of resources over and above its rate of return determined in a perfect competitive market. Economic rents are the result of deviations from the solution under perfect competition. Oligopolistic and monopolistic market conditions prevail, for example, for technological reasons (when increasing returns lead to an oligopoly in the provision of certain goods or services) or because of informational asymmetries (when markets fail for reasons of adverse selection). Monopoly positions can also be created deliberately by investment decisions that lead to specific and co-specialized assets. In this case, the fundamental transformation leads to an *ex post* bilateral monopoly that is the basis for economic rents. Economic rents are thus the result of specific investment decisions.

Such investment decisions by the various economic agents involved in the organizational design, however, do not occur automatically. Even if the investment is advantageous, the specificity that comes with it leads to situations of potential hold-up, rendering the economic rent unsafe. The result is the familiar underinvestment problem described by Williamson (1985). Necessary to the organizational design are therefore not only the correct incentives for such value-creating specific investments, but also the correct balance of power or other safeguards that lead those investing *ex ante* to appropriate their share of the economic rent *ex post* as well. This interplay between *ex-ante* investment incentives and *ex post* distribution rules for economic rent determines the efficiency of organizational designs.

Note here that economic rents are the basis for the competitive advantage of the whole organization. Collis and Montgomery (1998, p. 72) define competitive advantage as 'the way a company creates value through the configuration and coordination of its multi-business activities'. Systems theory can clearly be seen behind this definition: only if the elements are configured consistently can a competitive advantage for the organization be built up. The sustainability of such a competitive advantage is one of the main research areas in the literature on strategic management, described in more detail in Section 3.1. Here, the notion of path dependency features even more prominently.[67] The sustainability of competitive advantage also influences investment decisions, and thus the efficiency of the organizational design.

Efficiency

Efficiency in organizational design is achieved if the right investment decisions are made and the amount of economic rents that can be distributed to all agents connected in some way to the organization is maximized. This occurs whenever the complementarities between the various elements of organizational design are utilized, especially if the right balance between investment incentives (the decisions and related efforts that generate an economic rent) and decision-making power (the decisions and related efforts that distribute an economic rent) is struck.

In this case, the global maximum in the rugged landscapes of systems theory is reached.

The efficiency concept applied in this book is hence the maximization of total wealth for all agents connected in some way to the organization, and the efficiency of organizational design can be evaluated against this theoretical maximum. The micro-motives of the individual agents and their private maximization problems are, however, often at odds with the macro perspective of total value creation. An efficient organizational design takes these micro-motives into account in order to come as close as possible to macro efficiency.

When applying the thinking of systems theory, as described in the previous section, the concept of path dependency highlights the fact that efficiency in the present organizational design need not translate into an efficient design in the future. Changes in external conditions can make some other, totally distinct configuration the better design. Such 'earthquakes' that drastically change the look of the rugged landscape can occur in business and economics. One such example was the shift in production methods highlighted by Chandler (1990) and described in Section 2.1. Other recent shifts in the competitive environment are listed in Section 2.4 below. When evaluating the efficiency of organizational design, one must take into account dynamic aspects, such as the ability to change and the possibilities for adaptation, in order to avoid using a path that leads to a dead end.

Measuring value

With regard to organizational design, how can we measure the economic rents generated, and how can we evaluate the design's efficiency, compared to a theoretically ideal organizational model? Economic rents take many forms. They are part of the payments that the constituencies of the organization receive inasmuch as they are above the rate that would prevail in competitive markets or in the absence of specific investments. They are also of a more intangible nature when the preferences of individual agents are involved, when people have an intrinsic motivation to work for a certain firm or profession, for example, or when the social life of these agents is taken into account. This section therefore cannot describe comprehensively how the amount of economic rents an organizational design creates can be measured, as this is too daunting a task. Instead, listed here are some more or less vague measures for a guesstimate of economic rents and the efficiency of the design under investigation.

Profit as a measure of value

Profit is a very common measure of the success of a company. It is measured subject to well-established accounting standards and disclosed frequently. In the form of stock prices and the resulting market capitalization of companies listed on a stock exchange, immediate changes in value can be identified throughout the market's trading hours.

Profits are, however, related only imperfectly to economic rents. The accounting standards that have evolved since the 1920s are skewed: it is not value or economic rents generated by the organizational design that is measured, but rather profits that accrue to shareholders. It is only their part of the economic rent that is counted when taking the excess return to capital, adjusted for risk, into account. The elaborate accounting standards are of little use, since a large part of the value that is created in society does not show up in the balance sheets of organizations. The return on investments in human capital, for example, either does not show up at all or is treated as an expense. It is therefore necessary to look for other measures to complement profits in order to get a more accurate idea of the value created by a particular organizational configuration.

Other measures of value

Other potential measures for economic rents and value creation include:

- Market share in product markets and revenue growth rates of firms are measures of value creation and efficiency that are less sensitive to the question of who gets the rents generated in an organization. A high market share of any firm need not necessarily signal that it is the most efficient design. Especially in industries that are subject to increasing returns, either because of economies of scale and scope or network effects, or even both, market share might be caused by past success rather than present efficiency. Persistency caused by switching costs or complementarities might, in such a case, keep the inefficient organizational design alive. The same holds for revenue growth rates. In many emergent industries resting on the rise of the internet, the race to install a larger base than rival firms in order to profit from subsequent network effects among users wasted a lot of resources.
- The labour market might also offer a hint about successful organizational designs. And the decisions that young graduates make when deciding to join a particular industry and firm can be a good measure of success and value creation. However, it is also possible that bubbles lead to irrational decisions in the labour market. In the wake of the

internet boom, many people devoted their human capital to investment banking firms that subsequently let many of them go as the boom turned to bust. Tremendous amounts of human capital were wasted in this process.

- Reputation or positive press coverage are also measures that have a potential role to play in telling good organizations from bad. However, one must be aware that there is also a lot of statistical noise and potential herding behaviour in such press coverage. Star executives who were once revered on the front covers of business magazines later came to be implicated in scandals. And many firms, such as ABB, lauded by many researchers in academia for their good organizational design, later found themselves in trouble when external or internal conditions changed and the design could not keep up with the changes.

- Reports by companies on their social responsibilities and environmental impact can add to the understanding of the efficiency of an organizational design and whether the economic rents generated by it are genuine or are mortgaged from the future. Such reporting is, however, rather spurious, and no standards comparable to that for financial reporting exist. It is for this reason that many corporate reports amount to nothing more than corporate storytelling.

The deliberate decision not to measure

The measurement of value creation and the amount of economic rents generated by a particular design is also an element of that design. Complementarities exist with other parameters. It might therefore be necessary to configure measurement so that almost nothing is measured. While making it difficult to assess the efficiency of such a system, it is an important parameter that needs to be balanced with other elements. See, for example, Brickley *et al.* (2003) for a description of how the wrong alignment of measurements, goals and decision rights brought down a firm such as Enron.

In some cases it might therefore be better not to measure aspects that can easily be measured. Detailed measurement would distract attention and performance incentives away from elements that do not lend themselves to easy measurement. While measurement is often disregarded in the case of firms, at least compared to markets, this holds even more for other types of organizations. In academia, for example, the quality of teaching and research is difficult to measure. Instead of relying on imperfect substitutes such as the quantity of people taught or the number of papers published, a deliberate design feature is to refrain from narrow measurement at all. While this might lead many people to pursue their own goals and increase their leisure time, for others it also leads to academic freedom and the possibility of seeking truly innovative ideas, which is the ultimate purpose of an organizational design such as an academic institution. A similar argument for weak measurement is made in Chapter 6, where the organizational design of the German co-operative banking sector is described.

2.4   Changes in the business environment

Organizations are embedded in their environment. The environment influences organizations and the way in which agents operating within a particular organizational design make decisions – thereby determining the overall success of the organization and its constituencies, and the amount of economic rents that can be generated and distributed. Changes in the environment occur like earthquakes in the rugged landscape of competition and can render inadequate the efficacy of a particular organizational design. Other configurations and business models promise better success and efficiency.[68] It is therefore necessary to take possible changes in the business environment into account to understand the quality and robustness of a particular organizational design and how well it copes with the task of finding a new equilibrium.

The purpose of this section is to offer a non-comprehensive list of broad trends in the business environment and to describe how they affect organizations.[69] Factors such as increased technological progress, deregulation or changes in the financial system alter the competitive landscape and lead to changes in the relative importance of the economics upon which any organizational design rests. Dynamic efficiency becomes more important and the configuration of key elements in the organization needs to be geared towards flexibility and adaptability when the environment is prone to frequent change.[70]

Technological progress

One of the main features of today's business environment is the technological advancements that allow for new business models, in the same way that the invention of the telegraph and the steamship allowed for the replacement of the craft system with the system of mass production, as described in Section 2.1. The ability of organizations to innovate thus becomes a necessity for future success.

Creative destruction

In the best traditions of the Austrian school of economics, Schumpeter (1934) has described the forces that drive an economy out of equilibrium and the ongoing process of finding a new equilibrium. His starting point is technological advancement and the innovation possibilities for entrepreneurs made possible by such advancement. Entrepreneurs have an incentive to innovate: they can gain a monopolistic advantage from being the first and only supplier to offer a product based on their innovation, or from producing a good more cheaply in the case of a process innovation. This monopolistic advantage translates into an economic rent as a reward for innovation. But innovation also changes the competitive landscape. The demand for conventional products is replaced by one for the innovative product, and the former ways of doing business become unprofitable, leading such firms to adapt or to leave the business altogether – a process known as *creative destruction*.

Any monopolistic advantage based on such innovation is only temporary: the economic rent is eroded over time because other people and firms can copy the innovation, share in the economic rent, and lead the market to revert towards a competitive equilibrium – until the next entrepreneur arrives on the scene. The long-term rewards from the innovation thereby end up with the consumers, who enjoy better products at competitive prices.

Innovations can take many forms. It is not only the genius of a single entrepreneur, as described by Schumpeter (1934), who invents a new product or improves a production process that leads to the working of such forces of creative destruction. The rugged landscape of competition in complex organizational designs can also be changed when many different constituencies make small investments simultaneously: new peaks can emerge if many people pile up small stones in the same place.

The examples of Toyota implementing the system of modern manufacturing and of low-cost airlines successfully competing with the incumbent hub-and-spoke airlines, described above, illustrate the forces of creative destruction – especially if one considers the near bankruptcy of Toyota's rivals Chrysler and General Motors, and their subsequent adoption of the modern manufacturing system. The same holds true (albeit for other reasons, such as intensive regulation) for the full-service carrier in the airline industry. Incumbent firms in many industries, if they are not resilient enough to progress, find themselves vulnerable to upstarts doing business in a totally different way. Change in a disruptive manner[71] and the mechanism of creative destruction at work have become the notion of the day.

The emergence of the internet and its effect on information

One recent innovation not only introduced new products to the world and changed production processes for the better, but has already had a dramatic effect on many industries and will lead to more changes in the future. An innovation in the gathering, processing, and storing of information has occurred.

Example 2.6 An example of how the internet has changed the way that business is conducted is illustrated in the possibilities of using auctions. Whereas some stock exchanges can look back at a long tradition in trading highly fungible shares and providing a liquid market in such shares, such stock exchanges are limited in their geographical scope: people regularly assembled in a specific area or building during a pre-specified time. With the opportunity to link dispersed computers over private networks or, more recently, through the internet, stock exchanges and electronic communication networks (ECNs) were able to grow beyond these geographical limitations. But not only existing exchanges took advantage of this opportunity to expand. It suddenly became viable to create new markets based on the auction mechanism, that could not previously have existed because of liquidity problems related to low supply and demand in the geographical vicinity. The most prominent example of these new markets is without doubt eBay, where almost any good can be traded. Many services, which are usually more specific than goods, can also be acquired by auction. A company specializing in the matching of supply and demand in this area is Elance, where individual people can easily set up their own 'firm' in the same way that many people prosper by selling and reselling on the platform provided by eBay with their PowerSeller program.

Building on the Arpanet of the 1960s and replacing many proprietary electronic data interchange (EDI) networks, the internet in its current form was created in 1993 with the easy-to-use World Wide Web and its underlying range of protocols such as *http*, *smtp* and *ftp*. The internet has been a tremendous success almost since its introduction. The effect of this 'revolution'[72] has led to increased transparency in business, which simplifies the search in the 'foggy valleys' of the rugged landscape of competition. Dead ends can be identified more easily, and the knowledge of dispersed people can be combined to lead to new insights and innovations. This innovation in information is like equipping hikers in rugged landscapes with detailed maps and global positioning devices that broaden their horizons.

Recall from Section 2.1 that many theories of the firm were based on information, or the lack of it, to explain the existence and boundaries of firms. Innovations change relative prices, and innovations in information change the relative advantage of organizational designs. By making information more widespread and more evenly distributed, the use of market mechanisms becomes feasible where it was disregarded before. New interfaces between markets and hierarchies can be introduced, and complexity in organizational design reduced by modularization. This often frees up resources that can be redeployed towards more innovative activities.

Regulation and liberalization

A second major driving force in today's business environment is the liberalization of many markets and the changing nature of regulation in industries that were previously dominated by a single firm enjoying a (natural) monopoly.

Natural monopoly

Firms in various industries have to invest heavily in infrastructure in order to serve their customers. Telephone lines, electricity wires and gas pipes have to reach each and every household or plant, and railway tracks have to be laid between towns before any business can be done. It is often claimed that these utilities are natural monopolies. Other areas of the economy, such as the software industry or the securities transaction industry, also exhibit such features. These two industries are the subjects of case studies in the second part of this book.

The economics behind a natural monopoly have already been dealt with briefly in Section 2.2, where the concept of superadditivity was contrasted with that of supermodularity. A natural monopoly is based on the cost advantage that economies of scale or scope bring with them. This can be expressed mathematically by subadditive cost functions. In the case of a single product, the condition $c_1(x) + c_2(x) > c(2x)$ must hold, with $c_1(x)$ and $c_2(x)$ being the production costs two different firms would have, and $c(2x)$ being the costs a single firm would incur for the production of the same quantity.

In the case of more than one product, 'subadditivity refers to a situation in which a single firm is able to exploit both economies of scale and economies of scope and hence produce any combination of the same listing of goods more cheaply than the same listing of goods could be produced by *any* alternative industry configuration of more than one firm'.[73] If the condition of subadditivity holds, the market only supports a single firm supplying the good. This is usually the case if high fixed costs are combined with low marginal cost. The first firm investing in such infrastructure faces marginal costs close to zero and will readily lower its price if a second firm enters the market. Anticipating such behaviour by the incumbent, the potential entrant will refrain from entering, since it could not recoup its investment on the infrastructure.

Note also that the disadvantages of a natural monopoly can affect adjacent industries. To invest in specific infrastructure exposes the firm to potential hold-ups by its suppliers or customers. It is therefore quite common to integrate backwards and forwards along the value chain to safeguard the position in the activity that resembles a natural monopoly, an argument of transaction cost theory already described in Section 2.1 above. Vertically integrated monopolies thus came to prominence in industries such as telecommunications, utilities, the postal service and the railways.

However, monopolies, especially at many stages along the value chain, are usually an inefficient market design: too little of a product of inferior quality is offered for too high a price, and investment incentives for innovation are subdued by the lack of competition. Governments usually intervene to fix prices close to their competitive level in such a natural monopoly setting. Such intervention can take the form of nationalization of the monopolist, or the close regulation of a private firm. Both solutions have their disadvantages, since decision-making power, investment incentives and residual claims are misaligned.

The effect of liberalization or deregulation

With the introduction of the Single European Market, the former natural monopolies within the many national economies in the European Union (EU) were integrated into one market. The economics behind the production in the former nationalized natural monopolies were not affected by this opening of the market. Subadditivity of costs usually still prevails, and an inefficient market structure is the result. Setting up a pan-European natural monopolist is, however, difficult: too many vested interests are in place and too many economic rents are at stake. Instead of endless haggling between the various European governments to distribute these rents when organizing the market into a pan-European natural monopolist controlled by a body consisting of representatives of the various governments, the solution was to liberalize and deregulate such markets, characterized by the economics of a natural monopoly.[74]

With liberalization, the autonomy to structure economic activity in an efficient way returns. Areas of the rugged landscape of competition previously barred by decree are opened for exploration by liberalization. Entrepreneurs exploring the new territory might find a business model that allows them to compete effectively with the incumbent firm and even to appropriate a part of the economic rent. This allows for new forms of organizational design to be applied.

Many markets have been de- or re-regulated in recent years. Examples include, among others, the telecommunications sector, the energy sector, the airline industry, and the financial services sector. Often, as regulatory barriers fall, so do the barriers to entry into an industry. New business opportunities arise for innovative entrepreneurs or companies. Within these industries, falling prices, improved service, and much restructuring and reshaping of the boundaries of firms can be identified. In particular, an unbundling occurs of many activities that were previously performed by the natural monopolist to safeguard themselves against hold-up. Markets come into being where none existed before.

Example 2.7   A prime, but notorious, example is Enron. Before the accounting scandals and the related fraud that led to the demise of Enron, the company was creating a market for energy-related products. By actively trading spot and future contracts, Enron pioneered the world's largest online commodity trading site. Launched in November 1999, EnronOnline handled 548,000 transactions with a gross notional value of US$336 billion.[a] This allowed other companies to enter only certain business areas and to rely on the market to co-ordinate the generation, transmission and distribution of energy that was previously executed by the integrated natural monopolies.

---

[a]   See Enron (2001, p. 9).

Instead of owning the natural monopolist and providing only weakly powered incentives in a nationalized bureaucracy, governments withdraw to regulate only certain areas of competition (for example, in business involving households compared to a liberal regime for business among firms), and begin to level the playing field between the incumbent, often privatized, ex-monopolist and its upstart competitors. The pricing in particular of access and interconnection charges between different infrastructures are subject to approval by the regulator. Additionally, a universal service requirement is often put in place by the regulator to prevent companies from focusing solely on the attractive customers that generate high revenues at little cost.[75]

Standard setting

Another business trend, enhanced in a co-evolutionary way by technologies such as the internet and deregulation, is the growing necessity to agree on standards. Only if, for example, the basic vocabulary and syntax of websites are identical around the world, is it possible to use the internet effectively. Standards allow for the implementation of interfaces between distinct modules in a system's design and are thus a means of handling the complexity involved in today's business world. This allows new methods of co-operation across boundaries between different firms, and the disintegration of former natural monopolies becomes possible, a theme that will be taken up again in Section 3.2. It is the purpose of this section to highlight the economics behind the standards.

Network externalities

Standards are necessary if network externalities prevail. Although network effects often occur in industries that can be characterized as natural monopolies, the concept of network externalities highlights the benefit of a good for consumers – their utility is enhanced by other agents using the same good or technology. A natural monopoly, as explained above, is a property of the producers' cost curves, especially in the combination of high fixed costs with low or constant marginal costs. That 'the existence of network externalities cannot be claimed as a reason in favor of a monopoly market structure' is also explained by Economides (1996, p. 683).

Network externalities arise because of the complementary relationship between the different components of a network. As indicated in note 61 in this chapter, the telephone network is a prime example of these effects. A phone is only of value if it can be used to call somebody else – that is, there must be a second phone connected to the network. The utility increases in the number of phones connected, because more people can potentially be called. Specifically, in a network of n different, but connected nodes, $n(n-1)$ potential connections can be made. Any person joining the network increases the number of possible connections to $n(n+1)$. The resulting utility, not only for the marginal agent joining the network, but for all agents already in the network, is thereby increased. Economides (1996) compares different designs of networks where switches and bottlenecks exist. Of course, these more complex networks have their own economics, and each individual layout must be analysed for its peculiarities.

The complexity in networks and the access that switches or supernodes provide for other nodes in the network can be exploited strategically and can as such be the basis for economic rents. The decision whether or not to allow for an interconnection between different networks – that is, whether to implement an open or a proprietary standard – can in particular be of great strategic importance. Compatibility increases the benefit for agents in different networks, since all nodes can be reached via a suitable interconnection between the two networks. The decision to join an open standard or to retain a proprietary network with impeded compatibility not only has an effect on the company 'operating' the network but also on the people joining a specific network.

Industry-wide standard-setting makes sense: it encourages consumers to buy the new products or technologies immediately rather than delay their purchase until it becomes evident which network is the dominant standard. In this way, buyers are not locked into a product that lacks the support and co-specialized investments of other companies.

On the other hand, companies opting for proprietary standards must take these network externalities into account in order to reach a critical mass for the network. This is often done by initially subsidizing a special user group such as, for example, early adopters, who have a multiplier role. In the credit card industry, cardholders are often subsidized through generous interest rates. Losses incurred on this side of the network are compensated by fees taken on the side of merchants who accept such credit cards. See Rochet and Tirole (2003) for an exploration of two-sided markets where one side subsidizes the other to achieve overall success for the network.

Example 2.8 There was a fierce battle in the 1970s in the consumer electronics industry to establish the standard for VCRs among three competing technologies: the first to be introduced was Betamax by Sony, with Video2000 by Philips and VHS by Matsushita following later. Despite the headstart by Sony with its technical expertise, VHS eventually won the battle to become the industry standard as a result of clever marketing and an open licensing policy.[a] The process was reinforced by network effects and path dependencies when other agents, such as video rental stores, made co-specialized investments.

Today, even the biggest companies in the consumer electronics industry share the risks inherent in the network externalities of new technologies and opt for open industry-wide standards. The underlying technology of DVD players by Philips, for example, is based on a collaboration with five rivals, including Sony and Yamaha.[b] However, the desire to appropriate most of the economic rent that a successful standard creates leads other companies to keep the underlying technology of their product proprietary. Such a battle for the next standard is currently raging in the video games industry, where Nintendo, Sony and Microsoft are competing heavily with their GameCube, Playstation, and Xbox, respectively.[c]

---

[a] See Erhardt (2004, p. 282).
[b] See *The Economist* (2002e, p. 56).
[c] See Dietl and Royer (2003) for an in-depth analysis of the video games industry.

Note that the effect of standards is complementary to the other two changes in the business environment described so far. Standards allow for faster technological advances, since uncertainty about the winning standard is reduced and competing producers sometimes even join forces to develop new technology. At the same time, the dismantling of barriers through liberalization increases the benefits to industry-wide standards. They can serve as a focal point to simultaneous, but independent, decisions and as such act as a lighthouse some way into the uncharted territories of the area opened by liberalization. All three changes lead to a change in the rugged landscape of competition and necessitate a response in the system of organizational design.

The financial system

Another major force affecting business is change in the financial system. Legal requirements lead to increased disclosure and transparency, and the development of financial markets. The regulation of risk that banks are allowed to take leads to changes in the way that companies are financed. Both these aspects have an effect on the optimal allocation of ownership and control. These changes are subsumed here under the heading of the financial system.[76]

Importance of the financial system

Different financial systems require different corporate systems, and different constellations of the parameter settings in their subsystems. The Anglo-Saxon market-based system of, for example, the USA and the UK relies on external finance and outside information. Shareholdings are often fragmented and transactions take place frequently. Owners, assuming that shareholders occupy this role, usually have little influence. In contrast to that system, European and Japanese financial systems are based more on a long-term relationship between the providers of capital and the firm. Larger stakes by the shareholders and less liquid markets make shareholders more permanent owners who rely on inside information. Financial markets and markets in general are less developed, so that many constituencies of the firm do not have the option of a fast exit from the relationship. In this case, the parties to the firm behave more like partners.

These differences in the many parameters that make up consistent financial systems lead to different capabilities regarding the adaptability and flexibility in these systems when faced with major changes in the surrounding environment. Up to the 1980s, there was a period of relative stability in the world, with changes happening incrementally and at a slow pace. This placed a premium on the Japanese and German financial system. The Japanese method of employment and industrial relations, in particular, was regarded as best practice, and it was felt that all other nations should implement it as well if they did not want to fall behind economically. In a study of the automobile industry, Womack *et al.* (1990) describe how these practices had to be adopted by American firms if they wanted to remain competitive.

Example 2.9 Baker (1992) describes how Beatrice – a small American dairy that over the years had become a huge conglomerate – created value first by scaling up the business in the same way as described by Chandler (1990) for the oil business. After the Second World War, it added value by buying and consolidating many small companies that lacked access to a financial market which was at that time less developed than today. The company, however, overreached itself, and too many unrelated investments that were no longer manageable resulted in the CEO's resignation in 1985. The company was made private shortly afterwards by Kohlberg Kravis Roberts & Co. (KKR) with the individual divisions spun-off and divested.

Relative advantage of a particular system?

Porter (1992) describes in his article 'Capital Disadvantage: America's Failing Capital Investment System' the many shortcomings of the Anglo-Saxon financial system: too much emphasis on 'numbers' leads to the biased way in which the internal capital market allocates scarce resources towards investments that pay off over a short period, while neglecting investments in, for example, training people, which is less perfectly measurable and usually requires a longer time horizon than the one that the highly-developed markets for capital and labour 'allow' for. The conclusion that Porter drew was a need to change the American system into a system that resembled aspects of the Japanese and German financial systems. This view was corrected to some extent by Miller (1994), who states that, while there are flaws in the form of short-termism, the ultimate checks for competitiveness and for the managers running large organizations are the product markets where consumers make their choices.

At the time of writing, however, the Japanese economy has encountered severe difficulties and the European economies operating the relationship-based financial system are lagging behind American (and to a lesser extent British) performance.[77] What happened in the interim? This change resulted from a dramatic alteration in the speed of change during the 1990s. Disruptive political and technological changes favoured the more flexible approach of the Anglo-Saxon financial system. The possibility for change is more likely when relying on arm's-length contracts than on long-term relationships in which both sides are hesitant to sever ties because of the many roles such relationships have for the various partners. Employees are not easily dismissed because of their role in corporate governance and as providers of capital in the form of pension obligations – and a system of human resource development that relies on some form of apprenticeship with lower wages than the marginal productivity paid at the beginning of a career, and relatively higher wages than the marginal productivity paid close to retirement. The same dual role, as provider of finance and as important member in the governance system, was assigned to the banks. When faced with the necessity of rapid change, these arrangements simply did not allow adaptation as quickly as the Anglo-Saxon financial system was able to. Again, today, a system change, this time Japan and Europe abandoning their relationship-based model for the American alternative, is being advocated by many economists and politicians.

Changes in the financial system also alter the business environment in which organizations have to operate. Their design, including their strategy and structure, their boundaries and governance, is the subject of the next chapter.

2.5 The inadequacy of traditional theories of the firm

This chapter has introduced the foundations of organizational design that will be used in this book. It has highlighted various traditional theories of the firm that each focuses on a relatively narrow aspect or idea, and that explain analytically the existence and boundaries of firms. As a second module, the ideas of systems theory have been described. They suggest that such an analytical approach might not be enough to capture the complexity of organizational design. In the last section, some sweeping changes to the environment in which firms operate have been mentioned, which also expose some shortcomings in the traditional theories of the firm.

Putting together these different modules, it is sensible to take stock and show explicitly the inadequacy of the traditional, mainly analytical, theories of the firm in light of the many changes in the business environment that demand a co-ordinated response in the system of organizational design.

Specific investments and power

Value in the form of economic rents is created by investments that are specific to a certain relationship or a certain firm. Such specificity, however, can be a problem when complete contracts cannot be written on all future contingencies, and when no credible commitment to distribute economic rents in the future can be made *ex ante*, as was highlighted by Hart (1995) in the incomplete contracting approach.

Because of the nature of this contractual incompleteness, the issue of residual decision-making arises and economic analysis is no longer trivial. As a result, many advantageous investments with a positive net present value are not undertaken. Decision-making in future circumstances that cannot be covered in contracts therefore introduces the necessity of assigning this power and authority to a specific party to the contract whenever joint decisions are impossible because of divergent interests.

To be sure where the challenge for any organizational designer lies, let us reformulate this dilemma: whenever there is an economic rent created that will be realized in the future, the power to make decisions affecting that future date and thereby to influence the distribution of this economic rent must be taken into account for the present investment decision. Where markets for these investments exist, they are of a general nature. The threat of having the 'power' to exit the relationship via the market is enough in this case to ensure the efficient investment pattern. However, competitive markets seldom allow for the existence of economic rents.

On the other hand, if investments are specific inside a relationship, an economic rent is generated, but the power that outside markets bring with them is usually not enough to protect this economic rent. The default solution of refraining *ex ante* from such value-enhancing specific investments, in this case for fear of expropriation *ex post* by a more powerful principal, leads to underinvestment and an inefficient organizational design. The issue of to whom power is allocated is therefore at the heart of any organizational design.

Traditional solutions

Many theories of the firm described in Section 2.1 have offered possible solutions. The transaction cost economics, for example, propagated vertical integration and an adjustment of the boundaries of the organization. This has worked well in many industries, as proposed by Chandler (1990) and explained at the beginning of this chapter. In these industries, relying mainly on financial capital, the constituency with the *ex-post* power to appropriate any economic rents simply acquired the asset in question and undertook the specification itself. This unified the claim to economic rents generated by specific investments with the power to appropriate these rents into one economic principal. Ownership, the combination of residual claims with residual decision rights, is thus a good means of implementing efficient investments.

However, other problems arose out of this attempt to unify residual claims and residual decision rights. Financial constraints often do not allow for a unified ownership but lead to dispersed shareholdings and the reliance on professional managers. This brings the problem of information economics to the fore, especially the asymmetrical distribution of information and the unobservable characteristics or behaviour of other agents.[78] Incentives other than ownership are needed to mitigate such problems. Agency theory has developed good ideas and elaborate models that have led to the introduction of many instruments (such as stock options to reward good decisions, or tournaments for the promotion of the best agents) that make organizational design more efficient when such information asymmetries exist.

One class of successful organizational design has thus emerged: corporations have only a single-dimensional objective and are driven by the maximization of shareholder value. They reside in industries of the 'old economy', where physical or financial capital is the most important and often the only strategic asset. The owners of this capital have the right incentives to undertake the optimal specific investments, and any power rests formally with them. These providers of the specific investment that is the basis for the economic rent hire other agents such as workers or subcontractors in well-functioning markets – markets that, especially in the Anglo-Saxon financial system, are well developed and liquid. Such an optimized organizational design seems to lie on a peak in the rugged landscape of competition.

What is 'wrong' with traditional solutions?

The interesting question is whether or not this peak is the global maximum in these hills, and whether or not it remains the global maximum when changes in the business environments, highlighted in Section 2.4, are taken into account.

One crucial but largely implicit assumption is the notion of power that is used in the incomplete contracting approach. In this approach, the residual decision-making power is conferred on a single economic principal – be it an individual entrepreneur or a group of people with similar characteristics, such as shareholders, who are all interested in financial profit. Incentives for this principal are optimized through the allocation of ownership rights. The behaviour of other economic agents is prescribed by complete contracts and mechanisms that solve for any information asymmetries and are offered by the principal who ensures, through his/her ownership rights, that any economic rent accrued over the usual market returns reverts to him/her. In a grand *ex-ante* contract the optimal future decisions for all agents are calculated in such a way that they will optimally choose the desired behaviour that maximizes the economic rent of the principal. This supposes that the business landscape allows for good foresight and has a single, clearly visible peak. In such a setting, the allocation of power is clear.

However, this ideal world of agency theory does not coincide with the real world and the changing business environment. Technological progress and liberalization make local information and knowledge a key parameter in a rugged landscape. No grand *ex-ante* contract is possible any more.

If economic rents are generated through the complementary specific investments of many principals, an organizational design that assigns ownership and the related power only to a single principal is inadequate. Such an allocation of authority adversely influences the incentives of other people: they underinvest if they feel unprotected and vulnerable to expropriation of their economic rents generated by their specific investments. Striking a balance of power is crucial in an organizational design when specific investments by multiple constituencies are necessary to generate economic rents.

With the creation of new markets made possible by liberalization and the better use of information, it becomes feasible to use markets and the power they bring with their exit option to provide for a countervailing source of power and strike a delicate balance of power in the organizational design. As many activities are shifted back to markets, the increased reliance on these markets leads to a shift in the boundary of hitherto integrated firms. Langlois (2003) speaks in this context of 'an *unmaking* of Chandler's revolution'.[79] Having started this chapter with the thesis proposed by Chandler (1990), we have returned full circle and are confronted with its antithesis!

A balance of power

What, then, is the best organizational design resting on 'new foundations', to borrow the title of Zingales (2000)? Where should power reside and which forms of incentives should be given to advance specific investments by multiple constituencies? And how can we – in best dialectic tradition – find the synthesis from the thesis of Chandler and the antithesis of Langlois?

As previously suggested, many of the changes in the business environment lead to an increased importance of information and knowledge. Human capital is the repository of knowledge. Changes that lead to a premium on information and knowledge hence lead to a change in the importance of human capital, especially relative to financial capital. This holds even more true as many institutions, such as rating agencies or private equity funds, enhance the functioning of financial markets, thereby allowing for sophisticated financial arrangements, such as search funds,[80] that in turn allow for a better use of human capital.

Unlike financial assets, the solution proposed by transaction cost economics of vertical integration is not feasible. Knowledge is often too tacit in nature and thus inseparable from the person owning it. Human capital cannot be sold. Therefore, an adjustment of the boundaries cannot be the solution to unifying both residual power and specific investment opportunities in one economic entity. In the 'new economy' the providers of financial capital, the entrepreneur with his/her business idea, and the human capital involved in making the idea work are all bound together in a nexus of multiple specific investments. The success of such an organization does not rest only on the brilliance of the entrepreneur's idea, the enthusiasm of the people working for the company or the access to finance to quickly roll out products and services, but on a combination of these factors together. A successful organization operating in a business setting such as the 'new economy' will have to find a way to balance the different powers and to build checks against them, so that all can be assured of their share of the economic rents generated by their specific investment.

It is the very nature of this system – the necessity of different economic principals, all investing simultaneously in specific assets with the investments made being complementary to each other – that makes the assignment of power in an organizational design overwhelmingly important. Every economic agent has some characteristics of a principal, rendering the concept of who is principal and who is agent obsolete and even misleading if not applied carefully. The analysis undertaken in agency models can be dangerous, and a synthesis, as prescribed by systems theory, is necessary. Only with this systemic view can the various instruments strike a balance of incentives, and a balance of power in organizations be taken into account. This result is summarized best by Rajan and Zingales (2001b): 'Thus, unlike the ownership of unique alienable assets, which can be allocated simply by sale, control over other critical resources has to be built up through a variety of mechanisms such as internal organization, work rules, and incentive schemes.'[81] It is to these and other instruments and building blocks of organizational design that we turn next.

Notes

1. See Chandler (1990) for an historic account of the emergence of the modern firm.
2. Another argument in favour of vertical integration was the specialized nature of such investments, and this specificity made the system vulnerable to delay by other parties. As a possible solution to this threat, the integration of different activities in the value chain into one hierarchy seemed to be a good idea. More on this transaction cost argument follows in the third subsection of Section 2.1.
3. Note the crucial difference between rents and profits that is relevant here: profit refers to the accounting notion of that portion of rents created that accrues to the shareholders. However, economic rents can also be generated by and distributed to other stakeholders in an enterprise. The use of the term 'economic rent' is preferred here, since the emphasis is not on one constituency alone, but on the overall welfare. See also Section 2.3 for this distinction.
4. Coase (1937, p. 391).
5. Coase (1937, p. 392).
6. Alchian and Demsetz (1972, p. 779).
7. Opportunism is described as 'self-interest seeking with guile'. See Williamson (1985, p. 47).
8. Bounded rationality is described by Simon (1961, p. xxiv) as human behaviour that is 'intendedly rational, but only limitedly so'. The importance and necessity of this assumption is questioned by several authors, however. See, for example, Hart (1990).
9. See Alchian and Woodward (1987, p. 113; 1988, p. 67).
10. Williamson (1984, pp. 207ff.).
11. Whinston (2003, p. 3).
12. The use of hostages as an incentive mechanism was first described by Schelling (1956). See Williamson (1985, pp. 169–75) for a formal hostage model.
13. Franchises and other hybrid arrangements are, of course, much more complex than the illustration given here. For a description of such hybrid solutions see, for example, in the case of franchising, Klein (1980); for joint ventures, Hennart (1988); and for strategic alliances, Gerybadze (1995).
14. See Klein and Murphy (1997, p. 417) for a more detailed description of relational contracts.
15. See Dow (1993) for an analysis under which conditions capitalist firms emerge and when labour-managed firms prevail. Capitalist firms owned by shareholders are better when specific investments in physical assets are most important, whereas firms managed and owned by 'labour' can only be found when physical assets are of a general-purpose nature, and specificity of human capital is the key factor.
16. Such endogenous emergence of the monitoring task is also used in describing why banks exist. When free-riding incentives are too large, it makes sense to give a principal the control rights and the residual claim, and have contracts – in the case of banks, debt contracts – with all other agents. See Diamond (1984) for this notion.
17. See Spence (1973) for the conditions and costs that lead to a separating equilibrium in which only the types of higher quality find it worthwhile to acquire such a guarantee for their characteristics.

18. See Jensen and Meckling (1976, p. 308).
19. As such it is a formalization of the ideas first expressed by Berle and Means (1932) and much earlier by Smith ([1776] 1937, p. 700).
20. Jensen and Meckling (1976, p. 308).
21. See Jensen (1986, p. 324) for the role of debt in motivating organizational efficiency.
22. See Holmström (1982), who models the primary role of the principal in team production of many agents to break the budget-balancing constraint.
23. See Fama and Jensen (1983b, pp. 303ff.) and Fama and Jensen (1983a).
24. See Section 3.3 for a more thorough analysis of the multi-tasking problem.
25. Laffont and Tirole (2001, p. 44).
26. This is further developed in the work of Rajan and Zingales, especially in Rajan and Zingales (1998). See also Section 3.4.
27. See Hill (1996, p. 2). On the knowledge-based theory of the firm in general, see Casson (1997, pp. 76–116).
28. See Bolton and Dewatripont (1994).
29. Demsetz (1993, p. 172).
30. Demsetz (1993, p. 173).
31. Conner and Prahalad (1996, p. 478).
32. See Kogut and Zander (1996). The role that corporate culture plays as a co-ordination device that complements the hierarchy in any organization is analysed more deeply in Section 3.3.
33. Austrian economics goes back to Menger and von Böhm-Bawerk, and was sharpened greatly by von Mises, Schumpeter and especially Hayek. See Kirzner (1987) for a description of the main ideas put forward by the Austrian school of economics.
34. See Foss (1998, pp. 14ff.).
35. Liebeskind (1996, p. 94).
36. See Section 3.3 for parameters of job design.
37. Foss (1998, p. 13).
38. Williamson (1999, pp. 1097ff.).
39. Williamson (1999, p. 1106).
40. See Foss (1996b, p. 475).
41. See also Foss (2002, pp. 3ff.), who argues that a blending of both strands of literature is necessary to incorporate the concepts of knowledge and innovation into mainstream organizational economics.
42. See Holmström and Milgrom (1994, p. 972).
43. Confer Holmström and Milgrom (1991).
44. Holmström and Milgrom (1994, p. 973).
45. See Milgrom and Roberts (1992, pp. 228–32).
46. See Patel (2006, ch. 1) for the theory and principles of design.
47. Baldwin and Clark (2000, p. 63).
48. See Simon (1962) for the classic example of the watchmakers, Tempus and Hora. The example illustrates how reductions in complexity through an appropriate organizational design can increase organizational efficiency tremendously. See also Langlois (2002).
49. See Roberts (2004, pp. 54–5).
50. See also Milgrom and Roberts (1995a, pp. 181–3).
51. See Topkis (1998, p. 54).
52. See Allen and Sherer (1995).

53. See Teece (1986).
54. See Allen (1994) and Nelson (1994).
55. See Arthur *et al.* (1997) and Foss (1997).
56. Athey and Stern (1998) offer an empirical framework for the validation of complementarities and systems analysis.
57. See Durlauf (1998) and Arthur *et al.* (1997).
58. See the contributions to Krahnen and Schmidt (2004) on several elements and modules of the German financial system; Schmidt *et al.* (2002) on the convergence of financial systems in Europe; and Hackethal and Schmidt (2000) on the interaction of the financial system with other systems, especially the system that characterizes a firm. See Hackethal (2000) and Tyrell (2003) for the various roles that banks and markets play in different financial systems.
59. Arthur (1996, p. 100).
60. Economies of scale are expressed in mathematical terms as $c(x') + c(x') > c(2x')$. The costs that two separate firms have to incur in the production of a good or service are greater than the costs a combined firm would have to incur.
61. The existence of network effects leads to an increase in utility for all agents in the network. The existence of a single telephone, for example, is of no use to anybody. However, as more and more people join the telephone network, possible connections between the different nodes grow over-proportionately larger, thereby more than proportionately increasing the utility for everybody. Network effects are the subject of Section 2.4.
62. See Anderson (1999).
63. See Morel and Ramanujam (1999), and McKelvey (1999).
64. Milgrom and Roberts (1995b, p. 248).
65. See Bushnell and Shepard (1995) and Topkis (1995), and the reply by Milgrom and Roberts (1995c).
66. Gittell (1998, p. 31).
67. See Black and Boal (1994).
68. There are, of course, also changes that improve the relative position of a firm. See Tushman and Anderson (1986) and d'Aveni (1999) for a distinction between competence-destroying and competence-enhancing discontinuities in the business environment.
69. See Prahalad and Oosterveld (1999, pp. 32–4) and Prahalad and Hamel (1994b, pp. 6–11) for more detailed lists of sources for competitive discontinuity.
70. See also Markides (1999) on this dynamic view, and how the organization can 'get ready for the unknown'.
71. See Christensen (1997) for the distinction between adaptive and disruptive technology changes.
72. See Evans and Wurster (2000) and their introduction of example of how the business of *Encyclopedia Britannica* was almost destroyed by CD-Roms such as Microsoft's Encarta given away as a promotional item with purchases of new computers.
73. Brätland (2003, pp. 9–10; emphasis in the original).
74. What happens when such natural monopolies suddenly find themselves in an integrated market is described in Chapter 5 for the securities transaction

industry. Three different organizational designs for this scenario are presented there, and a guesstimate of which design is 'the best' is presented.

75. For an investigation of the economics behind deregulation in the case of the telecommunications industry, see Laffont and Tirole (2001).

76. On the many aspects of financial systems in general, and a comparison of the American and English with the German and French financial systems, see, for example, Schmidt *et al.* (2002) and Krahnen and Schmidt (2004). As examples of the much broader literature on the 'varieties of capitalism' see the contributions to Hall and Soskice (2001) and Amable (2003).

77. For an appraisal of the current state of the American financial system, see Holmström and Kaplan (2003).

78. See the Nobel lecture by Stiglitz (2002).

79. Langlois (2003, p. 352; emphasis in the original).

80. A search fund is usually put together by a recently graduated business or law school student who wants to buy out the owners of a company, effectively making it private, to employ his/her skills in running the company. With nothing more than his/her human capital, s/he looks for investors willing to lend him/her the money for the search. As a return on their investments, they are allowed to invest in the target company at favourable terms. After a few years, the company is sold again – it is hoped with a return for both investors and the searching graduate. See Rajan and Zingales (2003, pp. 5–6) for an example.

81. Rajan and Zingales (2001b, pp. 2–3).

3
Building Blocks of Organizational Design

3.1 The strategy of the organization

One of the building blocks the description of any organizational design has to take into account is the strategy of the system. In the literature of strategic management, many different facets of strategy are highlighted: the strategy has to formulate the purpose of the organization – its *raison d'être*. The strategy has to formulate which resources the organization uses to create value and to generate an economic rent, and in which markets the organization must be embedded to offer its outputs and appropriate this economic rent. These formulations of strategy under investigation in this section are closely and complementarily inter-twined with the implementations of strategy through the boundaries, the internal structure and the governance of the organization that are the subjects of the following sections.

The description of important strategic themes in this section is highly eclectic – only a few of the many concepts, ideas and matrices that have been developed in the literature on strategic management are considered here. A good introduction, from an economic perspective to the field of strategy, is offered by Besanko *et al.* (2000) who also apply a systemic view to strategy and illustrate it with many examples in their book.

Defining strategy

In the formulation of strategy, conscious choices have to be made about the right configuration for the elements and modules of the organiza-tional system that take any complementarities into consideration to achieve the most efficient design, given available resources and market positions. As Porter (1996, p. 64) explains: 'Competitive strategy is about being different. It means deliberately choosing a different set of activi-ties to deliver a unique mix of value.' The same holds true for market positions and resources. Only a unique configuration allows for the generation of an economic rent above the usual return on competitive markets. But because of the underlying complementarities, such unique configurations often cannot be mixed with one other. Trade-offs have therefore to be made between activities, positions or resources that are incompatible with each other.

Sustainable competitive advantage thus arises from different sources. On the one hand, unique market positions, as many models in the industrial organization literature show, allow firms to appropriate the economic rent generated by a lack of competition. Specific resources, as explained by the capabilities perspective, allow the firm to appropriate the economic rent generated by the singular competence. These two views are analytical in nature and an extensive literature exists for both. The main ideas of both strategic approaches are highlighted below.

On the other hand, further value is created by fitting unique market positions and specific resources together consistently. This task is not as easy as it sounds, however; returns from supermodularity are difficult to obtain. In the presence of complementarities, any arbitrary combination of different activities, market positions and firm resources is as likely to destroy value as to create it. In this spirit, Collis and Montgomery (1998) define corporate advantage as 'the way a company creates value through the configuration and coordination of its multi-business activities';[1] that is, by using its resources and competitive positions in the best way. Careful planning of the design is necessary to capture these extra returns from supermodular relationships between different value-generating elements and modules in the system that makes up the organization. This view on strategy is synthetical in nature, and to date little research has been undertaken in this direction.

Since a successful and consistent combination of unique positions and specific resources is even more difficult to imitate than the developing of such resources or the capturing of such positions, this kind of competitive advantage is less likely to be of a temporary nature in the process of creative destruction. As such, the organizational design itself can be the reason for any sustainable competitive advantage. Such an advantage can be even further entrenched because of causal ambiguity.[2] The complexity of the system design often does not allow for the pinpointing of the source of the advantage, or to determine which combination of the many different elements and modules causes the returns from supermodularity.

Strategy therefore creates a blueprint of organizational design where the result of the different choices are determined: the purpose of the organization and the resources and market positions it has to develop and sustain for value creation as well as the careful and conscious combination of these elements in a consistent way. In the strategy process, the design blueprint must be taken into consideration when working out the sequence of steps and leaps. Path-dependencies and dead ends in the rugged landscape have to be anticipated wherever possible, and the current assignment of power has to be taken into account to determine whether the chosen path is in fact feasible, given the vested interest of those currently endowed with power. These dynamic aspects of strategic management where complementary relations with the other building blocks of organizational design are greatest are largely left for investigation in Section 4.2.

Here, after considering briefly the importance of defining the purpose of any organization, the market-based, the resource-based and the account-ing- based perspectives of strategy are explored. Each perspective offers a distinct but complementary view on strategy, and highlights other aspects that could be the basis for any sustainable competitive advantage. An investigation of the strategic aspects of the construction of the value chain closes the section and leads to the next one, where the boundaries of the system are the main topic for exploration.

The purpose of the organization

An important element in every system that has a strong influence on other elements is understanding the reason for the very existence of the organization. For what purpose does the organization exist? And why and how does it create value for its various constituencies? Only if a satisfactory answer can be given to these questions, can the organizational design be further explored to see how sustainable any competitive advantage arising out of its value proposition will be.

To answer these questions regarding the *raison d'être*, the literature on strategic management proposes to develop statements of the vision and the mission of the organization, statements of the goals and objectives of the design:

- The vision of an organization is usually declared in a short and inspiring statement clarifying what the organization aspires to become and achieve at some point in the future. A good vision statement is clear about the strategic intent and the ends of the organizational design, but leaves room for flexibility regarding the means of achieving these ends.[3] It is broad, forward-thinking and ambitious.
- The mission statement is more explicit than the vision, albeit still short. The roles and value propositions for the various constituencies

are described within it. The heterogeneity, uniqueness and specificity of the organization, as defined here, eventually lead to a sustainable competitive advantage and to an economic rent for the organization. Additionally, the scope of the organization has to be defined. A good mission statement allows the constituencies of the organization to prioritize the different tasks and investment possibilities.

- The ideals of the vision and the mission statements, while maintaining the integrity of these statements, must be transferred into more specific goals. Objectives have to be formulated that are, while still ambitious, within reach for the organization in the shorter term. Only the fulfilment of short-term goals allows for measurement of success – however success is defined. Furthermore, the achievement of such milestones allows the organization to check whether or not it is still on the right track.

The content and form of these statements – whether they are written or unwritten, explicit or implicit – tells a lot about the openness and permeability of the boundaries of the organization as well as about the rigidity of the organizational structure. Like the constitution for a nation state, these statements reveal something about the balance of power in the organizational design.

Example 3.1   The Central Intelligence Agency (CIA) in the USA formulates its vision as 'to provide knowledge and take action to ensure the national security of the United States and the preservation of American life and ideals'. This nearly all-encompassing statement is complemented by a more focused mission: 'We are the eyes and ears of the nation and at times its hidden hand. We accomplish this mission by: (1) Collecting intelligence that matters. (2) Providing relevant, timely, and objective all-source analysis. (3) Conducting covert action at the direction of the President to preempt threats or achieve United States policy objectives.'[a]

More specific goals have been set through a 'Memorandum for the Director of Central Intelligence' issued in November 2004 by US President George W. Bush. In this memorandum he urges, among other things, to 'increase ... the number of fully qualified, all-source analysts by 50 percent' and to 'develop and employ information technology tools to assist in processing and use of information in foreign languages'.[b] Specific timelines for setting up detailed plans to fulfil these goals and objectives have been noted in the memorandum, so that a measurement of achievement becomes possible.

---

[a]   See http://www.cia.gov/cia/information/mission.html; accessed 9 December 2004.
[b]   See http://www.whitehouse.gov/news/releases/2004/11/20041123-5.html; accessed 9 December 2004.

The mutual consistency in these statements of the purpose of the organization should always be maintained. Only if all constituencies work towards a common vision can the complementary investments of each generate an economic rent. Through these statements the leadership can set the general direction that the organization intends to follow. In doing so, they offer a focal point for the co-ordination of various specific investments. In a suitable analogy, Bartlett and Ghoshal (2000, pp. 714–15) compare the vision of an organization to a lightning rod that captures the diffuse energy of all constituencies and channels it towards the powering of a single organizational engine.

The market-based perspective

It is beyond the scope of this book to examine in detail the market-based perspective of strategy. For our purposes here, some selected topics will subsequently be highlighted and put into the context of organizational design. The market-based perspective is based firmly in economics and the field of industrial organization. Numerous models, often using a game-theoretical framework, formally analyse various detailed aspects of the interaction between firms and the prevalent market structure. The books by Tirole (1988b) and, in the context of regulated industries, Laffont and Tirole (1993) provide a comprehensive overview of these models. A non-technical 'executive summary' is provided by Porter (1980) with his 'Five Forces Framework'.

The market-based perspective is mainly concerned with the markets in which the organization is embedded. The prevailing industry structure of these markets sets the rules of conduct for competitors within these same markets and thereby determines the performance of the firms in the industry. The market-based perspective is mainly used for the formulation of business-level strategy, and offers useful suggestions to find an attractive and rent-generating position for business units of corporations operating in many industries. Industrial organization models and the market-based view on strategy do not say much about the distribution of any economic rent – the internal allocation of power is largely unconsidered. However, viewing the organization as a black box allows us to concentrate on the single aspect of the power relationship between the organization as a whole and its environment.

Market position and economic rents

Trade in markets occurs when both partners to the exchange benefit from it. If the buyer values a particular good more than the seller of this good, the utility of both can be increased if the good is exchanged for some amount of money. Trade generates an economic rent measured by the increase in utility of both agents, thereby providing both with an incentive to trade. How this economic rent is split and distributed among the trading partners depends on their bargaining power. By threatening to abstain from the exchange – that is, by threatening not to generate any economic rent – a larger share of the total rent can be appropriated. However, if both potential trading partners pursue this strategy, no trade occurs and the potential for value creation is not realized.[4]

The distribution of economic rents is dependent on the markets in which the potential trading partners find themselves. In competitive markets, both can easily find a third party who either wants to buy or to sell the good, or has already done so recently. A price can thus be attached to the good, and the distribution of the economic rent is determined by such a price. The valuation of the buyer, minus the price paid, is the buyer's economic rent. The price received, minus the valuation of the seller, is the seller's economic rent. In this way, the existence of a competitive market bestows balanced power on individual agents by giving them outside options, and thereby granting them the right to leave and find a different trading partner.[5]

However, the absence of a competitive market with many potential trading partners changes the allocation of power. In the extreme case of a monopoly, there is only one agent offering the good. The monopolist can then increase the price to the level where it just equals the valuation of each buyer. At this price, or marginally below it, both trading partners still have an incentive to trade. The economic rent that is generated by the exchange of the good is, however, fully distributed to the monopolist. Having a unique position in the market and being the only potential trading partner confers huge powers on those in such a comfortable position.

Creating unique positions

Power goes hand-in-hand with economic rents. The idea in the literature on industrial organization, and the strategy implications derived from it, is to find or shape a market in such a way that a unique position can be obtained. By strategic actions, economic agents (be they firms or individuals) can increase their power to capture a larger share of the economic rent.

Such a unique position can be created through various means. In the following, only a few of the many instruments that are analysed in industrial organization models are mentioned. What is of interest here is how these instruments change the power relationship, and how this affects the generation and distribution of economic rents.

- By differentiation and investing in superior quality of the goods and services a firm produces, the firm makes it harder for consumers to find an alternative source from which this particular good or service may be obtained. Some monopolistic advantage can be created through the use of, for example, marketing, or the creation of a brand name. Such an investment changes the constellation of power – even when no real value is created. Competing products or services might then be perceived as inferior, and consumers would be willing to pay more for the branded good, allowing the differentiated firm to capture some of the consumers' rent even when no additional economic rent is generated.

- Market segmentation has a similar effect. If the firm can charge different prices to different groups of consumers, discriminating, for example, by age, they can obtain a larger share of the economic rent from the group that has to pay the higher price. As long as this segmentation encourages more people to buy the good or service from the firm, such behaviour can increase overall welfare.

- Through the erection of market entry barriers, firms can limit competition and thus change the balance of power to their benefit. By restricting potential trading partners for consumers, firms lower their outside options. Again, they can command a higher price and capture some share of the economic rent that would go to consumers in competitive market settings. Market entry barriers can be created by many means – for example, through the build-up of excess capacity – thereby acquiring the power to cut prices credibly if entry into such markets should occur.

- Regulation of industries in a similar way inhibits the market forces. Industries in which economic rents can be earned usually attract new competitors. If regulation prohibits new entries, the incumbents can earn economic rents subject to the power that the regulating agency gives them. The effect on overall welfare often depends on the quality of the regulation and the efficiency of the organizational design of the regulatory body.

- Firms can adjust their boundaries and integrate vertically forward or backward into distribution or procurement activities. By controlling the channels their competitors also have to use, these firms can increase their power over competitors and restrict competition in the initial stage of the value chain. Such a foreclosure strategy thus leverages the original power position, and a higher share of economic rents can be obtained.

These instruments allow an alteration in the power position relative to others. A caveat, however, needs to be considered: the generation of economic rents is not independent of its distribution, and the balance of power has an effect on the investment incentives. An efficient organizational design has to take into consideration the complementary relationship between the balance of power and the balance of investment incentives.

Power resulting from a unique market position can be malign if the overall level of welfare is lowered. Monopolists supply too little and of inferior quality at too high a price, and they lack the investment incentives to innovate. The amount of economic rent generated is thus too low compared with that generated by a superior industrial organization. Many firms are preoccupied with the distribution and appropriation of economic rents from other players, and not their generation. This was certainly the case in many regulated industries that resembled natural monopolies.

Effect of the changing environment

When new markets come into existence, they alter the power relationship. New technologies affect the information structure that often inhibited the functioning of markets. Information about the trading partner that values the good or service most highly can be obtained more easily. Geographic boundaries do not matter as much as before, and the internet allows for a virtually worldwide trade. Disintermediation becomes possible where the ultimate producers and consumers deal directly with each other. The power that intermediaries had because of problems in the information structure is diminishing fast in many industries – for example, in the business of travel agencies.

The liberalization of formerly regulated natural monopolies disentangles market entry barriers. New business models become feasible, and insurgents are acquiring positions of power that render the power of the incumbent obsolete. By allying with groups that have been in less powerful positions, these new competitors can create value for those groups as well as for themselves. The reliance on industry-wide standards as another major change allows for the modularization of many activities by creating a common interface between all firms. Activities that had to be performed in-house for fear of hold-up in uncompetitive markets can be transferred to the market. The changes in the business environment thus generally favour the functioning of markets, and consequently have a high impact on the balance of power between different firms.

Given these changes, the question thus looms whether we can still define industries according to traditional methods.[6] If the firm disintegrates into its parts or layers of the value chain, industries will converge and overlap. Business migration across the boundaries of an industry becomes easier, and new competition emerges from many sides, made possible by the changes in the business environment.

In many industries, therefore, new products and services rely on other companies operating in the same or related industries to make complementary investments that are specific to the new product or service. Different firms not only need to make co-ordinated investments specific to each other without relying on a 'hierarchy' and the related power to direct other people that are only successful if all investments have been undertaken. Network strategies – that is, the finding of the right strategic alliance partners – become increasingly important. Thus the question arises of what shapes power and authority in this setting? How are these specific investments co-ordinated, and how is the economic rent generated and allocated among the different players in this kind of competition between clusters of firms?

The resource-based perspective

In contrast to the market-based perspective, which is interested in the strategic position of business units in an industry, the resource-based perspective explores the basis of competitive advantage for the whole organization. This approach is relatively new in economics. Although the ideas were first put forward by Penrose (1959) and Wernerfelt (1984) to explain the scope of the firm and diversification into related industries, much of the research has been undertaken since the early 1990s. A good summary can be found in Collis and Montgomery (1997) as well as in Bamberger and Wrona (1996).

The resource-based view puts the emphasis on the importance of the resources, competencies and capabilities of a firm. If a firm can rely on superior resources or has developed better capabilities than its competitors, it has an advantage over them in relation to the competition. The resource-based view is best suited for an analysis of strategy at the corporate level, and how any 'parenting advantage' of the corporation as a whole can be given to the various business units by transferring resources and competencies between them.[7]

Resources, core competencies and capabilities

The idea that any sustainable advantage in competition arises somewhere inside the firm rather than from the position of the firm in the outside markets is the distinguishing feature of the resource-based view of strategy. The idea is developed in three broad branches of the literature – namely, in the resource-based view;[8] in the concept of core competencies;[9] and in the capabilities perspective[10] – which differ in contributing competitive advantage slightly to other factors.

Resources are defined by Amit and Shoemaker (1993, p. 35) as 'stocks of available factors that are owned or controlled by the firm'. Examples of resources are financial or physical assets such as property, plants or equipment, tradable know-how in the form of patents or licences, and knowledge embedded in human capital. Amit and Shoemaker (1993, p. 35) go on to define capabilities as the 'firm's capacity to deploy resources, usually in combination, using organizational processes, to effect a desired end. They are information-based … and are developed over time through complex interactions among the firm's resources.' Core competencies are defined by Prahalad and Hamel (1990): 'In the long run, competitiveness derives from an ability to build, at lower cost and more speedily than competitors, the core competencies that spawn unanticipated products.'[11] A competence is thus the 'organizational capability to combine and renew the firm's assets and capabilities in such a way that the firm obtains and sustains a competitive advantage'.[12]

The distinction between resources, competencies and capabilities has a lot to do with branding by different authors and less with the underlying substance. The main difference is the orientation towards processes that are more prominent in the core competence and capabilities perspective than in the resource-based view. What all these views have in common is the notion of uniqueness that translates into a competitive advantage by leveraging these resources, competencies or capabilities across business units and different product markets in a related diversification.[13] In what follows, no distinctions are made between these three similar concepts of strategic management emphasizing the internal functioning of the firm.

Firm resources and economic rents

The resource-based view explains why a particular resource – a machine, a licence or the knowledge of a manager – can be of strategic importance to a company. If certain resources or competencies are necessary for efficient production, only those firms that own or have access to such resources and competencies can produce efficiently. Other companies that might have to find some substitutes for these resources are at a competitive disadvantage when the substitutes are of inferior quality or involve higher costs. Firms that have the best resources can thus produce a particular good in the most efficient way and can earn – even in a competitive market setting – an economic rent. The generation of this economic rent is a result of the superiority of the resource or competence. The scarcer the resource, the higher the economic rent it generates, and the better the competitive advantage of the firm.

According to Peteraf (1993), there are four conditions that all have to hold in order that a resource can be the basis for a firm's sustainable competitive advantage:

- The resource must be heterogeneous. Only scarce or unique resources generate economic rents.
- The resource must be difficult to imitate. If replication or substitution is easy, the economic rent rapidly vanishes in *ex-post* competition – the competitive advantage is not sustainable.[14]
- The resource must not be perfectly mobile. Barriers restricting entry or exit and legal institutions hold back the valuable, rent-generating resource within the boundaries of the firm.
- The resource must not be tradable. If there is *ex ante* competition for the resource, the economic rent accrues to the original owner in the competitive bidding process.

Other authors pose similar conditions on resources to make them valuable for the firm. Amit and Shoemaker (1993), for example, list eight criteria for the generation of economic rents; and Black and Boal (1994) take a more dynamic view in their analysis of a sustainable competitive advantage.

Creating unique resources

Collis and Montgomery (1995) use this framework to describe how investments into new resources or the upgrading and leveraging of existing ones lead to competitive advantage. The inimitability of resources can be a result of, for example, physical uniqueness or an exclusive patent award. But there are often ways to circumvent a patent or possibilities of using a substitute for this particular resource. The competitive advantage and the economic rent are hence only of short duration. A better way to protect resources against such an erosion of their strategic value, according to Collis and Montgomery (1995, p. 122), is by continuous innovation that puts the firm on a path that competitors are not able to access through complementarities over time- or path-dependency. The unique resources might depreciate quickly when copied by others in a Schumpeterian competition of creative destruction, but the process of continuous and superior innovation is much harder to copy. This process is the truly important capability that underlies any sustainable competitive advantage. As Kay (1997, p. 45) remarks: 'It may be particular characteristics and complementarities associated with a combination of assets that are distinctive and difficult to replace as far as the firm is concerned.'

The criterium of appropriability or immobility for sustainable competitive advantage that both Peteraf (1993) and Collis and Montgomery (1995) apply is misleading: they view the firm as a black box with the underlying notion that any value that is generated belongs to the shareholders of the firm as the ultimate owners. But economic rents are not only profit, and value creation of an organizational design can benefit many constituencies. Using criteria such as appropriability and immobility of resources neglects the fact that other stakeholders in the firm can benefit tremendously from resources that meet the other criteria and thus form the basis for a sustainable competitive advantage. Good organizational designs should encompass this. This brings us back to the other side of any economic rent: again, we have to consider the balance of power, and how it is created and used in an organization that relies on unique resources for rent generation.

Economic rents and power

The distribution of these economic rents is subject to an *ex-post* bargaining process, and the relative bargaining power of the various constituencies is determined by several factors.[15] One such factor is the question of how much the resource loses if it leaves the relationship – that is, the value of the owner's outside option. If a resource can be utilized outside the firm at low cost and with little loss in economic rent, the bargaining position of its owner is enhanced. The possibility of building coalitions and threatening to leave en bloc similarly enhances bargaining power. Another factor determining the bargaining position is the loss of economic rent to the rest of the firm if the resource is withdrawn.[16]

Expectations about *ex-post* distribution of rents affect the *ex-ante* incentives to invest in the specificity that creates value. It is crucial to understand that investments in specific resources lead not only to the generation of an economic rent but at the same time lead to the acquisition of power. By making the resource co-specialized to others, the owner of the resource acquires the power to withhold the specific resource for production. The acquisition of power, however, is costly – not only because of the investment into specificity: at the same time that the owner of the now specific resource increases his/her power over other constituencies in the organizational design by threatening to withhold the rent-generating resource, s/he reduces his/her outside option and the power that competitive markets convey upon him/her. It is difficult for the now specific resource to live up to its full rent-generating potential in competitive markets that lack co-specialization with other resources in the firm. The resource owner thus faces an investment trade-off between increased power resulting from co-specialization and decreased power caused by lower outside options. How strong this trade-off is and whether it is skewed to one side depends on the configuration of other elements that make up the system of organizational design. We return to this problem throughout the book.

Example 3.2   In the investment banking or consulting industries, the most valuable resource is human capital. Office space, computers and nearly everything else can readily be acquired on competitive markets and is unlikely to generate an economic rent. The investment bankers or consultants, on the other hand, have unique knowledge and personal contacts. This knowledge generates the economic rent, which is also sustainable since it cannot easily be imitated or substituted. Knowledge residing in the brains of human capital and the personal contacts of clients are, however, not restricted to a certain company. The distribution of the rent is thus in favour of the bankers and consultants, and the investment banks and consulting firms receive less. Unlike workers in the automotive industry, who also have specific knowledge, there are no co-specialized assets such as machinery or specific tools that bind the valuable resource to a certain company.

This lack of other resources that investment bankers or consultants need in order to be productive makes them mobile and leverages their bargaining position. They change jobs easily to the employer offering the best conditions. Whole teams rather than individuals leave, since the knowledge of any team member is only complementary to the knowledge of his/her colleagues. Human capital in investment banking is very mobile, and a well-functioning job market leads to the distribution of the economic rent in the form of high salaries and bonuses to the team leaders or partners, and not to the firm.[a]

---

[a]   See also Chacar and Coff (2000) for an empirical study of rent generation and distribution in the investment banking industry.

Effect of the changing environment

What effect does the changing environment have on competition based on specific resources? Technological change is driven by innovation and combination of knowledge, and liberalization makes experimentation with new forms of doing business more valuable. The sophistication and completeness of financial markets within the financial system allow financing for good business ideas rather than allocating capital only to the largest companies.

All three changes thus lead to an increase in the importance and value of one resource – knowledge residing in human capital. When testing knowledge along the criteria described by Peteraf (1993) for its rent-generating potential, the result is that it is responsible for much of the heterogeneity between firms. In particular, tacit knowledge is rare and difficult to imitate, and the gathering of information and the ensuing learning process that builds up this knowledge is a path-dependent process that is a formidable barrier for competitors.[17]

What has changed, however, is the distribution of the generated economic rent. Investments into specific resources need *ex-post* power in some form to protect the resulting economic rent from expropriation. At the same time, investments into specific resources change the balance of power by creating a new source of power. Thus arrangements that allow for the mobility of human capital and knowledge have to be found. An efficient organizational design has to accommodate these changes by translating the adjusted strategy resting on a new set of value-creating resources into changes in the boundaries, internal structure and governance.

The accounting-based perspective

The third branch of strategy, which can be labelled as accounting- or finance-based, breaks down how much value each position and resource creates. The idea is to make the basis for sustainable competitive advantage more transparent.

Idea of Economic Value Added

Economic Value Added (EVA), conceptualized by the consulting company Stern Stewart, is the most prominent example in the area of value-based management.[18] The emphasis in this approach to strategy is on the measurement of value creation, and the approach is particularly good in analysing the impact that measurement of performance has on the overall competitive position of a firm. By bundling certain tasks into jobs, and certain activities or products into business units, the results can be measured more accurately and can be rewarded in a more consistent way given the amount of capital used and its costs.

Strategic business units where all activities are routine, and where the outcome can be monitored and measured quite easily and accurately, can be structured as a cost centre. Such units need an incentive system other than a job or business unit that engages in research and development, and should be structured and rewarded as a profit centre with fewer monitoring activities but more high-powered incentives in the rewards. The implementation of these ideas in the organizational structure and the main theme of this branch – measurement of success – are taken up in Section 3.3. More economic theory on these issues is discussed there.

Evaluation

But do the ideas of accounting-based perspective and value-based management still constitute good strategy? Sophisticated measurement and transparency make the amounts of economic rents that are generated visible and invite imitation if the design is good. Benchmarking, which is often a goal of proponents of value-based management, increases the tendency for economic rents to be eroded. As Porter (1996) and Collis and Montgomery (1998) all remark, operational effectiveness should not be mistaken for strategy.

While rigorous implementation of the ideas of Economic Value Added, and other ideas that have been in fashion in the business press for some time,[19] can increase the performance of the company and enable it to better control various business units and profit centres, it imposes rigid structures on the company. Depending on the business landscape, the necessity of staying on well-trodden pathways of financial control do not allow for experimentation or a search for new business models. Changes in the financial system and accounting standards that increase the need for elaborated measurement and transparency have led in many companies to the tendency where '[f]inancial reporting considerations have come to drive strategy, while obscuring true profitability and the actual amount of capital invested in the business'.[20] A too-tight measurement of success is bad for some activities and businesses. Good organizational design takes into account more possibilities to align incentives and measurement with each other. The construction of a value chain – or its deconstruction in a process of the 'unbundling of the corporation'[21] – is just one of them that has a large strategic component. It is to this topic that we turn next.

Construction and deconstruction of the value chain

Integrating different assets and activities into a single organization led to the construction of a value chain as a theoretical construct to explain and analyse the sequence of these activities.[22] Deconstruction refers to the process of taking apart the value chain while preserving the identity of the individual pieces. The intention is to take the deconstructed pieces and put them together in a different, more efficient design. Deconstruction is closely connected with the principle of modularization of systems.

Reassembling the value chain

In economics, deconstruction involves the disintegration of a value chain previously constructed by a single firm into its separate activities, so that each activity can be performed by the firm that has the best position and the best resources to undertake the particular activity when the environment changes. Deconstruction means using the advantages that particular companies have in performing different activities, to create interfaces between these activities, and to modularize the whole value chain.

Successful deconstruction has thus to find answers to the following questions: what is the value proposition of each activity in the value chain for the resources organized in the corporation and for the market positions of its business units? And, changing the perspective, what is the strategic activity that allows the market positions and firm resources to reach their full potential and generate economic rents?

The answer is initially quite simple: strategic activities are those activities that the organization can perform more efficiently compared to its competitors given its position in markets and the resources utilized by the firm. Different activities are best supported by distinct market positions and distinct sets of resources. The manufacturing activity for a mature product or service is best performed when the costs of production are lowest. Technological features of the production process often lead to economies of scale. Companies are able to exploit this by taking the module of production out of its own value chain; in fact, outsourcing all production activities to companies concentrating on these activities. These companies bundle the production for many other, now disintegrated, companies into their own few facilities that allow them to benefit from economies of scale – preferably in markets where labour unit costs for these mature products are lowest. Firms that still use their own plants produce at a suboptimal level and face a competitive disadvantage.

The same logic holds for other activities. In research and development (R&D), for example, the main driving force is the combination of knowledge to come up with innovative products. This combination is facilitated by the proximity of well-qualified human resources from many organizations in one location. Clusters – the most famous probably being Silicon Valley in California for information technology – allow the exchange of ideas across the boundaries of firms by making use of each company's own position within the cluster.[23] By nurturing the capability of using this external pool of knowledge as well as its internal one, the organization leverages its positions and resources, and gains an advantage from the speedy introduction of new products. In distribution activities, proximity to customers matters. Occupying a unique market segment in financial advisory services, for example, allows employees to gain expertise in products from different companies. Investing in a distribution network and a brand name that caters to these customers and this segment creates a specific resource that creates value by exploiting economies of scope between the different products.

Only the biggest companies can fulfil all three requirements to gain competitive advantage from its production activity where scale economies are prevalent, its distribution activity where scope economies matter, and the research activity where economies of speed are the driving force.[24] A better organizational design might thus deconstruct the value chain into individual modules and reassemble these into another design to make better use of the different economies underlying them. The interface for these modules are markets rather than the internal hierarchy along the value chain. Companies focusing only on one module can fit into this design by concentrating on a particular combination of market positions, firm resources and activities, thereby creating value and generating economic rents.

Example 3.3 At the very extreme of such a deconstructed value chain is the virtual company – a network of contracts made by a central principal. Managing this complex nexus of market positions, firm resources, and the efficient performance of the activities along the value chain thus becomes a value proposition of its own and generates an economic rent not only from the constituent parts but also from the whole.

Nike provides an example of this: 'While the public is likely to think of the company as a manufacturer of athletic footwear, the company is really a research and design studio with a sophisticated marketing formula and distribution mechanism.'[a] The manufacturing is outsourced to subcontractors: Nike itself owns or operates no factories or machines. The subcontractors use economies of scale and scope and take advantage of their geographical position in East Asia to gain access to cheap workers to perform the manufacturing activity in the most efficient way. The activities Nike itself performs allow the firm to leverage its resources, especially its designers of athletic wear. Marketing and the endorsement of celebrities create another important resource in the form of a valuable brand, and a large sales force training retailers to explain shoe technology to customers supports this strategy.[b]

---

[a] Rifkin (2000).
[b] See Evans and Wurster (2000) for this and other examples on deconstruction and unbundling in many industries.

Returns from supermodularity

The answer to the questions asked above, how firm resources, market positions and strategic activities belong together, also has a more subtle answer as well. A modular design reduces complexity, and thus reduces sources for causal ambiguity. Recall that complementarities among and between resources, positions and activities lead to a leveraging of the rent-generating potential of the unique positions and the unique resources. By exploiting the advantages of system design, these complementarities and path dependencies lead to a sustainable competitive advantage that does not only rest on the unique position or specific resource, but on a combination of both. Being placed at a higher altitude as a starting position and being able to climb the hill faster because of superior equipment allows the company staying on top wherever the peak turns out to be in the foggy and rugged landscape of competition.

The economic rent generated by this combination requires the assembly of different modules into one organizational design to lead to returns from supermodularity. Relying on the interface of the market to reduce complexity also reduces these possibilities. Particularly from a more dynamic perspective it becomes clear that an integrated value chain design can have advantages over a deconstructed one. Innovations and the co-specialized investments that are often necessary to exploit them commercially can pass down the value chain more easily if a chain of command is complementing them within a hierarchy or a suitable organizational structure. Thus a hub with a central co-ordinating management, as in the case of a virtual company, or a network of interdependent companies working together for their own benefit and indirectly for the benefit of the whole network,[25] are organizational designs that are better able to capture the returns from supermodularity when configured in a consistent way. This view is best summarized with a quote from Collis and Montgomery (1998, p. 72): 'An outstanding corporate strategy is not a random collection of individual building blocks but a carefully constructed system of interdependent parts.' It is to the other 'interdependent parts' that we turn in the following sections.

3.2   The boundaries of the organization

Boundaries determine power. Separating those on the inside from those that remain outside of the boundaries of the organizational design levies different degrees of power on them. The power those on the inside wield can be stronger; they are shielded from the power of outside markets, which increases the opportunities for value creation. The power those on the inside wield can also be weaker; they can become trapped inside the firm, which lowers the possibilities for value creation. Boundaries can thus provide shelter or incarcerate.

Boundaries shape investment incentives. Separating those on the inside from those that remain outside the boundaries of the organizational design provides different incentives for them. Incentives for those on the inside can be good; they have ready access to information about others in the organization and know how to interpret it. Co-specialized and co-ordinated investments are furthered, and nobody can overrule decisions that have been made. Incentives for those on the inside can also be suboptimal; they can too readily rely on the others and their decisions, and free-riding, rent-seeking and detrimental investments just to gain influence can be the result. Boundaries can thus provide incentives for value creation as well as value destruction.

The right configuration of the boundaries is hence a matter of utmost importance for organizational design and its efficiency. The complementary relationship between the balance of incentives and the balance of power in the system of organizational design is affected by the configuration of the boundaries. The art of organizational design is setting the boundary in such a manner that the benign effects of it prevail and complement the competitive advantages of the resources inside the organization and the market positions the organization occupies. The right degree of permeability of the boundaries allows for a flow of relevant resources across the boundaries to organizations and markets where their potential for value creation is greatest.

How can the boundaries be of use in shaping investment incentives to generate the most economic rents and to assign bargaining power to appropriate these rents? The purpose of this section is to explore how the boundaries of an organization are determined, where they are set, and how rigid they are. The effect of a changing business landscape can be expected to lead to a shifting or a blurring of the boundaries as other resources and positions become the basis for sustainable competitive advantage. A shift of the boundaries takes certain resources to the inside and releases others to the outside. A blurring of the boundaries allows certain resources to cross more easily from the inside to the outside, and vice versa. Incentives and power relations are affected in both cases. The following three sections deal with these tasks of setting, shifting and blurring of the boundaries,[26] and the effect on the efficiency of the organizational design.

Setting the boundaries

Ever since Coase (1937), the question of where the boundaries – horizontally as well as vertically – are to be set for an efficient organizational design has been an integral part of any theory of the firm. The idea of a firm with its hierarchical and carefully planned order is one extreme form of organizational design, and the idea of markets with their spontaneous order is another extreme form. But both ideals seldom appear in practice. Markets fail – for example, because of informational problems – and firms fail – for example, because of free-riding behaviour within them. Studying the idealized form, however, provides better insights by comparing theoretical extremes.

Markets and firms

Let us briefly and in a rough and sometimes oversimplifying manner recall the primary function of the boundary decision that previous theories of the firm have introduced,[27] before proceeding to the question of how the boundaries should be set or shifted in the light of the changes in the business environment.

- In transaction cost theory proposed by Klein *et al.* (1978) and Williamson (1985), the boundaries are determined by the necessity of integrating activities within the firm when problems of *ex-post* governance would prevent the investment in specific assets for fear of hold-up problems. By unifying governance through the integration of activities within the boundaries of one organizational design, these problems can be resolved and efficiency can be increased.
- One explanation of the boundaries of the firm that uses directly the insights of Coase (1937) rests on the relative efficiency of the internal market over the external one. Different agency effects prevail in the firm and the market regarding investment decisions. Whenever the internal capital market is more efficient in allocating capital, the project in question should be internalized within the boundaries of the firm.[28]
- The incomplete contracts approach to the firm proposed by Grossman and Hart (1986) explains the boundaries with the notion of asset ownership and the potential to provide *ex-ante* incentives. If investments by a particular stakeholder are indispensable, the allocation of ownership provides the incentives to undertake these investments. By unifying residual rights of control with the residual claim, the boundary of the organizational design is set to maximize value creation by optimizing incentives for this party while reducing the other parties' incentives. The trade-off between the incentives for the various constituencies through the instrument of asset ownership determines the boundary.
- The information-based view of the firm sees knowledge-creation as the organization's main purpose, and is closely related to the

resource-based perspective of strategy.[29] It sets the boundaries of any organizational design in such a way that the knowledge necessary for efficient production that would not be exchanged on markets because of their informational imperfection is encapsulated within the firm where other means of assuring the quality of information are feasible. Whenever information and knowledge can be codified and transferred easily, separate organizations can exist.

- The incentive system view of the firm by Holmström and Milgrom (1994) looks at asset ownership as only one of many instruments to set incentives. Whenever more balanced incentives have to be provided, the integration of a particular constituency or a particular activity within the confines of the firm achieves that. Within the firm, lower-powered incentives can be provided and a balance of incentives achieved that would not be possible in markets, since 'parties choose to transact in firms precisely when transacting in a market would produce misdirected incentives'.[30] The boundaries are thus determined by the levelling of incentives within the confines of one organization.

Every established theory of the firm thus sets the boundaries of the firm in such a manner as to mitigate problems that might arise in a pure market setting. Firms are better than markets at some tasks.

Using comparative statics, the boundaries that these theories have in mind are rigid and seldom allow a crossing.[31] Resources are either inside the firm or outside on the market. Positions of firms in markets, once occupied, are changed only infrequently. This is certainly not the case in reality. Other solutions and alternatives to integration exist. For example, instead of integration to alleviate problems of information transfer between different organizations, the resources that carry this information and knowledge can move between the organizations, thereby helping to achieve efficient production. These other solutions and alternatives must, however, be explored for any interdependencies with other parameters of the organizational design, which often render them inferior to integration within the boundaries of a single organization.

Example 3.4 The transfer of resources across the boundaries of the organization instead of integrating them within can be seen when scientists move from universities and academic research laboratories to commercial companies. Companies in many industries can profit from applying the results of basic research to commercial products. But this knowledge is often difficult to write down, especially when processes are involved. Employing

Continued

the researchers within the boundaries of the firm might thus seem necessary to gain access to this knowledge.

Basic research, however, is costly, not only in itself but also in terms of agency costs: how can one be sure that the effort exerted by the researchers is optimal when nobody, not even the researcher, knows the optimal level? Integrating these resources is thus a problem. In this case, a more efficient design is the transfer of the resources that carry the knowledge from academia to business rather than integrating them upfront.

Boundaries, investments and power

Boundaries determine the efficiency of an organizational design. Hart and Holmström (2002) show that overall welfare crucially depends on setting the right boundaries between different firms, units or collection of assets. Investments in these units maximize the amount of economic rent in each. But economic rents are not profits and can take other, less measurable, forms as well. Hart and Holmström (2002) label them 'private benefits' in their model. A boundary between two firms or units can have a profound effect on the efficiency of this design. The separation of two units by a boundary between them leads both units to neglect any external effects between them. However, the overall welfare – including private benefits – of the units are maximized separately. With integration, the interdependencies between the different firms are considered, but total economic rents might not be maximized. Private benefits that are not transferable with ownership are usually not taken into account by the joint decision-maker, who does not profit from them. By suitable modelling of this trade-off, Hart and Holmström (2002) are able to set the boundaries in such a way as to maximize, through appropriate investments, the amount of economic rents that are generated.[32]

But boundaries do not only shape investment incentives; they also assign power. The assignment of power feeds back to the incentives to invest, and ultimately to the efficiency of any organizational system. A different sort of power prevails in markets compared to firms. Trade on markets needs to benefit both parties, and requires these parties to agree on the spot on the distribution of the value that is created by the trade. The only form of power existing in pure market settings with anonymous trading partners meeting only once is the option of withdrawing from a trade.

Firms have more possibilities of generating and using power because of the continuing relationship between the constituencies forming the organization. The sources of power and the best use of it are investigated in Section 3.3. Note, however, that the wrong concentration of power within the firm allows the person wielding it to move resources around within the firm and to reposition the organization. This would be suboptimal, since the investments of others would be depreciated and economic rents destroyed by these actions. Boundaries thus determine the strategic resources of a firm. Only the right balance of power induces investments into rent-generating resources. With an unbalanced power distribution, hold-up within firms is possible as well as that occurring in markets. This kind of hold-up is even possible for resources of a general nature in the case of an almost worthless outside option caused by a malfunctioning market.

Boundaries also determine the strategic position of a firm. The literature on industrial organization shows how the setting of the horizontal boundary can lead to a huge competitive advantage. When economies of scale prevail, increasing the assets under control allows bigger firms to produce more cheaply than their smaller rivals. Models in the tradition of industrial organization also show how the setting of the vertical boundary influences the power distribution in the industry between the firms themselves, and between firms and consumers. Integrating backwards or forwards along the value chain can lead to a monopoly position at an adjacent stage of the value chain. The power that is connected to this monopoly position can be leveraged to the advantage of the enlarged firm. Such a foreclosure strategy allows the gaining of power by a suitable setting of the boundary of the firm.

Mixing markets and firms

Boundaries in reality are not as insurmountable, and the choice between firms and markets is not as strong, as was portrayed above. The relationship between firms and markets is more complex and intertwined since markets and firms are not only a means of conveying incentives for investment but they also operate in a particular way.[33] In business, we not only find firms operating within markets, but also markets working within firms.

Many organizations try to emulate the market by introducing internal markets for capital and labour. These internal markets provide incentives that would otherwise be too muted. Employees longing for a better-paid job find different rules applying in the internal and the external labour markets. The difference, if carefully crafted by the organization, allows the provision of more high-powered incentives. Internal markets for capital and labour have other advantages as well. How they achieve these and what the rules are that distinguish them from external markets is the subject of Section 3.3. It is sufficient to note here that markets help to improve the original and pure idea of firms.

The same argument holds true for markets. Stock exchanges, for example, are firms which operate markets, and implement a certain market microstructure with their trading systems that impose a particular information structure. These markets are managed, and market-makers help to improve the original and pure idea of markets. By levelling the playing field and the information structure for all investors, an increase in the efficiency of financial markets often results. The idea of improving on the extreme form of a market or a firm by connecting them in a particular manner is taken up again below. Let us now turn to the shifting of the boundaries when changes occur in the business environment.

Shifting the boundaries

Changes in the rugged landscape of competition lead to boundaries that – once set optimally – are no longer appropriate for altered conditions in business. Technological advances and the liberalization of several industries led to the emergence of competitive markets where none previously existed. The necessity of human capital for success has increased tremendously for firms. The changes described in Section 2.4 thus led to a change in the relative importance of resources within firms, and to a change in the relative merits of firms over markets in many cases. This section provides some evidence on the shifting of the boundaries that is the answer to these changes.

Outsourcing

Chandler describes the modern business enterprise as integrating different units that 'carry out a specific *function* involved in the distribution of a specific *product* in a specific *geographical* area'.[34] Whereas the questions about the geographical reach of firms and the different products a company manufactures or distributes are discussed controversially in the literature,[35] it has largely been taken for granted that firms have to perform many different functions, described along with the concept of the value chain by Porter (1980).

This view was challenged by changes in the business environment. The terminology of 'outsourcing' usually refers to the process of shifting the procurement of intermediate goods or services from within the firm to the market. Its characteristic is the realignment of the boundary between firms and markets. Activities previously performed by resources within the confines of the firm using the assets of the firm are now performed at arm's length on the market.

The question in many industries subject to rapid and disruptive changes is: which activities must still be provided in-house, and which can be outsourced to the market? The answer provided by managers or consultants is often to delegate to the market every task and activity that is not 'strategic' in nature. Anything involving the core competencies of the organization is still kept within its boundaries. Non-core activities are not essential to the rent-generating process of the firm and might even distract the company from activities that are truly value-enhancing. Thus it has become increasingly fashionable to explore in detail the underlying linkages between the different functions and evaluate them against the alternative mode of organization via a market for that inter-mediate good or service.[36] The emergence of markets allowed companies to do this and to subdivide their value chain.

Example 3.5 Outsourcing is prevalent in the motor vehicle industry. Speciality cars such as the Porsche Boxster are designed and marketed by the owner of the brand, while the manufacture and assembly is carried out by specialist firms – in the case of the Porsche Boxster by Valmet, a Finnish engineering firm.[a] The efficiency of the old organizational system of design-ing, producing and marketing cars within one company can be improved by outsourcing the activities that are subject to economies of scale and scope. Valmet can use its plants to produce speciality cars at an efficient level not only for Porsche but also for General Motors, with its Saab Convertible.[b]

---

[a]   See *The Economist* (2002d).
[b]   See http://www.valmet-automotive.com.

Note that at the same time as markets emerge for hitherto specific resources that can now be procured on these markets, the markets also smooth out the differences between firms. Any potential for strategic differentiation is eroded by this process, and former sources of economic rents are exhausted. Outsourcing thus shifts bargaining power and the connected economic rents not only between different firms but also between firms and consumers, thereby enhancing overall welfare.

Deconstruction

The gradation of outsourcing of a particular activity is the deconstruction of the whole value chain. Whereas with outsourcing the boundary between firm and market is affected, deconstruction takes this a step further: deconstruction usually involves the shifting of a set of resources or assets previously employed or owned by one firm to another firm on a grand scale. The realignment of boundaries between firms is characteristic.

With deconstruction, the value chain of the firm is sliced into small, distinct modules and then re-established for specific functions: the same stage on the value chain becomes more similar horizontally compared to other industries than vertically towards its own industry, which enforces deconstruction and rebuilding along these horizontal lines.[37] The administration of human resources and the payment of salaries is one example where the effect of the industry recedes and where efficiency can be increased by bundling these services for many firms in many industries together into just one firm in the value chain that specializes in this activity. The unbundling of hitherto vertically integrated activities allows the new organizations to focus better on their specific task without compromising it by considering other activities that also increase complexity and distract management. This modularization allows for a decrease in the complexity of the whole system.

Example 3.6   In the consumer-electronics industry, many firms – Sony might be the most prominent example – 'are selling their plants to independent electronics-manufacturing service (EMS) companies and then buying the products made in their former factories'[a]. The plants were bought by Solectron, an American company specializing in production for original equipment manufacturers (OEM) worldwide. The industries in which Solectron operates range through automotive electronics, telecommunications, consumer electronics, computers and networks, and medical equipment. Besides Sony, the customers of Solectron include, among others, IBM, Cisco Systems, Ericsson, Hewlett-Packard, Motorola and NEC.[b]

---

[a]   *The Economist* (2001a, p. 73).
[b]   See Solectron (2004, p. 2); see also http://www.solectron.com.

The new, more focused organization can shape its business model in such a way as to optimize its organizational design; its strategic positioning and resources can match the tasks better, and related adjustments in its organizational structure and corporate governance improve efficiency even further. Power is also assigned differently. As power shifts downwards to teams, or even to an individual level – either because markets become more complete and provide enhanced outside opportunities for people, or because this shift is made deliberately by a conscious decision about organizational design – the complementary relationships within the system lead to a change in the possibility of exploiting growth options inside or outside the firm. Resources are no longer imprisoned in the organization. If the owners of the firm – whoever they are – do not want to see key human resources or ideas leave the boundaries of the firm, they must reassign some of the economic surplus generated within the firm. Power and investment incentives are altered by deconstruction and can lead to more efficient organizational design.

Hagel and Singer (1999) explain how this unbundling and modularization reshapes whole industries. Entry barriers are torn down as specialists appear who focus their efforts on production with immense economies of scale, and sell their products to marketers who have the expertise, contacts, brand name and distribution channels to offer a wide range of products and exploit economies of scope between the different products. The task then is to find the boundaries of modules which allow for the reduction of complexity of the whole system without neglecting crucial interdependencies that could be the basis of returns from supermodularity.

Disintermediation

Disintermediation is the third effect that the changing business landscape has on many industries and businesses. By eliminating a whole set of boundaries that separated consumers and producers and allowed intermediaries to thrive, power distribution has been changed profoundly.

In the old system, when markets were non-existent or imperfect, intermediaries generated value by bringing goods and services from the producers of these goods or services to the consumers. A whole series of wholesalers, warehouses and retailers appeared between producer and customer, inflating the value chain. Intermediaries had access to both sides of the market, and they also had information that the other participants in this organizational design lacked. This placed them in a position of power and allowed them to extract economic rents. With better technology and the forces of liberalization at work, markets could emerge where none had existed before, or become more perfect and complete, thereby altering in a feedback loop the whole system of firms, markets and the various boundaries between them.

Example 3.7   Travel agents find themselves bypassed by travellers booking flights directly with the airlines. In the case of low-cost airlines, nearly every ticket is sold through the internet, and if travel agencies book on behalf of their customers, they rarely enjoy more favourable conditions. This has led many travel agencies to change their pricing schedules and charge their clients directly rather than rely on the airlines to pay a commission for every ticket sold, as was the case in the old system. Travel agencies have to rely increasingly on providing value-added services, such as putting together a whole package including the flight, hotels and rental car, and charging a fee for these services. By specializing in a particular niche, such as, for example, scuba-diving in Indonesia, they can still generate value for themselves as well as their customers.

In the new system of competition, intermediaries who could add value by stepping between the participants in imperfect markets are no longer necessary or even appropriate in the changed environment. When new peaks emerge in the rugged landscape of competition, the guides of old are of little use in the changed conditions, and of little help in conquering new territories, and disintermediation – the process of eliminating these intermediaries – sets in. Such disintermediation alters the power relationship. By gaining access to better information, individuals and firms alike can rely more on the market mechanism. Intermediaries that used to take their share of economic rents are bypassed.[38]

To summarize, note that all three described tendencies – outsourcing, deconstruction and disintermediation – shift the boundaries between firms and markets: boundaries that once protected positions to extract economic rents or imprisoned resources from appropriating their share of value creation are shifted or even eliminated. With the change in the boundaries of organizations and a change in the distribution of power, the incentives to invest are also altered. If these investments are positively reinforcing the changing conditions, the use of boundaries as a means of conveying power remains an important instrument in organizational design.

Blurring the boundaries

Besides altering the demarcation between different firms, or between firms and markets, another parameter in the design of boundaries is also of importance to improve the efficiency of an organizational design.[39] The boundaries of an organization are often portrayed as being rigid and closed. This holds true for some resources such as people employed in a hierarchy who work every day in the same office or factory for the same firm. But boundaries between different firms, or between firms and markets, never have been entirely closed. Raw materials or intermediate goods, at least, were allowed to flow into the firm, and the finished products to flow out of it.

With changing conditions in the business environment, the openness and permeability of boundaries has increased. Even resources that have remained firmly within the confines of a particular firm are starting to become more flexible and cross its boundaries more often. Additionally, resources are often not connected to one organization alone and excluded from other firms but are frequently shared between them. Assets are similarly not owned by a single firm and directed solely by its hierarchy, but frequently belong to no organization at all, such as standards, for example, that are developed jointly within a particular industry.

Again, formerly sheltered positions and resources lose their privileged possibility of extracting economic rents, and formerly incarcerated resources are set free to flow between organizations and to cross boundaries more seamlessly to wherever they can create the highest value and appropriate it.

In this section, the permeability of boundaries is explored. First, hybrids and alliances that have been investigated in the theory of the firm for a long time are characterized briefly, and second, clusters and networks are the subject of analysis.

Hybrids and alliances

The first aspect of the blurring of the boundaries refers to the boundaries between different firms. The legal concept of ownership involves the right to exclude others from using a particular resource or asset. The boundaries between firms can thus be deduced by observing the assets and resources owned by these firms. In the case of many goods and resources, the owner can easily be identified. The case is, however, more difficult for less tangible goods such as the information and knowledge embedded in human resources and whose ownership in the legal sense cannot easily be transferred. Does the firm that employs scientists for its research own these resources? When does it own the innovative result of the efforts of the scientists? As environmental conditions change and industries converge, human capital becomes transferable between different industries. To find innovative products and processes requires the exchange of knowledge or the flow of resources that carry this knowledge. Boundaries need to allow for this.

As Helper *et al.* (1998) observe, firms are engaging increasingly in collaboration with their input suppliers even as they are reducing the extent to which they are vertically integrated with those suppliers: 'Car manufacturers today collaborate more closely with their suppliers than did car manufacturers twenty years ago, and the intimacy of collaboration is increasing.'[40] This makes the notion of a boundary misleading, and the legal concept of ownership is of little use when determining the economic boundaries of an organizational design. The characteristic of permeability of the boundary between different firms allows for the sharing of resources and positions across these boundaries. Firms can co-operate in many hybrid forms such as joint ventures, franchises or licensing agreements, and strategic alliances that stop short of full integration. With these hybrids they can perform some activities jointly, such as research and development of new products, which each firm will produce and market on its own behalf. They can also use specific resources such as an intimate knowledge of the local conditions in such a joint venture that benefits both parties and allows them to create value.

The combination of legal separation and economic integration allows the setting of investment incentives and power in such a way as to maximize the economic rents generated by this organizational design. While the boundaries in relation to other firms and the market remain closed, the internal interface is structured to allow for a much better flow of resources to those market positions where they create the most value. The combination of separation and integration at the same time allows the avoidance of the problem analysed by Hart and Holmström (2002): collaboration to take into account external effects between two firms is possible, while joint decision-making also considers economic rents and private benefits that would otherwise be neglected. Hybrid forms of organization can thus increase efficiency by stimulating value-enhancing investments by firms as a whole. But such forms can also provide incentives for individual agents within these firms. By such a careful opening of the boundary, the owners of the resources held in the firm – such as the employees with their human capital – can find it more worthwhile to invest specifically, as they are no longer bound to a particular firm. This gives them power by providing another option of using this specific resource, and the threat of a hold-up by a single firm is reduced. At the same time, the investment is still sheltered from the outside markets with their tendency to erode economic rents.

By adjusting and blurring the boundaries between different firms, specific investments are stimulated that create value and power. *Ex-post* appropriation possibilities are given to those who decide *ex ante* over these investments. The efficiency of the overall organizational design is thus improved.

Clusters and networks

The second aspect of the blurring of the boundaries refers to the boundary between firms and markets. In the same way that firms can alter the boundary between themselves to an interface that allows for the exchange of resources and positions while still preserving a safe haven, markets can also be altered to allow for a more efficient organizational design. This happens when markets emerge between firms that are not characterized by a one-off, anonymous exchange of goods between people or firms. Firms build clusters or networks where they interconnect with each other to such an extent that it is difficult to tell whether a particular transaction is a market exchange or whether it has taken place within a huge, but loosely connected, single organization.

Unlike the hybrid form of organization described above, decision-making remains scattered, and the firms involved are legally and economically separate entities. Such an arrangement is usually open to the outside, so that new members can easily take part in this cluster or network, whereas the boundaries of the different firms remain closed unless they can benefit from the closer co-operation described above.

Porter (1998, p. 78) defines clusters as 'geographic concentrations of interconnected companies and institutions in a particular field. Clusters encompass an array of linked industries and other entities important to competition'. Such clusters enhance the productivity of the firms and institutions that form them: better access to suppliers, employees, specialized information and public goods can be gained by choosing to take part in such a cluster or network. Since the participating firms in a cluster are complementary to each other rather than direct competitors, they are mutually dependent on each other, and the success of one firm also boosts the performance of the others and attracts even more firms to the cluster. The idea of this mutually reinforcing success and the complementary notion of co-operation can easily be transferred from the context of a cluster based on geographic proximity – in which Porter (1998) was interested – to a network that does not rely on spatial economics but that makes use of proximity in other contexts – for example, in the case of investing in an industry-wide standard.

As described in Section 2.4, this becomes important when technological progress demands such standards, and when industries are liberalized. In regulated industries, the regulator provides a focal point on which the firms in the industry can base their decisions. But this is no longer possible when the regulatory agency ceases to exist in liberalized markets. Other focal points have to be found to co-ordinate investments and to make use of the external effects that prevail. Clusters and networks can be formed that allow for these external effects while at the same time preserving the correct decisions that maximize welfare. Again, by the adjustment and blurring of the boundary, the problem formulated by Hart and Holmström (2002) can be mitigated.

Investment incentives and power relations are also affected positively by the use of networks. Co-ordinated, value-enhancing investments can be undertaken without relying on a single hierarchy. This allows individuals and firms to capture returns from supermodularity that rest on co-specialized and complementary investments. Risks are reduced by an improved information flow within the network, and the exposure to a single firm that could hold up the owner of a particular resource or specific asset to capture a larger share of the economic rents is reduced.

The outside option for the owners of the various specific resources is thus strengthened. When economic activities are clustered around specific locations, for example, people do not have to move location to get a new job.[41] This geographical clustering thus induces more specific investment and allows the capture of economic rents in the form of private benefits.

As a final remark, note that a network develops its own dynamics and can be seen as an efficient organizational design or a module in a larger system in which the participating institutions co-evolve by successive changes among interdependent units that adapt to each other over time and react to external shocks in a co-ordinated way.[42]

But not only the external boundaries of an organizational design are important: their internal 'boundaries' also matter. It is to this subject, among other topics of organizational structure, that we turn in the next section.

3.3　The internal structure of the organization

The third building block of organizational design is the internal structure of organizations and the way that the processes are organized within them. The internal structure supports the strategy of the organizational design and helps to achieve its vision and goals. The internal structure sets boundaries within firms that often have similar functions and effects to the external boundaries. And internal structures support the governance of organizations by assigning decision rights and decision-making power. The many elements that make up the internal structure can be configured in various distinct ways to achieve efficiency for the overall system. A closer look at these elements and their configuration is the topic of this section.

The manipulation of incentives for investment and value creation of the constituencies taking part in the system is one of two main features affected by the right configuration of the internal organizational structure. Investments into value-creating assets, market positions and firm resources depend on the information about such opportunities. Hence a system for the generation of information and evaluation of actions is important for the incentive system. Investments in value-creating assets, market positions and firm resources depend also on the decision-making power of those with the relevant information. Hence the adequate setting of the power structure within the organization is important for the incentive system. By matching information with decision rights, and by setting incentives to use this knowledge and power wisely, value is created and economic rents are maximized.

The co-ordination of the investment decisions of the various constituencies is the other major task that a good internal organizational structure has to fulfil. Differences in the available information and differences in the decision-making power to transform this knowledge into implementable action potentially lead to decisions that do not support each other in a way that makes the best use of existing complementarities between these decisions and actions. Devices for co-ordination are therefore needed to create value and capture any returns from supermodularity.

This section is devoted to the task of describing the various elements that shape the incentives and allow for co-ordination while matching information with decision rights. The complementary relationship between these parameters is highlighted, and proposals for an efficient configuration within the overall organizational design are made by showing the systemic nature within each building block.

The systemic nature of the internal structure is well-recognized, and much of the literature deals with this. Brickley *et al.* (1997b), for example, draw attention to the necessity of achieving an alignment between decision rights, reward system and performance measurement, and Baron and Besanko (2001) use a case study of Citibank to underscore the relevance of fit between strategy, structure and incentives in an organization. How the various elements that make up the internal organizational structure fit together in a way that exploits the complementary relationship between these design parameters is the subject of this section.

The section evolves around the four themes of information and power, incentives and co-ordination, as illustrated in Figure 3.1. It starts with a

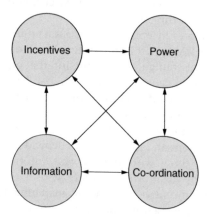

Figure 3.1 The four main themes of internal organization

closer look at information and knowledge, and how they affect the balance of power. The issues of incentives for the people involved in the organizational design, and of the co-ordination of their activities, follow. Both themes crucially depend on the available information and distribution of power that can manifest itself in the visible hierarchy within the firm.

Information and knowledge

The notion of information is used throughout this book in various places. The agency approach to the theory of the firm, the view of firms as knowledge-creating entities, and the resource-based approach to strategy have relied extensively on information to explain phenomena in organizational design. To describe the internal structures and processes of organizations, the notion of information, and its nature, source and distribution, is even more important. As a more solid basis for the rest of this chapter, a classification of information and knowledge is required.

Types of information and knowledge

Information – or knowledge[43] – is a peculiar good. One characteristic of knowledge is that it is difficult to evaluate. Evaluating and putting a price on any information before exchanging it is only possible when the information is known. If this is the case, however, no exchange needs to take place, since the information is already common knowledge and no one would pay any price for it.[44] This makes knowledge and information difficult to exchange in markets. Firms, however, have other means of coping with this problem: deferred compensation for the information or an *ex ante* employment contract with a fixed wage are just two possibilities. The firm as a knowledge-creating entity, as described in Section 2.1, is thus often a superior organizational design over markets.

A second characteristic of knowledge/information is that it needs a carrier and context to be useful. The location of knowledge is hence of importance. In large and complex organizations, the place where information/knowledge is generated matters, since complementarities with the allocation of decision-making rights exist. A ramification of the characteristic that knowledge needs a carrier and thus has a location is that information is often not only dispersed but also distributed unevenly. An asymmetric information structure – where some people know more than others – is the basis for the agency theoretical view of the firm. Agency models feature prominently in the realm of the internal structure of organizations, and many phenomena can be explained as mitigating problems of unevenly distributed local information.

A third characteristic of knowledge is whether it is explicit and codifiable in nature, or implicit and tacit.[45] Explicit knowledge can be codified easily. It can be written down, stored in databases, and be reused easily by other people. It can be sold or licensed to other companies, and can be acquired together with a whole company in a merger as with other resources that might be the basis for a competitive advantage. Tacit knowledge, on the other hand, is difficult to record, being embedded within its carrier and its context. Tacit knowledge is specific to a certain person or a certain organization. Tacitness has important ramifications regarding the possibility of transferring such specific knowledge. Jensen and Meckling (1999) accordingly define 'specific knowledge as knowledge that is costly to transfer among agents and that is not easily observable by other agents (particularly, by managers higher in the organization hierarchy). General knowledge is information that is transferable between agents at low cost or is easily observable by other agents'.[46] Note here that specific knowledge can be a source of competitive advantage, as are other specific investments.[47]

Knowledge and decision rights

For information/knowledge to be useful and to live up to its value-creating potential, it has to be matched with decision-making rights to exploit the complementary relationship between these two elements for the benefit of the overall system. Carrying some information but lacking the right to use it, or being required to make a decision but not having the necessary information is clearly inferior to a design where these two elements are aligned: the return to increases in the configuration of one element is enhanced if the configuration of the second element is also increased. Power and information are thus interdependent.

The location and carrier where information accrues and resides, and the distribution of decision rights is, however, often not identical. In this case, a redistribution of knowledge or power improves the efficiency of the overall design. The combination of information with decision rights can basically be achieved either by transferring the relevant information from those parts of the organization where it occurs to where decisions are made or, alternatively, by transferring the decision rights to where information is generated and stored. Parameters such as the costs of information transfer that depend on the degree of tacitness and the value of information in the context of decision-making alter the relative advantage of one solution over another. If the cost of information transfer is high, decentralizing decision rights is often the better solution. A description of such empowerment is postponed to the next section, where the advantages and disadvantages of centralization or decentralization and the impact on the authority relationship is considered.

For the first solution – the transfer of the information itself – three distinct methods can be distinguished. First, the person with the information can simply communicate the relevant information to someone else who needs it, and thus educate him/her. This requires the sender and receiver to be in direct contact, and the receiver to absorb the information, which can be difficult in the case of tacit knowledge.[48] Second, the information can be 'disembodied' from both sender and receiver. The use of the price mechanism, as described by Hayek (1945), allows for this. Third, direction – that is, the applied information – can be a substitute for communication, as explained by Demsetz (1993). The last two possibilities are exploited by the two basic forms of organizational design:

- In markets, a mechanism exists that alleviates the problem of collocating decision rights with specific and local knowledge. Hayek (1945) describes the importance of the price mechanism for the transfer of information. This mechanism makes it no longer necessary to communicate the information itself – a change in relative prices is all that is needed to influence the decisions and behaviour. It is not important why the relative prices have changed: the knowledge is embedded in the relative prices people observe, and they can use the disembodied information with their decentralized decision rights. The price mechanism forces economic agents to bear the monetary consequences that acting on the information embedded in the relative prices brings with it. This ensures compatibility of incentives. However, the price mechanism sometimes fails to ensure good co-ordination between interdependent decisions.
- In firms, the mechanism of direction can substitute for the transfer of the information itself. Especially if the relevant information accrues at a single location or is easy to transfer, the centralization of decision-making power is superior to the dispersed solution. Gathering and processing information centrally takes advantage of economies of scale and avoids duplication. The best response for the overall system can be calculated, and the efficient behaviour for every constituency can be determined. The relevant knowledge is then embedded in the orders and directions agents receive. This mechanism of direction ensures good co-ordination between interdependent decisions because of central planning. However, it can sometimes fail if agents have only weak incentives to make decisions and to act optimally when they do not bear the monetary consequences of their actions.[49]

Note that, in the case of truly dispersed knowledge, which occurs in the rugged landscape of competition in today's business environment, the necessity of good and co-ordinated decisions can make both idealized mechanisms inappropriate. Other structures and processes in organizational design have then to make up for such shortcomings. Elaborate knowledge management within a firm can, for example, help to provide incentives to use information efficiently and to co-ordinate it in such a way that it allows the creation and sustaining of a competitive advantage and the generation of economic rents. By thus actively managing knowledge, strategy is linked to structure in organizational design.[50] We return to the theme of co-ordination at the end of this section.

Generation and transfer of information

The first solution to the requirement to match knowledge with power was described above as the adjustment in the information structure and the generation and transfer of information to those with decision-making power. Information is a resource that can be the basis for a competitive advantage if it is superior to that of competitors. Specific investments in information can increase the competitive advantage of organizations and help to create economic rents by increasing returns to good decision-making.

But how to collect the appropriate amount of information and channel it to those who can use it efficiently? Whereas the ideal of the market mechanism embeds all relevant information into prices that can be observed in liquid markets, in other forms of organizational design, such as firms, valuable information is not that easy to detect. But unlike markets that can also break down when information becomes crucial (see the example in Akerlof (1970) of the quality uncertainty that might lead to a failure of the market for used cars), firms generate a lot of information just because of their going-concern nature – for example, in an internal labour market or in a strategic alliance with a supplier. Recording such information and measuring the characteristics and behaviour of employees and external suppliers creates knowledge that cannot be matched in anonymous spot markets.

Firms can also invest in market positions that may be a means of gaining access to such superior information. The value-creating potential of intermediaries, for example, often rests on information about the two sides they are representing. The case for the firm can, furthermore, be made whenever 'the sharp incentives of markets limit the lateral sharing of local knowledge which is inherently difficult to measure or reward directly'.[51] The combination of information to create knowledge can therefore be fine-tuned in companies with the correct configuration of the many elements that make up the internal structure of firms.

Example 3.8   An important aspect of knowledge and information is whether information is, and should be, available at all. If external effects on other parties prevail, it might pay to conceal such information and classify it carefully. In the scientific referee process, information is withheld from both the author and referee: neither should know the identity of the other party. If both author and referee knew each other's identity, their decisions and behaviour might be different and allow them to develop reciprocity.[a] The intended goal and purpose of the design in question would be impaired.

---

[a]   See Tirole (1988a, p. 464f.).

But there exists a danger to information generation and its transfer. Imagine the case in which information is simply gathered with the aim of using it to increase the own share of the economic rent that can be distributed to the constituencies involved in the organizational design without contributing to value creation in the first place. The unsolicited sharing of information with decision-makers can be used to lobby them for individual advantage and to the detriment of others. Milgrom (1988) and Milgrom and Roberts (1990a) label the resulting costs from these activities as influence costs: costs that can lead in the extreme to outright sabotage of the investments of others merely to increase the own share of the total. By not limiting the amount of information and managing the access to knowledge carefully, such a design might in fact destroy value.

Performance measurement

Numerous agency models solve for the best contracts that allow for the use of information and the inducement of efficient behaviour. Small differences in assumptions about the information structure in these models can explain many organizational features applied in practice. A description or classification of these models is beyond the scope of this book, and a short description of important aspects to performance measurement must suffice here.

The direct measurement of the characteristics and actions of people employed in the firm avoids the problem of asymmetrical information. By careful screening, problems of *ex-ante* information asymmetries that might lead to an adverse selection problem are mitigated. By careful monitoring, problems of *ex-post* information asymmetries that might lead to moral hazard are alleviated. But how much performance measurement should be undertaken? And what should be measured? Screening and monitoring is costly, both directly and indirectly in terms of the risk that imperfect measurement brings with it. Thus it often makes sense to measure not the output of an agent but rather the effort that is the input into production. Relative performance measurement can improve the efficiency of the system further by filtering the underlying noise out of the measure. Aspects of performance measurement are taken up below in the context of rewarding agents, especially managers and employees.

Example 3.9 Monitoring becomes easier with advances in information technology, as the case of video shops shows. These shops rent out videotapes, and used to pay a large amount of money in advance to the wholesale distributors. This type of contract has disadvantages – for example, too few copies of each film were ordered. With the development of smart cash registers it is possible to alter such a contract and to base the amount paid on a smaller advance fee and an agreement to share the revenues dependent on the number of rentals made.[a]

---

[a]   See Siegele (2002, p. 16).

Careful screening and monitoring can thus generate information that is valuable to those having the power to direct and lead others in organizational design, and improve its efficiency by actively managing the knowledge and information inside the organization. As an old saying puts it: 'Knowledge is power'. This takes us into one of the central themes of this book.

Power and authority

Whenever the transfer of specific knowledge is difficult and expensive, 'the alternative to moving the knowledge is to move the decision rights to those agents who possess the relevant specific knowledge',[52] to match information with the complementary power. The assignment of decision rights, however, has a direct effect on the balance of power in the organizational design, which is often not desirable on its own. So how should power be distributed in the organization? Through which means can power be acquired, be assigned, and be used? And how can positions of power be kept in balance? This section aims to shed some light on these issues.

Sources of power

Before proceeding to the question of how to assign power deliberately within the organization to better match the information structure, it is helpful to recall where power comes from generically, and why it is necessary to get its distribution right.[53]

As argued earlier, investments into unique resources and positions lead to economic rents and can increase the efficiency of an organizational design. Vesting resources and occupying positions, however, sometimes exposes these resources and positions to change. The investment might not be worthwhile later – not only because of uncertainty about the future, but also because of the often very predictable behaviour of others. Power or 'authority defines the allocations, distribution or rules of the game *ex post*'.[54] When getting these *ex post* rules of the game right, value-creating investments are not neglected *ex ante* for fear of adverse *ex post* rules that lead to a diminished economic rent that renders the initial investment unadvantageous.

But how can the organizational design ensure that *ex post* power is allocated to those who need to invest specifically *ex ante* to create value? Fortunately, the power distribution matches this requirement to a certain extent generically: specific investments lead not only to economic rents, but specific investments also bring power with them. By making a resource or position unique, the owner of it can wield some power from this singular resource or position. However, the strength of this power depends on the power that others have obtained by specializing their resources or positions. Thus, not the absolute power that specificity brings with it, but the relative power, compared to the specific resources and positions of others, matters.

As an aside, note that specific investments alone are not enough to generate power. The absolute power created by them is embedded in markets with their power structure. The existence of surrounding markets determines hence the value of the power. Their competitiveness lends credibility to the threat of withdrawing the unique resource or position from the organization. The loss in economic rent from withdrawing is minimized, more of the sunk costs can be recovered, and the exit option is worth more.

Different cases with different numbers of specific investments can be imagined. The trivial solution has no specific investments into either resources or market positions. There is no generic power in such a system, and power is not needed, since no economic rent has been created that could be distributed. This design resembles an ideal competitive market. If only one specific investment by only one economic principal is undertaken, the economic rent accrues to that principal alone, and his/her power is not challenged by others in the design, since general inputs can be used at market prices. Problems arise when many absolute powers clash. If multiple specific investments are made, each contributes to the creation of an economic rent and creates power. This power, however, can be used in the *ex-post* game not only to safeguard the economic rent created by the own specific investment but also to appropriate some share of the rent generated by the investments of others. This is especially likely when these multiple specific investments are complementary to each other. The economic rent resulting from supermodularity cannot be separated out in this case.

Multiple specific and complementary investments into resources or positions could arguably create the most value, but power struggles between the different generic powers could also lead to a reduction of value. Furthermore, if everybody expects to lose the *ex post* game between many powers because their own power is estimated to be relatively weak, nobody invests *ex ante* and no economic rents are generated – the most inefficient design. In such a case it might be better to have one strong constituency who invests and can be sure to receive the rent. This is especially appealing if one particular specific investment is of paramount importance. This implicit assumption in most of the literature on economics, finance and industrial organization thus leads to the analysis of only a special case in which the potential for value creation is not fully exploited. Altering and balancing the power structure can increase the value and efficiency of any organizational design in which multiple specific and mutually reinforcing investments need to be undertaken.

Altering the power distribution

But how can the generic power structure be changed? How can multiple specific investments be encouraged? Here, some of the many means that are available for the design of organizations are described. One of the prime examples of creating derived power by redistributing generic power is captured in the ancient military rule of 'divide and conquer'. By introducing boundaries within the organization, the information structure and thus the power distribution can be changed. Boundaries can be both horizontal and vertical. In the former case, the familiar hierarchy within firms emerges. The superior has power over his/her subordinates simply through his/her position in the firm, regardless of the specific information s/he holds. Vertical boundaries are determined by the introduction of departments that divide the firm along functional, geographical or other lines. By restricting activities and opportunities for members of these departments, the organization can encourage specific investments by some constituencies while discouraging others.

Note that the permeability of these internal boundaries is again a crucial parameter in organizational design. The advancement from subordinate to superior, for example, has a direct effect on relative power, and its prospect alone can spur specific investments in a feedback loop.[55] Both sorts of boundaries – horizontal ones that create a hierarchy and vertical ones that create departments – are explored in later sections from various angles. Both means of shaping the power structure also affect the other three themes of internal structure – the information that organizations have, the incentives they provide, and the co-ordination they have to undertake.

Other means of altering the distribution of power include those that increase or decrease the degree of power in the overall organizational system. In order to maximize the total economic rent, it might pay to lower the power and investment incentives of the one party that would otherwise have absolute power in the organization's design. By forming coalitions, individual agents can increase their collective power and thus safeguard their specific investments. Particularly in industries that rely on human capital, such as investment banking, successful teams in research or project management can increase their power by specializing their human capital towards each other and collectively creating a unique resource. Such collective action is investigated in Section 3.4.

Deliberate attempts to reduce the power in a particular organization can be made with two familiar organizational forms – the corporation and the state bureaucracy: 'Bureaucracies are usually defined as organizations mainly run by rules, or at least by the absence of delegated authority.'[56] The degree of power in bureaucracies is weak, and the potential for rent-seeking reduced. Specific investments by many constituencies are encouraged, since the *ex post* sharing rules are relatively rigid. Such a design, however, only works in particular circumstances, especially when the degree of novelty of information and the frequency of changes in the business environment are low.

The second possible solution to reduce the degree of power in the organization is the vesting of formal power[57] in a third, independent principal. The corporation assigns ownership and the residual decision rights that supplement it to dispersed shareholders, who usually do not have the incentives or information to micro-manage the firm actively. As Athey and Roberts (2001, p. 200) argue: '[I]t may indeed be optimal to assign decision rights to someone other than the best-informed party.' Efficiency can be improved by introducing another source of power into the relationship of two managers who should both specialize their human capital towards the organization to increase the total economic rent. In the absence of a third party, both managers might be reluctant to invest, or one might dominate. In both cases, underinvestment and a loss in efficiency would be the result. The relatively uninformed third party who does not have generic power on his/her own but only the assigned decision authority can act as a tiebreaker for other constituencies and relieve them from the fear of the power of the other principals.[58]

Checks and balances in power distribution

Power can corrupt. Having the power to move resources around within the organization and to reposition the organization allows for a potentially huge creation or destruction of value. People in positions of power are often subject to lobbying and influence by others. Dysfunctional investments and value destruction can be the result. So, how can power be checked and balanced? And what assures that power is used wisely?

The previous example of two managers who assign formal power to an uninformed third party shows the necessity of finding the right balance for the relative power of each provider of a specific investment to the organization. If the distribution of power is not balanced, wrong investment incentives are set. The fear of *ex post* expropriation of economic rents leads to underinvestment, while possibilities for rent-seeking can lead to too much investment in the pursuit of economic rents belonging to other parties. Both cases represent inefficient organizational designs. Changes in the distribution of power should hence be explored for their effects on the investment incentives of all affected constituencies. A fine-tuning of the balance of power and the introduction of checks to any generic power also stimulates investment incentives of other constituencies. The overall rent available for distribution is thus maximized.

What mechanisms can lead to such checks to the power, and to a balance in its distribution? Naturally, the boundaries that departments and hierarchies introduce to convey derived power by restricting the accessibility to resources and positions can also provide checks on the relative power of individuals or groups of agents. The process of decision-making can be separated in the same way into various steps that can be reassembled in a way that takes into account the necessity to provide a counterweight to positions of power. The separation of decision management and decision control in the context of executive and non-executive or supervisory power, as proposed by Fama and Jensen (1983b) and modelled by Dewatripont and Tirole (2005) in the context of information transfer, follows this idea.

There are many more possibilities to provide checks and balances in the power distribution than these rather obvious ones. An example of a more complex design is provided by Dewatripont and Tirole (1999), who also touch on the themes of information and incentives.[59] Although their fine-tuned design is seemingly inefficient and duplicates the task of information collection, it can mitigate the problem of rent-seeking and influence costs raised by Milgrom (1988). Dewatripont and Tirole (1999) show that a design that gives potentially immense power to (and provides high-powered incentives for) advocates can be efficient. By relating the success of the two sides to the amount and relevance of information the advocates collect in favour of their case, power and incentives are consistently high, to exploit the complementarities in the design. By balancing potentially biased information from one side explicitly with another view, power is distributed, so that some checks and balances prevail. While power is balanced in such an organizational design, incentives to collect information are maximized. The *ex-ante* uninformed third party can thus make a good decision. As Dewatripont and Tirole (1999) show, such a design is appropriate whenever information has a high value for decision-making, but the problem of bias in information is high. An example for such a design based on advocacy is the judiciary system.

Centralization versus decentralization of power

The changes in the rugged landscape of competition have made information more important. In particular, local knowledge has become a potential source of competitive advantage. Returning to the problem of matching information with power, there is the question of how the generic power conveyed by the specific resource or position based on local information is embedded within the checks and balances of the organization's power structure. How can it be ensured that those with valuable local knowledge have the authority to act on this information to the advantage of the whole organization? As Jensen and Meckling (1991, p. 260) remark: '[T]here is no automatic decentralized process which tends to ensure that decision rights in the firm migrate to the agents that have the specific knowledge relevant to their exercise.' The answer to the above question lies in the careful design of the hierarchy within the organization.

While the formal design act of dividing along hierarchical lines conveys authority on the superiors, real power in the sense of Aghion and Tirole (1997) is determined by the structure of information, and rests with those who hold specific knowledge. Decentralization of decision rights becomes necessary when the distribution of knowledge is dispersed and the information is specific and tacit in nature. Such knowledge can be communicated neither directly nor indirectly in a disembodied or processed form. Directions and orders are thus to be substituted by the delegation of authority as the only alternative to communication.[60] By delegation, decision-making power is devolved to lower-rank employees within the firm, and the hierarchy usually becomes flatter with this process. Lower-rank employees are thus empowered to use their local and specific knowledge.

In this process of empowerment,[61] the opportunity must be given to use the generic power provided by specific information. The real power based on superior information needs either to be supplemented with additional assigned power or complemented by the credible commitment of others not to use their formal power. While the first option involves new sources of power and usually increases the complexity of the design, the second option of abstaining from the use of power can assure others of their relative power, and is less complex. According to Aghion and Tirole (1997), such a credible commitment to use the formal powers only in extraordinary circumstances can, for example, be achieved by the use of a wide span of control. A superior with formal power to overturn the decision of a subordinate will seldom use this authority when many subordinates compete for his/her attention, when individual subordinates have developed a reputation for good use of their real power and information, or when the urgency of the decision requires immediate action. As a side effect, the incentives of the agents thus empowered by the reduction of the degree of usable power in the system are also strengthened.[62] Note again that, in general, incentives to make a good decision and the co-ordination of the dispersed decisions by relying on a common vision as a focal point are also needed when matching power with information. The next two sections deal with these complementary aspects.

Leadership

Before turning to the themes of incentives and co-ordination, however, a brief statement of how power can be used to the advantage of the whole organizational design is necessary. What is a good use of power? Or, put differently, what is good leadership? Good leadership involves the correct use of all sorts of information, the right use of all sources of power, and the adequate use of all means of co-ordination embedded in the overall strategy of the organization. As such, leadership is strongly complementary with the elements of strategy,[63] and all four themes of internal structure. Experienced leaders undertake, with their decisions and actions, the very task of designing organizations.

Good leaders use their power to decide on the information they have acquired either directly through communication or indirectly through the decisions of others. Thus leadership does not only involve the issuance of orders and commands, but also the granting of freedom for others to decide about their superior information and accept or reject their decisions. Experienced leaders manage information in such a way as to select the most appropriate means of either transferring the information – directly communicating or indirectly embedding it in decisions and actions – or delegating authority and accepting the empowered decision. By managing information, leaders are gatekeepers who are able to steer other decision-makers in the desired direction. Note that, in a feedback loop in the organizational system, such a position of controlling access also provides power. A responsible use of this power can assure other constituencies of the benevolence of the leader and induce them to make complementary specific investments. One sign of such benevolence is the sacrificing of part of the leader's own share of the economic rents. Such 'leading by sacrifice' induces other people to follow, thus increasing the overall economic rent.[64]

Example 3.10 Bartlett and Ghoshal (1995) describe how successful firms such as IKEA and the Body Shop rely heavily on the capabilities of their top managers to communicate effectively with their employees. What they extract as a common trait in these business environments, and recommend as an effective leadership style, is that of a listening and teaching boss rather than one issuing commands and monitoring the results among their subordinates. Note, however, that such a leadership style is closely connected to the person in charge, and may lead the whole firm to under-perform or even to fail once the successful leader, who is often also the founder of the company, steps down. Bartlett and Ghoshal's prime example in many of their writings – ABB (Asea Brown Boveri) – was in dire straits after its CEO Percy Barnevik withdrew from the company.

Delegation of authority requires leaders to trust the people empowered to act on behalf of the whole organization. The theme of co-ordination is thus of paramount importance for good leadership. Good leaders use their power to co-ordinate the decisions that others make by providing a vision for them on which they can base these decisions.

As Foss (1999b, p. 16) recommends: '[T]he leader must establish the knowledge among his subordinates that they all expect each other to obey and that they all know this.' The aspects of the organization's strategy, namely its vision or mission and its objectives, become important for this task of aligning the investments and actions of dispersed decision-makers. How the necessary co-ordination can be achieved is further explored below in the section on co-ordination.

Incentives and motivation

Even if the information relevant for decision-making is matched with the power to make and implement decisions, the best investments do not necessarily emerge. Incentives to use information and power in the way most consistent with maximizing the sum of economic rents are needed. This is especially true if costs related to, and risks associated with, these investments have to be compensated. The economic rent that individuals or groups of individuals receive for their participation in the organization over time can be such a compensation for costs and risks. The distribution of the costs and risks and the distribution of the resultant economic rent among the various constituencies are, however, often different – with the result that the individually rational investment decisions and the socially optimal investment programme are discrepant. The credible commitment – possibly underlined by a balanced power structure – to share the economic rent can provide incentives to make the best decisions and take the best actions, and thus compensates for the associated costs and risks.

The monetary effect of the decisions and actions becomes apparent in competitive markets almost immediately as the information about the unravelling uncertainty finds its way into market prices, and any economic rent resulting from these investments can thus be collected. This provides strong incentives for the owner of resources to compare the costs and risks of investments with the potential benefits and to act accordingly. However, the external effects of these decisions on other people are neglected in this process. Firms, however, have the possibility of influencing the structure and timing of the economic rents that accrue to individuals or groups of individuals. By altering the structure and timing of the respective share of future economic rents, firms can reshape the incentives of the different constituencies of the organization and steer them towards more co-operative behaviour if the economic success for the individual is, for example, tied to the performance of a group. Decisions and actions are different in this case, and the efficiency of the organizational design can often be enhanced if the reshaped incentive scheme allows the taking into account of the external effects on the specific investments of others.

In firms, there exist different incentive devices ranging from the weak (when, for example, a fixed amount of the economic rent is promised regardless of the decision or action) to the strong (when, for example, ownership considerations drive investment considerations, much as they do in competitive markets). Incentives can be positive in the form of rewards, or negative in the form of punishments. They can be explicit when bonuses are paid or implicit when promotions are tied to past performance. They can be based on individuals or on teams. They can be tied to a particular task or to a full set of tasks. Even the allocation of decision rights themselves can be seen as an incentive device, as explained by Aghion and Tirole (1997).

The purpose of this section is to describe the means of setting incentives and of raising awareness to consider complementarities between different incentive devices. Highly eclectically, different means of providing incentives are explored. For a more thorough description, the interested reader is referred to Galbraith (1977, ch. 21), Gibbons (1998) or Roberts (2004, ch. 4).

Basic agency setting and rent-sharing

Specific investments allow for a more efficient production of goods or services. Selling these goods and services on markets generates a cash flow into the organization that can be distributed among the various constituencies as a return on their investment. The sharing of the monetary components of economic rents in the form of contingent payments – as a bonus for employees and managers or a dividend for shareholders – is the most obvious incentive device. In particular, the provision of monetary incentives for managers is explored in numerous models in agency theory that focus on the relationship between shareholders and managers.

In the basic setting of such models, a principal employs an agent to make decisions or take action on behalf of the principal, based on the specific knowledge of the agent. The principal, being in a position to offer a complete contract that possible agents can either accept or reject, can use the power provided by this structure: the particular agent employed by the principal is compensated with a competitive wage that would leave all the economic rent generated to the principal. But will the principal get the 'best' agent with the most appropriate capabilities, and will the agent then use his/her specific knowledge?[65] Is there any specific investment that creates an economic rent? If the costs of such investments are private and thus have to be borne by the agent, then the agent is better off not using the specific knowledge that can generate the economic rent – a rather inefficient design. Thus the principal is better advised to offer the agent a share of the economic rent as a compensation for the specific investment. If the agent can increase the odds of receiving this share of the economic rent by using specific knowledge, s/he will do so, and the problem of moral hazard is alleviated. A bonus for success in the form of a contingent cash payment for employees or share options for managers make both principal and agent better off.

The recent rise in the use of stock option programmes as an incentive device for top management[66] has often been criticized as rewarding management too much. It should, however, be seen as compensation for the investments that managers undertake to make the best use of their specific knowledge and capabilities in a business environment that puts a premium on these resources to achieve a sustainable competitive advantage for the whole organization.[67] The same holds true for the payment of an efficiency wage for employees. If the firm pays a wage above that prevailing in competitive markets, employees are discouraged from shirking by the raised costs of being dismissed: the economic rent associated with the efficiency wage would be forgone in that case. Additionally, the use of an efficiency wage increases the quality of the pool of applicants desiring to work for the organization.[68]

There are, of course, numerous agency models that depart from the basic setting briefly sketched here, which take a closer look at, for example, the attitude towards risk of both principal and agent. Many models deal with the question of how much reward is appropriate to stimulate the right decisions and actions, and which of the different possibilities and proxies to generate information to measure the efficiency of decisions and actions is the best in the particular circumstances. In particular, the last point – the generation and use of information in incentive contracts – shows the intertwined nature with other themes of internal structure. Similarly, the complementarity between the provision of incentives and the allocation of power is formulated explicitly in the property rights approach going back to Grossman and Hart (1986), and Hart and Moore (1990). Here, ownership – the assignment of residual control to a particular party – conveys the incentive to maximize the economic rent with the decisions taken. For a comprehensive treatment and an overview of the different models, see Salanié (1997) or Bolton and Dewatripont (2005).

Multiple investments in team production

A refinement of the basic agency setting is necessary to capture the demands of the changing business environment. If multiple specific investments by many different agents are compulsory for the generation of economic rents, how can incentives be provided to each of these agents? Is there still a role to play for the principal? One of the first to apply the thinking of agency theory to the team production problem identified by Alchian and Demsetz (1972) was Holmström (1982), who describes the problem of moral hazard in teams.

An agent who has to invest to produce a joint output is likely to underinvest in an attempt to free ride on the efforts of the other agents. If all agents engage in such behaviour, the efficiency of the organizational design is impaired. How, then, can incentives for optimal investment be set? Holmström (1982) shows the impossibility of achieving efficiency and distributing the joint output among all agents in equilibrium. An optimal incentive system would require that the marginal increase in team output accrues to the member responsible for this increase by balancing his/her marginal costs with the benefits of additional effort. However, this cannot be achieved for all members of the team. The innovation by Holmström (1982) was to reinterpret the role of the principal as a disinterested third party, to balance the budget. The principal absorbs any remaining surplus (when penalties are necessary) or steps in to replace any shortfall (when bonuses are needed) to provide balanced incentives for all agents.[69]

Similar to this line of reasoning is the argument put forward by Levin and Rayo (2003). They argue that such a budget-balance-breaking principal might fail to stimulate the agents to invest specifically, for a variety of reasons – s/he might abuse the power assigned to this role, or might lack the necessary information. Instead, Levin and Rayo (2003) propose to concentrate the power into a single party and provide incentives through repeated interaction among the various agents. The threat of losing future economic rents provides incentives for this empowered agent to abstain from expropriating the share of the other agents because of their specific investments. Such relational contracts resting on the continuation of a relationship can thus be a valuable means of shaping incentives in firms. See also Baker *et al.* (2002) on the use of relational contracts in organizations.

Internal labour markets

Markets provide high-powered incentives: the owner of a resource or position can feel the monetary consequences of a decision or action immediately if the market prices such resources and positions competitively and correctly. The capital market, especially for shares of large companies, is relatively well developed, and the monetary consequences of specific investment decisions of shareholders or their agents are often anticipated in the aggregate price prior to investment. Risks can be shared and allocated efficiently by relying on the market mechanism. Markets thus provide high-powered incentives to invest in the most efficient way. However, not all markets in practice come close to the theoretical ideal, and are as well developed as some segments of the market for capital. Markets can fail because of a lack of information, or are even non-existent where specific resources are concerned. The labour market, for example, is less good at pricing the value of specific investments. As a consequence, people are not inclined to invest their human capital specifically unless other incentive devices supplement the direct monetary rewards and compensate them for the costs and risks of these investments.

Such an incentive device that mimics the market mechanism within firms can be an internal market for labour.[70] Firms can operate an internal labour market and restrict potential candidates for positions higher up in the hierarchy to those people already employed by the firm. While this limits the pool of eligible people and erects entry barriers so that those best qualified for the job might be barred from it, it also shelters those already in the organization from competition. If specific investments are of paramount importance for the organization, the operation of an internal labour market induces such investments by thus safeguarding the economic rents. Promotions based on merit or seniority to higher levels of the hierarchy provide incentives to take the desired actions.[71] Note that the choice of operating an internal labour market is complementary to corporate strategy and the industries the organization is in. For firms with fast-growing businesses, the use of promotions as an incentive device is easier than for firms in stagnant and mature industries.[72] In the latter case, the promotion decision is more like a tournament in which the winner takes the whole prize. It is a zero-sum game in which the gain of the person promoted is the loss of the other people who were not chosen for the job.

Example 3.11 General Electric used a tournament[a] for choosing the successor to Jack Welch when he retired in December 2000 after leading the company for more than twenty years. Three candidates were identified to follow him, from whom Jeffrey Immelt was chosen after a tournament of roughly eighteen months. The other two, Robert Nardelli and James McNerney, left the company within a week of the decision being taken. They left for Home Depot and 3M, respectively, where each immediately became chairman of the board and chief executive officer.[b]

---

[a] See Nalebuff and Stiglitz (1983) on the economics of tournaments.
[b] See *Businessweek* (2000).

Internal labour markets have, of course, many more features and means to shape incentives than the instrument of promotions described here. See Baron and Kreps (1999, ch. 8) for a more comprehensive treatment of internal labour markets.

Employability

The uncertainty involved with promotions puts the economic rent from the specific investments of employees at risk again. If they are dismissed after a tournament or in an up-or-out scheme, operated often by consulting firms and investment banks, any economic rent attributable to the firm-specific investments is lost and efficiency is impaired. The problem of underinvestment looms again. To mitigate this problem and insure employees against this risk, the complementary promise of employability[73], a kind of guarantee by the employer to make sure that former employees have no difficulty in finding another job on the external labour market, should supplement such a strong version of an internal labour market.

Employability can be assured through different means. For example, specializing human capital to a particular team in an organization provides easier access to other people's knowledge and the possibility of learning from them. This increases the value of the human capital of the employee and provides incentives to undertake such specific investments. Another means of increasing employability is through higher transparency and visibility combined with an attribution of performance to individuals. A model on these lines that also takes the themes of power and information explicitly into account was developed by Ortega (2003): power increases the visibility of managers and thus creates information that can be used by the external labour market. This strengthens the outside option of these managers, leading to improved incentives to make the right decisions.

Leaving a particular organization destroys the economic rent that a continuation of the relationship would provide, but the increase in value of the human capital allows some part of it to be recouped in another team: the economic rent becomes portable across the boundaries of a particular organization, and managers or employees are less reluctant to undertake value-creating specific investments. If the complementary elements of a strong internal labour market with an up-or-out scheme and the credible promise of employability are in place in an internal labour market, both employee and employing organization gain from this combination: it induces the employee to make specific investments and stimulates the right actions and decisions, while making the economic rent transferable in some way across organizations through the promise of employability. It also creates a sustainable competitive advantage for the employing organization whenever the increased incentives for all employees and the resulting economic rents from those remaining with the organization outweigh the loss in relationship-specific investments from those being forced to leave it.

Career concerns

Related to the operation of an internal labour market is the notion of career concerns. The basic framework, first applied by Holmström (1999c), considers a sample of managers with different talents initially unknown to everybody. These managers are employed by firms that can only offer a fixed wage for a certain period when contingent contracts cannot be made *ex ante*. While the actions and investments of the agents are their private information, the performance of each is fully observable by all *ex post*. This leads to the familiar problem of moral hazard: managers are reluctant to exert effort or to make the right investments when this is associated with costs to them. Explicit incentives such as a bonus might alleviate this problem, as described above. Holmström (1999c) proposes that, under certain conditions, implicit incentives can be a substitute means of providing direct monetary rewards. If managers are concerned about the fixed wage offered by the employer in the next period, they are induced to exert effort to influence performance and thus increase this future wage offering. The pursuit of a career with higher wages over time leads employees to invest specifically and thus create value for themselves and the organization. The reliance on implicit incentives (such as promotions in an internal labour market within an organization, or the transfer of employable human capital across the boundaries of organizations that usually are associated with higher monetary rewards) can hence be a powerful incentive for both managers and employees.

Example 3.12　The value created by such career concerns for organizations may be estimated when analysing the value of someone from General Electric (GE) taking over the top job at another company. Cairncross (2003) reports that nineteen former managers from GE created US $24.5 billion for their respective new organizations after they left General Electric. The news alone that someone from GE would take the helm at these companies led to an increase of US $1.3 billion in their market capitalization – with no loss in GE's share price.[a]

---

[a]　See Cairncross (2003, pp. 13–16) and the references given there.

Dewatripont *et al.* (1999a) refine the model by Holmström (1999c) and formally analyse the impact of the information structure on implicit incentives. They show that, under certain conditions, the garbling of information (such as reporting only whether a test has been passed or failed rather than the actual grade) can in fact reduce the incentive to exert effort, since the link from performance to the market's inference about talent is weakened. In Dewatripont *et al.* (1999b) they apply the career concerns model to the multi-tasking problem of providing incentives in government agencies that have to pursue a broader set of goals than the simple profit motive of capitalist firms. In Section 3.4, the consequences are described of such deliberations on the choice of an organizational form.

Other refinements of the basic career concern model by Holmström (1999c) include Auriol *et al.* (2002), who provide an agency model on the effects that career concerns have on the incentive to co-operate in a team, and Ortega (2003), who shows that the unequal distribution of power and the accompanying visibility to some managers is an overall efficient design – while increasing incentives among the more powerful to make good decisions, it decreases the incentives of the less powerful.

Balancing incentives

After the above description of explicit and implicit incentive devices, the questions arise of which instrument is best in which situation, and how these instruments should be combined to achieve the most efficient outcome. The combination of various incentives can be summarized in different incentive schemes. Low-powered schemes provide insurance for the agent against the risk of adverse changes in business, but they lead to shirking and too little effort. Incentives that are too high-powered might decrease the propensity to work together co-operatively in a team, or pose problems whenever the agent has to fulfil more than one task. The choice of the best incentive scheme therefore matters. Using the example of multi-tasking – the necessity for a single agent to undertake different tasks, or face a task with several dimensions to it – illustrates the need to set incentives in a balanced way.

The bundling of various tasks together into one job may be necessary for technological reasons. The work of top managers includes a range of tasks to be executed. Besides trimming the costs of established processes and products, managers have to acquire new resources and occupy new positions to leverage the advantage of the organization. The maintenance of existing businesses and developing new ones compete for the attention of the manager, and finding the right set of tasks in the first place is often part of the manager's job. Similarly, production workers have to consider the tasks of producing a high volume of good quality while taking care of the machines used in production.

How should incentives be set when the agent has to deal with several tasks? Holmström and Milgrom (1991) argue that a balance of incentives is necessary to rule out unwanted behaviour. If it is relatively easy to measure the results of efforts to cut costs by a manager, or to count the volume of output the worker produces, explicit incentives such as a bonus or a piece-rate system could induce high effort by the agent. Rewarding cost-cutting or raising the output, however, draws attention away from the other tasks the agents face, where the result might be more difficult to observe. The worker can easily increase output in this situation by neglecting the quality of the product or the maintenance of the machines used in production. Similarly, the manager can easily cut costs by stopping research activities that might, in fact, pay off in the future. The provision of high-powered incentives for a single task is detrimental in this setting, since 'incentive pay serves not only to allocate risks and to motivate hard work, it also serves to direct the allocation of the agents' attention *among* their various duties'.[74] Holmström and Milgrom (1991) propose several solutions to this problem:

- Incentives for different tasks need to be balanced. Setting high-powered incentives along one dimension raises the marginal returns to provide incentives along other dimensions of effort. If this is not possible, the complementarity relationship requires the provision of low-powered incentives for all tasks. See also Cockburn *et al.* (1999) for the example of a balanced provision of incentives in pharmaceutical firms.

- Restricting the freedom of agents in the way that they pursue certain tasks complements the use of low-powered incentives. A worker earning a fixed wage is usually required to work in an office, where the pursuit of personal activities is restricted. In this case, these activities cannot compete for the attention of the agent. A salesperson earning commission, on the other hand, faces high-powered incentives and is expected to direct enough effort to the desired tasks. See Olsen and Torsvik (2000) for a model where the discretion of the agent co-varies with the intensity of incentives.

- If high-powered incentives are advantageous, it may be a good idea to adjust other parameters of organizational design such as the ownership of assets or a shift in the boundary. The high-powered incentives of independent contractors are then matched with the ownership of the tools of production, and enough effort is provided for the maintenance of these tools. See also Holmström and Milgrom (1994) for this argument.

- Jobs can be designed in such a way as to bundle the tasks where the result can be measured easily into one job, and the tasks where performance is difficult to observe into another. The use of high-powered incentives for the first job is then feasible, whereas the second job is rewarded with a low-powered incentive scheme.

The problem of multi-tasking is quite common, and becoming increasingly so with the changes in the rugged landscape of competition that shape the new business environment. Empowered employees face the task of defining their own jobs and allocating their time to various tasks. They are required to form temporary teams on an *ad hoc* basis to perform efficiently and induce others to invest in the task identified by them.

Although the earlier investigations have largely been from the perspective of providing motivation for managers and employees, the necessity of balancing incentives also applies to other constituencies and in other contexts. Laux and Walz (2004), for example, show that the success of universal banks entering the business of investment banking can be enhanced if advising clients is tied in with also providing risky debt for them. Specialized investment banks have an incentive to provide high-quality service in order to be able to generate economic rents from their client relationships in the future, similar to the argument of career concerns described above. Banks attracted to the investment banking industry by these rents initially lack these incentives: they do not value these relationships sufficiently and are therefore inclined to shirk on the quality of their advice, pursuing a strategy of hit and run. Laux and Walz (2004) show that tying the task of advising clients with the task of providing risky debt to the same clients restores the balance of incentives for the entrants. In this case '[r]isky debt can serve as a substitute for future rent in providing the bank with incentives not to shirk high-quality service'.[75]

Co-ordination and co-operation

Even if the information relevant for decision-making is matched with the power to make and implement decisions, the best investments do not necessarily emerge. The co-ordination of the different, dispersed decisions that use the information and power in a way that is most consistent with maximizing the overall economic rent is needed, to avoid contradicting decisions and investment behaviour. Co-ordination is thus necessary whenever investments are interdependent and involve complementarities. But which means allow decisions to be co-ordinated in an organizational design? Co-ordination may be achieved either through a simplification in design, through orders from a centre or through the pursuit of a common direction. All three means are described in more detail in this section, and all have their advantages and disadvantages when combined with other elements of organizational design.

First, the task of co-ordination can be greatly simplified when suitable interfaces are implemented in the design of organizations. This can be achieved through an internal structure that channels information flows and allocates power within autonomous modules such as departments, divisions or segments.[76] Within these smaller units, complexity is reduced and co-ordination becomes easier. Second, Dessein (2003) describes the way that co-ordination through the issuance of orders results in faster decision-making and a less distorted aggregation of information. Co-ordination is hence achieved by means of a hierarchy. However, hierarchical orders can have the drawback of being based on very little relevant information. The power to command subordinates is therefore most appropriate for situations that are complex in the sense that no single incremental adjustment will increase efficiency. Third, a design based on a well-communicated strategy and common vision helps to co-ordinate the individual investment decisions that must form a nexus of specific investments to create economic rents. Focal points such as the corporate culture thus guide dispersed and empowered decisions. Individuals and teams can become more self-managing while still working towards a common objective.

Departments and divisions

Departments and divisions set vertical internal boundaries and thus create discrete modules within firms. By structuring the firm into departments and divisions, the complexity of the overall corporate system can be reduced if appropriate interfaces between the different departments or divisions exist. This facilitates the co-ordination of the dispersed investments.

As the craft system in many industries was replaced by the more efficient system of mass production, the complexity in co-ordinating these larger entities also grew. As a reaction to coping with the increased information and co-ordinating the various investments, firms such as General Motors began to structure themselves along the lines of many divisions or strategic business units.[77] Such units are headed by executives who can run their line of the business autonomously. Segment reporting in financial statements allows for good performance measurement against other companies or business units operating in the same industry, and the incentive scheme can be based on this information. The role of the corporate top management in these firms – which are often conglomerates of unrelated businesses – is that of managing the portfolio of these business units. With an elaborate capital budgeting process, corporate managers evaluate, in the internal market for capital, investment projects suggested to them by division managers and sponsor the most promising one. Operating an internal capital market allows the setting of a budget for each unit's investment expenditures and lets the managers in the divisions who have the relevant information decide how to invest. Thus the efficiency of the organizational design is increased.[78] From the perspective of strategic management, this setting is captured by the well-known matrix developed by the Boston Consulting Group with cash-generating units subsidizing the expansion of future stars. In a simple business landscape with a single peak to climb visible from afar, this process has its merits.

Such divisions have their drawbacks, however, as Ghoshal and Bartlett (1995, p. 88) state: 'Divisions divide'. Corporate resources are fragmented and value-creating new combinations of resources are hindered if the structures are too rigid and impermeable. Resources can become trapped in the divisions if an unbalanced incentive scheme favours the own unit over others or the whole system. This is a particular problem in the rugged business landscape of today that puts a premium on the combination of dispersed knowledge to spot the most promising peaks to climb. To achieve an efficient design, it is thus necessary to keep the other themes of the internal structure of firms in mind. Incentives for co-operation can, for example, be set with a reward structure that also takes overall corporate success into account. Power should be distributed relatively evenly between divisions to avoid a 'tyranny of the inefficient'.[79] And the transfer of information – as well as improved incentives for co-operation – can be facilitated by job rotation between the divisions if the internal boundary is permeable enough to allow for this.

The case is similar for internal structures organized along functional lines, and the above arguments also hold for departments. Departments for production or marketing, for finance or personnel can also reduce the complexity of the firm and allow for a better co-ordination of decisions and actions. The specialization in functional areas even allows for the accumulation of expertise that can further increase the efficiency of the organization. In the analogy of hill-walking, this is akin to advancing speedily on a well-trodden path in a simple landscape. However, if the business environment changes and the landscape becomes more rugged and fragmented, the rationale for setting up departments fades. Reducing complexity and using standardized interfaces between different functions may then mean taking the process of introducing boundaries within an organization a step further: outsourcing supportive functions to external suppliers might then be best, to take complementarities between the co-ordination of dispersed investments and the boundary decision into account.

Industries and market segments

As an aside, note that, as divisions and departments introduce internal boundaries in a firm, markets also have such boundaries. Segmenting markets with the purpose of co-ordinating economic activity makes sense if distinct modules are therefore created. Whenever industries or market segments share a common body of knowledge, standards can be established that allow interfaces between different industries. Complexity is reduced and the task of co-ordination is made easier. But unlike the division or department boundaries in firms, the boundaries of industries and market segments are usually less clear cut, and evolve more through an 'invisible hand'.

But there are exceptions in the form of governments trying to improve on the design of markets. Regulation introduces boundaries in markets – for example, segmenting them into wholesale and retail, as is the case in deregulated energy markets in Europe. Such regulation makes sense when markets would reduce complexity too much and would not take interdependencies with other industries into account. Regulation remedies such market failure. By reintroducing a more complex design, however, the potential for inefficiencies and abuses increases: is it, for example, just a different interpretation of the available information and scientific evidence that has led to import restrictions for genetically modified food in many European countries, or is such regulation a form of rent-seeking and protection of the incumbents' interests?

Note that organizational design of markets also often exhibits some sort of hierarchy. In the motor vehicle industry, the large firms have focused their strategy on designing and assembling cars. Much work is outsourced to so-called 'tier one' suppliers, who produce complete submodules for the automobile firms and themselves rely on other firms to supply them with parts. Again, such a design allows for easier co-ordination and in addition offers incentives for suppliers to reach the status of a tier one supplier or to remain in this class.

Hierarchies

The underlying information that drives the investment of empowered decision-makers is dependent on its carrier and its context. People value and interpret information differently, given other pieces of information they possess and the specific context in which they find themselves. If the price for a particular good rises in the market, people are induced to invest in production facilities or in training to produce it. If such investment and training takes some time, the momentary shortage signalled by the high price could lead too many people to invest. The result is an oversupply later and the wasting of resources that have been invested into too many projects. Cycles are the effect of such unco-ordinated investment decisions. A central planning unit that does not only have the information embedded in the high price, but also knows how many dispersed investments are undertaken, could improve efficiency when ordering only as many investments as are beneficial. This central information processing and the co-ordination through orders is the main characteristic of a hierarchy in organizations.

When are hierarchies a good means of co-ordinating dispersed investment decisions? And how do they achieve co-ordination? Hierarchies introduce horizontal internal boundaries to the structure of firms. The role of the hierarchy is to assure the flow of information and to economize on it. By simply addressing employees in the space left by the incomplete contract signed between them and the firm, information is disseminated within the organization in the form of orders. Decisions made at the centre are implemented throughout the firm. The issuance of orders and the co-ordination by means of a hierarchy is of advantage if relevant information can be gathered centrally – if information is generated at the centre or easily communicated to it.[80] A hierarchical structure also has its merits if the interdependencies between dispersed investment decisions are large.

But relying on the means of a hierarchy is not always efficient. Obviously, if information is not generated at the centre and cannot easily be transferred to it because of its tacit nature, hierarchies are less good for co-ordination. The changes in the business environment that increased the importance of local knowledge has consequently led to a demise of many hierarchical layers and a 'flattening' of firms.[81] But the use of a hierarchy has more drawbacks than this obvious one. Hierarchies are just one element in the organizational system, and complementarities with other elements lead to ramifications that are not that apparent: a hierarchy in the internal structure of firms is linked inextricably to the organizational theme of power. Hierarchies convey formal power. The power distribution that arises if a hierarchy is introduced into organizations need not reflect the generic power distribution – and it is precisely this deviation that has an important role to play in inducing specific investments, as described above. The superiors in a hierarchy also have an incentive to be biased towards their own information and the projects they favour.[82] And superiors can be subject to rent-seeking by the subordinates on whose information they must rely. Influence costs reveal the darker sides of a hierarchy and can impair the efficiency of the design. Thus other co-ordination devices might be needed.

Organizational culture

If neither a simplification of organizational design nor the use of a hierarchy is feasible for good co-ordination of specific investments, a third possibility to co-ordinate dispersed, but empowered, decisions exists in providing a common focal point. With the described changes in the business landscape, sustainable competitive advantage for the organization lies in the use of dispersed yet interdependent knowledge and actions in a co-ordinated way. The provision of a focal point helps to guide decisions based on the dispersed knowledge that needs to be co-ordinated without the need to communicate the information in either raw or processed form, and without the need to modularize the system, thereby forgoing any returns from supermodularity.

There are different ways to set a focal point. Formulating a strategy that sets a clear vision for the organization and underlines this with certain objectives, as described in Section 3.1, can provide such a focal point. Another way is the reliance on a pronounced organizational culture that leads the members of the organization to pursue a common goal. In Kreps' (1990) view, the organization is not seen as a collection of physical assets but rather as a carrier of reputation capital that provides a history and memory of how the incompleteness of contracts is likely to be filled, and how the *ex-post* bargaining power over economic rents between the various constituencies will probably be used. A reputation for not abusing authority and power can be established under certain conditions. If the reward of future rents from repeated interaction is greater than the immediate gains achievable through appropriation of the economic rents of other people, it is better to stick with this situation: the implicit contracts underlying the relationship become self-enforcing.[83] This leads to improved efficiency in the organizational design where specific investments are undertaken with the knowledge that the result-ing economic rents can be appropriated even without formal safeguards.[84]

The frequent interactions between the various constituencies of a firm allows such self-enforcing or relational contracts to work. The corporate culture of firms is hence a crucial means of co-ordinating investments and makes the best use of dispersed information. Ghoshal *et al.* (1995, p. 756) even believe that firms exist primarily not 'to exploit economies of scale or to attenuate human opportunism through fiat and rational control. [The reason for their existence] lies, instead, in their ability to acquire, assimilate, and coordinate the use of dispersed knowledge.'

How can a focal point be established, and which organizational culture is the best for a particular situation? Goffee and Jones (1996) distinguish four different organizational cultures according to the degree of sociability and solidarity between the members of the organization. Sociability refers to the aspect that people 'tend to share certain ideas, attitudes, interests, and val-ues and to be inclined to associate on equal terms'.[85] Solidarity 'describes task-focused cooperation' between *unlike* individuals and groups'.[86] The configuration of both aspects shape the organizational culture, and (given the organization's purpose) the most appropriate culture can be chosen.

Using this framework, Goffee and Jones (1996) identify a 'fragmented organization', a type that can often be found in professional services or academia, where the individuals associate themselves more with their profession than with the current employer. The sense of belonging to a profession, and the codes and procedures established therein, allow for a rapid, mutual understanding of people across the boundaries of the organization. Co-ordinated changes in the overall strategy and structure of fragmented organizations are, however, difficult to achieve in dynam-ically changing business environments because of the high degree of autonomy of individuals and teams. A fragmented organizational culture is usually complementary to blurred boundaries of the organization and an internal structure where individual freedom is high and performance measurement and rewards are difficult to set because of multi-task problems.

Another possible organizational culture is that of a 'communal organ-ization', where both sociability and solidarity are high. In such an envi-ronment, teamwork is encouraged and people from different units meet often, both inside and outside the work context. Necessary changes to the operations of the firm in a dynamically changing environment are relatively easy to make, and the authority of the leaders is unlikely to be challenged. A more elaborate example of such a community is described in Chapter 7 with a case study on open-source systems.[87]

3.4   The governance of the organization

The last building block of organizational design is the governance of organizations. The matching of power with investment incentives on a macro basis complements the other means, discussed in the previous three sections, related to strategy, boundaries, and the internal structure of organizations. The primary instrument of governance to align power with incentives is the assignment of ownership.

Markets, where small and autonomous principals are the owners of resources and positions, function well through a reliance on property rights and ownership. The invisible hand of markets works when ownership considerations drive decisions and actions to achieve efficient investments. Whenever the interdependencies between different principals are relatively unimportant and external effects are weak, the autonomy of these small modules that own the means of production should be sustained. In this case, the use of markets is the best organizational design to promote efficiency.

External effects, however, can lead to the failure of markets. And technological or other reasons can make the integration of two or more of these small, autonomous modules a necessity. This raises governance issues in this relationship, such as, for example, the question of who should optimally be in control and own the larger, integrated unit. The necessity to deal with ownership issues is paramount in the case of the more complex design of firms: governance matters. Corporate governance answers the questions of how ownership is allocated, and whether it is shared between many parties or given exclusively to one particular principal in the case of a corporation. The allocation of ownership in corporate governance and the checks and balances on the power of the single owner or in a coalition of many owners therefore drives the efficiency of the overall organizational design.

Defining governance

There are substantially different views in the literature as to what corporate governance is. The narrow view expressed by Shleifer and Vishny (1997, p. 737) takes only into account 'the ways in which the suppliers of finance to corporations assure themselves of getting a return on their investment'. The shareholders, with their specific investment of capital, are assumed implicitly to be the owners of the corporation. Corporate governance therefore primarily considers agency problems between shareholders and managers – and to a lesser extent also debt-holders. In this view, the agency problem first identified by Jensen and Meckling (1976), and the problems existing in a world of incomplete contracting as described by Grossman and Hart (1986) and Hart and Moore (1990) are reflected. But are the challenges stemming from an agency setting with incomplete contracts between shareholders and managers the only problem? Is this the real problem with governance? It is, for example, rarely the case that all other constituencies in the firm have complete contracts enforceable by the courts within a nexus of formal contracts that protect their specific investments. Employees, for example, also face the danger of hold-up once they invest specifically. Other constituencies than the suppliers of finance also have to 'assure themselves of getting a return on their investment'.

Some authors have therefore moved on to define governance in a broader sense. Tirole (2001, p. 4) defines it as 'the design of institutions that induce or force management to internalize the welfare of stakeholders'. This definition places top management in a central position – a position it undoubtedly has in an organization. But is it the responsibility of the top managers also to take the welfare of other stakeholders into account? There are examples where this is not the case, and where the management adds relatively little value to the organization: in professional services such as accounting and law practices or consulting firms, for example, the management of the company is not of overwhelming importance for the production of the service. Governance problems between other constituencies, bypassing the management, are more pronounced.

The definition of governance that is meaningful for the purposes of this book must therefore be still more general: Zingales (1998) defines governance as 'the complex set of constraints that shape the *ex post* bargaining over the quasi-rents generated by a firm'.[88] Understood in this sense, corporate governance is 'the entire set of rules, procedures, and institutional arrangements that shape decision-making within the firm and the distribution of the returns generated by implementing these decisions'.[89]

It is the purpose of this section to describe ownership as one of several possible institutional arrangements that influence the investment decisions and bargaining over the resulting economic rents.[90] The section briefly recalls the importance of ownership in an incomplete contract setting before describing the characteristics of the different constituencies or stakeholders, and the relative importance of ownership for them as an incentive device. Other mechanisms shaping bargaining power and providing incentives are explored, which alleviate to a certain extent problems arising from the loss of ownership in a larger module and offer more efficient governance in organizations. The section ends with an overview of different organizational forms.

Specific investments, stakeholders and ownership

Stakeholders

Investments are generally undertaken if the expected return is positive. However, uncertainty and risk exist and can lead to situations where the investment, although with a positive expected net present value, does not pay off: the actual return is negative. This is the normal risk that economic activity brings with it. It is compensated by a risk premium over a risk-free rate that is, for example, paid to shareholders business and financial risks, or to employees performing dangerous or risky jobs.

Relationship-specific investments have the additional risk that, even in situations where the actual return is positive, the return to the original investor is negative: the economic rent generated by the specific investment is appropriated by someone else in the relationship. This additional risk means that the economic rent from the specific investment is at stake for the investor. All principals undertaking specific investments are hence stakeholders: their return depends on the actions of other constituencies in the organization. It is this stake in the ongoing relationship, and the uncertainty about the behaviour of the other partners in the organization, that makes the analysis of governance important: fearing an appropriation of the economic rent by other constituencies might lead to abstaining from the value-generating specific investment and thus to an inefficient outcome. For efficiency to be restored, mechanisms in the organizational design must be implemented that safeguard the stake against the possibility of expropriation by other constituencies. On a macro basis in the governance of organizations, ownership can be such a mechanism to alleviate the dilemma of balancing *ex-ante* investment incentives with *ex-post* rent appropriation power.

Ownership – combining power and incentives

Ownership is a very strong element in the organizational system. Ownership is usually defined as 'residual control rights to assets, that is, the right to determine the uses of assets under circumstances that are not specified in a contract'.[91] In the incomplete contracting approach pioneered by Grossman and Hart (1986) and described in Section 2.1, the allocation of *ex-post* rights of control defined as ownership drives the efficiency of the organizational design by influencing *ex-ante* investment incentives. By assigning residual rights of control over the use of assets, ownership has an important effect on the bargaining position of the various constituencies and their propensity to invest specifically. Naturally, incentives to invest specifically are strengthened for the party that has ownership rights – no one can appropriate the economic rents resulting from these specific investments.[92]

But the effect that the assignment of ownership of physical assets has on investment incentives is more subtle. Particularly in situations where only a combination of many assets generates value, fragmented ownership rights to these assets can lead to a situation of deadlock in which many powerful owners might use their position to extract economic rents from others in the combination. Fearing such expropriation, no one would be inclined to invest specifically, and little value would be created. Integrating the assets in one organization and combining the residual rights of control improves efficiency in this situation. But an important question then emerges: who should have the ownership rights over this bundle of assets? The answer is relatively straightforward for physical assets.[93] Ownership is assigned to that constituency whose specific investment matters most: a constituency that is indispensable to an asset should also own it, and unified ownership of complementary assets is optimal.[94]

Assigning ownership of all complementary assets to the most indispensable constituency raises two problems. Success might require multiple specific investments, and thus many indispensable parties exist. And ownership rights to human capital assets cannot be transferred, making integration into one organization with a unified ownership problematic. An alternative to allocating exclusive ownership rights to one constituency is the sharing of the ownership rights in a coalition of all parties investing specifically to each other. With this alternative, however, the above mentioned deadlock between powerful principals might occur again. These two possibilities – exclusive ownership of one party, or sharing of ownership to a coalition of many parties – are described in more detail below.

Exclusive ownership

The alternative of assigning ownership rights to one party exclusively makes sense in those situations where only one specific investment has to be made. If, for example, only the shareholders have to make a specific and sunk investment, and all other inputs for production are so general that they can easily be supplied or hired with complete contracts from competitive markets, the allocation of ownership to shareholders – a group with relatively well aligned interests – and the maximization of shareholder value is the most efficient organizational design. Assigning ownership rights to one party exclusively also makes sense whenever budget constraints do not rule out the bundling of multiple specific investments by one constituency. If, for example, an entrepreneur with a brilliant idea also has the financial capital to invest in the necessary facilities to exploit the idea, inefficiencies resulting from a mismatch of power and incentives do not prevail. Such straightforward settings, however, often cannot be found and, as explained in Section 2.1, the darker side of ownership gains prominence.

Ownership can only be assigned once. At the same time that ownership strengthens the *ex-ante* investment incentives of the owner by allocating *ex-post* residual rights of control to him/her, it weakens the power and incentives of others. Granting exclusive ownership rights to a particular party – be it an individual or a group with well-aligned interests – makes other constituencies reluctant to invest if the power conveyed by ownership is not countered by some other institutional feature. Potential mechanisms to counter the power of ownership rights are discussed below.

A coalition of owners

The alternative of assigning ownership rights collectively to all indispensable constituencies can be an efficient design in situations where multiple specific investments have to be made. A coalition of many powerful parties is able to change rapidly in a dynamic environment if consensus can be reached easily or if the changes in the environment affect them all in nearly identical ways.

However, if these conditions do not hold and if interests diverge too much, organizations with such a stakeholder regime, where ownership is shared between different constituencies, appear impractical. The mutual dependence of the various parties, who have to agree, can lead to a deadlock between the different parties and underinvestment by all: all might fear that the other parties will not stick to their side of the bargain. The economic rent created by an individual specific investment with associated private costs would be expropriated by the coalition of powerful owners and shared collectively between them – an inefficient design resembling the team production problem analysed by Alchian and Demsetz (1972).

Another issue that can make the assignment of ownership to a coalition of owners a problem is the possibility of side-contracting between different constituencies. If subcoalitions can form, the organization is torn apart internally, and the full potential for value creation is not realized. Even more likely, value is actively destroyed in the battle over the economic rent, and investments into positions of power outweigh investments that truly generate value.[95]

No ownership

A third possibility besides exclusive allocation of ownership or sharing it collectively in a coalition exists when ownership is not assigned at all. It may seem unconventional for an economist to discuss and promote the abolition of ownership in certain organizational designs. But recall the purpose of the economic rationale behind ownership: *ex ante* incentives for value-generating specific investments are to be set and matched with the *ex post* power to appropriate the resulting economic rent. If no one has any power *ex post* to appropriate the economic rent generated by the specific investment of other constituencies, such investments are always of value and will be undertaken. The organizational design eliminating ownership can achieve efficiency.

But which organizations disarm their constituencies in this way? The prime example is the organizational design behind markets. No one owns the 'invisible hand' of markets, yet no one would deny the efficiency achieved by this organizational design in many settings. On the contrary, improving the design of markets or industries by taking 'ownership' of the industry and subjecting it to regulation often fails: it grants residual rights of control to the regulators but does not match this power with incentives to find the best organizational outcome. The deregulation of many industries in recent years, described in Section 2.4, acknowledges this fact.

A second example can be found in the communities of academia or the open-source movement. No one owns the ideas behind basic research or the software code written by these communities. Any attempt to capture ownership rights would reduce tremendously the incentives for others to invest in this field of study or the programming of a particular piece of software. Investments are only undertaken if no one can claim ownership of the results and appropriate the economic rent. This strengthens the incentives of the individual. Commitments such as a professional culture or legal constructs that require the publishing of results freely thereby abolish ownership in these designs and promote efficiency.

The different constituencies

The term 'constituency' has been used a lot throughout this book as a proxy for the various groups that form an organization. It is helpful to clarify this notion and to provide examples of the necessary parties and the roles they play in organizations. In particular, describing which constituencies are necessary for a successful organization, whether they invest specifically, and how important ownership is for them as an incentive device and as a means of providing power is the purpose of this section. Other potential devices to set incentives and convey power that might complement ownership are analysed in the next section before describing in the closing section some organizational forms that allocate ownership to one or more specific constituencies.

Shareholders and other providers of finance

Shareholders are usually seen as the legitimate owners of companies[96] without questioning why the incentives and power conferred by ownership are necessary for shareholders and their role in the organization. Small shops prevailed in the craft system in which the master or his family invested in the tools of production and worked with these means to produce a good or service. The combination of both equity financing and labour provision led to an efficient design, given the business environment. The assignment of ownership was trivial. As larger projects and firms were needed to reap the fruits of technological progress and adjust to changes in the business landscape, this combination was no longer feasible. In the system of mass production, no one had enough capital to finance all the tools of production, and thus equity was shared among many 'share-holders'. In the system of mass production, no one had sufficient expertise to perform all the different tasks involved, and thus work was shared among many specialized employees. But why is it that ownership is usually associated with the providers of financial rather than human capital?

The answer lies in the higher specificity that often characterizes the investments of shareholders.[97] Investments in facilities and factories, in the tools of production or the reputation of a brand are often sunk costs and cannot be redeployed by another firm. Although secondary markets for shares are well developed and often very liquid, they do not convey the power to safeguard economic rents from specific investments. They allow individual shareholders to leave the company easily by selling their shares, but this does not hold true for the shareholders as a group. Whenever such investments are necessary to generate a sustainable competitive advantage over other organizations, the assignment of ownership to shareholders has its merits to stimulate these investments.

Furthermore, the constituency of shareholders usually consists of small and dispersed shareholdings that are not connected to the organization in other ways. Shareholders are thus outsiders who can set the general direction the organization takes but are often unable to influence the company's progress towards this target.[98] Other constituencies are better suited to steer the company on to a certain path that leads in another direction, thereby appropriating some of the economic rent. The strong and ultimate power provided by ownership and the residual rights of control are hence a sensible means to set investment incentives for the providers of capital.

But financial capital does not only come as equity. Banks and bond-holders issue debt to finance organizations. Although such debt can also be invested specifically, other covenants make the assignment of ownership rights less important. Only in situations of financial distress does control pass from shareholders to the providers of debt finance.[99] Depending on the likelihood of default and the riskiness of the business operations, lenders thus also have something at stake. In particular in the financial system in Germany and other continental European countries where relationship banking is more important than the bond market, this is recognized in the governance structures, as banks play an active role and often have several representatives on the supervisory board.[100]

Employees

Many companies state that human resources are their most important asset. This holds true especially in industries where superior information and knowledge is important. Services are now the biggest sector, surpassing manufacturing in terms of employment and value-added. The people employed in service industries often need a very different set of skills from those in manufacturing: the ability to cope with complexity and develop specialized solutions for clients and customers is needed instead of sometimes monotonous work on an assembly line. Where people *are* employed in manufacturing, they now also need different skills and know-how to supervise the automated manufacturing process done by specialized machines that need an investment in specific training to operate them. Today's employees are a different breed from those at the beginning of twentieth century, when the system of mass production emerged. Employees have become more indispensable for firms, and not all of the contingencies of their job can be covered in a complete contract. Their specific investment is often required to create a sustainable competitive advantage. This makes them stakeholders in the future success of the organization. Does this mean that employees as a group should have ownership rights, either exclusively or collectively in a coalition of many constituencies?

To answer this question, it is helpful to distinguish the power that general and specific human capital conveys. General human capital can by definition be used in many organizations and for many tasks. Basic capabilities such as reading and writing, as well as more sophisticated statistical and analytical concepts, belong in this category. Incentives to acquire such general human capital are generated through better employment possibilities and the prospect of earning higher wages. People who have invested in general human capital are usually protected by labour markets that allow them to gain the full economic rent generated by their investment. No other constituency is able to exploit this, because people are free to leave for other organizations, taking their general knowledge with them. The existence of markets and the competition between firms convey power for people investing in general knowledge, and any economic rent accrues to them. Ownership is not necessary to safeguard such an investment.

With specific human capital, the answer is different. Specific human capital is more valuable in a certain relationship or in combination with the other assets of a particular organization. The termination of this relationship leads inevitably to a destruction of specific human capital. The possibility of the total loss of the economic rent generated gives people with specific human capital a stake in the organization.[101] Without safeguarding mechanisms, *ex ante* investment incentives are weakened. The residual rights of control that come with ownership can be such a safeguarding device. But should ownership generally be used as such a means?

Unlike the shareholders, employees are engaged with the organization every day when they transform their information and knowledge into decisions and actions. They can steer the organization at the micro level. Furthermore, being less dispersed than shareholders, unified action is easier for them, and the formation of unions enhances their bargaining power. They are insiders and can use their *de facto* control to protect their economic rents against other constituencies. Ownership as a *de jure* means of aligning incentives with power and promoting specific investments for employees is thus not as important. Other elements in the organizational system can accomplish this alignment if another constituency needs ownership more urgently.

Management

Managers occupy a central and pivotal role in the organization. As providers of human capital, much of what has been discussed for the constituency of employees also holds for managers. As with employees in some functions and particular industries, managers are knowledge workers.[102] The tacit dimension of the knowledge of managers makes them indispensable for the organization, and their firm-specific human capital is often paramount for the success of the organization. Incentives to build this specific knowledge and the power to protect the economic rent associated with it are certainly needed.

But managers also differ from ordinary employees: because of their pivotal role, their bargaining power *vis-à-vis* the providers of the complementary resources is also increased. This makes the threat to leave the organization more credible, and thus the economic rent attributable to their specific investment less vulnerable. Managers, furthermore, can use centralized information to make decisions that have a much greater impact than those of employees. Ownership rights are thus not needed for managers.

On the contrary, this greater impact of managers would make appropriation of the economic rents of other constituencies much easier. In nearly all circumstances, the provision of ownership or residual rights of control would therefore impair the efficiency of the organizational design. Ownership would be such a strong and formal power on top of the real power[103] of the managers that it would discourage specific investment by other constituencies.

The argument is strengthened by Rajan and Zingales (1998, p. 412) who argue that 'allocating ownership to one manager has the effect of giving her too much power to start with and, thus, of crowding out the incentives for the other managers to accumulate power through specific investments'. The power for a particular manager that specific investments generate would stand no chance against the combination of generic power and ownership rights of the other manager. If the total of specific investments is relevant for the efficiency of the organizational design, it is better to vest ownership rights into a neutral constituency – someone who does not even need to have a stake in the organization. Dispersed and distant shareholders are thus the best owners whenever ownership might tilt the balance of power towards a particular constituency in the coalition of stakeholders or among different managers. A disinterested third party disarms managers and, while reducing their power, induces them to invest specifically. As Blair (1999) summarizes, the function of a passive third-party owner 'is to keep control of the assets out of the hands of any of the active participants in the firm, precisely so that those active parties will not use control over the assets to gain strategic advantage for themselves at the expense of the other participants and thereby cause the coalition to fall apart'.[104]

Other potential stakeholders

Competitive markets usually make it unnecessary for other constituencies to invest specifically and become stakeholders of an organization. But there are exceptions. A familiar example is suppliers in the automobile industry. They co-specialize their production facilities to the assembly line of the manufacturer, and increasingly also subcontract the design of parts and modules and become a tier one supplier for the car companies. Such investments are specific to another organization, and economic rents can be collected with this superior organizational design. Providing exclusive ownership rights for the supplier, however, amounts to forward integration – the adjustment of the boundary complements the provision of residual rights of control. The question of whether suppliers should take part in a coalition of many stakeholders is more complicated to answer and depends on the relevance of ownership rights for other constituencies and the relative advantage of other mechanisms to balance power and investment incentives.

Similarly, customers can also acquire a stake in the organization. If they co-specialize their products or processes to the intermediate good, the switch to the product of another company as a substitute involves high costs. Examples of this situation are provided by airlines, which build their business model around a hub. They are the customers of the organization managing the airport and reconfiguring the airline's business system to another hub is expensive. The airline thus has a stake in the airport company, and the generation of value of the two organizations becomes intertwined. Assigning exclusive ownership rights again amounts to integration and the adjustment of the boundaries of the system. Participating in a coalition of owners can be a solution but, again, the efficiency of such a design depends on which other constituencies are also stakeholders, and whether more appropriate mechanisms exist to align power and incentives.

Example 3.13 The symbiotic relationship between different organizations and mutual stakeholdings are illustrated by Prahalad and Ramaswamy (2000). More than 650,000 customers tested a beta-version of Microsoft's Windows 2000 and shared ideas and problems with Microsoft that could improve the product. But customers also gained from being given early access to a product. As Prahalad and Ramaswamy (2000) report, many customers were prepared to pay for this privilege, as they could thus influence and customize the product to their needs.

Depending on the purpose of the organization, other constituencies might exist. For example, several charities cater for the well-being of certain groups of people – such as Amnesty International caring for those who have been stripped of their human rights. Such beneficiaries thus acquire a stake in the organization – their livelihood or even their life depends on it. The assignment of ownership and the provision of other incentive mechanisms of these non-profit organizations requires careful design to serve the needs of the beneficiaries.

As a final remark, note that in many organizations some of these roles are combined, and people or legal entities belong to several constituencies at the same time. People holding shares can also buy the goods and services produced by the organization as customers. Managers and employees can also be encouraged to hold shares. And different classes of securities ranging from equity to debt are held by venture capitalists. While this combination increases the complexity of the organizational design, it also allows the better structuring of power and incentives to promote efficiency. For people who are engaged with an organization in more than one function, many possibilities exist to invest specifically. Assigning ownership in this setting has to take the interdependencies between the different roles into account. Complementarities might exist that allow benefiting from returns from supermodularity. In the insider control governance systems of continental Europe and Japan, the bundling of various roles into the same group is a characteristic feature in the design of their respective financial systems. In the context of organizational design, the same deliberations apply. The organizational form of co-operatives[105] is a prime example, showing how, in particular situations, efficiency can be improved through various roles being played by the same group of people.

Governance mechanisms

Ownership aligns *ex ante* incentives with *ex post* power. It encourages value-generating specific investments and allows the appropriation of the resulting economic rents. But residual rights of control can be assigned only once. And the allocation of ownership is a strong governance mechanism: while it strengthens the power of the owner, at the same time it weakens investment incentives for other constituencies. It is the purpose of this section to describe governance mechanisms that can be used as an alternative to ownership, but that can also provide checks and balances on the absolute power of the owner. These alternative mechanisms to align incentives with power include enforceable contracts, the reliance on either exit or voice, and the provision of access.[106] Using these means, the power and investment incentives for other stakeholders can be aligned more evenly. And complementarities between the governance mechanisms can be used to increase the efficiency of the organizational design by combining these means.

Enforceable contracts

The seemingly most trivial mechanism is to rely on complete contracts that are enforceable by outside jurisdiction. This counters the residual rights of control of the owner of an organization by specifying explicitly the investments and distributing any economic rents *ex ante*. If investments can be observed and verified, this assures efficiency.

But designing efficient organizations is not that easy. Bernheim and Whinston (1998) argue that, in the presence of even a single non-verifiable aspect – imagine several specific investments by a single principal of which only the specific human capital component cannot be verified – it is of advantage to further increase the ambiguity and leave the underlying contract more incomplete than would otherwise be necessary. The reasoning behind the model by Bernheim and Whinston (1998) is akin to that of Holmström and Milgrom (1991) and the multitasking argument for balancing incentives. Bernheim and Whinston (1998) add to their argument the necessity also to balance the power between the contract partners. If one of them could easily get a verdict from a court, since the contract is complete in spelling out his/her rights but not all of his/her duties, the balance of power is skewed in his/her favour: the other contract partner cannot have recourse to the court and the governance mechanism of enforceable contract is not applicable. To get the balance of power level again, it is necessary to leave the contract incomplete and ambiguous in the other parameters as well, and restore the fit in the design of the organizational system.

In a similar vein is the reasoning behind the model by Rajan and Zingales (2000b). Even if it were possible to write a complete contract for a particular transaction, efficiency can nevertheless be impaired whenever the parties to the contract have to deal with each other in the future. The monetary transfer necessary for efficient production in the period when enforceable contracts are feasible can be used to alter the balance of power in the future. If such investments in power cannot be ruled out, the reliance on enforceable contracts is not advisable in such a situation. Power-seeking distorts incentives and impairs efficiency.

The option of exit

Specific investments create generic power. By threatening to withdraw the specific resource or position from the relationship, thus diminishing the value of co-specialized assets, this power can be used to protect the economic rent. The threat of destruction is more credible the better the outside opportunities are. The value of the outside option is determined by several factors.[107] First, the existence and quality of outside markets strengthen the exit option. Markets make the redeployment of the resource or position possible. The power of markets thus supplements the generic power and, in the extreme case of a perfect market, the investment is general in nature and thus perfectly safeguarded against appropriation. Second, the value of the outside option depends on the degree of specificity of the resource or position in relation to other assets in the relationship. If other investments are even more specific, the threat to withdraw the specific assets becomes more credible and the bargaining power is enhanced.

Note that the actual use of outside options is a very crude mechanism. The economic rent that is created by the specificity of the resource or position is destroyed if the relationship is indeed terminated. The use of exit thus resembles a nuclear bomb, and often the simple but credible threat is enough of a deterrent to balance the power with other con-stituencies relying on exit options or on other governance mechanisms to protect economic rents from specific investments. If shareholders are not happy with managers or other constituencies, they can trigger this option individually and exit the relationship by selling their shares on the secondary market. This causes share prices to fall. Consequently, the accumulation of shares in the market for corporate control becomes less costly. The concentration of the ownership rights in larger block hold-ings increases the value and power of ownership and thus restores a balance of power: managers who abuse their power can be dismissed. Of course, the market for corporate control is a very crude mechanism, and the increased likelihood of a hostile takeover alone might discipline managers and reign-in their power.

Outside options exist also for the providers of human capital. Employ-ability conveys such an outside option. Employability is defined by Kanter (1989, p. 92) as 'increased value in internal and external labor markets'. If managers and employees can recoup their investment in some other organization as well, they are inclined to invest specifically in advanced skills that are 'superior to those widely available on the market'.[108] It is in the interests of the organization to ensure employa-bility and increase the value of the outside option since this stimulates value-creating specific investments. Other, co-specialized resources or positions that belong to other constituencies in the firm can thus gain as well. Such functional or technical expertise is portable across the bound-aries of a particular organization, and the economic rent associated with investments in these specific resources can be transferred along with the employee or manager who changes jobs, sometimes taking some of the co-specialized resources and positions with him.[109] Value is not destroyed by exiting the organization if conditions of employability prevail – the value is simply shifted between different organizations.[110]

Raising the voice

Exit is often the last resort for the constituencies of an organization to protect their economic rent. However, value is destroyed by it. It is hence sensible to have some other governance mechanism providing constituencies with power. Before exiting a relationship, actively pointing out the problem might be better. The governance mechanism of voice provides this alternative. Voice is defined by Roberts and van den Steen (2000, p. 3) as 'the right and ability to affect decisions and distributions and thereby the means to protect their interest'.

The voice mechanism is usually employed in a coalition of various stakeholders. Being responsible for the governance of the organization as a group necessitates the use of voice. Sharing information and discussing its relevance and appropriate action in the joint decision-making body (board of directors) allows the different stakeholder groups to influence decisions and to protect their share of the economic rent. Inside information allows the active monitoring of the other constituencies, to keep their powers in check. A further advantage is the broader base of information that can be used to determine the best investments.

The reliance on voice as a governance mechanism is no panacea. It has its costs and disadvantages. A strong position of many constituencies that can increase their voice to shape decisions and distributions can lead to deadlock on the board. This tendency is exacerbated if the constituencies are heterogeneous in composition. Shareholders as a group are relatively homogeneous; largely caring about the financial gain. Other stakeholders – managers, employees, suppliers or customers – vary much more in their individual objectives. Allowing them to voice their concerns – especially in situations, where a dynamic environment requires a rapid response – might be detrimental: if voice amounts to a veto right for every stakeholder, deadlock for the whole organization is a real possibility and a danger. Decisions agreeable to all concerned are difficult to find, and the possibility of rent-seeking behaviour and the resulting influence costs becomes a drag on the efficiency of the organizational design.

Fortunately, the voice mechanism as defined by Roberts and van den Steen (2000) does not only cover the situation of an insider-controlled stakeholder regime with a common board where all stakeholders meet and use their voice. It is also applicable in companies that allocate ownership to a distant, singular owner, as with the shareholders in outside-controlled firms. Although deprived of ownership rights, managers and employees can still use the inside information that they frequently gather and apply as part of their job 'to affect decisions and distributions'. Through various, often small, decisions and actions they contribute to the success of the organization and steer the system to avoid any detrimental action to their share of value creation. Setting the agenda of the organization and defining its purpose allows managers and key employees to build up and defend their own stakes in the system. The use of instruments of the internal structure described in Section 3.3, such as the hierarchy and the distinction between formal and real authority, thus efficiently complements the use of voice by insiders in the shareholder-owned firm.[111]

Access

An alternative mechanism to ownership is the provision of access. As Rajan and Zingales (1998) explain, access to critical resources and positions is often a superior mechanism to shape incentives and stimulate investments, especially into specific human capital, which is not limited in the way that ownership is: access to indispensable assets can be granted to several parties at the same time. Rajan and Zingales (1998, p. 388) define access as 'the ability to use, or work with, a critical resource'. Regulating and restricting access to critical assets induces investments into specific human capital and creates *ex post* power contingent on the right investments. Such co-specialized investments convey generic power as argued in Section 3.3: a withdrawal would reduce the total economic rent generated by an organization. The control of the co-specialized resource hence provides bargaining power.

To stimulate those value-creating investments that convey generic power, Rajan and Zingales (1998) recommend the regulation of access to critical resources and positions, such as a particular machine, for example. They distinguish three cases that resemble different technologies. First, if investments are substitutes for each other, then granting the exclusive right to co-specialize to only one employee is optimal. Multiple access would depress the incentives of every party to specialize. If the chosen employee invests specifically, s/he not only increases the overall economic rent but also gains enough bargaining power to protect his/her share of it. The specialization makes this employee the ideal choice for this job, and both parties – the owner and the employee – have an interest in continuing the relationship. Second, in the case of an additive investment technology, aggregate investment is increased if many parties are allowed to access the critical asset, while each individual's incentives are slightly weakened. When investments are, third, complementary to each other, however, restriction of access to one employee is again the best design. The reason is that too much power would be generated by multiple parties who can block each other in an attempt to extract a larger share of the economic rent. *Ex ante* investment incentives would again be impaired.

How can access be regulated in organizations? Different elements of the internal structure of organizations, such as the assignment of tasks to particular people, grant exclusive access. Being the manager in charge of a particular business division stimulates incentives to invest specifically in that unit. By confining the possibility of investing specifically in this business unit to this particular manager, *ex ante* incentives and *ex post* power are better aligned and efficiency is increased. Similarly, the setting of the boundary of the organization or the shifting through outsourcing allows such exclusive access to be assigned.

Systemic nature of governance mechanisms

The various governance mechanisms of ownership and access, and of exit and voice complement each other. A successful organization adjusts these one against the other to shape the overall balance of power and to determine incentives. The complementary relationship between ownership and access is acknowledged by Rajan and Zingales (1998, p. 416): 'Both ownership and the regulation of access to critical tasks within the organization are integral to making the firm successful. Both can be seen as mechanisms to regulate power and to coordinate investment in the organization so as to maximize organizational output.'

The other mechanisms also exhibit complementarities. In most of the literature on corporate governance, ownership and formal authority are assigned to shareholders. Managers are understood to be their agents and have real control over the organization through their decisions and actions. Governance understood in this way mainly deals with problems of aligning the interests of managers with those of shareholders. Many contributions surveyed by Shleifer and Vishny (1997) deal with overcoming this problem of the separation of ownership and control identified first by Berle and Means (1932).

But if the efficiency of organizational design is of interest and an unprejudiced view is applied, then – perhaps unconventionally for an economist – it is not the problem that Berle and Means (1932) identified, but rather the solution. Both managers and shareholders gain with a design that allocates ownership to the shareholders and control to the managers. Because of their distance from the daily operations of the organization and their outsider status, dispersed shareholders are arguably in the weakest position. Encouraging them to invest specifically thus requires the strongest governance mechanism available.[112] Assigning real authority, in the sense of Aghion and Tirole (1997), to the managers counters this strong position and allows the managers themselves to invest specifically without fearing being expropriated by strong owners. Furthermore, shareholders help managers to prevent rent-seeking and power acquisition among themselves. If complementary investments by different managers are necessary for success, ownership by them would be too strong and discourage the investment incentives of all insiders. Instead of a reliance on the exit mechanism or a pronounced use of voice, a cacophony would result. Outside shareholders act in this situation as tie-breakers and budget-breakers and mediate the power between different managers.

Of course, this is a very brief and to some extent oversimplifying view. The design of governance mechanisms is more complex and also depends on the configuration of elements of the other building blocks and the business environment.[113] If shareholdings are, for example, not small and dispersed, as in many firms in the Anglo-Saxon outside-control system, ownership rights are considerably strengthened and more power than that provided by real authority is necessary to protect the investments of other stakeholders. A board where multiple constituencies meet and use their voice, as is the case in many firms within the inside-control system, restores the balance of power. As another check on the ownership rights of shareholders, the restriction of the exit option for shareholders applies: an active takeover market is absent. It would lead to situations where outsiders could gain ownership and control and expropriate the economic rents resulting from specific investments by other constituencies.[114]

Organizational forms

The last two sections have argued that, first, constituencies vary in their relative importance for the organization, and their stakes differ along with the resources and positions they provide and the technology the organization applies to meet its ends. Second, mechanisms of governance can be combined in different ways to strike a balance, protect the interests of the organization's stakeholders and spur their investment into value-creating assets. Different organizational forms can now be distinguished where particular constituencies use distinct combinations of governance mechanisms to achieve such a balance and protect their stake. A brief description of the most widespread organizational forms is the purpose of this section. For an analytical framework, see Hansmann (1996).

Private firms

Overcoming the dilemma of aligning incentives for specific investments with power to protect and appropriate the resulting economic rent is relatively trivial, with closely held private firms that operate in markets. Incentives and power distribution are allocated to the private owner, who combines the roles of main shareholder and general manager. Formal contracts and reliance on outside markets for other inputs supplement this solution. Wealth constraints, however, limit the amount of equity capital that can be provided and make this organizational form mainly feasible for small and medium sized enterprises.

Private firms are the backbone of many economies and a major feature in the financial system. Not only in Italy and in Germany, with the important role of the Mittelstand, but also in developing and transition economies, such small, private firms are often dominated by a particular family. This remedies the wealth constraints to some extent and broadens the capital base. Profits are often reinvested to take advantage of growth opportunities.

Private firms often employ other members of the family as well, and the additional social interaction complements other means of incentives and power. Succession in private firms usually leads the children of the family patriarch to become the owners at some time in the future and thus aligns the interests within the family. The near-certainty with which promotion to the status of owner will come encourages specific investments by the younger generation. This further increases the efficiency of the design.

The corporation

The capitalist firm owned by investors in equities is the most widely studied organizational form among economists. The use of this organizational form is most appropriate if financial capital is the most important input for the organization, and the scale of the enterprise matters. The financing of large projects requires the transfer of the financial capital into specific physical assets, which makes the providers of finance vulnerable to hold-up by the other constituencies. To protect their return from the investment, they rely on the assignment of ownership as the most potent governance mechanism. Shareholders are thus the owners of corporations and exercise their formal rights of control through the board of directors. Management acts on behalf of the shareholders and has fiduciary duties towards them. The objective of maximizing shareholder value has primacy.[115]

The manifestation of corporations varies widely with different financial systems. In the financial system of the USA, for example, a single-tier board prevails, while in countries such as Germany a two-tier structure with a separate supervisory board is the norm. Different laws, such as the one regulating the co-determination of employees in German supervisory boards, further increase the variety in the design of corporations. The existence and generally better development of markets in the Anglo-Saxon financial system increase the outside possibilities for constituencies of corporations operating in such a financial system. The reliance on the exit mechanism is hence more pronounced. The German and Japanese financial systems, on the other hand, rely less on markets. The outside option for different stakeholders is less valuable and the use of the voice governance mechanism more common.

A comprehensive treatment of the various manifestations of corporations, the relative importance of the various constituencies and their stakes in the corporation (which might also vary with the industries served and technologies applied), and the best combination of the many governance mechanisms, is beyond the scope of this book. The interested reader is referred to Schmidt (1997) and especially to Schmidt and Weiss (2003). See also Allen and Gale (2000b) for a comparison of corporations in the major financial systems.

Partnerships

If financial capital is of lesser importance relative to human capital, the organizational form of a corporation with the powerful position of shareholders becomes less appropriate. Ownership is too strong a governance mechanism, and the relatively more important investments into human capital would be crowded out. The organizational form of a partnership recognizes the shift in the relative importance of the constituencies. In partnerships, the managers and key employees are assigned the ownership rights collectively.

Partnerships can be found in human capital-intensive industries, especially in professional services such as law firms or consulting companies. The partnership is owned by the knowledge workers. Physical assets can be leased from competitive markets, so that no upfront investments require large capital outlays, and the necessary equity can be obtained by pooling the financial capital of the managers and key employees. The governance system of partnerships is characterized by a complex combination of all the governance mechanisms. Intensive use of voice among the different owners prevails to protect their share of the economic rent and is complemented by a reliance on the access mechanism, especially when contacts with potential clients are the critical resource. Regulating the acquisition of ownership status through the management of access is an incentive device to induce specific investments. Furthermore, having specialized their human capital more towards the profession than the firm, excellent outside options are often also available as a last resort should the use of the other governance mechanisms fail. For a more comprehensive theory of partnerships, especially in human-capital-intensive industries, see Levin and Tadelis (2005).

Government ownership

Another possible organizational form is the assignment of subdued ownership rights to a government or an agency that regulates business on behalf of the government. In this case, bureaucracies perform the activities which are usually characterized by strong network effects and subadditivity of costs, so that a situation of a natural monopoly prevails. The telecommunications industry and the post and railway network as well as utilities (electricity, gas, and water) are prominent examples of where the government or municipalities own and employ the necessary means of production for these goods and services. Other organizational forms would assign the powerful ownership rights to a particular constituency, which could be tempted to extract economic rents from other constituencies – especially consumers who are stripped of the exit options that competitive markets convey.

While politicians usually remain outside of the bureaucracy, their power is kept in check by the democratic process and investigative journalism. The power of other, inside, constituencies such as managers and employees is lowered through various governance mechanisms and instruments of internal structure such as the restriction of a job to some well-defined tasks with detailed rules, few outside opportunities, and the possibility of using their voice only in exceptional circumstances.[116] As Novaes and Zingales (2004, p. 247) summarize: 'An excessively bureaucratic organization ... arises to reduce the manager's bargaining power.' The organizational form of government ownership is further explored in Chapter 5, in the context of the European securities transaction industry.

Co-operatives

Co-operatives are usually founded by groups of individuals to pursue common goals. In agriculture, for example, farmers set up co-operatives to purchase necessary equipment and to market their produce. In the financial services industry, co-operative banks and insurance mutuals play an important role in channeling funds and spreading risks between their members. While these members also provide the necessary financial capital for the organization, their other role is usually more important for them.[117] The advancement of the welfare of their members rather than the strict pursuit of profit is hence the main objective of co-operatives.

The diminished importance of the provision of capital, in contrast to the pursuit of the interests as a consumer or supplier, is reflected in the way that ownership rights are allocated: those members who provide the capital become shareholders of the co-operative and are assigned the ownership rights. But unlike corporations, where the control rights are exercised on a basis of one vote per share, co-operatives assign voting rights on the basis of one vote per member regardless of the amount of capital invested. Ownership rights are thus weakened.

This decrease in ownership power is balanced by restricting the use of other governance mechanisms as well. As Rey and Tirole (2000) argue, erecting small exit barriers to accommodate negative externalities among the remaining members weakens the outside option but nevertheless increases efficiency and induces investment. See also Fama and Jensen (1983a) as to how co-operatives deal with agency problems. The organizational form of co-operatives is further explored in Chapter 6, in the context of the German co-operative banking group.

Non-profit organizations

Many economic activities in areas such as education, health care or disaster relief are provided by non-profit organizations. Any profit earned in the course of business is usually required by statutes to be retained in the organization to finance the provision of these services in the future and to expand the organization. Hansmann (1988, p. 270) describes these organizations thus: 'Nonprofit firms are characterized by the fact that the persons who have formal control of the firm are barred from receiving its residual earnings.' In other words, the assignment of both residual rights of control and residual claims to one constituency is impossible. This has an important impact on the efficiency of the design, and other instruments and mechanisms have to be adjusted to accommodate for the lack of ownership.

The customers of non-profit firms, usually referred to as donors, provide the organization with capital and 'buy' charitable services such as education for a particular community, or disaster relief for a particular group of victims. Customers are often too dispersed and their contributions often too small to induce them to monitor the inside constituencies as effectively as managers, who have real authority. Similarly, the beneficiaries of such charitable services – especially in the case of a disaster – often have no power at all to counter the power of managers. How can efficiency be achieved? Hansmann (1996, p. 228) argues that 'the nonprofit firm abandons any benefits of full ownership in favor of stricter fiduciary constraints on management'. A discussion of these stricter constraints can be found in Massmann (2003) and Fama and Jensen (1983a). Note that formal restrictions such as bureaucratic rules for managers and employees, as well as reputation effects for providing these services in an efficient way, play a prominent role.

Communities and networks

Organizing economic activity in communities or networks is the last of numerous organizational forms described here. Examples of such communities can be found in the form of associations or clubs whose aim it is, for example, to promote the tourism industry in a particular place. The local hoteliers – while still being competitors – nevertheless work together to attract guests to their resort. Other examples include companies that want to create an industry-wide standard to overcome the reluctance of customers to adopt a new technology.[118] Organizing in a community, association, cluster or network allows competitors to work together where positive network externalities prevail.

Different organizations with diverse incentive systems and diverse governance structures can be part of such communities and networks: nonprofit and government organizations such as universities and ordinary firms of varying sizes and legal status can complement each other and work towards a common goal. As in non-profit firms, the mechanism of ownership is of little importance in the governance of communities. There is no owner. Economic rents accrue directly to the individual person or firm in the community. The governance system is complemented by mechanisms that make entry and exit possibilities for the community members easy, and residual rights of control are often allocated to and appropriated by those who invest most in the common project.

The importance of communities and networks is further explored in Chapter 7 in the context of the open-source movement in the software industry.

Notes

1. Collis and Montgomery (1998, p. 72).
2. See Lippman and Rumelt (1982) for a model of this kind of ambiguity, which leads to superior rates of return without inducing market entry by new competitors despite the absence of any barriers to entry.

3. See Hamel and Prahalad (1989, p. 66).
4. Note that there are other aspects that shape the power of trading partners and might lead to the failure of markets; for example, the fact that the valuations of the good are the private information of the buyer and the seller.
5. The use of outside options and the 'exit' possibility that markets offer are discussed in Section 3.4.
6. See, for example, Bresser *et al.* (2000, p. 2).
7. See Campbell *et al.* (1995).
8. See, for example, Barney (1991).
9. The concept of core competence was developed by Prahalad and Hamel (1990), and illustrated with many examples in Prahalad and Hamel (1994a).
10. See Stalk *et al.* (1992) for principles of capability-based competition, and Teece *et al.* (1997) for the framework of 'dynamic capabilities'.
11. Prahalad and Hamel (1990, p. 81).
12. Den Hond (1996, p. 50).
13. See Markides and Williamson (1994).
14. See also Barney (1991).
15. See also Coff (1999) on the connection between competitive advantage and the bargaining power of the stakeholders.
16. See Pfeffer (1992) and Chacar and Coff (2000, p. 249).
17. See Chacar and Coff (2000, p. 246f.) for an analysis in the context of the investment banking industry.
18. See, for example, Glassman (1997) for a description how EVA can add to the value of organizations.
19. Brickley *et al.* (1997a) provide data on the life-cycle of management fads such as Total Quality Management (TQM), Just-in-Time, and Economic Value Added (EVA). They show that many of these and other concepts can quickly gain popularity among business leaders but often fail to deliver the promises made.
20. Porter (2001, p. 21).
21. See Hagel and Singer (1999).
22. See Porter (1985) on the concept of the value chain in a firm in a strategic context.
23. See Porter (1998) for the underlying economies of clusters.
24. See Hagel and Singer (1999) for this line of argument.
25. See Mintzberg and van der Heyden (1999) for an attempt to illustrate graphically these new manifestations of organizational structures.
26. See also Hamel and Prahalad (1996) for a description of the changing, shifting, blurring and crumbling nature of boundaries.
27. An excellent account of the boundaries in the theory of the firm is given by Holmström and Roberts (1998). See also Gibbons (2005) for a synopsis of the various theories.
28. This capital allocation-based perspective of corporate boundaries was developed by Bolton and Scharfstein (1998) and Stein (2003).
29. See Barney (1999) for a discussion of the capabilities perspective with regard to the boundary decision and a comparison with the view of transaction cost economics. See Eliasson (1996) and his example of the Swedish aircraft industry for the advantages of integrated production when knowledge and competencies are difficult to communicate outside the organizational context.
30. Gibbons (2004, p. 10).

31. See Gertner (2002, p. 14) who highlights the high correlation and comple-mentarity between vertical integration and exclusivity. Exclusivity refers to the case where 'the company does not sell the input to others nor does it buy the input from outside suppliers'.

32. Note, however, that such a static optimization of the boundaries needs to be corrected whenever changes in the business landscape occur. The optimum might never be reached, as adjustments of boundaries take time. Other parameters of the boundary decision not considered by Hart and Holmström (2002) – such as blurring them deliberately – also allow for a mitigation of this problem.

33. The mechanism by which the incentives are given is also an important parameter influencing the choice between markets and firms. The function-ing of these mechanisms is the subject of Section 3.3.

34. Chandler (1990, p. 14; emphasis in the original).

35. The topic of geographical spread is discussed in the literature on interna-tional management; see, for example, Rugman *et al.* (1985) and the contributions to Porter (1986) and Buckley (1991). The product dimension is discussed in textbooks on microeconomics; see, for example, Besanko *et al.* (2000, ch. 5). In a strategic context it is emphasized in industrial organization; for a comprehensive treatment, see Tirole (1988b).

36. See Foss (2001) for advantages, disadvantages and strategic dimensions of outsourcing.

37. See Ehrensberger *et al.* (2000).

38. See Evans and Wurster (2000, pp. 69–97) for some interesting examples of how disintermediation affects the competitive position in various industries.

39. See Day and Wendler (1998) for relational forms of organization.

40. Helper *et al.* (1998, p. 4).

41. Chacar and Coff (2000, p. 252) cite as an example the investment banking industry in New York City, where Frank Quattrone and his team changed their employer but still worked in the same building.

42. See Eisenhardt and Galunic (2000) on such co-evolution and how it can be used by a single firm in the context of co-ordinating its business units.

43. Some authors – such as, for example, Ackoff (1989) – make a distinction between data, information and knowledge. Data refers to important observa-tions of the environment – such as temperature, barometric pressure and the altitudes of starting point and peak when one is setting out to hike in moun-tainous terrain. Information puts this data into a meaningful context by com-bining the different data and comparing it with past experience. Temperature, barometric pressure and altitudes are thus translated into useful information to determine the best time and path to use to climb to the top of the mountain. In contrast to this information, real knowledge about the conditions of the path is then obtained by actually hiking to the peak. For the purposes of this book, however, the terms information and knowledge are used interchangeably.

44. See Arrow (1962, p. 615).

45. The seminal work on tacit knowledge is by Polanyi (1966), but see also Ryle (1946) for a distinction between 'knowledge that' and 'knowledge how'.

46. Jensen and Meckling (1999, p. 9).

47. See Wruck and Jensen (1994) in the context of Total Quality Management (TQM). There are, of course, other classifications of information and

knowledge. Another example comes from Zack (1999a), who distinguishes between core knowledge, advanced knowledge and innovative knowledge; see also Zack (1999b). The emphasis is often on the importance of knowledge for strategic management. Focusing here on the internal structure, such features are excluded.

48. The capacity to absorb new information and to use this knowledge also rests on the existing knowledge and capabilities of the human being or the firm. The more symmetrically the knowledge is distributed between two agents, the better the absorptive capacity. See Cohen and Levinthal (1990).

49. See also Foss (1999c, p. 464).

50. See Hansen *et al.* (1999) for a discussion of how firms such as McKinsey and Accenture use personalization or a codification strategy, respectively, to transform the technical aspects of doing business in the consulting industry into a competitive advantage. This is only one of many examples of how knowledge can be used to generate rents by exploiting its characteristics. The extensive literature on knowledge management is beyond the scope of this book and will not be considered further here.

51. Ghoshal *et al.* (1995, p. 752, citing Holmström and Milgrom (1991)).

52. Jensen and Meckling (1999, p. 9).

53. See also Pfeffer (1992, ch. 4) for a discussion of the sources of power.

54. Tirole (1988a, p. 464).

55. An intriguing model along this line is provided by Rajan and Zingales (2001a). See also Rajan and Zingales (1998) for the notion of access to specific investments of other constituencies that bring forth power. The governance mechanism of access is described in more detail in Section 3.4.

56. Tirole (1988a, p. 466).

57. See Aghion and Tirole (1997) for the distinction of formal and real power.

58. See Rajan and Zingales (1998) for a model to explain the advantages of third-party ownership.

59. See also Rotemberg and Saloner (1995).

60. See Dessein (2002) for the trade-off between delegation and communication. Refer to Roider (2006) for a model of delegation as an optimal response to potential underinvestment by two distinct parties.

61. Empowerment is different from re-engineering: in the latter, a redesign of jobs and tasks and a change in responsibility for their execution leads to an increase in efficiency. Empowerment, however, leaves the specification of the task, or even the quest for the right task, to the individual. See Argyris (1998) for a discussion of when and how empowerment can work.

62. See Aghion and Tirole (1997, p. 20). See also Baker *et al.* (1999), who propose self-enforcing relational contracts that make the use of real or – according to Baker *et al.* (1999) – informal power feasible in an incomplete contract setting.

63. For the process of setting strategy through good leadership, see, for example, Eisenhardt (1999).

64. See Hermalin (1998) and Rotemberg and Saloner (2000).

65. Note that there are two distinct strands in the agency literature. The first deals with *ex ante* uncertainty about the capabilities and prior investments of the agent, and how potential adverse selection processes can be mitigated. The second branch deals with *ex post* uncertainty about the actions, decisions and investments within the organization of the agent, and how

any problems of moral hazard in its various forms can be alleviated. Both strands are relevant in achieving a good organizational design. For conciseness, the focus here is on the *ex post* uncertainty.

66. Stock options currently account for more than half of the compensation package for CEOs in large US companies. See Rappaport (1999, p. 91).

67. See also Bebchuck *et al.* (2002) on this issue. Executive compensation that is linked to the stock market through the use of stock options is predominantly seen as an alignment of managers' interests with those of the shareholders. However, it can also be a deliberate means to distribute economic rents to managers as compensation for their specific investments.

68. On the efficiency wage hypothesis, see, for example, Baron and Kreps (1999, pp. 76–77), and in the original macroeconomic context, Shapiro and Stiglitz (1984).

69. Note that the Holmström (1982) results are identical to those of Alchian and Demsetz (1972). The underlying argument is, however, different: even if the joint output can readily be observed, the principal as proposed by Holmström (1982) allows the fine-tuning of the incentives of every agent by breaking the balanced-budget condition. The argument proposed by Alchian and Demsetz (1972), however, rests on active monitoring by the principal to induce agents to exert effort.

70. See Baker and Holmström (1995) for interesting evidence on internal labour markets.

71. See Prendergast (1993) for the role of promotions to overcome the moral hazard problems inherent in a situation in which the worker should be compensated for specific investments through a higher wage, but the employer could claim *ex post* that such investments have not been made to reduce his/her wage costs.

72. See also Auriol and Renault (2001) for the effects of the hierarchical structure on incentives through promotions based on either merit or seniority in this context.

73. See Ghoshal *et al.* (2001) for the concept of employability.

74. Holmström and Milgrom (1991, p. 25; emphasis in the original).

75. Laux and Walz (2004, p. 4).

76. See Dessein *et al.* (2005) for a model that analyses the advantages of different structural forms while taking into account their effects on incentives, power and co-ordination.

77. See Chandler (1962).

78. The argument is, of course, not that simple. See, for example, Bolton and Scharfstein (1998) and Stein (2002) for a more thorough analysis of internal capital markets and the problems they bring.

79. See Rajan and Zingales (2000b) and their earlier working paper version (Rajan and Zingales, 1996) for examples and a model of how co-operation is neglected because of the fear that other divisions thereby accumulate too much power, which they could wield to the detriment of the co-operative division.

80. See Stein (2002) for the advantages of hierarchies in handling 'hard' information that can be verified easily in the context of an internal capital market. To keep incentives to gather information intact, firms focusing on

production technologies that rely on 'soft' information have to be more decentralized and instead use the external capital markets.

81. See Rajan and Wulf (2006) for empirical evidence. See also Garicano (2000) for changes in knowledge-based hierarchies when the costs of acquiring and communicating information decrease.
82. See Dessein (2003) for a model of the trade-off between faster decision-making through authority in a hierarchy and more unbiased decision-making by consensus in committees.
83. See Baker *et al.* (2002) for the use of relational contracts in markets and firms.
84. See also Hermalin (2001) for a discussion of the complementarity of corporate culture with other issues of the internal structure of organizations such as leadership and delegation of authority.
85. Goffee and Jones (2001, p. 4).
86. Goffee and Jones (2001, p. 4; emphasis in the original).
87. See Goffee and Jones (1996) for a more detailed description of the merits and shortcomings of the other types of organizational culture.
88. Zingales (1998, p. 498; emphasis in the original).
89. Roberts and van den Steen (2000, p. 3).
90. For a comprehensive survey of governance that considers narrow and broader views alike, see Becht *et al.* (2003). The systemic nature of different governance systems is analysed by Allen and Gale (2002), John and Kedia (2005), and Heinrich (2002). See also John and Kedia (2003), who take the complexity and complementarities within the 'set of constraints' explicitly into account and provide a theoretical framework for joint optimality in the design of different governance mechanisms.
91. Foss and Foss (1999, p. 1).
92. But see also Foss and Foss (1999) for a critique of the incomplete contracting approach and their notion of 'appropriable control rights'.
93. See Grossman and Hart (1986) and Hart (1995).
94. See Hart and Moore (1990) for an illustrative example and a model determining the optimal ownership structure, given the need for multiple specific investments and the existence of outside markets. Note, however, that this general result need not hold true. Depending on the bargaining nature and the use of outside options instead of the inside option of an ongoing relationship, de Meza and Lockwood (1998) reverse the result obtained by Hart and Moore (1990), that ownership always motivates investment weakly. They show that under particular bargaining structures the outside option of spot markets can be binding. In that case, to motivate the principal to invest specifically makes it 'necessary that he does *not* own the asset' (de Meza and Lockwood, 1998, p. 365; emphasis in the original).
95. Recall the influence costs analysed by Milgrom (1988), described in Section 3.3.
96. See, for example, Hart (2001, p. 1079).
97. See Dow (1993).
98. Of course, many companies exist that have only a small number of shareholders. Across different financial systems, families or other companies control organizations through large block holdings, and hedge funds adapt their investment strategies to influence the organization actively.

99. See Blair (1995, pp. 23–26) for the governance aspects of bankruptcy.
100. There is, however, a lively discussion as to whether banks should have this role. More recently, empirical evidence suggests that banks have reduced their involvement in the governance of German companies. See, for example, Hackethal *et al.* (2005).
101. See also Blair (1995, p. 238).
102. See Drucker (1999) for the characteristics of knowledge workers.
103. See Aghion and Tirole (1997) and Aghion and Tirole (1995) for the distinction between formal and real authority. Although formal power in the form of ownership is vested with shareholders, several factors such as their distance from the organization and their dispersion allows the managers to use their own superior information and wield real power in the management of the organization.
104. Blair (1999, pp. 84f.).
105. See below for a theoretical description and see Chapter 6 for a practical application.
106. There exist other lists of governance mechanisms. Especially if the narrow view of corporate governance is applied, the analysis is more focused on potential agency conflicts between shareholders and managers. The structure of the board of directors, the way executives are compensated, the market for corporate control, and concentrated shareholdings feature prominently as governance mechanisms in this narrow view. See, for example, Allen and Gale (2000b).
107. See Hirschman (1970) for a description of the exit mechanism.
108. Ghoshal *et al.* (2001, p. 92).
109. Note that the deconstruction of the value chain that occurs in many industries is the visible outcome of this governance mechanism and complements the boundary decision. See also Rajan and Zingales (2000a) for the example of the bond trading group at Salomon Brothers where almost the entire team left to found a new venture.
110. For further elaboration on the use of the exit option in the form of employability as a governance mechanism, see Schmidt and Weiss (2003, p. 125).
111. See also Schmidt and Weiss (2003, pp. 123–5).
112. See also Gans (2005) for a model where this results from an auction among potential owners.
113. For two models that capture complementarities between different governance mechanisms, see John and Kedia (2005) and John and Kedia (2003). Both papers derive optimal designs with distinct configurations of governance mechanisms depending on the development of markets and the technology that firms use. The authors, however, adhere to the narrow view of corporate governance and the mechanisms they analyse are thus not as broad as the ones presented here. Optimal governance systems derived by them include a system with concentrated shareholdings and monitoring by a bank as an insider system, and dispersed shareholdings and the reliance on the takeover mechanism as an outsider system. As a third optimal system, ownership by managers without the need for internal or external monitoring is presented. See also Franks and Mayer (1995) for a description of the two distinct governance systems of outside and inside control.
114. Refer to the argument of value redistribution as a cause for hostile takeovers by Shleifer and Summers (1988), and the two models on this topic provided by Chemla (2004) and Chemla (2005).

115. Maximizing shareholder value is identical to maximizing the total value creation of the corporation only in certain circumstances. See Blair (1995), Massmann and Schmidt (1999) and Prahalad (1994) for critical comments on the primacy of shareholder value.
116. See also Weber (1922) as the classic reference on bureaucracies, and Dewatripont *et al.* (1999b) for a discussion of stylized facts of government agencies.
117. See Rey and Tirole (2001), who look at the financing of co-operatives and explore the interdependent roles of agents taking part in co-operatives.
118. See also Section 2.4.

4
Designing Efficient Organizations

4.1 Synthesis of the building blocks – designing for fit

This chapter sets the capstone on top of the foundations laid in Chapter 2 and the building blocks erected in Chapter 3, before breathing some life into this design with case studies of different organizations in the second part of this book. Cohesion between the different building blocks – the strategy and boundary decisions, the internal structure and governance – is necessary to keep incentives for value-creating investments and the distribution of power in balance. As a capstone in an arch supports the layout of the other bricks with its weight, only a consistent synthesis of the building blocks of organizational design with their different instruments allows the resulting organization to fulfil its function efficiently and to create the most value.

Most of the investigation into efficient organizational design has been accomplished and many complementary relations between organizational parameters – not only within the building blocks but also between them – have been described at length and with the inevitable redundancy that the description of the same phenomenon from different perspectives brings with it. In this section, the different building blocks of organizational design described previously, and the complementarities between them, are briefly summarized. The existence of complementarities lead to distinct configurations and successful business models, among which a choice can be made considering the costs of complexity and the returns from supermodularity. The next section takes the role of environmental changes into account and describes briefly problems that arise when traversing from one, perhaps outdated, model to another, more promising, system. The chapter closes with some stylized organizational designs that suit well the changes to a more rugged landscape of competition and thus promise to create value.

Taking stock

Different organizational parameters ...

Let us recall briefly the most important themes of each building block described previously. The configuration of these parameters of organizational design determines the success of the whole organization. Important themes of strategy besides the purpose of the organization include the activities, resources and positions that are performed, acquired or occupied by the organization. The construction of a value chain (or in recent years, the deconstruction of it) of different activities has important effects on the determination of the boundaries of the firm. Configuration possibilities in this building block include the setting, the shifting and the blurring of boundaries. If boundaries are configured to be permeable, for example, resources can move to their best use, and positions can be redeployed in the context of another organization.

However, boundaries alter incentives for investment in many ways – both benign and malign. Incentives within the confines of a firm are different from those on outside markets. The same holds true for the distribution of power. The themes of investment incentives and power, along with those of information and co-ordination, are the most important elements in the building block of the internal structure of organizations. Many parameters can be configured to influence the design and efficiency of the organization. In the building block of corporate governance, the relative importance of the different constituencies, the constructs of distinct legal forms and the use of several governance mechanisms are the most important themes. The right configurations of these elements allows organizations to be designed where the distribution of power is balanced and where incentives to create value are optimized. Table 4.1 summarizes the most important themes and representative parameters that the designer of an organization has to consider for this task.

... and their design features

In the analysis in Chapter 3 of the different building blocks, many complementary relationships were highlighted between the different elements that make up these modules. But for the design of efficient organizations, the synthesis of these building blocks is also necessary. Complementarities do not only exist between the elements within a single module but also prevail between elements of different building blocks. Thus the configuration of parameters in one of these modules depends on the configuration of parameters in another.

Two alternatives are generally available to handle these linkages. The first is to reduce such interdependencies where possible. This decreases

Table 4.1   Important organizational design parameters

Building block	Main themes	Design parameters
Strategy	Purpose	Vision and mission
	Activities	Integration and construction of the value chain
	Positions	Markets and industries
	Resources	Leverage across business units
Boundaries	Setting	Vertical and horizontal integration
	Shifting	Outsourcing, deconstruction, disintermediation
	Blurring	Degree of permeability
Internal structure	Information	Tacitness, asymmetry, performance measurement
	Power	Degree of centralization, leadership
	Incentives	Reward structure, career concerns, internal markets
	Co-ordination	Departments and divisions, hierarchy, organizational culture
Governance	Constituencies	Relative importance of stakeholders
	Mechanisms	Complete or relational contracts, exit, voice, access, ownership
	Forms	Legal constructs

the complexity of the overall system and makes it easier to manage. The example of deconstruction of the value chain that affects the strategy and the boundaries of organizations simultaneously helps to clarify this point: a thoroughly implemented strategy of deconstruction allows for a reliance on the interface of standardized markets. Interdependencies between different activities, resources and positions that would have to be managed within a single firm are reduced, thereby avoiding complexity. Design parameters such as the strategic motives in two different firms can be configured separately, with the result that resources and positions do not need to be confined within a single entity if they could be put to their best use elsewhere. A modularized design thus has its merits.

The second option is to exploit these interdependencies. The inherent complexity can be a source for the further creation of economic rents. Supermodularity becomes an important issue. Applying a systemic view of organizations, and taking any interdependencies between the building blocks and their parameters into account, allows firms to be designed that generate returns from supermodularity. The generation of returns from supermodularity, however, depends critically on the correct and consistent configuration. A random combination of differently configured building blocks usually disregards potential complementarities between the building blocks and their elements. Fit between the strategic motives, the determination of boundaries, the many instruments of internal organization and the various governance mechanisms is also required. Such a synthesis alone leads to superiority in design and more efficiency in the organization of economic activities.

Complementarities between the building blocks

There are, of course, many linkages within and between the four building blocks of organizational design. The existence and different strengths of complementarities make some combinations and configurations weakly preferable, while others appear to be strongly mandatory. A consistent configuration of elements stretching over several modules further strengthens the mortar between the different building blocks. Figure 4.1 illustrates the effect of consistency as the capstone in organizational design.

In the following six paragraphs, complementary relationship between any pair of building blocks are investigated. Most of these linkages have already been described above from different angles, such as, for example, deconstruction or the importance of market mechanisms that have been investigated in the context of different building blocks. The analysis of complementary relationships between the building blocks, their main themes and their design parameters offered in this section is by no means comprehensive – depending on the particular design under

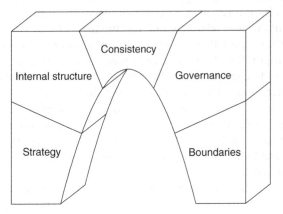

Figure 4.1   Consistency as the capstone of organizational design

investigation, other elements with supermodular properties between them may be more prominent than the ones sketched here. Furthermore, the ambiguity of cause and effect that often prevails and complicates the analysis of the parameters of organizational design can even be the basis for sustainable competitive advantage and efficiency.

Complementarities between strategy and internal structure

Does structure follow strategy, or vice versa? This question does not matter when a systems perspective is applied. Strategy and internal structure influence each other through complementarities among their various parameters. To fully understand organizations and to design them for efficiency, no particular theory – either from the strategic management literature (such as, for example, the capabilities perspective of the firm) or from organizational economics describing incentive systems in the internal structure – is sufficient on its own. Instead, an integrated approach that picks eclectically important insights from both strands and evaluates them for potential complementarities is necessary. This view is supported by Gibbons (1998) and Foss (1999a), respectively proponents of organizational economics and the resource-based view. Gibbons (1998, pp. 129f.) argues: 'The systems perspective also has broader implications: not only should complementary instruments be used in incentive contracting, but the firm's strategy towards incentive contracting should complement its strategies towards human resource management, manufacturing, product development, and competition.'

Interdependencies between strategy and internal structure include the following, among many others: first, the purpose of the organization necessitates a particular approach to the decision-making powers and incentives for human resources. In manufacturing firms, power for the average employee is relatively low and the hierarchy can be quite steep to co-ordinate specialized resources. In universities and other research institutions, on the other hand, high-powered incentives for employees prevail, and fiat authority provided by a hierarchy is relatively low. The chosen strategy of concentrating on cost reduction or striving for excellence demands different internal structures. The former strategy calls for 'guardians' while the latter puts a premium on 'stars' to use the terminology of Baron and Kreps (1999, pp. 26–9). Designing organizations to allow for 'stardom' encourages leadership and is reinforced by a consistent organizational culture.

Second, the right configuration of the internal structure of firms can be a credible means to implement a certain strategy and occupy valuable market positions. By committing itself through a rigid structure of highly independent business divisions with strongly decentralized decision-making powers, the firm (or a network of many firms in a cluster) can signal the production of a certain quantity, leading its competitors to withdraw or to pursue a less aggressive strategy.[1] Prevailing complementarities thus increase the returns to such a strategy and allow the shaping of the market structure if the configuration of parameters such as the reward system signals this commitment in the internal structure.

Third, strategies relying on the superiority of human resources demand an internal structure that manages information and knowledge in a consistent way.[2] Cross-functional teams and an organizational culture of sharing information support these strategies through better creation, dissemination and utilization of knowledge in the form of specific human capital that generates economic rents.

And finally, the construction of a value chain of several activities within the firm to exploit economies of scope between them is reinforced by an internal structure where a hierarchy and departments are designed to manage the resulting complexities. Design parameters such as job rotation of employees and cross-functional teams allow the transfer of specific knowledge effectively within the organization, and the making of decisions based on the best information while still exploiting the benefits of specialization.

Complementarities between internal structure and governance

The interdependencies and complementarities between the internal structure and the governance of the organization have already been discussed in detail. The theme of power is a crucial element in both building blocks. Assigning power through means of an internal structure such as a hierarchy, for example, complements the use of power in the external structure of governance. Managers and employees are insiders in the governance, and generate and use information for decisions and actions that affect the success of the organization. The recent changes in the business environment make the use of specific information advantageous and therefore demand also an increase in the decision-making power of managers and employees. The complementary relationship between internal structure and governance, however, necessitates in this case a corresponding increase in the power of outsiders through appropriate, stronger governance mechanisms in order to compensate for the empowerment of the insiders. This can be achieved through a strong executive board which provides the general direction of the company and exercises decision control. Improved ownership rights for external shareholders in corporations allow them to act as tie-breakers and budget-breakers, which prevents deadlock between the empowered insiders. The budgeting process in the internal capital market approved by the organization's board is an example of such a device to assign power and influence incentives in the internal structure.[3] If power is thus increased for one individual or constituency as a response to changes in the business environment, as a general rule the power of the other constituencies should similarly be increased to restore the balance of power.

Other interdependencies between the internal structure of organizations and their governance include the complementarity between the issues of co-ordination and organizational form. For some firms, strict divisions and departments in the internal structure are the most appropriate means of supporting their choices about the use of an internal labour market, with well-defined career paths that shape incentives and inside possibilities, while also increasing the exit option through improved employability. For other organizations, legally separate subsidiaries are the best organizational form to complement the other design parameters. In the case of professional partnerships such as auditing or consulting firms, for example, an organizational form of a loose network of firms makes it easy for teams that already share the same background of general knowledge to co-ordinate on the acquisition of specific knowledge while retaining the individual incentives to invest. Empirical evidence supports such deliberations: Rajan and Wulf (2006) analyse panel data that lead to the conclusion that layers of hierarchy in the internal structure have been abandoned at the same time as firms have become more like partnerships, networks or clusters.

Complementarities between governance and boundaries

Numerous interdependencies also exist between the building blocks of governance and boundaries. The question of which assets should be bundled together under joint ownership in an organization has driven many researchers in the tradition of the incomplete contracting approach. Setting appropriate boundaries – that is, increasing their efficiency – allows the sheltering of specific investments inside the organization and protecting of associated stakes for the investing constituency by also raising the expected return from such investments. Assigning residual rights of control for these assets matters, and, as Holmström (1999a) argues, the return from assigning these rights to outside shareholders increases with changes in the business environment. Shareholders are more likely to reshape the boundaries and 'freely and "unemotionally" move the resources they control to higher-valued uses'[4].

Boundaries are, furthermore, a tool to grant access to resources and positions in the organization. This enhances the governance mechanism of access and increases the returns from using it. The organizational form of a network or cluster blurs the boundaries between different firms in the network and thus makes it more efficient to allow simultaneously for more permeable boundaries to exploit fully the complementarity relationship between governance and boundaries.

Finally, Gibbons (2000) emphasizes that relational contracts are used within and between different organizations and their constituencies. The pay-off from using relational contracts increases with more efficient boundaries if environmental change occurs. In much the same fashion, Ghoshal and Bartlett (1997) provide in their book a blueprint for an 'individualized' organization whose boundaries are fundamentally re-evaluated. In such an organization the roles of different constituencies – especially those of employees and top managers – in the governance of firms are subject to a 'new moral contract'. Like a constitution for a nation, this contract complements the use of shifted and blurred boundaries, and applying both yields returns from supermodularity. Ghoshal and Bartlett (1997) and Ghoshal *et al.* (1999) demand that such a contract inspires organizations to act more towards value creation than towards the appropriation of value. Here, the interdependence between the purpose of the organization and other strategic themes comes into play. It is to this topic that we turn next.

Complementarities between boundaries and strategy

Boundary decisions have many complementarities with the different themes of strategy. An appropriate setting of the boundaries that includes all relevant constituencies, resources and positions is paramount to achieve the purpose of the organization. Recall that boundaries can prevent resources and positions being put to their best use. Some visions of the organization can thus best be fulfilled if boundaries are rearranged or sufficiently blurred to allow for the exchange of resources.

The widening of boundaries can help to protect the core of the organization. The setting of wide horizontal boundaries and the inclusion of many strategic business units within the organization can similarly allocate resources and positions efficiently, and increase the returns for elements such as functioning internal markets that help managers to cope with the inherent complexity of such a design. Even a conglomerate strategy that integrates seemingly unrelated businesses into one firm can make sense. It reduces risks for the firm and thus safeguards specific investments. The whole organization is not destroyed if changes occur, and there is time for repair or replacement of capabilities – a fact that might validate many conglomerates, especially in developing and transition countries where the rate of change is high.

The construction or deconstruction of the value chain is another interdependency between the strategy and the boundaries of an organization that has been highlighted extensively above. Note that complementarities or synergies exist between many activities: an increase in the quality of the performance of one activity of the value chain very often also increases the returns from raising the quality of another activity. If boundaries are set rigidly, the returns to a vertical widening of boundaries and the integration of these activities into one value chain performed by a single organization are hence also increased. If the ease with which boundaries can be shifted and blurred is increased, complementarities between strategy and boundaries also increase the returns from deconstructing the value chain into several organizations.

Complementarities between strategy and governance

Every constituency has to determine for itself how the relationship with others in the context of the organization creates value for it, and whether to take part in the organization. Constituencies who decide to invest in value-creating resources and positions specific to an organization become stakeholders in the continuing success of the organization. Their resulting economic rent needs to be protected to keep investment incentives intact. Various governance mechanisms help to strike a balance for the specific investments of many constituencies, as explained in Section 3.4.

Complementarities between strategy and governance often increase the returns to the use of a particular governance mechanism if the strategy of the organization is adapted simultaneously through choosing a suitable business model. The use of voice in a coalition of owners, for example, not only helps to safeguard economic rents but its efficiency can be further improved if the constituencies take an active part in the formulation and implementation of a strategy for the organization that is consistent with it. Setting the purpose and general direction for the organization complements the use of voice as a mechanism to protect the share of economic rents *ex post*. The same holds true for corporations, where residual rights of control are allocated only to shareholders: if changes in the business environment demand the use of the specific knowledge of managers and employees for a strategy exploiting innovations, a more active role for them in the strategy process is mandatory to complement this empowerment and generate returns from supermodularity.

There are, of course, numerous other links between strategy and governance in organizational design. Strategies influence the market structure, thereby potentially decreasing the competitiveness of outside markets. This lowers the value of the exit option and leads to switching costs for customers and suppliers. A realignment of power through the use of other governance mechanisms or different organizational forms becomes advisable to keep appropriate incentives for specific investments. In the industry for standardized software applications, such alternative measures can be found in open-source communities, as explained in Chapter 7.

Complementarities between internal structure and boundaries

The last pair of building blocks where complementarities increase the consistency and efficiency of organizational design are between the internal structure and the boundaries of the organization. The interdependency is recognized by Stein (2003, p. 152) in the context of internal capital markets: '[T]he boundaries of the firm are determined by the following trade-off between managers vs. markets as allocators of capital. On the one hand, by giving a CEO control over assets, and the authority to redistribute capital across these assets, one sets her up with high-powered incentives to become a delegated expert. On the other hand, the very fact that she has the authority to move capital around makes her vulnerable to rent-seeking.' Both benign and malign effects of power are influenced by the setting of boundaries. Widening the boundaries of the organization increases the returns from other incentive instruments, up to a certain limit.

Boundaries also determine the flow of information. In situations where returns to the use of information increase, the complementary relationship also leads to increased returns from blurring the boundary and making it more permeable. This is the case in many hybrid and network designs that allow for the flow of information and its use for innovative purposes while sheltering any economic rents created by that use. The captivity of resources and positions, far from imprisoning them, provides incentives, as Holmström and Roberts (1998, pp. 83–4) illustrate. They characterize the systemic nature of firm boundaries, investment incentives and power with many examples from a range of industries.

To use the specific information and co-ordinate dispersed investments, Ghoshal and Bartlett (1995) advocate a restructuring of the firm along the lines of processes that cut across the boundaries of the various strategic business units and stimulate entrepreneurial and competence-building processes. By flattening hierarchies and breaking down barriers between formerly separated fiefs, an organization increases its true value-creating potential. In today's environment, one has to go even further than prescribed by Ghoshal and Bartlett (1995): true value creation for individual agents must not stop at the boundaries of the firm, which too often become a means for a group of managers to shield their share of economic rents from competition. It is very often the open structures and open processes cutting across the confines of a particular organization that underlie many successful business ventures today.

Configuration of business models

Effects of complementarities

Complementarities within and between the building blocks of organizational design and their parameters have been established both here and in Chapter 3. The question now is, what to do with these numerous complementarities. Recall the consequences of complementarity between two elements in a system: if complementarity exists, increases in the value of one parameter also raises the marginal return from increasing the other parameter. This is tantamount to being a positive cross-derivative in well-behaved functions – that is, functions that are continuous and twice differentiable.

But the notion of complementarity is also applicable if the underlying functions to an economic optimization problem are not well-behaved in this sense. This makes the concept especially valuable for situations in which binary decisions have to be analysed. Plenty of these binary decisions exist in business, and many parameters described above demand such a choice between two variables before adjusting the level of the element as well. Examples include decisions such as:

- whether to enter a market and occupy a position in it;
- whether to adjust the boundaries by a merger or acquisition to integrate a related activity vertically;
- whether to introduce particular elements of internal organization such as, for example, pay-for-performance; and
- whether to employ a particular legal organizational form or to allow a particular constituency's voice to be heard in the governance.

If complementarities exist, introducing one parameter also raises the marginal return from introducing the other parameter. This leads to sets of configurations of parameters of organizational design that should be applied together to achieve consistency in the system. Certain elements have to be matched with others to increase efficiency and exploit returns from supermodularity. Such sets of consistent configurations can be observed in practice in the form of business models.

Example 4.1 Two separate business models can be found in the marketing of professional sports competition: individual marketing by each club, and central marketing by an association of individual clubs. The former model can be found in many European soccer leagues, where individual clubs such as Manchester United build their brand successfully. This design induces high-powered incentives for the individual clubs and its players to strive for stardom. In contrast, the latter approach is found in Major League Baseball in the USA with the first-year player draft[a] and can create a more level playing field by redistributing some of the revenue among the clubs and their players. By intentionally weakening the spoils that can be gained, the resulting tournament is less skewed in favour of big and rich clubs, leading to a better chance of success for the poorer and smaller clubs – which enhances their incentive to compete. The overall investment effort and the economic rent for distribution are thus potentially maximized in such a structure, which at first sight seems to reduce individual incentives to perform.[b]

---

[a] See http://mlb.mlb.com/NASApp/mlb/mlb/draftday/rules.jsp; accessed 29 April 2005.
[b] For a model in this direction, see Gürtler (2004).

Examples of business models have already been provided in Section 2.2. In the modern manufacturing system, flexible machines with low set-up costs are matched by short production runs, low inventories and skilled workers to exploit the supermodular relationship between these parameters. In the low-cost business model in the airline industry, a set of configurations has been chosen that matches the renunciation of on-board meals, seat assignments or baggage transfer across different legs of a flight, with the use of secondary airports to reduce inefficiency in terms of the time that the aircraft is grounded.

Distinction in business models

Certainly, many distinct sets of different configurations can exist that allow for several successful business models, just as many peaks of differing height can exist in mountainous terrain. When comparing business models, however, a restriction to two sets of configurations is often made for didactic reasons. This has also been the case in the illustration of only two peaks in Figure 2.2 (see page 40), although a more appropriate picture would look more like the rugged landscape depicted in Figure 2.3 (see page 44).

Example 4.2   The classical case for the matching of different elements to a consistent organizational design that deviates substantially in many parameters from the standard business model in manufacturing is that of the Lincoln Electric Company. As Fast (1975) illustrates, Lincoln Electric's design rests on exploiting the supermodular relationship between elements of manufacturing, marketing, finance, human resource management, and the company's strategy and philosophy. The complex system deployed by the Lincoln Electric Company creates value with this uncommon configuration, as Milgrom and Roberts (1995a, pp. 199–205) describe exhaustively.

That a mixture of elements used in an inconsistent way leads often to failure is also demonstrated by Lincoln Electric. From 1987, Lincoln Electric acquired profitable businesses in other countries. When trying to install its successful organizational design in these subsidiaries, however, Lincoln Electric found this difficult: overseas operations incurred losses that more than offset the profits from the original sites. Consequently, some of the acquired companies were closed.[a]

---

[a] See the account of Hastings (1999), a former chairman of the Lincoln Electric Company.

The analogy to business models in the metaphor of hiking in mountainous terrain is the necessity of matching the correct degrees of latitude and longitude to reach the peak of a hill. Business models are characterized by a whole set of elements that have to be configured consistently to maximize the efficiency of the organizational design. An efficient system requires that no incremental deviation in the configuration of a single parameter can improve the success of the system – the design is at a local optimum. Similarly, no arbitrary mixture of elements of two business models is likely to improve the design. This usually makes it detrimental to apply 'best practices' without thinking thoroughly about the consequences of tearing apart complementary elements and combining them in configurations where they do not match consistently. The hiker in the rugged landscape who matches the degree of longitude of one peak with the degree of latitude of another finds him-/or herself potentially at the bottom of the valley between the two hills instead.

It is not the purpose of this chapter to describe particular business models. This has been done already in many examples throughout the text and will be done in more extensive form in the context of the case studies in the second part of the book. The focus is, instead, on some theoretical deliberations regarding the advantages and disadvantages of business models. The complementarities underlying business models require choice among the possible configurations. It is hence a good idea to explore their characteristics in detail to make a good and informed choice. We turn now to a brief description of these characteristics.

Characteristics of business models

The most visible and often most important distinction among several consistent systems regards the amount of economic rents these designs create.[5] Just as peaks in the rugged landscape have different heights, so business models differ in the amount of value they create. The model of modern manufacturing described by Milgrom and Roberts (1990b) and Womack *et al.* (1990) allowed companies that implemented it, such as Toyota, to make a higher profit than companies following the mass production business model. The differences in value creation were so strong that nearly all motor vehicle companies have now switched to the more appropriate business model of modern manufacturing.

But the verdict is not so easy in the airline industry. Although some low-cost airlines currently make more profit than established full-service carriers and have surpassed them in terms of market capitalization, the evaluation of the impact on overall welfare is more subtle. The profit for shareholders of airlines on its own does not take into account the economic rents earned by other stakeholders. In the business model of full-service carriers, travel intermediaries appropriate some of the economic rents that air traffic generates as commissions when issuing tickets. And travellers save time when flying from the main airports instead of travelling to a distant secondary airfield. As an aside, note that in a larger design where no particular firm is of concern but rather the total industry, the very choice between different models also creates some value. Choice allows customers to self-select from among the competing designs. They can choose the one most appropriate for them depending on whether they are on business trips or on holiday.

In any case, both systems in the airline industry are consistent in the sense that no small deviation in a single parameter can further increase economic rents. But the amount of economic rents a business model generates is not enough on its own when choosing among business models. Some other characteristics, briefly listed here, also have to be considered to evaluate the relative efficiency of these organizational designs:

- The height of a peak is not the only concern of a hiker. What also matters is the steepness of the incline and the danger of falling. Thus, if an exact configuration of particular organizational parameters are crucial for success, but difficult to achieve, it might pay instead to opt for a less demanding design. As well as the return from the design, its riskiness or robustness also matters. In the rugged landscape of competition, this amounts to climbing a lower peak that becomes a plateau instead of a higher one with a very steep incline that makes advancing dangerous.

- Connected to this point is the ease of reach of a particular peak or a particular configuration. If a certain business model is easy to configure, too many competitors will probably follow it, thus making it less worthwhile. Every new venture during the dot.com bubble was based on revenues from advertising. While perhaps sustainable for a few firms, this model could not support so many: a cablecar to the top of the peak might spoil the remoteness of the place.

- Another characteristic to be considered when evaluating business models for their attractiveness is the likelihood of changes in the business environment. Impending changes can make a business model less worthwhile, as firms in the music industry found out after the internet allowed the easy downloading of music. Changes in the rugged landscape of competition can happen glacially but can also be very explosive – like, for example, the eruption of the volcano on Thera around 1600 BC, which destroyed the Minoan culture on the island.

The latter point leads into the consequences of changes in complementarities that can be induced by changes in the business environment. As slow erosions over time or sudden volcano eruptions can reshape the surface of the earth, changes in the business environment can render the consistency or appropriateness of a business model obsolete and necessitate changes in the configuration of the parameters of organizational design.

4.2 Adaption to the environment – designing for change

Constant change in the business environment alters the consistency or appropriateness of different business models. A consistent synthesis of the building blocks that considers complementarities between their parameters can thus, over time, fail to achieve efficiency. Efficiency can be impaired by configurations that, while being statically optimal, lead to either inconsistencies in or inappropriateness of the future design, which hence falls short of creating the most value. This dynamic aspect of efficiency is highlighted in the context of strategic management by Ghoshal *et al.* (1999, p. 12): 'Static efficiency is about exploiting available economic options as efficiently as possible – making the economy more efficient by shifting existing resources to their highest valued use.

Dynamic efficiency comes from the innovations that create new options and new resources – moving the economy to a different level.'

Having explored in the previous section the question of how organizations should take into account the complementarities between the parameters of organizational design to implement an efficient business model (that is, how hikers can reach the peak), two questions in particular remain:

- how to stay at the top of the peak – that is, how to adjust the business model continuously whenever adaptive change makes the current one inconsistent; and
- how to traverse peaks – that is, how to adjust the business model radically whenever disruptive change makes the current one inappropriate.

This section highlights first the importance of changes as a design feature for the systems of the whole economy and explores the trade-off between static and dynamic efficiency that firms or other organizational forms, as submodules of the whole economy, have to consider for their own organizational design. Next, to answer the first question, solutions to overcome inconsistencies in the design resulting from adaptive change over time are investigated. The section closes by answering the second question with a discussion of possibilities of coping with inappropriateness of the design resulting from disruptive change.

Constant change as a design feature

Creative destruction ...

There is constant change in the larger design that constitutes the capitalistic system of the overall economy. This constant change is an important design feature in the larger system which comprises the organizational designs of many smaller firms or other types of organization, which have been described throughout this book. This constant change determines the power and incentives for the submodules of individuals or groups of individuals who participate in a firm, a network or some other organizational form. Thus it is important to understand the impact of changes in the business environment for the efficiency of the smaller organizational systems, and how these changes affect the balance of power and the balance of incentives in these designs.

Creative destruction, as sketched briefly already in Section 2.4, ensures these balances in the capitalistic system. Creative destruction provides incentives for submodules to innovate, be they individual entrepreneurs or well-established firms. Creative destruction also shifts power automatically over time between the submodules, as Schumpeter (1934) has argued, from the entrepreneur or his/her firm to the consumers by means of a competitive market. This second characteristic of creative destruction feeds back on the first, and the shift in power reinforces incentives for the incumbent to remain in power, or restores incentives for insurgents to acquire power through innovative and specific investments. Creative destruction thereby assures that efficiency is maintained over time.

How does this mechanism work? Sustainable competitive advantage and the resulting economic rents result from specific resources or unique positions. They are generated if a particular organization and its constituencies invest in such value-generating assets and use their specific information in an innovative way. It is not only a bright idea by a single genius that can lead to innovation and the creation of an economic rent: a sequence of many co-ordinated and co-specialized small investments by different constituencies also leads to innovation within a particular organizational design. For this situation to occur, however, it is necessary that the power to appropriate these rents is used as a suitable incentive device for investment, as has been reasoned throughout this book.

The power generated by these specific resources and unique positions is, however, only conveyed temporarily. Other firms start to exploit the relevant knowledge as well and begin to compete with the person or firm where the information was first applied. Competition between different organizations shifts power between organizations and ultimately to consumers, who are thus able to capture most of the value that has been created by the initial application of the specific resource or position in the context of a firm. Organizations that fail to renew themselves constantly by adjusting the balance of power and the balance of incentives in their design might be forced out of business. Competition thus ensures that only organizations survive that in fact create value.[6] By automatically repealing power from the incumbents, the forces of creative destruction constantly level the field of competition and thus restore the incentives for investment. Creative destruction and the forces of constant change are hence an important organizational parameter in the larger design of the overall capitalistic system.

... and its counterforces

The forces of creative destruction can take time to restore the balance of power and incentives in the larger capitalistic system. Markets can seemingly fail, and the mechanism of creative destruction can seem to be defunct and the invisible hand too weak. Natural monopolies based on network effects or large switching costs between competing standards are examples of situations where market failure can occur. Well-meaning attempts to create an organizational design that is more efficient and that corrects for a balance of power skewed in favour of the natural monopolist are often the result. Regulation is introduced to deal with these shortcomings. In the short term, this often improves the design by countering the power of the natural monopolist with the power of the regulator. But in the longer term, it leads to inefficient organizations that continue to occupy positions of power and whose constituencies are able to block change to protect their share of an economic rent that could otherwise be much greater. Value is often destroyed in an attempt to protect it. Numerous declining industries in many countries, where enormous amounts of subsidies are wasted, bear witness to this. But also in financial systems that are less flexible and less able to adapt to change (such as the German and Japanese systems) these positions of power inhibit the working of the forces of creative destruction. Power can be wielded only because of the negligence of an important parameter of organizational design – the gale force of creative destruction.

But the power of the invisible hand of creative destruction is stronger than is often supposed. As Langlois (2003, p. 353) observes: '[W]hen markets are given time and a larger extent, they tend to "catch up", and it starts to pay to delegate more and more activities rather than to direct them administratively.' Thus, even in situations where a natural monopoly seems to prevail, regulation more often than not increases the inefficiencies in the design. Instead of a balance between the powers of the natural monopolist, the regulator and the invisible hand of competition, a powerful alliance of the natural monopolist with the regulator counters the forces of creative destruction, making it indeed too weak. While improving static efficiency in the short term, dynamic efficiency in the long run is seriously impaired.

Therefore, abstaining from the temptation to improve the design through the introduction of a regulator to restore the balance of power in the short term increases the incentives for other individuals or firms to search for an organizational solution that bypasses the power of the natural monopolist. This is possible if exploration in the rugged landscape of competition is feasible. Many examples of recently liberalized industries illustrate the power of creative destruction: disruptive changes in the business environment are often the result after such liberalizations. The smaller organizational designs of individual firms have to consider these forces of creative destruction when balancing their power structures and incentive schemes.

Staying at the peak – continuous adjustments

How can organizations ensure that their statically optimized organizational design does not impair dynamic efficiency? In this section, the problem of inconsistency in the organizational design that arises with change in the business environment is highlighted, and three possible solutions to overcoming these inconsistencies are proposed. Adjusting its design continuously to deal with adaptive change allows an organization to stay at the peak of competitive advantage and helps to restore its efficiency when faced with such a change.

Inconsistencies in organizational design over time

As the external environment of organizations changes, the elements in these organizational systems can become inconsistent with each other over time. Adjustments of different organizational parameters are needed to restore an efficient design. This is rarely a trivial task. Path-dependent processes have led to configurations for some organizational elements that cannot readily be altered. Through their complementarities, these elements affect the configuration of other parameters, thereby improving the consistency (or, in the case of adverse changes, enhancing the inconsistency) of the organizational design.

Recall, for example, that power is acquired either generically through specific investment or can be derived by configuring organizational parameters such as the introduction of a hierarchy in organizations. Power stimulates incentives to invest specifically only if it is balanced between the various constituencies that have to invest for value creation. The balance of power that is appropriate for some business settings might, however, not be appropriate for others: as change occurs, the distribution of power might not match the necessary incentives to invest; power might have been accumulated by those constituencies whose investments are no longer of paramount importance for the success of the organization.

The prevailing power distribution discourages specific investments of other constituencies that have become desirable with the changes in the business landscape. For those without control, the generic power that specific investments convey is not enough to offset the accumulated power of those who invested in the past. For those in control, the possibility of appropriating the economic rents generated by the specific investments of others becomes more attractive relative to the generation of economic rents through their own specific investment. The balance of power thus ossifies and becomes skewed and inconsistent as time goes by. Efficiency is impaired.

Three solutions in the organizational design are possible to overcome these inconsistencies and to adjust continuously to adaptive change:

- organizations can be designed for dissolution after they have achieved their purposes, so that inconsistencies cannot occur over time;
- organizations can be designed for flexibility, so that any inconsistencies arising over time can easily be corrected; and
- organizations can be designed for commitment, so that inconsistencies will have to be overcome eventually.

Designing for dissolution

If implementing adjustments in a design is a problem, the dismantling of an organization is a possible solution to overcome the effects of an ossified balance of power that discourages new value-creating specific investments. The forced dissolution in the capitalistic system through creative destruction by competitive markets works on this premiss. But even in a smaller organizational system, the deliberate dissolution of a design that has fulfilled its purpose can make sense if the rate of change is expected to be high and the importance of specific investments by different parties varies. Project management is one organizational form that is designed explicitly for dissolution.

Example 4.3   Movies are made in an organizational design that is assembled *ad hoc* just for the purpose of shooting one film, and it is usually dismantled after it has fulfilled this purpose. Movie sets are characterized by a nexus of specific investments that all constituencies – for example, the director and the main actor – have to undertake, and that determines the overall success. The distribution of economic rents is subject to *ex-ante* bargaining with some part of the rents accruing inalienably to the individuals taking part in the venture by determining the career of actors or directors and their bargaining power in future productions.

Although movie sets are created for each project from scratch, the people who could take part within the venture are from a limited pool in which good communication links exist. This feature balances the power and makes the possibility of a hold-up a less severe problem. A second stabilizing force within these webs of specific investment are large media firms that act as carriers of reputation;[a] media companies have sunk costs in studios and cinemas and are equally exploitable, especially if the movie turns out to be such a great success that a sequel is made, in which case the power relationship changes dramatically.

---

[a]   See Kreps (1990).

The dismantling of old organizations and the creation of new ones is thus a sensible way to circumvent the problem of the skewed and inconsistent distribution of power described above. This especially holds true for less successful organizations. If it is not discernible whether adverse circumstances or an inconsistent design is the cause of failure, dismantling the project, the business unit or the whole organization and starting again from scratch is often the better alternative to tinkering with the organizational parameters in an effort to adjust the initial configuration.

Note that the option of dissolving an organizational design has also its disadvantages. This kind of organizational design often depends on the support of complementary institutions, such as well-developed markets or private equity capitalists. If external parameters do not allow for an easy deconstruction and subsequent reconstruction, such a design has its costs: too many favourable investments might be wasted by it, and the redeployment of assets imposes friction in such a design. The continual renewal of existing organizations to adapt to the changes provoked by creative destruction is therefore often the better option.

Designing for flexibility

A second solution to overcome the effects of an ossifying power balance apart from the deliberate dissolution of the organization is to design the organization for flexibility.[7]

Organizations designed for flexibility rely on a certain configuration of their parameters. The strategy of flexible organizations is geared towards change. Path-dependent processes are often disregarded, and resources and positions acquired in markets by the frequent deconstruction and subsequent reconstruction of firms or their parts. The boundaries are configured to allow for flexibility and permeability. Organizations use alliances with each other and take part in loose networks to self-regulate the industry or to develop common standards.[8]

Example 4.4   An example of flexibility in design is provided by Disney. Responding to changes that allow for the digital production of animated movies, the necessary creative work was spun-off into smaller, sometimes independent, companies. One example is Pixar, which was founded (among others) by a former Disney employee, John Lasseter, and which retains a close relationship with Disney.[a] These adjustments in the boundaries and the internal structure amounted to a redistribution of economic rents. While the shareholders of Disney arguably lost value, they were in no position to block

Continued

adjustments that restored efficiency. Power was conveyed through the possibility of exit for innovative employees who undertook their value-generating specific investments at some independent venture.

***

[a]   See Pixar (2005) and *The Economist* (2002a, p. 68).

The internal structure abstains from configurations that are too complex. All constituencies are rewarded immediately for their contribution to value creation, and the use of elements of deferred compensation, such as seniority pay or defined benefits in a pension plan,[9] is restricted. In the governance of flexible organizations, a reliance on the value and power of exit options can be found. Organizational forms such as the shareholder-owned corporation complement the other building blocks. A corporation, where ownership rights are assigned to shareholders, does not tie the resources of its constituencies too tightly to the firm.[10] Many companies have altered their original business purpose to such an extent that their founders would no longer recognize them. One of the most prominent examples is Nokia, which transformed itself from being a wood-pulp mill and rubber company in Finland to become the leading mobile handset maker in the world.

Designing organizations for flexibility relies on certain parameters in the system of the overall economy. As with the possibility of dissolving organizations when they have achieved their purpose, flexible organizations need well-developed markets that help them with the ongoing task of deconstruction and reconstruction of organizations. Flexible organizations also need other firms that are designed in a similar way. Both these needs can be found in the Anglo-Saxon financial system, where these individual organizational configurations are a necessary element for the consistency of the overall financial system.

The expectation of the rate of change also influences the choice of how many complementary relationships to exploit. If rapid and ongoing changes are expected, a premium on flexibility will be readily incurred, to leave the option for future adjustments open. Thus organizations designed for flexibility exhibit a high degree of modularization between the different building blocks and the submodules of these. While deliberately forgoing returns from supermodularity in a more complex and statically efficient design, emphasis is put on dynamic efficiency.[11] In some settings it might, however, be optimal to commit to a more complex design and rely on its self-correcting power as adaptive change occurs. Such organizations are designed for commitment.

Designing for commitment

The third option for designing organizations for adaptive change in the environment is to choose a configuration of their parameters that strongly commits the organization and its constituencies. Organizations designed for commitment rely on distinct configurations of their parameters. The internal structure makes use of a high-commitment work system,[12] and the incentives are reshaped extensively towards deferred compensation in order to increase them, thereby reinforcing the achievement of the organization's purpose.

Strategy is geared towards actively influencing developments in the business environment, thus allowing these organizations to be a motor of change.[13] The commitment is further enhanced by relatively rigid and impermeable boundaries and the use of proprietary standards. Resources and positions have to be developed in-house. Appropriate elements of the governance complement this commitment introduced by the other parameters. Organizational forms such as a sole proprietorship or a professional partnership require the owners to dedicate their human and financial capital towards the firm. They are locked into this position and cannot easily remove their resources.[14] This increases, in a loop of positive feedback, their incentives to perform efficiently and to innovate in order to have an active influence on the changes in the environment.

Organizations designed for commitment deliberately destroy options for flexibility. Exit is complicated, and the best use of resources and positions is within the confines of the organization. As with a roped team climbing a mountain, enough is at stake for every constituent to agree to changes in the delicate balance of power if the necessity for adjustments arises. This is achieved by increasing the inherent value of the organizational design through exploiting many complementarities between the different elements, and thereby generating returns from supermodularity.

Example 4.5 The value of commitment in organizational design is demonstrated by the Lincoln Electric Company. Having run into trouble with its ambitious but poorly aligned global expansion, Lincoln Electric did not have sufficient cash flow in 1992 to pay the bonuses promised to its employees. To retain their trust and maintain the validity of its organizational system, Lincoln Electric eventually decided to borrow the money from banks to pay the bonus.[a] The ongoing commitment of all its constituencies allowed Lincoln to regain its competitive advantage based on its unique organizational design.

---

[a] See Hastings (1999, pp. 168–70).

This solution has its merits if the business environment can be influenced sufficiently. It is the alternative with the greatest complexity of design. Causal ambiguity among the distinct configuration of various elements often allows such organizations to remain at the forefront of change, and to set the rules instead of being the recipient of them.[15] Once an organization is committed to change in the environment, there are strong complementarities to innovate. Increasing the returns on innovative activity also increases the returns on other elements in the system because of the complementarities between the parameters of organizational design. Therefore, an organization designed consistently for such commitment explores the rugged landscape of competition and evolves by actively experimenting and searching for a better design.[16]

Organizations designed for commitment also have their weaknesses, however. Analogously to the reinforcement of the value of flexibility that occurs when many organizations adhere to it, the alternative of designing for commitment similarly thrives best if other organizations in the overall system rely on it as well. This is the case in, for example, the German or Japanese financial systems. When faced with change that is dictated to rather than innovated by these organizations, difficulties in the adjustment arise as some constituencies see better options outside the old system, and their commitment begins to wane.

Switching peaks – radical adjustments

How can organizations ensure that any continuously adjusted business model they follow is the most efficient one? The problem of inappropriateness that arises in their business models with disruptive change in the business landscape is highlighted, and possible solutions to overcome this inappropriateness are proposed in this section. Radically adjusting their whole design to deal with disruptive change allows organizations to reach to a higher peak of competitive advantage and helps to improve their efficiency in the light of such change.

Sudden inappropriateness of the configuration

Not only occasional flooding or erosion alters the face of a landscape over time; earthquakes and eruptions of volcanoes also leave an impact on it. New peaks emerge. Change in business, as described above, is similarly not always adaptive but can be of a disruptive nature as well. The result of disruptive change is that the business model employed by an organization loses its attractiveness so rapidly and overwhelmingly that continuous adjustments are no longer an option to cope with this kind of change. More radical ways of switching between different business models and pursuing the global optimum have to be considered.

Radical change occurs, for example, if unchartered areas in the rugged landscape of competition are opened for exploration by liberalization or deregulation. Business models previously barred can be implemented. Following the deregulation of the airline industry in the USA in 1978, for example, American Airlines 'invented' the business model of a hub-and-spoke system to take advantage of its new freedom. Other airlines, such as US Airways, readily accepted this way of competing and adapted to it. It was, however, only the truly disruptive way of breaking this existing paradigm that led Southwestern Airlines to reinvent the whole airline industry with the introduction of the low-cost business model.[17]

Other disruptive changes occur with advancements in technology and related innovations that make new ways of performing economic activities feasible. A clash of different financial systems, made possible by globalization and the integration of previously separate markets, is similarly a disruptive change. Recall from the previous section that organizational modes to deal with changes – that is, flexibility or commitment – fared best when other organizations also followed these modes. If, however, a critical mass of organizations supports a different mode, the original business model becomes inappropriate. A crisis can occur among these organizations because of this inappropriateness.

The effect of disruptive change is an organizational design that is not self-sustaining. If, for example, human resources are no longer attracted to an organization, its internal labour market breaks down. Inconsistencies in the design can therefore follow inappropriateness of design. Organizations remaining on a lower local peak lose out in competition with the organizations that have made the switch to the higher peak or global optimum.

Various possible ways of overcoming the inappropriateness of the organizational design can be imagined. The dissolution of the organization is again an option, especially if most of the value inherent in the design has been destroyed by adverse changes in the business environment, and if inconsistencies in the design follow its inappropriateness. See the preceding section for a discussion of this alternative. Another possibility is to stick with the design. This is a viable option if the design's inappropriateness is not too great compared to more efficient systems. Being content with remaining on a lower peak can also have its advantages, especially since climbing to another peak has its own risks and adjustment costs. Only a crisis and the threat of the total destruction of the design stimulate the necessary adjustments by the organization and its constituencies.

Depending on the severity of the crisis, however, the prevailing balances of incentives and power can be an obstacle to adjustment.

Two solutions exist to change the inappropriateness in the organizational design and to adjust it radically in order to react to disruptive change. Organizations can:

- alter their design through a series of small steps, changing the configuration of one parameter at a time; or
- alter their design through a single big leap, changing the configuration of many parameters simultaneously.

Small steps

According to Milgrom and Roberts (1995b), one solution for radically adjusting the design of an organization is through a series of adjustments in the configuration of different parameters, one at a time. Progressing with small steps allows a thorough configuration of each parameter with its correct value.[18] Switching peaks through a series of small steps has serious impediments, however. Recall that the starting point of the original business model from which the traverse begins is, despite its inappropriateness, still a consistently configured system. Altering just one parameter does not improve the efficiency, and is in fact, more likely to impair it. Consistent systems represent local peaks in the rugged landscape of competition from which the only path is downhill. The original business model therefore exhibits persistence.[19]

The route of small steps takes the company through a period of lower performance than would have been likely had it left the old, consistent system in place. This may well create resistance from those stakeholders who have something to lose. If enough power is assigned to or built up by them, they could reverse the process of adjustment through the restoration of the original configuration.

Much depends, therefore, on the configuration of organizational parameters and the resulting balance of power and incentives. The amount of economic rents that can be gained through a switch of the business model and the possibility of distributing them credibly *ex ante* further determine the advantage of adjustments through small steps. Redundancy in the organizational design provides for enough resources and positions that can be of value at the time of transition and help the organization through a trough between two different peaks.[20] Adhering, for example, to seemingly unrelated diversification within one firm is often penalized by financial markets with a conglomerate discount. However, taking the maximization of all rents into account, and not only the share that accrues to shareholders, can make such a strategy valuable. In the same way that scouts in a rugged landscape explore dead ends and provide foresight, such diversification allows organizations to recognize potentially easier means of accomplishing the switch from one business model to another, more appropriate one. Having erected, for example, seemingly unnecessary bridges over a valley might impair the static efficiency of the design and lead to such a conglomerate discount. At the same time it also allows for an easier traverse between different peaks and an enhancement of dynamic efficiency.

Example 4.6   With the introduction of the Single European Market and the advent of low-cost airlines, the business model of many national-flag carriers from smaller countries in the European Union rapidly lost its attractiveness. As their protection through bilateral open-sky agreements was abandoned, adjustments in their business model became necessary. The Irish airline Aer Lingus responded to these disruptive changes with a switch from the original system of a full-service carrier to become a low-cost airline through a series of small steps.

Features of this model were introduced over time. Direct sales through the internet increased from 8 per cent of all bookings in 2001 to 66 per cent in 2004. During the same period, 3,300 people were laid off, nearly halving the number of employees. The fleet was adjusted by taking Boeing aircraft out of service and switching to Airbus, thus reducing the different types of aircraft used to four, down from six. Elements from the original business model, such as a frequent flyer programme and the handling of cargo, are, however, still in place, and while employee ownership of shares has increased to 14.9 per cent, the Irish government is still the main shareholder. Profits are down to €1.2 million in 2004 as a result of the change in the business model.[a]

---

[a]   See Aer Lingus (2005) and Connolly (2004) for more details of the switch in business models.

Big leap

The second solution for radically adjusting the design in light of disruptive change is also described by Milgrom and Roberts (1995b). Instead of moving from one peak to another through a series of small steps, the necessary adjustments can be made with one big leap. With a big leap, the configurations of many parameters in the original business model are altered simultaneously. This kind of radical adjustment has the advantage that it immediately restores consistency between the building blocks and the different parameters of organizational design. The danger with simultaneous adjustments in many configurations lies, however, in missing the global optimum and ending up in a wilderness of dismal performance. This is especially a problem whenever the new business model requires a careful and exact configuration – that is, whenever it is risky and not robust enough to handle deviations in the configuration of its parameters. Making a big leap to a new peak with steep inclines is more dangerous than leaping to a plateau on top of a mountain.

Example 4.7 RJR Nabisco, the example used at the start of this book, provides an illustration of how radical adjustments can be implemented through the simultaneous reconfiguration of many organizational parameters. RJR Nabisco was a conglomerate of different activities in the food and tobacco industry, with little overlap between these activities. When markets had become more efficient by the mid-1980s, this altered the rugged landscape of competition and designs with smaller, more focused companies relying on the market interface became more appropriate.

With the takeover battle for RJR Nabisco in 1989 a big leap was made.[a] The most important adjustment to complement the change in strategic direction was a change in the ownership structure and the way the company was financed. The private equity firm Kohlberg Kravis Roberts & Co. (KKR) took control of RJR Nabisco and financed the purchase price of US$31.5 billion with US$30 billion of debt. Such a financial structure altered the balance of incentives tremendously: after the acquisition, KKR had to break up the company and implement other necessary adjustments in order to repay the debt.[b]

---

[a] See Burrough and Helyar (1990) for a detailed illustration of the takeover battle and the various adjustments.
[b] See also Bishop (2004) for the importance of private equity to support adjustments in the organizational design through big leaps.

Reacting to disruptive change with big leaps requires co-ordination of the adjustments with regard to the correct timing and exact configuration. This is more difficult in some designs than in others. Co-ordination of the adjustments in the complementary parameters becomes crucial. More centralized organizations that have assigned a high value to leadership promise more success with this adjustment mode. Leadership provides guidance to and co-ordination of dispersed decision-makers. A strong organizational culture and the use of the governance mechanism of voice by a coalition of owners can similarly achieve the necessary co-ordination. Depending on the actual configuration, the success of big leaps can be influenced, and disruptions in the business landscape can be countered, by a transition to a more appropriate business model.

4.3　Efficient organizational design

This book has been about organizational design. Organizations are complex systems composed of various elements and modules. The strategy and boundaries, internal structure and governance are the main modules, and these four building blocks make up the organization. The actual configurations of the different parameters within these building blocks determine the balance of power in organizations. Power influences the decision to invest specifically into resources and positions, and helps to safeguard the resulting economic rents from such investments. An efficient balance of power leads, therefore, to an efficient balance of incentives that maximizes the sum of the economic rents generated by the organizational design.

A configuration of the numerous organizational parameters that considers interdependencies and potential complementarities between them is more efficient and creates a larger amount of economic rents for distribution among the constituencies of the organization. Designing organizations to take into account such complementarities increases efficiency by generating economic rents from this supermodular relationship between complementary elements.

This book has in its first part analysed different organizational parameters for potential complementarities between them, and synthesized these elements into consistent systems. Designing organizations for consistency among their building blocks and organizational parameters leads to superior business models in the rugged landscape of competition. Changes in this business landscape, such as technological advances or liberalizations that lead to an increased importance of human capital relative to financial capital, alter the relative efficiency of different organizational designs. Such changes demand adjustments to the design in order to restore consistency between the elements of the different building blocks, to rebalance the power of the various constituencies, and to keep the investment incentives of these constituencies intact.

Having analysed the building blocks and synthesized the design of consistent organizational systems theoretically in the first part of this book allows us to use this framework for an investigation of the different business models that can be found in practice. A decision about which design is the most efficient is, in the absence of an absolute benchmark, only possible from case to case in a comparative organizational analysis of distinct designs. Case studies are the best way to study organizations and the success or failure of their business model. How such business models compete with each other and whether a particular business model is more efficient than another is the topic of the three case studies in the second part of the book, which supplement the examples given throughout the first part.

The first case study deals with the European securities transaction industry. This industry and the different firms in it have had to adjust to the introduction of the Single European Market. Business models that have been consistent and appropriate for separated markets in Europe are no longer appropriate. Three possible systems are illustrated in Chapter 5 and evaluated against each other. The second case study describes the German co-operative banking group as a network of many autonomous banks with a subtle balance of power in the group. This business model is compared in Chapter 6 to the system of the Deutsche Bank, an organization of approximately equal size that is, however, designed with often a completely contrary configuration of the key organizational parameters. The third case study deals in Chapter 7 with open-source projects, and a description of how in these communities power and incentives can be set to compete with organizations that follow a business model more in line with that described by traditional theories of the firm.

Notes

1. See Higl and Welzel (2004) for an application in the context of co-operatives.
2. See Eliasson (1996) and his example of research and development teams in the Swedish aircraft industry.
3. As Holmström (1999b, pp. 75–6) explains: 'The firm gains power over human capital through ownership and control of assets ... It uses the power to set "internal rules of the game" and design incentives in a manner that internalizes some of the contractual externalities that are present in markets due to asymmetric information.'
4. Roberts and van den Steen (2000, p. 20), citing Holmström (1999a).
5. Recall for the purposes of the following arguments the examples of modern manufacturing and the airline industry described in Section 2.2.
6. See also Moran and Ghoshal (1996) and Allen and Gale (2000a) for a description of the complementary relationship between firms and markets in the financial system.
7. Formal treatments of flexibility and its value are provided by Boot and Thakor (2003), and by Krahnen *et al.* (1985). See also Wernerfelt (1997) for a game-theoretic model of different organizational designs, and their respective flexibility and adjustment costs.
8. See, for example, Hamel (1999), who proposes to design organizations in such a way as to resemble the network that forms the cluster in Silicon Valley.
9. Recent examples of General Motors and Ford, as well as unionized airlines in the USA, show that such legacies from the past can become unsustainable if not adjusted in time. Carson (2004, p. 5) reports, for example, that General Motors has 2.4 pensioners for every current employee, and, as illustrated by

The Economist (2005, p. 74), United Airlines, in bankruptcy since 2002, finally defaulted on four employee pension plans to the amount of US$9.8 billion in May 2005.

10. See Allen and Sherer (1995).
11. See also Roberts (2004), who speaks of 'tight' and 'loose' coupling between different elements or modules to illustrate the trade-off between static and dynamic optimization.
12. On consistent high-commitment work systems and their advantages, see Appelbaum *et al.* (2000). See also the various contributions to Blair and Kochan (2000).
13. See d'Aveni (1999) for many examples of how organizations can maintain a continuous advantage by strategic influence of their business environment.
14. See Allen and Sherer (1995).
15. See Hamel (1996).
16. See also Foss (1998).
17. See Greifenstein and Weiss (2004) for a comparison between the two distinct business models and the way the systemic interaction and fit leads to success in the different models. See also Section 2.2.
18. See also Eisenhardt and Sull (2001, p. 114), who cite the example of Enron which 'shift[s] among opportunities ... relied on small moves, which are faster and safer than large ones'.
19. See Section 2.2, and Schmidt and Spindler (2002) for the effects of persistence.
20. See Cyert and March (1963) and Burton and Obel (1984, pp. 177ff.) for the value of 'slack'.

Part II
Practice of Organizational Design

5
The European Securities Transaction Industry

5.1 Introduction

Despite a lot of restructuring and many innovations in recent years, the securities transaction industry in the European Union (EU) is still a highly inefficient and inconsistently configured system for cross-border transactions. Many EU politicians eagerly promote the completion of the Single European Market, but – apart from a few exceptions – the industry structure still closely resembles the former fragmented market structure of largely independent organizations operating along national lines. This causes higher costs in the handling of cross-border securities[1] which ultimately translate into higher costs of capital – a significant competitive disadvantage for European firms compared to companies in the USA.

Industry experts point to several aspects that impede the realization of an efficient securities transaction system. While trading is widely seen as efficient, clearing and settlement processes across different countries are still too costly. The fragmented industry structure, which does not allow for capturing the significant benefits from scale, scope and network effects, is paralysed by several obstacles to consolidation. As well as the political, cultural and legal barriers among the different countries, the motives of the market participants such as infrastructure providers and direct users sometimes contribute to the impediment of consolidation efforts and thus prevent a socially optimal solution.

What has become increasingly visible is the lack of a common communication standard among service providers. This could be a result of vertically integrated providers with incompatible information dissemination standards and post-trading routines. As a consequence, typical cross-border trade requires substantial interaction among the different trading, clearing and settlement systems which can only be dealt with effectively by additional intermediaries such as (sub)custodians. This extends the length of the value chain and thereby increases costs for the investors. More interaction requirements are also more risky because of the higher complexity of the trade and a higher likelihood of failures. Higher risks usually mean additional collateral requirements, which is a further cost driver.

Not surprisingly, there are diverging opinions on how to cope with the current inefficiencies. Don Cruickshank, former CEO of the London Stock Exchange, favours a market structure that separates trading from post-trading activities, while the latter should be organized as a utility comparable to the Depository Trust & Clearing Corporation (DTCC) in the USA:

> If the single market in financial services is to be delivered, then competition and regulatory policies must be allowed to work side by side. Where we can see some spring shoots of such an approach is in moves to allow exchanges to compete on a harmonised utility clearing and settlement layer as the most effective way of reducing transaction costs in the securities industry as a whole and maximising the potential for competition elsewhere in the securities value chain.[2]

This stands in strong contrast to the view of Werner Seifert, former CEO of Deutsche Börse, who claims that an efficient solution can be delivered by vertical integration of the activities, and that the culprits are the myriads of different regulators in the EU:

> Many people claim that clearing and settlement should be done by a single, Europe-wide utility, like in the US, and that greedy private operators help themselves from the till by insisting that trading, clearing, and settlement remain integrated. Not so! At Deutsche Börse we have looked at this very closely, and the overwhelming problem in the integration of European capital markets is driven by different regulations, even different applications of identical rules where they exist – the whole messy business of EU regulation, with actual implementation left to the member states.[3]

What these two views reveal is that different and sometimes intertwined forces are at play in the European securities transaction industry. The motives of the different opponents can be biased by strategic deliberations and the desire to advance the industry structure to the opponents' own advantage. This study sheds some light on these opposing claims by applying economic tools to identify the underlying economies in the industry and to comment on an efficient securities transaction system for the EU. Our contribution is to provide a framework for the analysis of this industry which identifies and structures the different elements, interprets efficiency in a broader sense, and offers policy advice by proposing consistently configured trading, clearing and settlement systems (TCS-systems) that achieve high levels of efficiency from the perspective of a benevolent organizational designer. Applying the methodology of systems theory, we provide answers to the following questions: (i)What are the economic characteristics of the relevant activities, and which constituencies are involved in these activities? (ii) Which strategic decisions can be conducted by the industry players; and what are the consequences of these? and (iii) What are consistently configured organizational designs that provide superior efficiency to alternative set-ups?

Our framework presents three systems for the European securities transaction industry that are configured in a consistent way: the first assigns a prominent role towards regulation and allows the capture of the economies in the industry to a great extent by integrating and consolidating the activities in the different national markets. The second lets the market forces work and – although more fragmented – allows for a high level of innovation and a more dynamic industry. The third consistent system is also characterized by consolidation and integration, but instead of heavy regulation it is kept open to market forces by adjusting the necessary elements, so that any ensuing monopoly remains contestable. We conclude that the third design has its advantages over the other two: policy-makers in the European Union should strive to implement the various elements of it to make a consistent whole, to the benefit of the European capital market.

Related literature

Public authorities and academics alike have taken an interest in the European securities transaction industry. Different regulatory bodies and committees established by the European Commission focus mainly on the identification of structural weaknesses in the industry and outline concrete recommendations to overcome these problems: in response to ECOFIN's request to provide regulatory proposals for the European Securities Markets in 2001, the Committee of Wise Men, chaired by Alexandre Lamfalussy, demands further restructuring and scrutiny for the requirement of a regulatory framework in the clearing and settlement area. Furthermore, they point towards competitive issues and general systemic risk aspects that may evolve in the context of monetary policy and the functioning of payment systems.[4] The Giovannini Group, a consultative group headed by Alberto Giovannini and appointed by the European Commission, analyses cross-border clearing and settlement arrangements in the EU and finds that international transactions are more complex and costly than domestic transactions as a result of fifteen barriers, and that these inefficiencies represent a paramount barrier to an integrated financial market.[5]

The European Shadow Financial Regulatory Committee (ESFRC) disagrees with the claim of some market participants that a forced consolidation into a pan-European regulated utility would solve these problems. Instead, they are pushing for an ownership separation between trading and post-trading facilities in order to foster fair competition.[6] The Committee on Payment and Settlement Systems (CPSS) and the Technical Committee of the International Organization of Securities Commissions (IOSCO) jointly developed recommendations for securities settlement systems that aim to improve the safety and efficiency of these systems. In particular, the report recommends minimum requirements that these systems should be obliged to fulfil, and the best practices for which they should strive.[7] Based on these recommendations, the Committee of European Securities Regulators (CESR) and the European Central Bank (ECB) published nineteen standards,[8] which also incorporated comments on standardization, communication and messaging, and business continuity,[9] as well as on standards for risk management controls.[10] Market participants were consulted on draft versions, and many institutions used this opportunity to respond. Some organizations also published their own reports and white papers on the industry.[11]

Academic papers usually highlight particular aspects of the industry by focusing on a certain aspect in the securities transaction value chain while inevitably neglecting other potentially interrelated factors. Some contributions provide empirical research on the main activities: Hasan and Malkamäki (2001) investigate potential economies of scale and scope at stock exchanges, while Schmiedel *et al.* (2006) focus on the same subject in the case of settlement systems. A related study was conducted on network effects at exchanges by Hasan and Schmiedel (2003). Additionally, formal models are presented for various topics such as on the economics of financial networks by Economides (1993); on vertical integration by Koeppl and Monnet (2004) and Tapking and Yang (2004); on competition between central securities depositories (CSDs) by Kauko (2005); and on competition between custodians and CSDs by Holthausen and Tapking (2004). Furthermore, moral hazard aspects were modelled to distinguish between net and gross settlement by Kahn *et al.* (2003).

There are, however, also contributions that apply a more holistic approach and thus are more closely related to the framework used in this chapter. One of the first academic contributions is by Giddy *et al.* (1996): they analyse four alternative models for the European clearing and settlement market, mainly from the perspective of the users of these services. Differences between their models exist in the way that linkages between the CSDs are structured. Our approach is similar to theirs in respect of evaluating trading, clearing and settlement along three dimensions and deriving distinct organizational designs for a future industry setting. But unlike their approach, we take microeconomic incentives of the key industry players into account in more detail and base the analysis of possible systems on sounder foundations with regard to these aspects.

The paper by Milne (2002) establishes analogies between other utility network industries, such as the telecommunication sector and the securities settlement market. These markets, he argues, have similarities in possessing a natural monopoly that has to be regulated. Milne identifies the book-entry function and the transmission of corporate actions as the two activities of the value chain that need to be regulated via access pricing and the establishment of common communication standards. He concludes that this minimal regulatory effort should suffice to create a level playing field on all other stages such as clearing, settlement and custody, rendering further public interventions unnecessary. While we agree on this notion, we extend his policy advice by presenting and applying a more comprehensive framework that – together with the methodology of systems theory – allows for broader policy advice.

The paper closest to ours in spirit and result is by van Cayseele (2004), who agrees with our reasoning proposed in a previously published working paper version of this chapter.[12] Van Cayseele starts from the same premiss as this chapter, by asking what an economically optimal outcome for the clearing and settlement industry would be. Relying on the concepts of 'essential facilities' and 'two-sided markets',[13] he concludes that the advantage of a market solution relying on contestability of the industry is to be preferred over a single regulated monopoly with the potential costs of government failure.

Outline

Section 5.2 briefly describes the three efficiency concepts deployed in this chapter. We concentrate on the activities of trading, clearing and settlement (TCS) along the value chain, and the providing institutions.[14] In Section 5.3 we explain the underlying economies of the activities at each level of the value chain and the interdependencies across the whole chain. The role of regulators is also discussed briefly. Section 5.4 considers possible strategies and associated actions to highlight the microeconomic incentives of the infrastructure providers. Three important decisions about the configuration of the design have to be made – where to set the boundaries, whether to adopt an industry-wide standard, and how to assign ownership rights. We show consistent TCS systems in Section 5.5 that are efficient from the viewpoint of social welfare. Their individual components are complementary and thus reinforce each other. Potential drawbacks and implications for social welfare are discussed. Section 5.6 concludes with a comparative organizational analysis.

5.2 Three concepts for evaluation

Economic rents are created through 'good' investment decisions by the various constituencies, and allocated to them through 'good' distribution rules. This interplay between *ex-ante* incentives and *ex-post* distribution also determines the efficiency of possible TCS systems. We analyse efficiency along the three lines of static, dynamic and systemic efficiency to (i) evaluate the generated economic rents; and (ii) estimate the resulting overall efficiency. We describe briefly each concept and the potential trade-offs between them.

Static efficiency

A certain activity is performed in a statically efficient way if there is no solution that would allow a less costly implementation. It is under this notion that the commonly used concept of cost efficiency is considered. Parameters influencing the static efficiency are the costs of production, which in turn are influenced by the underlying technologies and the economies arising from them. In the securities transaction industry, network externalities[15] are prevalent. They lead in many areas, such as the trading of a single derivative instrument or the settlement of a particular stock, to an efficient market structure that is a natural monopoly.

Static efficiency generally increases if the number of companies conducting business along the securities transaction value chain decreases because of the underlying economies. The costs of any regulation that has to be set up to keep the remaining companies and their rent-extracting potential in check, however, lead to a lowering of static efficiency.

Dynamic efficiency

Activities are performed in a dynamically efficient way if today's structures and investments do not hamper the efficient performance of these activities in the future. By investing in a certain technology or by institutionalizing a certain industry structure, the ability to change and to adapt becomes affected. In particular, the dominance of a network provider may have detrimental effects on the innovativeness of the market.[16] Industry structures and processes that do not allow for innovation and for quality improvement in the future thus are not efficient under the notion of dynamic efficiency. Competition in the market usually helps to alleviate problems such as low innovativeness or poor quality of the goods and services. The absence of competition may lead to complacency and to less innovation as is common in a monopolistic environment. When estimating dynamic efficiency, key parameters are (i) the industry structure that determines the difficulty of entering the TCS industry; (ii) the rate of technological innovation; and (iii) the propensity of all constituencies to invest and the resulting sum of all investments.

Systemic efficiency

Our third evaluation concept, denoted systemic efficiency, provides an insight on systemic risk issues that are inherent at various stages of the value chain and takes into account the stability of the TCS industry when faced with adverse systemic events. We define systemic efficiency as the degree of robustness of the activities in the securities transaction industry to systemic risks that are born out of strong adverse systemic events.[17] A systemic event occurs when a 'bad event' for one or more market participant(s) has subsequent negative repercussions on other market participants. Such an event may vary in severity, ranging from a delay in payment or delivery of the securities in question to a full-blown failure of a party to meet the agreed-on obligations. Potential contagion effects have to be taken seriously, most notably in cases of strong negative systemic events such as the failure of an institution. Systemic risk issues are treated with great care by both public and private entities. Both *ex-ante* (crisis prevention) and *ex-post* (crisis management) measures have to be introduced in order to deal with systemic risks. Appropriate regulation has to ensure this.

Interdependencies

Note that the three concepts of efficiency are interdependent:

(i) The statically efficient solution of a monopoly conveys only minor incentives to innovate, whereas a few players in an oligopoly can interact in heavy competition and try to develop better products and processes, thereby increasing dynamic efficiency. They also compete for monopoly rents that are non-existent in an environment of perfect competition, where the users of the infrastructure gain the main part of economic rents. The potential profit that can be gained is therefore a big enough incentive to undertake the large technological investments needed up-front.

(ii) Static efficiency can decline when measures are taken to increase systemic efficiency: the provision of collateral, for example, increases the stability of the industry against adverse shocks, but levies opportunity costs on the market participants. The existence of economic rents also facilitates the build-up of a financial buffer that allows these companies to be more stable in times of systemic crises.

(iii) Perfect competition would contribute potentially more in terms of innovativeness, thereby increasing dynamic efficiency, but the systemic efficiency could be damaged: a more fragmented structure may impose more work on regulators to keep the overall system sound. However, competition also fosters innovations in risk management tools which are beneficial to systemic efficiency.

5.3   The securities transaction industry

To analyse the securities transaction industry we define the securities transaction value chain and the constituencies that are involved in these activities. The value chain has three main activities: securities need to be traded, the results of the trade have to be confirmed and calculated by a clearing process, and the delivery of money and paper to the parties to a trade has to be settled. Institutions such as exchanges, clearing houses and central securities depositories (CSDs) provide these services. Two more constituencies are involved in the value chain, namely the users and regulators. The users are the clients of the infrastructure provider and can be further subdivided into banks and brokers as direct users,[18] and investors and issuers as indirect users. The regulators monitor the processes in the industry to ensure a sound and efficient transaction environment. Their role is discussed at the end of this section.

Economies of the securities transaction value chain
Network effects

There exist strong positive network externalities in each of the three stages: in trading, network effects can be both observed on the investors' as well as on the issuers' side. For the former, becoming a member of an already large network of investors who trade on the same platform increases both the member's own and the others' utility by providing additional liquidity to the market.[19] The latter group benefits from larger networks, as these can more easily absorb the issuers' need for capital.

There are viable positive network externalities on the user side for both clearing and settlement. A concentration on a few transaction systems allows for a higher proportion of clearing and settlement instructions to be processed internally. This increases the utility of all users because costly links to other networks become less necessary. In the extreme, a single clearing and settlement network would be faster and less costly in comparison to processes that require interaction with several clearing and settlement systems.

Economies of scale

The providers of TCS facilities can gain significant economies of scale as the set-up costs for a transaction platform have a substantial portion of fixed costs, so that average costs fall with increasing transaction volume. This view is confirmed by empirical investigations. Malkamäki's analysis of the processing of trades at stock exchanges shows scale economies for increasing trading volume.[20] Another contribution, by Schmiedel *et al.* (2006), measured significant economies of scale for settlement systems: platforms with high transaction volumes will be able to offer lower transaction costs to users than will low-volume competitors. For non-automated transaction systems – that is, floor-based trading – this effect is not as pronounced as for automated trading systems, since the ratio of fixed costs to variable costs is higher for the computerized system.

Economies of scale are also present in counter-party risk management. In particular, if a central counter-party (CCP) is used at the clearing stage, the users of the facility can save resources on the management and control of counter-party risks. By pooling risk management facilities at the CCP, costs can be eliminated by risk management specialization effects. Additionally, if netting mechanisms are used, the users will enjoy reduced capital provision requirements, and therefore lower opportunity costs.[21] As a consequence, scale economies may be even more pronounced in clearing than in other stages.

Economies of scope

All three activities also exhibit potential economies of scope. Providers are able to process different types of securities on the same platform while incurring only relatively low incremental costs. Clearing facilities that process different classes of securities such as stocks, bonds and derivatives have additional leeway for scope economies as they are able to implement innovative risk management procedures such as cross-collateralizing along different classes of securities. This would lead to an overall decrease in capital provision requirements to the users and would consequently save costs.

The upshot of the results above suggests a tendency towards a strong concentration of the activities or even a natural monopoly at each stage of the value chain because of the underlying and mutually reinforcing economies. According to our definition in Section 5.2, a concentration in the industry translates into high static efficiency.

Contestability of the market

A concentrated market in turn lowers dynamic efficiency, as the latter falls with decreasing levels of competition. The existence of substantial network externalities or scale and scope economies creates a barrier to entry and offers established platforms some protection from competitors.[22] Nevertheless, high levels of dynamic efficiency can be achieved if the market for securities transactions remains contestable – that is, if competitive and innovative infrastructure providers can gain market share at the expense of established competitors.

The diversion of transaction volume is more likely if more of the following aspects coincide: (i) the competitor demands lower fees – Domowitz and Steil (1999, pp. 8–9) give several examples of this behaviour; (ii) a competing provider offers a significantly better service for users based on a better technology which manifests itself in faster, more reliable or more convenient transaction handling; (iii) the competitor offers new products or services that have not yet been supplied and 'monopolized' by an established provider; and (iv) clearing and settlement institutions reduce their capital provision requirements by introducing netting processes. However, this point may be a matter of regulatory concern as competing institutions might want to apply less stringent risk management to underbid successfully the fee structure of competitors.

Systemic risk issues

Systemic efficiency is particularly relevant in the clearing and settlement of securities and appendant funds. There are several sources of, and alleviation efforts towards, systemic risks. Clearing and settlement institutions have developed risk management tools that attempt to reduce both *ex ante* and *ex post* the various types of settlement risk. Since the various types of systemic risks, such as counter-party, custody and cross-border risks, have been elaborated in detail by other contributors,[23] we focus on the relationship between systemic efficiency and market concentration. The relationship is not straightforward. Both a fragmented and a consolidated industry structure have to deal with trade-offs.

A concentrated industry structure can exploit economies in centralizing risk management efforts as it is more cost efficient to have one party collect the information and to monitor the other parties instead of having all parties monitoring each other. Thus a central risk manager will be more cost efficient and more sophisticated. However, the central risk manager may bank too strongly on its dominant position and believe that public entities would bail it out in case of a failure, and moral hazard may materialize in the form of reduced monitoring efforts.[24] Therefore regulatory effort – albeit rather simple, as only one institution has to be controlled – might be necessary.[25] Additionally, a higher degree of consolidation leads to less complexity in the interaction between the providers and thus reduces the probability of failures in communication and asset transfers.

A fragmented industry structure, on the other hand, may provide systemic efficiency that is superior to a concentrated market. More industry players will usually lead to higher levels of competition. A possible parameter of competition can be the provision of sound and stable transaction systems among providers, which boosts systemic efficiency. Another positive aspect of fragmentation is the existence of redundancies which – if communication protocols between different transaction systems are compatible – can be used to re-route transactions from a failed to an intact system. Multiple transaction systems may thus increase the robustness of the industry, though potential contagion effects between the providers may weaken this advantage.

Vertical interdependencies in the value chain

In several European countries, the dominant trading institution often also exercises control over the activities further downstream – that is, the exchange is integrated vertically into the domestic clearing and settlement activities. This setting is mainly driven by efficiency motives as it enables the whole transaction to be processed straight through in a faster, more cost-efficient and more reliable manner. Straight-through processing (STP) at a single institution offers significant economies to both users and providers, in comparison to the processing between separate entities, because: (i) it lowers communication costs between the respective activities, thereby improving static efficiency; (ii) innovations concerning the processing of transactions are easier to implement since co-ordination efforts with other providers along the value chain are not necessary. This shortens the implementation period and therefore increases dynamic efficiency; and (iii) it makes transaction failures less frequent, since the data transmission process is optimized in-house – for example, by implementing a proprietary communication standard. This represents an improvement in systemic efficiency.

However, with the decline in IT infrastructure costs in recent years, the arguments for vertical integration are not as strong as they were some years ago, because transmission costs to outside institutions are now significantly less costly and not necessarily higher than those in-house.

Furthermore, as trading habits of investors gradually shift from a domestic towards a more international approach, the national 'silos', as the vertically integrated entities are also called, not only no longer represent the investors' scope of transaction activities but even hamper frictionless processing of cross-border transactions in Europe. This is because of the incompatible proprietary communication standards that each national silo had developed to communicate along its own controlled value chain – a legacy that makes communication between silos a highly complex and inefficient task.

Differing communication standards between vertical silos also de facto impede the contestability of downstream activities – that is, the clearing and settlement markets. They represent an effective entry barrier against other providers that strive to enter the market of an established silo. They are unable to do so because once a trade is made on the established trading platform, competitors are restricted to offering their services for the downstream functions because of the existing proprietary communication standard of the established provider. Therefore, the clearing and settlement activities of the established provider are protected by its trading activity and are thus hardly subject to contestability. This may result in dynamic inefficiencies.

Regulation

Efficient trading, clearing and settlement of securities is important for the functioning of the whole economy. Companies need to gain access to finance, and private households need a vehicle by which they can save their financial surplus. This assigns financial markets in general, and the TCS industry in particular, a pivotal role. The well-being of other industries and many people depends on it. Adverse effects spill over into other parts of the economy, implying negative externalities. Therefore, regulation of the TCS industry is a means of avoiding or mitigating these external effects.

These spill-over effects are material to the settlement stage of the securities transaction value chain when the payment system is involved. A failure of one party to meet its obligations might lead to contagion that has negative effects on the liquidity of the banking system and threaten the economy through this transmission channel. The central bank as lender of last resort has an incentive to deal with these regulatory issues.

It therefore needs to be (and is) one of the key regulating institutions, since central bank money is frequently involved in settling the cash side of securities transactions. Other regulatory bodies are concerned with different aspects: for example, the performance of each activity for all users – which are of a considerably heterogeneous degree – in a fair manner needs to be ensured – that is, access to the infrastructure must be open and non-discriminating. The European Commission, with various reports – the Lamfalussy Report, the two reports of the Giovannini Group, and the Investment Services Directive – is committed to this task in the Single European Market. National agencies implement actions to put these aspects into practice today. Regulators often join forces to set standards after consulting the relevant industry players – for example, the joint working group set up by the European Central Bank and the Committee of European Securities Regulators (CESR). A single European Financial Services Authority might one day take over this job. In all cases, the right balance between static, dynamic and systemic efficiency must be chosen by the regulators.

Regulation lowers static efficiency since it is costly to set up a bureaucracy – or a publicly owned entity in the extreme – to achieve the performance of the three activities in the value chain. The 'outsourcing' of regulation to the providers and the users of the infrastructure could be a cost-efficient alternative. Possible means for this outsourcing lie in self-regulation by the infrastructure provider. Whenever they can compete on quality, as many exchanges do with different market segments and the attached regulatory conditions, regulation need not be of the costly public variant. As a second means, the infrastructure can also be user-governed. In this setting, the club of users writes its own rules. Whenever little entry in this club is required, this can again be better than publicly provided regulation.

The current system with competing regulatory regimes in Europe – with sometimes overlapping competencies, sometimes unattended areas – is seen nearly unanimously by the industry as a major barrier to business, since a level playing field is not provided. We come back to the question of regulation in the context of the three efficient systems in Section 5.5.

5.4 Strategic conduct – the provider's action set

In this section we analyse the three key parameters in our framework that the providers of the infrastructure, the users and the regulators can use to interact strategically to shape the future of the securities transaction industry. The focus is on the providers of the infrastructure, but possible actions and reactions of the other constituencies are taken into account where necessary. The three parameters in the action set that we look at are (i) the boundary decision of the infrastructure providers; (ii) the decision regarding whether to adopt an open standard or to develop a proprietary communication tool; and (iii) the governance of the infrastructure providers.

Boundary decisions

The institutions providing the infrastructure for trading, clearing and settling the different financial instruments face the problem of whether to integrate different activities in the organizational design of one firm or whether to concentrate on just one function or one specific financial instrument. We describe two distinct business models – the vertically integrated silo and the vertically focused firm.

The vertically integrated silo

The first business model is the vertical silo – the combination of TCS together in one firm. It is applied, for example, by Deutsche Börse. The advantage of such a model is that it allows the reaping of benefits that derive from the economies of scope between the three functions, as described above in Section 5.3. Communication is easier when the three functions are performed in close proximity within the same organization. Specific forms of data exchanges between the three stages of the value chain and straight-through processing allow for the emergence of economic rents.[26]

However, one of the adverse effects such a business model has, which might be a prevalent microeconomic motive behind this strategy, is the leverage of a (natural) monopoly on one stage of the value chain upstream or downstream to other stages. In particular, a vertical silo may cross-subsidize its trading costs – thereby attracting customers from other platforms – through its monopoly profits on the clearing and settlement stage or vice versa.[27] By this strategy, an institution following the business model of vertical integration effectively strengthens its competitive position. Furthermore, the vertical silo forecloses the market to competitors: by restricting access for them in one activity, users can be forced also to 'buy' the solution for another activity from the same institution. If there is no choice for them but to deal with the same provider, a monopoly rent can be extracted from the users, further increasing the economic rents generated in this model because of the specificity inherent in it.

Therefore, the interesting question arises as to whether Deutsche Börse can deliver its promises given that it controls downstream activities and de facto can foreclose the market because of its monopoly at the following stage in the value chain. When faced with the specific and co-specialized investments they have to undertake, banks and brokers could be reluctant to join in this venture.

The vertically focused firm

The other business model that has promising features is that of more focused infrastructure providers and the use of market mechanisms between them. A prominent example for this industry setting was used in England where three independent institutions, namely the London Stock Exchange, London Clearing House and Crest, provided infrastructure services only for a single stage of the value chain.[28] If a good solution for the data transfer between the three activities of the securities transaction value chain is implemented, this model has appeal because it does not place too much power in the hands of a single entity that can control access to its infrastructure – an infrastructure that exhibits strong network effects. For each activity, the users can choose the institution that provides it in the most efficient way. Competition forces less efficient institutions out of business and sets high-powered incentives for those that survive. As such firms do not have to worry about any interdependencies between their different lines of business, they are more eager to adopt new and better technologies and processes; and cannibalization of value propositions within the same firm cannot happen. These institutions therefore increase both static and dynamic efficiency. A possible drawback that might have to be taken into account by the regulators is less systemic stability that incentives that are too high-powered might induce. How the problem of establishing a market mechanism for the intermediate goods – the information transfer from one stage to the next in the value chain – can be dealt with is the topic of the next section.

Communication standards and accessibility

The interaction between the stages of the value chain is of crucial importance to the way business is performed in the TCS industry. It necessitates infrastructure providers making decisions both on the information transfer mode (that is, the type of communication standard) and the degree of accessibility of their activities to competitors.

Proprietary versus open communication standards

Proprietary standards infer that the information format of the transactions cannot be interpreted without co-specialized investments, so competitors are discriminated against, whereas an open standard enables competitors to process the information and allows users to switch providers more easily.[29]

The decision of whether to adopt an open standard or to set up a proprietary system is intertwined with the vertical boundary decision. In the case of a vertically focused infrastructure provider, the solution is simple. Such an institution has to rely on the market for the performance of upstream and downstream activities, and the communication protocol has to be in an open and understandable format.[30] The situation is different for companies following the business model of a vertical silo: such companies can develop a solution that allows them to keep private the information that has to be passed along the securities transaction value chain. By doing so, it can develop an idiosyncratic data exchange format that allows the generation of an economic rent because of its specific nature.

However, an economic rent could also be generated by foreclosing the market for an upstream or downstream activity. Users are forced to rely on the same institution and buy the bundled product at a one-stop shop. They have to invest in co-specialized computer systems that allow them to handle this proprietary data format. With an open communication standard between the different stages of the value chain, deconstruction becomes possible. There would be a choice that allowed customers to deal with the best and most efficient institution.

Analysing open and proprietary communication standards on the basis of our three efficiency concepts reveals that there are two major advantages for proprietary compared to open communication standards: (i) they can be more specific in relation to a certain financial instrument or a certain institution than open communication standards, and thus be more statically efficient; and (ii) a higher dynamic efficiency can be obtained, since a proprietary communication standard allows for the complete appropriation of the economic rent that is generated by innovations. Additionally, the benefits of innovations made with open standards could be enjoyed by every participant without being obliged to invest in this innovation. Thus underinvestment problems may arise with open standards.

However, proprietary communication has also two major drawbacks when compared to open standards:

(i) Proprietary standards provide more incentives for strategic behaviour to infrastructure providers, which can be to the detriment of the users. Thus market foreclosure strategies and mutual reinforcements of monopolies at different stages of the value chain can have a negative impact on users. Both static and dynamic efficiency may be impaired. A communication standard that is open to all market participants prevents, or at least alleviates, this strategic behaviour: it is easier for competitors of the infrastructure provider or for the users themselves by means of internalization to work around such a foreclosure.

(ii) Proprietary standards raise more regulatory concerns if a regulator wants to ensure the proper functioning of the market and access for other constituencies. Therefore, static efficiency may be lowered because of the increased regulation costs. Additionally, systemic efficiency may be low if regulators do not control the proprietary standard sufficiently.

Restricted versus open accessibility

Accessibility is the reverse of communications and refers to interactions between competitors across different stages of the value chain – that is, between trading and clearing, or between clearing and settlement. Open access describes the ability of institutions to provide their services at one stage of a transaction while other stages of the value chain are performed by competitors. This stands in contrast to transactions where access is restricted by a provider. Restriction of access is possible whenever a provider is able to leverage its dominant position on other stages of the value chain. This may, for example, occur if a dominant trading facility prevents other providers of downstream activities from receiving the transaction and route it automatically instead to their own clearing facility. Another example of dominance can be found in the opposite direction if a settlement provider has the monopoly on a certain security and refuses to accept transactions that are traded or cleared from anyone apart from its own upstream activity provider. Therefore, restricted accessibility can strongly impede fair competition among providers in the TCS industry.[31]

Accessibility as well as the communication standard decision depend primarily on the industry structure,[32] the allocation of power between the different constituencies, and the governance and ownership of the providers of the infrastructure. Using (or being forced by a regulator to use) a common means of communication technology effectively opens markets. The power that is conveyed by open markets to users allows them to search for the best price and quality. This in turn eventually forces a redistribution of economic rents away from the incumbent providers who would otherwise hang on to an inefficient allocation of resources from a welfare perspective. It is to these governance aspects that we turn next.

Ownership structure and governance

Ownership of a good is an incentive device: if residual decision rights are aligned with the rights to residual income, decisions are made in such a way as to maximize this share. The maximization of it optimizes social welfare whenever these decisions can be made independently of others. It therefore matters who ultimately has control over a certain good or resource. This is also the case for a firm – a much more complex 'good' and a whole bundle of resources. For our analysis, we take into account the ownership structure of a provider of the infrastructure in the securities transaction value chain to check whether economically sound decisions will be made by this institution. Three distinct forms of ownership can be identified: (i) a for-profit firm that operates to maximize profits, which are distributable to its shareholders as dividends; (ii) a non-profit mutual that operates to maximize the utility of its members; and (iii) a publicly-owned entity that provides a good or service that would not be provided efficiently by a private firm because of its public good nature and the underlying external effects.

Public ownership of an infrastructure provider can be a means of delivering a service that must be provided by a natural monopolist. The public policy-maker, acting in the interest of society as a whole, is not interested in narrow profit motives but rather tries to provide this service in an efficient quantity. This gain is, however, very likely to be offset by inefficiencies that public bodies bring with them. Without a profit motive, the resulting incentives in the publicly owned firm are weakened and inefficiencies are reintroduced.

In recent years, many publicly-owned monopolies in diverse industries have been privatized, and for-profit firms established in their place. In this form of ownership – the standard capitalist form most commonly analysed in economic theory – the residual decision rights are aligned with the residual claims, and better incentives are thereby conveyed. The public interest of the provision of the right quantity for the correct price in these network industries is better served by a regulator who has less decision power (and less potential for meddling) than an outright publicly-owned enterprise. The shift in control and power away from a public authority towards the private agents that use and provide the infrastructure increases overall welfare by nurturing better decisions because the resulting economic rents are exploitable by these decision-makers.

The third possible ownership arrangement is that of mutual ownership. In the mutual form, the users of the infrastructure provide the necessary investments themselves, so that the statically efficient quantity is produced for a price that is lower than the monopoly price. The direct users are members in the providing institution and take into account the supplementing function that the infrastructure has for the core business in which they ultimately want to generate economic rents. The amount of economic rent generated in such a mutually-owned institution is therefore lower compared to a for-profit firm, while inefficiencies are reduced in comparison with a publicly-owned and overregulated authority. Such a structure has its drawbacks, however. The membership of the mutual firm can ossify, and new entrants may be discouraged from using the same infrastructure. If the members are too heterogeneous, the governance of 'one member, one vote' instead of 'one share, one vote' can cause decisions to be distorted by the divergent interests, and the larger players can be held up by the smaller constituencies.[33] In recent years there has been a wave of demutualizations, especially among exchanges, because of these problems.[34]

Why are ownership and governance aspects important?

The governance of the infrastructure providers is of particular importance for the efficiency with which securities transactions are performed. The Council of Institutional Investors, representing 130 pension funds holding US$3 trillion in assets in the USA, criticizes the fact that of the three constituencies of the New York Stock Exchange – members (intermediaries like broker-dealers and specialists), listed companies and investors – only the members are allowed to vote and to choose the board. This structure has a potential negative effect on the self-regulation of the exchange, since that is biased towards the members' interests.[35]

The governance structure also influences the ability of a firm to innovate and to be efficient in a more dynamic sense. Too much power in the wrong hands hinders necessary innovation in the face of disruptive technologies. The introduction of electronic trading systems, for example, was heavily resisted by floor-based brokers, who have an important voice in the governance of exchanges. If these are not only the users of the infrastructure but can also exert power through a mutual ownership arrangement, they can block the innovations that would make them worse off but lead to big gains for other users.

Interdependencies in the action set

The three described action parameters are not independent of each other. We want to highlight some interdependencies here as a precursor to the comparative analysis of the three organizational designs in Section 5.6.

Boundary decisions and communication standards

Open standards are a means to credibly commit an institution performing a certain function in the securities transaction value chain not to pursue a foreclosure strategy through vertical integration. The leveraging of a natural monopoly at one stage of the value chain for a certain financial instrument cannot be used to force customers to use the infrastructure of the same institution in the previous or next stage in the value chain as well. The choice for customers and the threat of market entry by upstarts do not allow institutions to use their power to extract more than their 'fair' share of economic rents generated by the activities of the securities transaction value chain. This makes a strategy of vertical integration less attractive. On the contrary, in such a setting it would be necessary for the integrated institution to compete with many focused firms that know their activities by heart. Any advantage in terms of higher economic rents that these focused institutions can gain can only come from better service, which leads them to pursue a strategy that puts a premium on innovation. Even if the vertically integrated firm also pursued aggressive R&D activities, it would be faced with the dilemma of cannibalizing its own success whenever it came across an innovation at one stage of the securities transaction value chain that would force it to restructure the relationship between the integrated stages. The need to meddle with transfer prices weakens incentives for middle managers, or even leads to outright sabotage of the new product or process by the managers of a less innovative stage.

Ownership structure and communication standards

Economic rents can be generated by for-profit firms by using the ideas of industrial organization theory to structure the industry and thus make it more difficult to enter the market. One such tool is a proprietary standard, probably in combination with a strategy of vertical integration. In the other two ownership forms we described – public and mutual ownership – these incentives to foreclose the market by opting for a proprietary communication standard are not that prominent, since the appropriation possibilities of any rents generated are less good for the owners of such institutions. In the case of a publicly provided infrastructure of the natural monopoly functions, this institution will settle on its own (proprietary) standard, but fair access is usually granted by the provider of the public good. In the case of a mutual ownership structure, the tendency is for an open communication standard because the users themselves will gain from less diversity between different providers: in this case they have to invest only in one system to cope with data from numerous institutions in the other stages of the securities transaction value chain. However, incentives to develop the common standard and to take into account better possibilities in data exchange through broadband connections and better encryption and decompression algorithms are needed. One possibility is the use of open-source-like structures. Franck and Jungwirth (2003) see the advantage of such structures in donations that are made by interested constituencies without a crowding-out of valuable investments in the case of an emerging standard. Co-operatives are then a preferable organizational form that allows the establishment of a standard without the effects of competition that would lead to a fragmentation or to a lock-in into an inefficient system.[36]

Boundary decisions and ownership structure

Mutually owned organizations have their drawbacks in terms of slow decision-making and weakened incentives because of the lack of a profit motive. Vertical integration augments this disadvantage by making the organization even more complex. The users of the infrastructure for the securities transaction value chain are therefore more likely to set up several co-operatives, each highly focused along the value chain and probably having different members and relying on open standards for the exchange of information between them. The users themselves restrict the activities of a co-operative to the absolute minimum.

The solution of public ownership is more likely to be vertically integrated, but a sensible and economically minded policy-maker would again opt for a deconstruction of the value chain and private provision for the activities where this is the best option. Unregulated private organizations run in the best interests of their shareholders are very likely to pursue a strategy to shape the industry in their favour and to erect entry barriers whenever possible. As mentioned above, a foreclosure strategy of leveraging a monopoly position from one activity to the next makes perfect sense for such institutions. Privately owned companies are therefore likely to increase their scale and scope by integrating actively along the value chain when no countervailing forces prevail.

We have now outlined the constituents of our framework and discussed them in detail. In the following section we put these parameters together to concentrate on the systemic relationships between them that make some configurations more efficient than others when seen from a perspective of maximizing overall welfare.

5.5   Proposals for an efficient organizational design

Systems in general consist of various modules. Between these modules or elements there can be a complementary relationship. Complementarity between any two such elements implies that the simultaneous increase in both elements leads to an overall superior performance. In the case that such a complementary relation between the elements of a system exists, the right configuration of these modules matters. Only if they are adjusted for supermodularity will the design in question be internally consistent. Such a consistent system will perform better than any system in which deviations from the coherent configuration in one or a few parameters occur.[37]

This section presents three idealized systems where the configurations of selected elements, especially the parameters of the action set described above, are arranged so that the complementary relationship is taken into account and the overall system is efficient from the viewpoint of a benevolent system designer. Small deviations from the configurations suggested lead overall to a less efficient solution.

System 1 – Regulated monopoly

Description

The system of a regulated monopoly has two distinct features implied by its name: (i) there is no competition in the provision of the activities on those levels of the securities transaction value chain that are consolidated; and (ii) the role of the regulator is very pronounced in these stages. Usually the roles of regulators and providers are combined, and the infrastructure is publicly owned.

The horizontally consolidated and possibly even vertically integrated structure can take several forms depending on the scale of integration in each activity. In the USA, for example, the Depositories Trust & Clearing Corporation is the monopoly for clearing and settlement activities, and trading occurs on several exchanges. Many national markets in Europe were structured as a vertical silo with all three activities integrated into one entity. What are the advantages of such a system?

The consolidation in each activity allows the gaining of economies of scale and scope for the providers along the securities transaction value chain. Users, on the other hand, enjoy the strong benefits of a single network. The public ownership and the lack of competition lead to low incentives for innovation activity. The threat of entry is reduced, since the underlying economies as well as the publicly sanctioned role as the sole provider strengthen this institution.

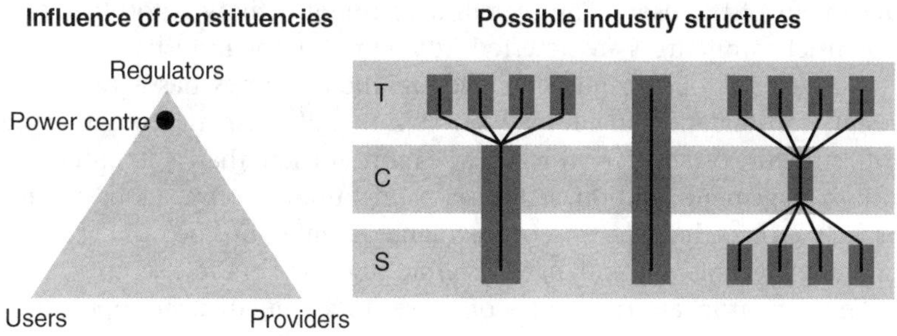

Influence of constituencies   **Possible industry structures**

Figure 5.1   Regulated monopoly
Note: T = trading; C = clearing; S = settlement.

Vertical integration enhances this entrenchment further, but leads also to the possibility of straight-through processing and an efficient use and dissemination of information from one stage of the value chain to the next. The low rate of innovation and the resulting stability in the industry makes it feasible to write detailed plans. The low innovation activity is also consistent with a low investment propensity among all players, and low total investments. The users of the infrastructure are willing to undertake the necessary co-specialized investments. The standardization process is organized by the regulator, which uses its powerful position to enforce and set the standard means of communication. The sum of total investments is low, since no company can compete with such a vertically integrated, publicly owned organization that uses the underlying economies of scale and scope.

Figure 5.1 provides an illustration of possible industry outcomes of a regulated monopoly as well as the position of the power centre between the constituencies.

Efficiency analysis

Static efficiency in these settings is relatively high because of the strong exploitation of network effects and economies of scale and scope. The significant market power of the providers has its counterweight in the public ownership structure, so that the inefficiencies of a monopoly do not prevail. However, the incentive structure within a big public agency also brings some costs in terms of lost efficiency. It depends on the actual processes and organizational structures of this body as to whether the combined effect is still positive.

Dynamic efficiency is quite low because of the lack of competition. The pressure for product or service innovations remains limited, to the detriment of the users. The overall investment activity is too low, and potential competitors are deterred from entering the industry.

The analysis of systemic efficiency in these settings has a two-sided result. Consolidation enables the centralization of risk management by the infrastructure providers – which can be more efficient than a decentralized risk management solution. However, as mentioned above, moral hazard aspects such as the reduction of risk management efforts because of a too-big-to-fail feeling may endanger systemic efficiency in these settings.

The regulators are the centre of power in a regulated monopoly system. Ideally, this should reduce potential moral hazard issues in risk management and ensure fair transaction prices for the users – that is, the users should benefit from exploited scale economies. However, regulation itself is costly, so that increasing systemic efficiency will lead to a loss in both static and dynamic efficiency. This organizational design is most notably interesting when static efficiency aspects outweigh dynamic considerations. This may be the case when disruptive innovations are expected to be rather rare in the future, and the processes in the industry are settled and stable.

System 2 – Competitive fragmentation

Description

In contrast to System 1, the market structure of System 2 is rather scattered – that is, it features polypolistic characteristics, including several providers for trading, clearing and settlement. A high level of competition at all stages of the securities transaction value chain leads to a high rate of technological innovation. The fragmented industry structure necessitates the use of open standards, since otherwise the users would have to undertake co-specialized investments to several providers. Open standards and good access possibilities allow new competitors to enter the market easily whenever they see fit. This is consistent with the high rate of innovation that is increased by such new entrants. The tendency to invest is high, since it can be the basis for Schumpeterian rents. The resulting overall investment level is therefore possibly too high when too many uncoordinated investments are undertaken. Overinvestment and a resulting bubble can lead to cycles of investments that exacerbate the economic cycle and the ups and downs of financial markets.

The ownership of these firms rests in private hands, since this is the most efficient incentive tool to sustain the necessary rate of technological progress to keep the system stable. The role of the regulators is very reserved; any exaggerated activity by them would lead to a lowering of investment incentives for the private companies, which would then have to worry about meddling by the regulators. The only activity they

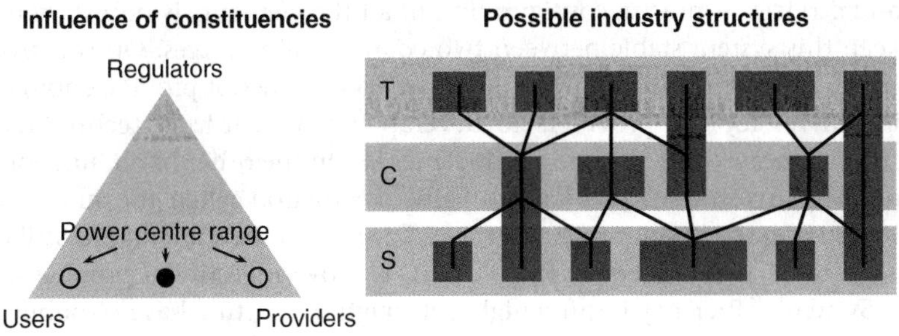

Influence of constituencies

Possible industry structures

Figure 5.2 Competitive fragmentation

Note: T = trading; C = clearing; S = settlement.

should engage in is to ensure the open access. Self-regulation by the competing providers is a means by which to differentiate themselves from competitors, and attract more users and a better competitive advantage. The epicentre of power lies with the privately-owned providers or with the users, depending on the providers' ownership structure. The tendency to integrate the securities transaction value chain vertically is low – cross-subsidies from one stage to the next are not possible because of the fierce competition at each stage, and the reluctance for change in such a vertically integrated institution that is faced with cannibalizing its own success whenever new processes or products occur, makes it a suboptimal solution.

Figure 5.2 provides an illustration of the industry setting as well as the position of the power centre.

Efficiency analysis

Static efficiency is low in this setting. The relatively small size of the providers does not allow for the benefit of economies of scale and scope. Also, positive network effects for the users remain unexploited because of the large number of smaller networks in this fragmented industry set-up. Consolidation efforts exist, but a constant stream of new industry entrants armed with innovative products and new services prevent the creation of one dominant monopoly. A system with several relatively small market participants prevails.

Dynamic efficiency, on the other hand, is high because of fierce competition and low entry barriers to the market. Open communication standards ensure that providers with better services will be able to offer their service to users without being hampered by established providers. Users such as banks can effectively threaten providers that they will internalize transactions should they not be satisfied with existing products and services. A precise configuration of all the elements is necessary to keep this system stable between two countervailing forces. On the one hand, an industry setting with open standards may not provide enough incentives for the providers to develop the standardized technology further because of free-riding inducements. On the other hand, uncoordinated investments can lead to value destruction when too much is invested in the boom times of a cycle. The system therefore has to strike a delicate balance between these under- and overinvestment problems.

Systemic efficiency is quite high. Although this setting has no (public) regulator and is mainly self-regulated, the robustness in the provision of securities transaction possibilities is nevertheless fairly high. The driving factor is the competition among providers – in this case, competition for the most stable and secure transaction system. Thus infrastructure providers have an incentive to compete on quality and create a safe TCS environment for their clients. However, an important precondition for this scenario is the transparency of the providers' risk management efforts to the users. If it is difficult for the latter to evaluate the quality of risk management, the providers may have the adverse incentive to boost profitability by cutting down on costly risk management procedures and endangering systemic efficiency. This race-to-the-bottom effect may be prevented by a user-dominated governance structure.

Another positive effect of the competitive fragmentation on systemic efficiency is that the fragmented market structure that is characterized by high levels of infrastructure redundancies and open standards enables a relatively easy re-routing of transactions in cases of emergency. Ample substitution possibilities for the users and low switching costs because of open communication standards ensure systemic robustness in times of failure of one institution. However, depending on the nature of an adverse systemic event, contagion between the different transaction systems may occur, and thus neutralize the positive redundancy aspects.

A system of competitive fragmentation is particularly interesting in a dynamically changing environment when returns on innovations are high and static efficiency considerations dominated by dynamic efficiency aspects.

System 3 – Contestable monopolies

Description

There are two crucial characteristics to the third system we propose: (i) the market for infrastructure providers is more or less consolidated; and (ii) communication between the industry participants – both horizontally and vertically – is performed via open standards. New entrants to the market are able to communicate with the others and are granted access to established providers. The efficient size with respect to scale and scope economies limits the number of direct competitors on each horizontal stage, and natural monopolies prevail. The users benefit from the merits of a single large network. Vertical integration is rather detrimental in such a system, since the monopoly positions at different stages could be used strategically by the providers to reinforce rent extraction possibilities in other activities, to the disadvantage of the users. Two possibilities exist by which such behaviour can be ruled out: first, a public regulator can ensure open access and limit any vertical integration attempts; and second, the users themselves can mutually own the necessary infrastructure and restrict such behaviour by the management of the provider in question. Depending on which concept is used to restrict the infrastructure provider from capturing too large a share of the economic rents, the epicentre of power is somewhere between the regulators and the users.

Open standards and guaranteed access allow new entrants to enter the market and further limit the rent appropriation potential of the incumbent. With better products or processes they are in a good position to challenge the incumbent and eventually to gain the upper hand. The rate of technological progress and innovation is therefore higher than in System 1 of a regulated monopoly. The investment propensity and total investment are higher, since the incumbent has to keep up with the innovative progress or risks becoming obsolete and losing his/her position to an upstart. Again, self-regulation can be a means of competition, with better quality and stability gaining an advantage. This allows the reduction of public regulation and its associated costs.

Figure 5.3 shows idealized industry structures as an analogy to System 1. The boxes with dashed lines illustrate potential new entrants into the industry.

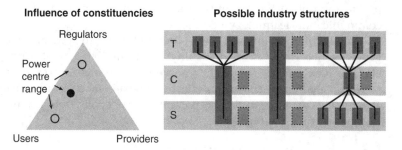

Figure 5.3   Contestable monopolies
Note: T = trading; C = clearing; S = settlement.

Efficiency analysis

Static efficiency in a system of contestable monopolies is enhanced in this setting because of the high level of consolidation in the three stages of the value chain. The existence of a quasi-monopolistic infrastructure enables the full exploitation of existing economies of scale and scope, and network effects. Static efficiency gains are passed on to the users in this system, as each level on the value chain is contestable to market entries because of open communication standards. Furthermore, the costs of regulation can be kept to a minimum and do not distort investment incentives for the providers.

Dynamic efficiency is also high and is achieved by the open standards architecture which results in contestability in each activity and low barriers to entry. This prevents the existing monopolist from appropriating too large a portion of the monopoly rent, as potential entrants with better service offerings pose an effective threat. Nevertheless, some barriers to entry, such as liquidity, still exist in a particular security at the trading level and allow a monopolist to benefit from rents from his dominant market position. These rents further ensure that the incumbent has a strong incentive to maintain this position, and to react to the incentives provided by it. As mentioned in Section 5.4, there are also some drawbacks to open communication standards with regard to dynamic efficiency aspects, such as potential free-riding behaviour, in the development of innovations.

Systemic efficiency is high in this system; it benefits from being sufficiently consolidated and having open communication standards. The former aspect enables the industry to centralize its risk management in one institution, while the latter ensures competition for the most stable transaction system, so that the quasi-monopolist is forced to maintain a high quality of risk management in order not to lose users to other providers. Additionally, open communication standards enable a wider proliferation of knowledge on the transmission of transaction data. As communication technology becomes common knowledge, it is likely that market participants will react faster and better to systemic emergency events. However, contestability of the market may also bring along adverse aspects such as the race-to-the-bottom incentives for the provider, mentioned above. An effective no-bail-out commitment by governments or central banks may prevent the monopolist from assuming him/herself to be too big to fail.

5.6   Comparative organizational analysis

The three systems described above are all consistent systems that maximize social welfare in the sense that an incremental deviation from the configuration of its elements would not lead to further improvements. As such, they are better than the inefficient industry structure employed at the time of writing in the European securities transaction industry, which both fails to capture the static efficiency benefits from a full-blown consolidation and the dynamic efficiency gains from competitive fragmentation. In this section we compare the three systems derived from our framework and evaluate their relative merits and drawbacks to come to a conclusion as to which system policy-makers in the EU should strive to implement. In particular, we pose the following questions:

- How robust are these three systems when small deviations from the optimal configuration occur, and how likely is a system to deteriorate into an inconsistent system that is inefficient given the micro-motives of the different constituencies?
- Which of the three systems dominates the other two if social welfare is to be maximized; that is, which system is the global optimum?

Stability of the systems and the threat of inefficient systems

The first system of a regulated monopoly is very stable and not in danger of falling apart easily once its elements are configured in a consistent way. By its ownership of the infrastructure providers or by the power it devolves to its regulators, the government makes a credible commitment to staying in the system. New entrants cannot upset the system, and the incumbent monopolist has only weak incentives to engage in innovative activities. The stability itself puts a positive feedback into the system, since long-range planning and routinization become possible, which lower the cost imposed by regulations.

The system is not likely to deteriorate into an inefficient system: in many European countries dominant regulated monopolies along the securities transaction value chain ensured that the underlying economies of scale and scope could benefit the domestic level without incurring a too big a social welfare loss, because of efficient regulation. By striking the right balance between these costs, securities trading, clearing and settlement in national markets are highly efficient, at least from a static and systemic point of view. History has shown that such a system needs a very big shock – such as the integration of formerly separate financial markets into the single European one – to overcome its inertia.

The second system of competitive fragmentation is not very stable, and small deviations from the consistent configuration can lead to a deterioration into an inefficient setting. If, for example, too many unco-ordinated investments are undertaken, the problem of overinvestment arises. If a bubble builds and subsequently bursts because of a sufficient macroeconomic shock, it can force these investors to sell many assets below their value. Many providers become insolvent and are forced to leave the industry. A consolidation process is started by the institutions that are in a better position.

These firms start to consolidate horizontally to achieve greater economies of scale and increase the degree of static efficiency. They also integrate vertically to safeguard this horizontal expansion and to leverage the resulting market power. Since all institutions concentrate on becoming financially sound again, the rate of technological innovation drops, new entries look less attractive, and the whole system can evolve into one of the other systems or fall into inefficiency if no regulation is introduced to keep the market contestable or if the ownership is reorganized to a more mutual structure (which is a less likely possibility). The surviving institutions can extract too much of the economic rent, and their monopoly power is not compensated by a regulator.

The third system of contestable monopolies is equally hard to sustain. A monopolist at one stage of the securities transaction value chain might be tempted to integrate forwards or backwards. Such a merger of two dominant monopolies might look good at first sight: by integrating the two institutions, the communication between them can be streamlined, and straight-through processing might be facilitated, to the benefit of the users. Open access is guaranteed by the acquiring institution and formally assured by the small regulator. However, the realization might look different in practice and many potential entrants are deterred by the more entrenched position of the merged institution. This protection induces the incumbent to divert its efforts towards rent-seeking and engage in investments in the 'open' communication standard that slightly favours its own business. If regulation is not adjusted accordingly towards a stronger regime, such an institution can lower the overall amount of economic rent that is generated, thereby decreasing social welfare. At the same time, it can gain an economic rent for itself that is bigger than it would be in a consistently configured system at the expense of a relatively larger loss in the economic rents that the users can enjoy.

Like the system of competitive fragmentation, the system of contestable monopolies is likely to deteriorate when even small deviations from the consistent configuration occur. The micro-motives of the infrastructure providers will generally lead to a situation in which a monopoly prevails that is entrenched through vertical integration, a proprietary communication standard, and an ownership structure that places too little weight on the benefit of the users and society as a whole. Such a mixture of different configurations will not maximize overall welfare.

Evaluation of the systems and global optimum

So far we have not discussed whether one of the idealized systems is better than the others. Calculating an exact figure for social welfare in each of the three systems is almost impossible: too many parameters would need to be measured, and too many errors would be made in measuring the efficiency of the organizational design. We therefore restrict ourselves to indications only. Which of the three systems might be the global optimum that dominates the others? The system of a regulated monopoly produces at an efficient level, so that economies of scale and scope can be gained. However, it fares poorly when dynamic aspects of efficiency are taken into account. No investment incentives are set, and the cost of regulation or public ownership further decreases the overall welfare generated by this system.

The system of competitive fragmentation scores especially highly when aspects of dynamic efficiency are important. However, because of the small scale of the providers, too little of the underlying economies are utilized. The system also suffers from co-ordination problems between the different firms, so that too many duplicate and incompatible investments are undertaken. The system of contestable monopolies does not have these drawbacks once configured in a consistent way: a small number of institutions deploy the underlying economies of scale and scope, and the limited role of the regulator also ensures that these costs are kept to a minimum. The market stays open for new entrants, so that improvements resulting from innovations do not need to be forgone.

This guesstimate leads to the conclusion that the third system of contestable monopolies is the best and should be implemented in the TCS industry in the EU. A caveat must be applied, since this system is of a rather unstable nature and likely to slide down towards an inefficient system of unregulated monopoly if not adjusted in a consistent way. Table 5.1 summarizes the merits and drawbacks of the three systems.

The transformation of the securities transaction industry

The introduction of the Single European Market was a strong catalyst that upset the system of a regulated monopoly many European countries had in place. Many features of the established system were suddenly and simultaneously changed. By simply opening the markets and leaving everything else unchanged, the result, however, is inefficient. Too many inconsistent configurations of important elements are in

Table 5.1 Comparison of the three idealized TCS (trading, clearing and settlement) systems

	Regulated monopoly	Competitive fragmentation	Contestable monopolies
Action set			
Boundary decision	Strong horizontal consolidation, vertical integration, STP possibility, no need for transfer prices	Low horizontal consolidation, vertical integration detrimental: cross-subsidies and cannibalization effects	Strong horizontal consolidation, vertical integration detrimental: incentive to appropriate open standard
Standard/ accessibility	Proprietary standard, closed system	Open standard, open access	Open standard, regulated access
Ownership/ governance	Public ownership, not for profit, heavy public regulation	Private ownership, for profit, self-regulation as parameter of competition	Private ownership (possibly as mutual), for profit; 'regulation light' or self-regulation
Constituencies			
Users	Low level of decision-making power (DMP), low investment propensity	Low to medium level of DMP, (too) high investment propensity	High level of DMP if mutual ownership, otherwise lower; low to medium investment propensity

Providers	Very few players (possibly only one), low to medium level of DMP, low investment propensity	Many players, high level of DMP, high investment propensity	Very few players, low to medium level of DMP, low to medium investment propensity
Regulators	High level of DMP	Very low level of DMP	Medium level of DMP if providers are not mutually owned, otherwise lower
Comparative analysis			
Static efficiency	High because of realized economies, lessened by regulatory costs	Low because of unrealized economies	High because of realized economies, low regulatory costs
Dynamic efficiency	Very low because of lack of competition, low technological progress, high entry barriers	Very high because of competition, high technological progress, low entry barriers	High because of threat from potential competitors, medium technological progress, low to medium entry barriers
Systemic efficiency	High because of centralized risk management, possible moral hazard problems	High because of redundancies and open standards, lessened by low co-ordination among players (overinvestment)	High because of centralized risk management; moral hazard issues unlikely because of entry threat by potential competitors
System stability	Rather robust against changes in parameters	Robust as long as high degree of innovation is existent, bubble-prone	Rather fragile; precise configuraion necessary; regulation must ensure accessibility for potential competitors

place; too many regulators increase the costs and thereby decrease social welfare. Publicly owned or heavily regulated institutions do not have the incentives to make the right decisions. And previously vertically integrated institutions can bar others from using parts of their infrastructure. Divergent objectives of the many regulators, or unhealthy competition between them, decreases efficiency even further.

The response by many regulators was to withdraw a little and let the market mechanism work. The system in the securities industry in the EU in the 1990s therefore had some characteristics of a system of competitive fragmentation: the rate of innovations such as automated trading and the demutualization of exchanges increased dramatically, and many new entrants tried to do business in the industry. The total amount of new investments was high, and duplication of investments occurred in the process of battling for the dominant position in a segment of the market. The users were fully aware of the costs imposed by the incompatible communication standards between the national institutions, and tried to shape the industry to their liking.

Now that the investment boom is over and the rate of technological progress has receded a little, the securities industry in the EU is again at a crossroads. The rate of consolidation – horizontally as well as vertically – remains high, and many unsuccessful ventures are forced to close and leave the industry. New entrants who could keep up the pressure to innovate cannot be seen. The surviving providers try to entrench their monopoly position by vertical integration and proprietary communication standards.

It is an open question how, and if, their rent appropriation possibilities will be countered either by tougher regulations that would place the European securities industry back in a system of regulated monopoly (although now at the European level) or whether the users of the infrastructure can ensure together with a cut-down regulator that a system of contestable monopolies can be reached, which is our policy advice. It is crucial that a consistent configuration of key parameters is achieved, to avoid a system with a quasi-unregulated monopoly that might be preferred by infrastructure providers but certainly not by the users and society at large.

Notes

1. Lannoo and Levin (2001, pp. 14–30) and Deutsche Börse Group and Clearstream International (2002, pp. 15–29) present a cost analysis of cross-border transactions.
2. Cruickshank (2003).

3. Seifert (2003, p. 82).
4. See Lamfalussy (2001).
5. See Giovannini Group (2001) and Giovannini Group (2003) for details of these barriers in different areas.
6. See European Shadow Financial Regulatory Committee (2001).
7. See Committee on Payment and Settlement Systems and International Organization of Securities Commissions (2001).
8. See Committee of European Securities Regulators and European Central Bank (2004).
9. These issues in particular were raised by the G30, an international body composed of senior figures from both the private and public sectors, and academia.
10. The European Association of Central Counterparty Clearing Houses (EACH) was one of the initiators of this point.
11. See, for example, the White Paper by Deutsche Börse Group (2005), which describes the post-trade market. While trying to influence policy-making, such efforts are often rather biased.
12. See Serifsoy and Weiss (2003).
13. See also Rochet and Tirole (2003).
14. Custody functions follow the settlement process. These ensure the distribution of coupon payments, the implementation of corporate actions and the lending of securities as well as the trading-induced transfer of ownership. We shall subsume these transaction-induced custody aspects under settlement activity and ignore the other services in custody. Taking into account all aspects of custody would add to the complexity, while providing only limited value-added for our purposes.
15. For a detailed discussion on network externalities, see Shapiro and Varian (1999, pp. 173–225).
16. See Economides (1993, p. 92).
17. The terminology used is adapted from de Bandt and Hartmann (2000), albeit the authors discuss this issue in much greater depth. See de Bandt and Hartmann (2000, pp. 10–17) for further details.
18. Banks and brokers are the main institutions using the infrastructure as immediate users. They play a pivotal role in the securities transaction value chain for institutional as well as retail investors on the one side, and for companies with their underwriting business on the other. By internalizing security transactions and acting as subcustodians, banks are to a certain degree also direct competitors of the infrastructure providers. A model of the competitive relationship between CSDs and custodians can be found in Holthausen and Tapking (2004).
19. The pivotal role of liquidity stems from the potentially large costs that can arise from illiquidity during trading. According to the Deutsche Börse Group and Clearstream International (2002, pp. 17–22) their proportion of total trading costs is substantial. Liquidity can be characterized along four dimensions – namely, width, depth, immediacy and resilience; see Harris (1991, p. 3). For a model of such two-sided markets, see Rochet and Tirole (2003).
20. However, he confines his findings to very large stock exchanges. See Malkamäki (1999) for further details.
21. See van Cauwenberge (2003, p. 94).

22. This view is shared by Economides (1993, pp. 92–3). He states that, as a consequence of the reinforcing nature, a financial 'network exhibits positive critical mass'. A further consequence of networks 'is that history matters ... because of significant switching costs' which protect established players in the market.

23. See Giovannini Group (2001, pp. 18–19) and de Bandt and Hartmann (2000).

24. See Diamond (1984) on the use of such delegated monitoring as a rationale for the existence of banks.

25. See de Bandt and Hartmann (2000, p. 17) for further details.

26. See Williamson (1985) for the role of specificity in explaining vertical integration.

27. The detrimental effect of vertical integration on horizontal consolidation between different infrastructure providers at the same stage of the securities transaction value chain is formalized by Koeppl and Monnet (2004) in a mechanism design model taking into account the asymmetry of information between the different players.

28. The London Clearing House has recently teamed up with Euronext's Clearnet, and Crest merged with Euroclear in 2002.

29. The battle for a unique communication standard and the different competing approaches are described in Weitzel *et al.* (2003).

30. One could also imagine a situation where a proprietary standard is used. In this case, the outcome would be a hybrid solution along the lines of Williamson (1985): long-term contracts or strategic alliances are necessary to account for the hold-up problem, since specific investments have to be made.

31. See also Milne (2002) who proposes to regulate access to the book transfer (which would fall under the notion of settlement in our argument) as he identifies it as the natural monopoly within the clearing and settlement industry.

32. There is a strong interdependency and complementarity between accessibility, communication standards and the vertical boundary decisions of the providers: we observe the tendency that a vertically integrated firm often employs a proprietary standard with restricted access, while a vertically focused firm prefers open standards and open accessibility.

33. Hart and Moore (1996) present a model in which the heterogeneity of users makes a mutual structure less preferable.

34. See also Domowitz and Steil (1999, pp. 14–16) on this issue.

35. See *The Economist* (2003c, p. 59) for this example.

36. For a theoretical underpinning of co-operatives and their investment incentives in emerging standards, see the work of Rey and Tirole (2001).

37. Recall that, mathematically, complementarity relates to a positive cross-derivative: the first-order returns for the increase in one element are further enhanced if the second element is also increased. Consistency is the characteristic where any pairwise combination between any two elements has a non-negative cross-derivative – also referred to as a supermodular relationship – between them. See Section 2.2 and Topkis (1998) for a mathematical approach.

6
The German Co-operative Banking Group

6.1 Introduction

Different organizational designs have often evolved over time for the performance of the same economic or social activity. Such different organizational arrangements can also be found in the provision of financial services. By applying the methodology of comparative organizational analysis, crucial differences between different economic systems can be established. This chapter follows this path by comparing a publicly listed bank (the Deutsche Bank) with the co-operative banking group in Germany. It is striking that the biggest German bank, Deutsche Bank, had total assets of €804 billion at the end of 2003, whereas the credit co-operatives with their central banks and other special finance companies in their group had an aggregated, non-consolidated total assets of approximately €988 billion. This is because the co-operative banking group is not a single legal entity but is made up of about 1,400 independent banks. And this is not the only difference. Also in respect of their strategy, organizational structure, owners and corporate governance, and, last but not least, an understanding of why they are in business at all, the organizational designs differ remarkably.[1] In this chapter, the different structures and processes that make up the different organizational designs are compared, and the questions of whether one banking group is more efficient than the other, or whether both institutions have advantages and disadvantages, are answered. The investigation undertaken in this chapter takes into account the organizational designs as seen in the period 2000 to 2003. A slightly modified version of this chapter has been published previously as Weiss (2005).

Related literature

A lot of work on German co-operative banks is carried out by a specialized chair at the University of Münster. Theurl and Kring (2002), for example, describe the governance structures of various banks operating in the German co-operative banking group. For selected institutions at all levels of the German co-operative banking group, they list the formal and informal arrangements that shape the governance of the institution in question, and the governance of the whole net of institutions. In particular, the use of different legal by-laws allows for a fine-tuned governance of each individual entity but also for a delicate set of checks and balances in the whole group.

Greve (2002) has a similar approach to analysing the German co-operative banking group. By applying insights from the new institutional economics literature, he shows that the co-operative form is an efficient institution when asymmetric information about the creditworthiness of clients prevails. Using the same argument, he shows that the formation of a co-operative banking group with central banking institutions is an effective response for dealing with that uncertainty. The imminent hold-up problem that any specific investment of small co-operative banks causes to the monopoly of the central bank can be dealt with through the assignment of the ownership of the central bank to the local credit co-operatives. Greve (2002) sees the principle of membership and the identity of members and customers as the core competence of the credit co-operatives.

This case study goes beyond that narrow focus on governance aspects in the German co-operative banking group. By contrasting the co-operative banking group, as one organizational design for performing an economic activity, with another design – the Deutsche Bank as a firm more in line with traditional economic theory – it analyses whether both ways to produce and distribute financial services are efficient and consistent systems. The governance of co-operatives can be only one element in such a corporate system. Of equal importance are the strategies pursued and the purposes fulfilled by the economic system as well as the allocation of power in the system conveyed either at a micro level by the internal structure or at the macro level by corporate governance.

Deutsche Bank

Deutsche Bank AG was founded in 1870 in Berlin 'to transact banking business of all kinds, in particular to promote and facilitate trade relations between Germany, other European countries, and overseas markets'.[2] Spreading out from its headquarters, it has opened branches in all the important German cities as well as in major capitals abroad. Over the years it has grown to become the market leader in Germany in many areas of banking and asset management, and has become a respectable bank with global ambitions. The bank has approximately 503,000 shareholders, with the bulk (82 per cent) of its shares being held by institutional investors. The bank serves more than 13 million customers, for personal and private banking, in more than 1,500 branches, mainly in Germany and the EU. In addition, many institutional investors rely on Deutsche Bank to manage their assets. In recent years, Deutsche Bank has made considerable efforts to build up an investment banking division by acquiring first the London-based Morgan Grenfell and later a US bank, Bankers Trust. At the end of 2003, the bank employed 67,682 people, of which more than half worked outside Germany. The corporate culture of Deutsche Bank is geared towards performance, and leadership plays a strong role in the group: both issues are manifested in the bank's former slogan 'Leading to results' and the current one, 'A passion to perform'.

The co-operative banking group

'In terms of the number of people, co-operatives are the largest economic organization in Germany with approximately 20 million members. Co-operative banks represent the largest group of co-operative companies with 15 million members and 200,000 employees.'[3] The co-operative banks rest on the idea of Friedrich Wilhelm Raiffeisen, that what the individual cannot achieve alone may become possible for the many. In 1850, Hermann Schulze-Delitzsch founded the first Volksbank in Saxony. He later described this experience in a publication that led to the autonomous foundation of many local banks based on these principles. The credit co-operatives grew locally, and the top tier was established later, but only when a need for these institutions emerged.[4] At the end of 2003 there were 1,393 independent co-operative banks (*Kreditgenossenschaften*) with an average volume of total assets of €406.5 million. They are supported by two central banks (DZ Bank, the product of a merger of DG Bank and GZ Bank in September 2001, and WGZ-Bank), three mortgage banks (DG Hyp, WL Bank and Münchner Hypothekenbank), Germany's biggest building society with a market share of 25 per cent (Bausparkasse Schwäbisch Hall), one insurance company (R + V), the third-biggest German investment funds manager (Union Investment, DIFA, and DEVIF together in the Union-Fonds-Holding AG) and several special finance companies for leasing (VR Leasing), factoring and other financial services – for example, the BAG

Bankaktiengesellschaft in Hamm, for problem loans. This *Finanzverbund* is completed by four companies performing IT services (for example, Fiducia) and by the seven regional associations (*Genossenschaftsverband*) that perform consulting and auditing services for their members. The credit co-operatives are organized in the Bundesverband der Volks- und Raiffeisenbanken (BVR – Federal Association of German Co-operative Banks).

In total, the co-operative banks and their top-tier institutions have around 15,000 branches and offices in Germany (down from 17,500 in 2000) serving 30 million customers. With a market share of roughly 18 per cent of client deposits in Germany in April 2004, the credit co-operatives and their two central banks were second only to the savings banks – also a group of independent banks structured in a similar fashion to the co-operative banking group. The four biggest private banks together (among them Deutsche Bank) had a share of 14.4 per cent in deposits. In loans to private households and corporations, the big four had a market share of 12.7 per cent, compared to 16.1 per cent of the co-operative banking group.[5] Table 6.1 provides key figures for both banking groups for the period 2001 to 2003.

Methodology

The goals of this chapter are the description of the different organizational designs that the two banking groups have chosen as their business model, and a comparative analysis to decide whether one organizational design is superior to the other in terms of economic performance. The emphasis is put on the co-operative banking group as being the business

Table 6.1   Key facts and figures for the banking groups

	Deutsche Bank			Co-operative banking group		
	2001	2002	2003	2001	2002	2003
Total assets[a]	918,222	758,355	803,614	903,000	909,000	890,000
Income before tax[a]	1,803	3,549	2,756	0.37%[b]	0.47%[b]	0.52%[b]
Number of						
customers	12,000,000	12,500,000	13,000,000	30,000,000	30,000,000	30,000,000
shareholders	523,059	512,519	503,000	15,154,624	15,184,846	15,281,857
employees	94,782	77,442	67,682	170,000	170,000	175,000
branches	2,099	1,711	1,576	16,707	15,866	14,979

Notes: [a] in € millions
        [b] of total assets of primary banks

Source: Annual Reports of Deutsche Bank and BVR.

model less in line with standard economic theory. The publicly listed Deutsche Bank is used as a reference point and benchmark, since in this business model performance measures such as profit are much more pronounced.

The methodology used for this comparative organizational analysis is that of systems theory. A system consists of various elements that share certain characteristics. One such characteristic can be a complementary relationship between two elements. Mathematically, this amounts to a positive cross-derivative or a supermodular relation between these two elements.[6] From the viewpoint of economics, this characteristic leads to the fact that increasing one element also increases the benefit from increasing the other as well. If many elements form a complementary relationship with each other, the right configuration of all is important for the proper functioning of the whole system. Such a system that makes use of the complementarity between its various modules is a consistent system. No small deviation in the configuration of any single element can lead to a better performance of the whole system but impairs the success of the system by making it inconsistent. If such complementary relationships prevail among the elements, a co-ordinated configuration becomes necessary. This is the issue of organizational design.

The first authors to use this mathematical approach in the realm of economics were Milgrom and Roberts (1990b). They showed how the Japanese system of manufacturing, as applied by Toyota, was indeed a design with the main parameters configured in a consistent way. In the area of banking, Aoki and Patrick (1994) applied this thinking to describe the Japanese banking system. The various contributors in Krahnen and Schmidt (2004) use this methodology to describe the merits of the German financial system. A comparison between the different financial systems in Europe is provided by Schmidt *et al.* (2002). For the use of this methodology in the context of corporations as systems, see Roberts (2004) and see the theory of organizational design developed in the first part of this book. The organizational design of consistent systems is usually a bimodal distribution with two distinct configurations. In this case study the two systems in question are the organizational designs of Deutsche Bank and the co-operative banking group. Such consistent systems are local optima: any incremental variation in only one element will lead to inferior performance in the system as a whole.

The idea of combining the framework of comparative organizational analysis with systems theory can provide an answer to whether one consistent system is better than the other – that is, whether a global optimum exists. In the context of this case study, this translates into a question of whether the organizational design of Deutsche Bank or the co-operative banking group is more efficient.

Outline

Section 6.2 analyses in depth the question as to which strategy these organizations pursue and how this strategy is reflected in the respective structures – either internally within the confines of one large bank or over the external boundaries of many smaller ones. The issue of corporate governance of the two organizational designs is dealt with in Section 6.3. Here, the questions of how control is allocated and how leadership is exercised are analysed. In both sections, a short description of the benchmark of Deutsche Bank is given, before concentrating on the configuration of the elements in the organizational design of the co-operative banking group. Section 6.4 compares in which situations one or the other arrangement has an advantage, or whether one organizational design must be seen as grossly inefficient.

6.2   Strategy and internal structure

Deutsche Bank

Strategy and business understanding

Deutsche Bank is structured as a virtual holding company with two business groups: a 'Corporate and Investment Bank' and 'Private Client and Asset Management'. The strategy Deutsche pursues with this concept is customer-focused, with both business groups closely connected to create substantial revenue and cost synergies.[7] With the new concept, however, the responsibility for information technology (IT) infrastructure was decentralized to the two business groups 'to enable product and client-related IT developments to be implemented faster and more efficiently.'[8] From the remaining parts of the virtual holding structure Corporate Centre and Corporate Investments perform crucial tasks such as planning, controlling and managing the industrial holdings and venture capital activities, while DB Services is open to attract business volume in scale-intensive activities from other banks as well.

Internal structure of the bank

Deutsche Bank's structure is centralized, with important strategic and operational decisions being made in its corporate or divisional headquarters in Frankfurt or – in the case of investment banking – in the more important markets such as London and New York. Deutsche Bank pursues a strategy with global ambitions. Having acquired Morgan Grenfell and Bankers Trust, it directs many resources into the investment banking business with its potentially higher margins. In the annual rankings of the investment banking business, Deutsche Bank has climbed in recent years into the 'bulge bracket' and looks well-positioned to cater for the largest clients on a worldwide basis. Unlike some of its Wall Street rivals, it is backed by a huge balance sheet that allows intermediate financing of a client in the short and medium term whenever market conditions do not allow an immediate issue of securities in the capital markets.

Human resource policy and career paths

Human capital at Deutsche Bank is well qualified to meet the goal set by the overall strategic direction; more than half of all employees are university graduates. The responsibility for training and the acquisition of necessary skills is left mainly to the individual, but certain executive development programmes, together with Ashridge Management College and Duke University exist, with Deutsche Bank sponsoring some of the expenses. Deutsche Bank states on its website: 'A new view of career is gaining importance: development of one's own capabilities, expanding the basis of one's knowledge, and gaining prestige for one's abilities, knowledge, and personality.'[9] This emphasizes the acquisition of general rather than bank-specific knowledge, and puts weight on the employability of its human resources.[10]

Consistent with the relatively high degree of decision-making power, the human resource policy is shaped by equity-based compensation elements such as the DB Share Scheme and DB Global Share Plan for top managers. The value of such compensation is subject to change related to market conditions or poor performance: in 2003, the bank released €20 million in earnings related to amounts previously accrued for such options.[11] This exposes employees to risks, which in turn leads to the self-selection of people applying to work with Deutsche Bank. Employees in general are encouraged to buy shares of Deutsche Bank through a special scheme, with 65 per cent of employees participating in it worldwide in 2000. Even at the retail level, pay-for-performance schemes were introduced for unionized workers at around this time.[12] The idea behind this strong emphasis on variable pay elements and high empowerment is to encourage innovation in products and processes.

Although there are established career paths within Deutsche Bank and an up-or-out rule, at least in the investment banking division, it does not operate a strict internal labour market. Too much emphasis on growth via acquisitions and much restructuring prohibit the effective use of this. A further sign that Deutsche Bank is not committed to such an internal labour market is the appointment of the spokesman of the board at the time of writing, Josef Ackermann, who joined Deutsche Bank only in 1996 on leaving Crédit Suisse.[13] Economic theory predicts that in such an environment implicit contracts about future promotions are not good as instruments to give incentives to either employees or management. Incentives must therefore be provided by pay-for-performance and stock options, as mentioned above, which is consistent with the emphasis on employability.

The co-operative banking group

Strategy and business understanding

The strategy for the co-operative banking group as a whole is formulated and co-ordinated by their association, the Bundesverband der Volks- und Raiffeisenbanken (BVR).[14] The new strategy of 'Concentrating Forces' was endorsed overwhelmingly by 97 per cent of the members of the BVR at their 2001 general meeting. Seven special projects[15] were started, to deal with particular problems. Teams were built with people from many *Finanzverbund* institutions. In all the teams, the representatives of the local banks are the biggest group. Responsibilities for these projects and co-ordination is undertaken by the BVR, the regional associations, the central banks or the IT services – whichever the greatest competence.

An understanding of why the co-operative banks are in business is stated by one of the largest credit co-operatives on its website: 'The cooperative form rests on a special principle. For us as a cooperative bank the pursuit of profit in a shareholder-value sense is not everything. More important is the economic advancement of our members ... Our responsibility to our members does not only include the payment of an attractive dividend. It also involves a strong orientation towards our business area and the accompanying of our target group – the entrepreneurial and private middle class.'[16]

At the top level, the DZ Bank describes its role as follows: '[I]t is the central clearing bank, liquidity manager, and service provider for the local co-operative banking sector. As a group it also covers business involving investments, mortgage banks, savings and loans as well as leasing, factoring, insurance, and financing for equity capital and projects. These services are provided by specialists in the subsidiaries in Germany and abroad.'[17]

Both statements have in common that profitability is only seen as a necessity to stay in business. The more important goal lies in fostering the interests of their members and helping their clients (or, from the perspective of the central institutions, the local credit co-operatives) to succeed.

Internal structure of the group

In its annual report, the BVR makes the following statement about the structure of the *Finanzverbund:* 'The ideal of the cooperative banking group is and will be the legally and economically autonomous Volksbank or Raiffeisenbank in its local community. The cooperative banking group is no concern, and it will not become one in the future. The autonomy of the BVR members and its agents remains untouched.'[18]

The structure of the German co-operative banking group is decentralized. At the end of 2003 there were 1,393 Volks- und Raiffeisenbanken, the local credit co-operatives that are independent legal entities. Their 15 million members are the ultimate owners of the whole co-operative banking group, since the shares of the central banks are held by the primary banks. The majority of the special financial institutions are in turn controlled jointly by the central banks and the local credit co-operatives, or are subsidiaries of the central institutions.

The role of the local credit co-operatives is to promote the business and welfare of its members by offering them the best products. They have the local knowledge to make the right decisions for this goal and to give the best advice to their customers. Therefore, the marketing of financial products is in the realm of the local co-operative banks. They specialize in serving their customers in the best way.

The role of the central banks in the organization is that of an agent to the small autonomous units that make up the *Finanzverbund*: 'According to its statutes, DZ Bank's traditional mandate is to promote the German co-operative system. It supports its partner banks in times of high credit demand or of excess liquidity and provides them with the whole multitude of products and banking services because it would be inefficient to let every local credit co-operative develop these individually.'[19] DZ Bank sees its main tasks as performing the central bank function for the 1,131 Volksbanken und Raiffeisenbanken in its area, and to carry out all commercial bank functions in Germany and abroad for them and their clients.

The role of the special financing institutions is to build up expertise in various areas of financial services. They develop new products such as mutual funds, insurances, and special finance (such as factoring and leasing) and concentrate on the efficient execution of related tasks. It is here that the special knowledge about products and the legal and tax environment resides. These special organizations act as a centre of competence within the *Finanzverbund*, and their number is growing, as recent formations of new companies and the outsourcing of various activities show.

Human resource policy and career paths

Most employees in the local credit co-operatives are from that particular region and know their customers not only through business but also meet them regularly in their social lives. Unlike employees from the Deutsche Bank who are often 'imported' from another branch and have many incentives and outside options to leave for another job after a few years, the employees in the credit co-operatives show a greater loyalty to their bank. Meaningful relationships between customers and their bankers can develop and often endure for many generations. The co-operative banks rely less on university graduates but put more emphasis on the apprenticeship system, with subsequent training done within the *Finanzverbund* by the Akademie Deutscher Genossenschaften (ADG), or provided by external sources at a level below that of universities. This fits well into the internal labour market that the *Finanzverbund* operates for the directors of the local banks, their central banks and their association. The president of the BVR at the time of writing, for example, has worked in the DG Bank and institutions that previously merged with it before being appointed to the top job at the BVR. The Bankaktiengesellschaft AG in Hamm, a centre of competence for bad loans, as another example, sent several employees in 2000 to work on a temporary basis as executives in the top management of other banks.[20]

Systemic features in the co-operative banking group

The deconstruction of the value chain that is so popular today among many big industrial groups has been in place in the co-operative banking group since before the twentieth century. The unbundling of activities allows banks to concentrate on how best to achieve the economies that underlie respective business. In the case of marketing, these economies are mainly ones of scope. Value for customers is best created by selling them the most appropriate goods. The dense branch network and the fact that the local co-operative banks and their employees are firmly rooted in the local community allows them to gather the necessary specific information that make possible the realization of these economies of scope. By concentrating on the production of financial services and the related back-office activities, the central banks and special finance institutions achieve economies of scale. They step in whenever the local banks are either too small for the efficient production of financial services, or are restrained by the limited geographical reach of each bank.

The research and development activities and production activities are organized in the central banks and the special financial institutions. By pooling the best human resources in centres of competence it becomes possible to create a competitive edge for the local credit co-operatives and for the other institutions within the Verbund. Innovation and entrepreneurship is probably enhanced by the decentralized structure of the Verbund, with the formal delegation of decision rights to the managers of local banks and branches. With trial and error, it is possible to adapt to changes and to find the solution that best suits each particular change. The way innovation is handled in the Verbund can be shown through the example of the recently founded VR Kreditwerk, a joint venture between DG Hyp and Bausparkasse Schwäbisch Hall, which specializes in the provision of back-office work related to all aspects of real-estate financing. Kreditwerk states on its website that the 'open architecture' of the Kreditwerk makes it possible for other co-operative mortgage banks and all interested credit co-operatives to participate in this innovative service concept.[21]

6.3   Corporate governance

Deutsche Bank

In the corporate governance of the Deutsche Bank, four stakeholders are explicitly acknowledged: 'Deutsche Bank regards its shareholders, customers, staff, and society as its four key stakeholders with equal status and with whom it engages in dialogue and partnership. Maintaining a balance among this quartet of interests is, for us, a demanding and compelling challenge. Part of our corporate identity is to create lasting added value for all four interest groups.'[22] As in any corporation, formal control rights rest ultimately with the shareholders who provide the equity capital necessary for the bank's operations. They can exercise their rights at the annual general meeting. In 2003, about 39 per cent of the registered shares made use of these rights at the AGM of Deutsche Bank.

The shareholders elect their representatives into the Supervisory Board, the *Aufsichtsrat*. Together with the representatives of the employees, according to the German co-determination law, they jointly control the Board of Managing Directors – *Vorstand* – consisting (as of June 2004) of four people who are ultimately responsible for the decisions taken at the bank. This is supplemented by the Group Executive Committee which has eleven members and includes the managing directors as well as the business heads of the group divisions. It reviews the development of the various businesses, discusses strategy, and prepares recommendations for final decision by the Board of Managing Directors. The Deutsche Bank *Vorstand* exercises strong leadership in a relatively small board compared to other German boards: the spokesman Josef Ackermann has claimed a more CEO-like role for himself. As in the internal hierarchy, there are clear responsibilities defined for specific tasks.

The stakeholder group of customers can rely on the exit possibilities that the competitive banking market in Germany provides. The power of Deutsche Bank to extract rents from them is thus limited. Besides its representatives on the supervisory board, the staff has broad decision-making powers assigned by various elements of the internal structure and can thus safeguard its investments, which are of a rather general nature because of the employability concept pursued by Deutsche Bank.[23]

The distribution of power between these four stakeholders is of interest: the question remains whether Deutsche Bank ultimately is a company run in the interests of its shareholders. They stated on their website in 2002: 'A bank's growth depends on its shareholders' willingness to provide sufficient capital. Shareholders, however, will only do that if they receive a return that corresponds at least to the usual capital market yield. Only then will Deutsche Bank shares remain an attractive investment for private and institutional investors.'[24] Nothing is said about maximizing shareholder value. Instead, it is implied that the shareholders get the 'usual capital market yield'. That is quite a long way from their role as residual claimant prescribed to them by economic theory.

The co-operative banking group

With more than 15 million members, the co-operative banking group has one of the most dispersed shareholdings in the world.[25] As in a capitalist firm, the Volksbanken und Raiffeisenbanken delegate functions and responsibility to people who are competent and who enjoy the confidence of the members. The members select a supervisory board, and this selects the executive board of the bank.[26] The executive board and supervisory board are responsible to the yearly members or representatives meeting for their activities. The responsible persons are checked in a democratic way. Each member is equal and has one vote, regardless of the number of shares held. The democratic co-operative form functions through a system of checks and the reconciliation of interests.[27]

However, this democratic element also has its drawbacks. Because unlike the situation in an incorporated bank, the equity base of credit co-operatives is variable: capital in the co-operative banks can be redeemed by its members. This makes the co-operative vulnerable to withdrawals of its capital base, which determines its growth possibilities.[28] There is therefore a strong incentive for management to retain its earnings and thus secure the opportunity for future growth.[29] This tendency is further strengthened because the member's share is redeemed at its nominal value. The lack of a secondary market leaves any accumulated surplus with the co-operative. The result is a rather unattractive financial claim that does not provide any strong incentives for investors to use their formal powers and raise their voice in the general meeting of members.

This fact is enhanced by the allocation of decision rights between the members of the co-operative. Regardless of the capital that an individual supplies, s/he has only one vote in the general assembly. The resulting feature of a credit co-operative is therefore a very autonomous management that is not subjected to external control by the capital markets nor to internal control by the general meeting.[30] Is this an inefficient outcome or are there other checks and balances in place to keep the power of managerial discretion weak?

This is indeed the case; the acquisition of information about the behaviour of the management is comparatively cheap. The members and shareholders of the bank live close to their bank, and the managers share the social life in the town or region where the members live. Any excesses or too many fringe benefits enjoyed by the management can be seen immediately by the members and put into the regional context and standards. Furthermore, the members perform different functions: they are not only the providers of equity capital, but are also the depositors and borrowers of the bank. As shareholders, they accept more risk than they would prefer in their role as depositors. By bundling these three functions into one, the agency conflict between shareholders and debtors is minimized. The remaining agency problem between members and management is dealt with by the fact that credit co-operative banks are firmly rooted in a limited area. That makes it easier to gather the necessary information for monitoring the managers and puts some limits on the possibility of excessive growth. Other elements at work in restricting the discretion of the local management are (i) the existence of an internal labour market that rewards the building of a reputation; and (ii) the pressure that is put on by the BVR to merge the local credit co-operatives to form bigger, more efficient units. Here again, only the best managers will remain in the driving seat.

Corporate governance in the top tier of institutions suffers from another agency conflict: the owners are the primary credit co-operatives that are represented by their managers, who are ultimately responsible to their co-operatives' members. As described earlier, they do not have strong incentives to perform in the interest of their owners, so one might conclude that the control mechanism to be applied in the top institutions is also weak, as in the central banks. Looking at the financial history of DG Bank, the former top institute, one can see that here a lack of control correlates with poor results. After being embroiled in a financial scandal about securities lending in the late 1980s and a string of bad loans in the 1990s, the bank was merged with GZ Bank, itself the product of a recent merger between two of the second-tier central banks, to become DZ Bank.

6.4   Comparative organizational analysis

The narrow view of efficiency

In 2000, the net income before tax Deutsche Bank made was €4,949 million. The credit co-operatives generated an annual profit of 0.2 per cent of the average total assets,[31] which amounted to €1,070 million. This wide discrepancy might lead one to the easy and obvious conclusion that credit co-operatives are a grossly inefficient way of organizing modern financial services and should be seen as the inferior organizational design. Two caveats are necessary: first, a sizeable amount of Deutsche Bank's profit is the result of a bumper year in investment banking. The Global Corporates and Institutions division accounted in this year for a profit of roughly 60 per cent. In 2003, however, €2,756 million by Deutsche Bank compares with €2,801 million for the primary co-operatives.

Second, the profit made by the central banks and the special financial institutions in the co-operative banking group is only included in the figure as far as it was distributed in the form of dividends to the local credit co-operatives. Since there are no consolidated accounts for the group as a whole, the part of the profits that was retained by these top-tier institutions is not included. When comparing the organizational settings from a welfare point of view, that easy and obvious conclusion must be further challenged. The question arises as to how the creation of value can be measured in a meaningful way. The profit figures given by the financial data are based on the assumption that value is created solely for shareholders, which even in the case of Deutsche Bank is probably not true, as mentioned earlier. Accounting rules prescribe that personnel expenses, for example, are seen as costs. Other value created might not even show up in the accounts – one example is the forgone revenue for a bank that does not charge a fee for basic payment services for its customers – a practice of which many co-operative banks approve. These figures also exclude the value appropriated by the state; the co-operative banks in Germany paid four times as much tax as the big four private banks taken together.[32]

Differences in the designs

The role of leadership

Certainly, differences are great when the role of leadership is taken into consideration. At Deutsche Bank, the role that the board and the CEO-like spokesman play in setting the strategic direction is very large. Their power evolves out of the strong emphasis on a centralized hierarchy as well as on their human capital and the ability to succeed the selection process to make it to the top. Capacity restraints are an important reason why many decision rights are delegated to lower levels, such as the newly created Group Executive Committee, either with or without formal authority.[33]

In the Finanzverbund, on the other hand, leadership is not allocated clearly. Power is spread by design more widely across the whole Verbund, as in a heterarchy. Decision control and decision management is separated in the sense of Fama and Jensen (1983b): the BVR proposes and manages new strategies while the leaders of the individual co-operative banks agree on the general direction and implement the necessary changes to progress in this new direction. The managers of the individual retail banks, however, are offered a wide degree of freedom and can choose whether to use the products on offer in the Finanzverbund. For example, only around 60 per cent of the retail banks offer their clients products tailored by the building society Schwäbisch Hall,[34] a situation unimaginable in the Deutsche Bank.

Flexibility and adaptability

Another potential weakness of the spreading of power is the lack of rapid adaptability. Whenever urgent decisions have to be taken and whenever co-ordinated action is necessary, the system used by Deutsche Bank is probably the best. An example of this is provided by the time it took the Finanzverbund to agree on a common platform for e-banking. The VR-Net was rather late compared to the pioneering role that Deutsche Bank played when it established Bank 24 in 1995. The formation of a company to co-ordinate the internet activities of the Verbund took place as late as July 2001, with the first banking activities beginning in April 2002.[35] However, as this particular example shows, it can sometimes also be an advantage not to jump immediately on to the bandwagon of the latest management fads and to waste money and other resources on ill-fated business ideas, as many private banks did during the stock market bubble of the late 1990s.

Before this central solution was implemented, many primary banks, especially the bigger ones in the major cities with more sophisticated customers, built online banking facilities on their own. This experimentation led to a duplication of effort and money on the one hand, but on the other the different investments undertaken by many institutions led to innovative ideas, of which the best were implemented in the common standard. The case of VR-Net shows that the balance between autonomous innovation and co-ordinated investments is rather tricky. In this example, a more centralized and co-ordinated approach – either by direction as in the case of Deutsche Bank or by evolution, but with binding standards – would have been better. Still, not every large primary bank (such as, for example, Berliner Volksbank) that has established online banking on its own has switched to the common solution with a single appearance provided by VR-Net. At the end of 2002, only 347 co-operative banks had licensed the technology provided.[36]

The role of benchmarking to establish the best practice within the Finanzverbund is consequently a sensible topic. In one project of the BVR, Bundeseinheitliche Geschäftsprozesse (common business processes), such effort is undertaken with the aim of structuring the whole Finanzverbund more efficiently, and to gather data for improved control.[37]

The human resource strategies

Human resources are one of the crucial success factors in banking. As noted earlier, Deutsche Bank relies heavily on university graduates and on the knowledge and ideas they bring with them. The turnover rate in particular jobs is relatively high, and people are evaluated by their results. In the investment banking industry an active labour market exists, with many possibilities for individuals and whole teams to switch employers. This active market allows them to command much of the rent that is generated by their scarce human capital. In the co-operative banking sector the emphasis is more on people who join the bank after leaving school and are trained internally in the bank. There is much less emphasis on establishing connections with universities for recruiting. All in all, Deutsche Bank relies more on the market for labour than do the co-operative banks, which operate an internal labour market.

The product strategy

Deutsche Bank has made intensive efforts to establish itself as one of the banks in the 'bulge bracket' of investment banking. In this segment, human and social capital is the important resource that underpins the basis for a competitive advantage. For many activities, such as advising in mergers and acquisitions, banks do not need much financial capital. This allows investment bankers to capture a big slice of the economic value that is added by their work. Hence, the way that Deutsche Bank treats its employees with regard to measuring the contribution of the individual or the team towards performance, and the way those people are rewarded with bonuses and generous stock option packages complements this product strategy.

The co-operative banks perform more the traditional tasks of commercial banking, which rely more on financial relative to human capital. The measurement and in particular the rewards structure is consistent with this market strategy and the overall objective; the banks in the Finanzverbund emphasize more the value generated for customers. The use of stock options is not possible; even the banks that are registered as a corporation do not have their shares listed on a stock exchange. Even if the market for those shares were liquid enough to support the provision of incentives to employees by means of stock options, the co-operative banks would probably not make much use of it – too much inequality in the remuneration of employees would contradict the objective of pooling individual strengths for the benefit of the group.

Complementarities between the building blocks

We can distinguish between two different organizational designs – systems that are characterized by complementarities between their elements and by consistency in the way these elements are configured. As described above, Deutsche Bank's strategy can be described as global, with a tendency to shift resources from commercial and retail banking to its investment banking division. In this line of business, human capital is relatively more important than financial capital. The global ambition and reach allows it to implement career paths and a corporate culture that uses exactly this strategy to attract and retain scarce human capital. Much emphasis is put on the performance of the individual or the team, and leadership plays a very strong part; both themes are manifested in its former slogan 'Leading to results'. The complementarities provided by rewarding empowered employees with scarce human and social capital (especially in the investment banking division) with bonuses and stock options are used. The measurement of performance, especially in financial terms, is very elaborate. In corporate governance, Deutsche Bank explicitly recognizes that as well as the shareholders, who are rewarded with an adequate return on their capital, there exist other stakeholders, such as employees. Especially when taking into account how much of the value generation depends on the employees in investment banking, the recognition of their stake and the rewards of their investment seems appropriate, in particular when comparing them to pure investment banks run in the traditional Anglo-Saxon way, which are often organized as partnerships.

The *Finanzverbund* and the system it establishes is similarly characterized by complementarities and consistency. By establishing individual legal and economic entities with formal decision-rights based in the local community and not in some distant headquarters, the Volks- und Raiffeisenbanken have a credible commitment to act in the interests of the local community and their customers. A bad decision by the management spells the demise of the entire bank, and not just a branch. Its strategy of customer focus is strengthened by this regional principle. Placing the decision rights that effect the whole group into the formally rather weak hands of the president of their federal association and the board members of their central institutions allows the credit co-operative system to achieve a distinct set of checks and balances in their governance that also enhances the value of their strategy of value creation for their local customers. The measurement of performance is rather weak, no consolidated accounts are prepared, and the collection and publication of data takes some time. Although there are some efforts to introduce benchmarking and to actively compare the different co-operative banks, the negligence of more sophisticated financial performance measurement is consistent with the configuration of other important elements. Too much focus on narrow financial performance would run counter to the broad value maximization strategy and the autonomy of the local credit co-operatives. The mutually reinforcing elements of both systems are summarized in Table 6.2.

The broader view of efficiency

In times of rapid change, the integrated system of the Deutsche Bank offers many advantages – the central leadership has the autonomy to give direction and to co-ordinate the necessary changes. This is especially important if complementarities between the elements of the organizational design exist, as was shown above. In this case, it is a competitive advantage not to rely on consensus, as the example of the establishment of online banking has revealed. The possibility of making a big leap instead of taking small steps[38] was valuable. On the other hand, at times of relative stability the autonomous system of the co-operative

Table 6.2 Systemic features of the two banking groups

	Deutsche Bank	Co-operative banking group
Corporate objective	Financial performance	Broad value maximization
Relevant knowledge	More general	More specific
Decision-making	Centralized, top-down	Decentralized, bottom-up
Leadership	Strong and central	Dispersed
Personnel policy	External recruiting	'Internal' labour market
Salaries/wages	Matching market, more variable	Deferred elements, more fixed
Performance measures	Financial performance measures	No overall performance measures
Key stakeholders	Quartet of stakeholders	Diverse roles of members

banking group can reveal its advantages. The formal delegation of decision rights is an advantage when analysed from an economic perspective. Motivation and the incentive to invest in customer relationships and the specific information that goes along with it are not weakened, as in the integrated approach.[39] The slow growth and the small steps that the Finanzverbund undertakes are also because it is limited in its international expansion by the existence of co-operative banking groups in other countries. The agreement on alliances seems to be the only option in the mid-term for an international expansion. The possibility of simply buying its way into new markets and products, as Deutsche Bank has done with the acquisition of, for example, Bankers Trust, does not seem a viable option.[40]

Both models must therefore be seen as consistent systems to perform financial services. When analysing which is the more efficient, one has to define in what circumstances and over what span of time. Taking into account that both ways of organizing the provision of financial services can look back on a history of more than 130 years, both organizational designs should be considered as systems that are able to perform the economic functions of banks rather well. This conclusion is further strengthened by the geographical spread of both business models. The corporate system of Deutsche Bank has been followed successfully by other global financial institutions and is widely studied in the economic literature, while the co-operative idea, on the other hand, has spread to probably every country on earth in some form. The relatively improved performance of one system over the other depends on the pace with which changes in the business environment take place. Institutions have to evolve over time. As this pace varies, the fortunes of each particular organizational design can be reversed.

Notes

1. They are also changing over time and adapt to new challenges and opportunities as the whole German financial system and banking industry change. This case study analyses a snapshot of both organizational arrangements around 2002.
2. See http://www.deutsche-bank.de.
3. See http://www.dzbank.de.
4. See Aschhoff and Henningsen (1996) for a more detailed history of the co-operative banks in Germany.
5. Figures and calculations are from Deutsche Bundesbank (2004).
6. See Topkis (1998) for the mathematics of complementary and supermodularity, and see Section 2.2.
7. Deutsche Bank (2004).
8. Deutsche Bank (2001, p. 8).
9. See http://www.deutsche-bank.de.
10. See Ghoshal *et al.* (2001) for the concept of employability. See also Section 3.3.
11. See Deutsche Bank (2004, pp. 83–91) for the use of the various equity-based compensation elements.
12. See Deutsche Bank (2001).
13. See *The Economist* (2002b) for a portrait of Josef Ackermann.
14. See Bundesverband der Deutschen Volks- und Raiffeisenbanken (2001, p. 5).
15. See Bundesverband der Deutschen Volks- und Raiffeisenbanken (2001, p. 10).
16. http://www.frankfurter-volksbank.de.
17. See http://www.dzbank.de.
18. Bundesverband der Deutschen Volks- und Raiffeisenbanken (2001, p. 9).
19. See http://www.dzbank.de.
20. See BAG Bankaktiengesellschaft (2001, p. 12).
21. See http://www.vr-kreditwerk.de.
22. Deutsche Bank (2001, p. 12).
23. On the substitutability of power conveyed through corporate governance and power conveyed through the internal structure, see Schmidt and Weiss (2003).
24. Deutsche Bank (2001, p. 12).
25. See Bundesverband der Deutschen Volks- und Raiffeisenbanken (2001, p. 55).
26. See Theurl and Kring (2002, pp. 8–11) for more information on the governance of co-operatives.
27. See http://www.bvr.de.
28. See Rey and Tirole (2000) for a model of how this weakness of co-operatives can be overcome.
29. As Pleister (2001, p. 20) notes, 'there is a rule of thumb when it comes to the distribution of the economic results: a third is used for the internal strengthening, a third is used for the equity capital and another third is assigned to customers/members.'
30. For more on the issue of control in co-operatives, see Krahnen and Schmidt (1994, pp. 55–60).
31. See Bundesverband der Deutschen Volks- und Raiffeisenbanken (2001, p. 53).
32. See Pleister (2001, p. 14).

33. See Aghion and Tirole (1997) for a distinction between real and formal authority, and the ramifications that delegation of control rights provides.
34. See Bundesverband der Deutschen Volks- und Raiffeisenbanken (2002, p. 72).
35. See Bundesverband der Deutschen Volks- und Raiffeisenbanken (2002, p. 80).
36. See Bundesverband der Deutschen Volks- und Raiffeisenbanken (2003, pp. 79–80).
37. See Bundesverband der Deutschen Volks- und Raiffeisenbanken (2002, pp. 29–33) for more details on this project.
38. See Milgrom and Roberts (1995b) for this distinction, and see also Section 4.2.
39. See Aghion and Tirole (1997).
40. Growth by acquisition, however, was undertaken when the Norisbank was acquired by the DZ Bank from HypoVereinsbank in October 2003.

7
Open-source Projects

7.1 Introduction

From Netscape to Mozilla

The browser war between Netscape and Microsoft ended with a devastating defeat for the former company in 1999, when its market share fell within a year from around 60 per cent to only 10 per cent. With the introduction of the World Wide Web (www) in 1993, a new range of protocols, such as the hypertext transfer protocol (http), had emerged, which subsequently became standards. These protocols allowed for the easy specification of a path to resources on the World Wide Web. Older protocols such as telnet, usenet or gopher were largely displaced over time by the use of the hypertext transfer protocol. The use of this protocol allowed the display of resources on the internet in a graphical user interface if particular software, a web browser, was used.

Mosaic was the name of the first popular web browser that allowed the use of these new possibilities. It was developed in 1992 at the National Center for Supercomputing Applications (NCSA) at the University of Illinois by a team led by Marc Andreesen. The NCSA licensed the Mosaic browser on generous terms for various computer platforms. Non-commercial use was allowed without charge, and access to the source code, the underlying set of instructions for the software, was possible, although the licence was held proprietorially by the NCSA.

Seeing the potential of the internet, Marc Andreesen founded Netscape Communications Corporation in April 1994 to exploit the possibilities that web browsers offered commercially. Their product, Netscape Navigator, was officially released at the end of 1994. It was an easy-to-use product that soon became the dominant web browser with at times a market share of nearly 70 per cent. The innovation of showing some resources of websites while other resources were still being downloaded allowed for a more rapid display of the content and allowed the text to be read while waiting for the graphics to arrive. This simplification and the decision to give the browser away free of charge reinforced the adoption of the internet by numerous users. Despite adhering broadly to industry-wide standards, having the biggest share of the browser market allowed Netscape to influence the future direction of these evolving standards and gave it a superior position in the industry. Netscape maintained its technical leadership and used its dominant position to introduce technologies such as cookies, frames and JavaScript in order to leverage this position. In this way it threatened to level the playing field between different operating systems.

This threat and the powerful position Netscape had acquired over the internet made Microsoft, the company dominating the software industry with its operating system, Windows, nervous. Fearing the dilution of its power, Microsoft introduced a web browser of its own in 1995, Internet Explorer. Like the Netscape Navigator, the Internet Explorer was based on the source code of the original Mosaic browser. Microsoft has licensed this code from Spyglass, the company set up by the University of Illinois to commercialize the Mosaic web browser. While clearly inferior at the beginning, the Internet Explorer from version 4.0 onwards gained ground against Netscape's Navigator. Decisions by Microsoft to bundle Internet Explorer into its Windows operating system and to allow internet service providers (ISPs) and computer vendors to customize Internet Explorer to their products clearly helped it in the battle with Netscape.

While Internet Explorer was getting better, Netscape lost its technological lead. The decision to offer an e-mail client and a website composer along with its Navigator in its application suite Netscape Communicator made the source code complex. As a consequence, the Navigator browser become buggy, prone to crashes, and could not handle the increasingly complex code of websites that relied on JavaScript and tables. Finally, web developers started to use Microsoft's proprietary extensions of the hypertext markup language (html) that favoured Internet Explorer and accelerated Netscape's demise, leading to a radical switch in the dominant system.

After its defeat, Netscape announced on 22 January 1998 that it would reveal the source code of Communicator under an open-source licence[1] in order to gather development effort from outside Netscape. These efforts culminated in the Mozilla project.[2] Netscape Communications

Corporation was finally acquired in 1999 by AOL, an internet service provider, which eventually discontinued the development in 2003.

Having undertaken the dramatic step of opening the source code, some difficulties existed from the start. Building the Mozilla web browser from Navigator's source code, for example, still required a proprietary library from a third party,[3] and did not work properly because of the huge and complex code base that proved difficult to disentangle. Most of the core developers therefore decided to scrap this legacy code and to rewrite important libraries and the rendering engine.[4] A short time after that decision, on 7 December 1998, the new Gecko engine was released, which was noticeably faster and smaller in terms of lines of code than its predecessor.

With AOL's decision to close its browser division, the Mozilla Foundation took over the responsibility for the development of a web browser as an alternative to Microsoft's Internet Explorer. Being fully independent of any commercial interests, the Mozilla Foundation can follow the significantly different production processes in open source. The integrated applications suite of Mozilla, which encompasses a browser, an e-mail client, a newsreader and an html editor, was split into more manageable modules that still rely on common underlying technologies such as the Gecko rendering engine, but allow for a more reliable and secure program. The e-mail client has since been released as Thunderbird and the web browser, on 9 November 2004, as Firefox. During the first 24 hours after release, Firefox was downloaded more than a million times, and more than 50 million downloads occurred in the first half year after its release. As Table 7.1 shows, the percentage of people switching from Internet Explorer to a web browser based on the Gecko rendering engine developed and maintained by the Mozilla open-source community is on the rise.

Objective of this case study

Where does this recent success of Firefox and Mozilla come from? How did the open-source project Mozilla succeed, where its closed-source

Table 7.1 Market share of different web browsers (per cent)

Web browser	Nov 2003	May 2004	Nov 2004	May 2005
Internet Explorer	82.0%	74.0%	71.0%	66.0%
Gecko (Firefox, Mozilla)	14.0%	20.0%	24.0%	29.0%
Opera	2.0%	2.0%	2.2%	2.7%
KHTML (Konqueror, Safari)	1.1%	3.5%	2.6%	3.1%

Source: See http://www.safalra.com/website/browsermarket/index.html; accessed 15 June 2005.

predecessor Netscape failed? And, in an industry characterized by network effects and economies of scale and scope in production that in many segments of the industry lead to a quasi-natural monopoly, with which organizational design could the position of the powerful incumbent be overcome without resorting to heavy regulation?

Open-source projects are not only confined to web browsers. Other successful products are developed and maintained by various open-source communities. The most prominent and biggest open-source project in terms of the number of developers who are involved in it is the operating system Linux,[5] which similarly has gained market share against Microsoft's equivalent program, the Windows operating system,[6] or the web server software by Apache that approaches a market share of 70 per cent in comparison to its best closed-source competitor, Microsoft's Internet Information Server (IIS) with a 20 per cent market share.[7]

What is common to all these projects, and thus arguably the secret of the success of open-source products in general, is the adherence to a particular organizational design. The system of open source for software development relies on a certain configuration of the organizational parameters that reinforces the value of each element, and exercises positive feedback on the value of other elements. Open-source software is different in many respects: it is distributed together with the source code, so that it is possible for people to change features of the program they do not like, or to enhance it if they wish to do so – something that is next to impossible when the access to the source code is denied and the program is distributed in binary form only. Furthermore, no transfer of money or other compensation is required for this – source code and program are simply downloaded from the internet. As such, open-source software can be read, redistributed, modified and used freely. There are, however, some strings attached to this: open-source programs are not subject to any commercial licence that grants their holder the exclusive right of use and modification, but to a different kind of licence. Examples are the GNU General Public License (GPL) for most open-source products, or similar licences such as the Mozilla Public License (MPL). Licences such as the GPL specify that any modifications must be re-released under the GPL. While this seems to be a strong impediment to commercial exploitation of any value that is created by modifications or minor changes, it guarantees that changes introduced by a programmer donating his or her code cannot be exploited by someone else who appropriates the economic rents from such improvement. But open source is more than just the issue of providing access to the source code of a software program and the legal constructs surrounding it. Open source also promotes, for example, the reliability and quality of software by supporting an independent peer review process that allows for a rapid evolution of the source code. This and other pillars of open source that together form a consistent organizational design are described in this chapter.

The aim of this case study is a comparative organizational analysis of open source in contrast to more traditional ways of developing and maintaining software. As the introductory example has shown, open source, implemented correctly, can be a means of stimulating competition in an industry where network effects and economies of scale and scope exist. Where traditional firms, striving to make a profit, have failed (like Netscape) or would not even dare to tangle with the economies prevailing in the industry that were so much against them, open-source communities such as the ones of Mozilla or Apache can nevertheless constitute an organizational design that bypasses such economies.

Why can a system resting on small and emerging communities such as Mozilla or Linux be such a formidable competitor to large, incumbent firms such as Microsoft? This chapter identifies the critical success factors that are necessary to enable open source to work successfully. Using the methodology of systems theory,[8] it is argued that the emulation by commercial firms of open source through the adoption of only some of its elements will not be enough to cope with the competitive threat such communities offer to the incumbent software companies. And in fact any misalignment of important elements will lead to deteriorating performance among such firms. This chapter concentrates on the following issues:

- to show why the system of open-source software production is a consistent system in which it is necessary to configure its elements for complementarity; and
- to compare the organizational design in a comparative organizational analysis to the traditional model of software production, and thereby pinpoint those elements whose configurations are crucial for the success of each consistent system.

Some remarks on how the prevalence of both an open-source as well as a closed-source system leads to a more efficient organizational design of the overall economy conclude the chapter.

Some related literature

The phenomenon of open source has received a lot of attention in recent years. The number of open-source projects and programmers has increased, as well as the number of engineers, sociologists and researchers from other academic disciplines, who all wonder about the rise of open-source software. And economists are no exception; different theories and methodologies, ranging from field studies based on interviews with programmers to case studies of specific projects and economic models, have been applied to deal with the phenomenon of open source.[9]

For many researchers in different academic domains, the motivation for taking part in an open-source community at all is most surprising. Many contributions exist in this first strand of the literature. Osterloh *et al.* (2002b) distinguish three different motives: intrinsic motivation; low costs for participation; and signalling of abilities.[10] The first of these motives has recourse to anthropological motives. Altruism or ideology provide an intrinsic motivation high enough to induce people to exert effort and participate in open-source communities.[11] The argument of low costs for participation has gained prominence with communication via the internet becoming ever easier and less costly. The argument of low costs is often supplemented by the benefits, or the external rewards, that can be obtained. Lakhani and von Hippel (2003), for example, emphasize the advantages of a system in which the developers of software are also its main users, and in which one user helps another by providing valuable feedback. Open-source programmers profit from this both by learning on the production side and by obtaining a better product on the consumption side. Rapid feedback by the best in each specific field or project allows for rapid advancement along the learning curve by individual programmers, and alleviates the free-rider problem. This effect is modelled by Johnson (2002). He shows that under certain circumstances the free-riding problem in the provision of a public good such as open-source software can be overcome: whenever the ratio of the individual benefits from the use of such software to the individual costs of production is sufficiently high in comparison to the likelihood that some other agent develops a solution, the programmer takes part in an open-source project.

While these theories stress the benefit of being involved in an active community, other academic contributions take this idea a step further and concentrate on the third motive, suggested by Osterloh *et al.* (2002b). Not only is the recognition by insiders valuable. If a signal can credibly be acquired that is also understood by outsiders, higher economic rents may be obtained in the future. Open source thus acts as a signalling device.[12]

A second major strand of literature deals with the economics of open source and how promising business models, especially contrasted with those of traditional, closed-source firms, can look. Various models exist that focus on the competition between different regimes of software production. Mustonen (2003), for example, provides a model on the competitive interplay between a closed-source monopolist and a competing program based in open source. Parameters such as occupational choices made by programmers, the implementation costs of users, and the wage offered by the monopolist, determine the quality of each product and therefore the equilibrium between open and closed sources. Other aspects of competition between open source and closed source are highlighted in models by Dalle and Jullien (2001) and van Wegberg and Berends (2000). While certainly contributing to the understanding of the phenomenon of open source, such models are often too analytical, necessarily neglecting the interplay of a larger number of parameters.

Case studies offer a methodology that allows the interdependencies between such a larger number of parameters to be taken into consideration. While many case studies of individual projects can be found,[13] a description of key open source configurations common to many projects is rarer. A comprehensive open source framework is provided by Rothfuss (2002) who, however, describes open source from the perspective of computer science. Lerner and Tirole (2002) provide valuable thoughts on the economics behind a number of important elements in the open-source process, but they lack a more systemic perspective.

Garzarelli (2003) comes closer to this task. He relates open source to the economics of organization and stresses the importance of knowledge in the production of software. Organizational forms such as clubs or communities allow people in the software profession to absorb easily any knowledge embedded in the program and its source code. This helps to make progress in developing the code and reinforces the value of the program. A spontaneous order within these communities and a certain degree of self-selection of programmers among different tasks then result. A second contribution that is closely related to the aim of this chapter to describe the systemic features of open source is the well-known metaphor of Raymond (2000a). He compares the functioning of the open-source model to a bazaar, and contrasts this with the business model of traditional software firms. It is the purpose of this chapter to extend this line of argument and to explore the differences in organizational designs between the open-source and the traditional model of software production using the methodology provided by systems theory.

Outline

Section 7.2 provides some background information on the software industry and the development and maintenance of software in general, and the phenomenon and licensing of open source in particular. Additionally, two distinct modes of innovation are characterized. Sections 7.3 and 7.4 describe the traditional business model of keeping the source code proprietary, and the new business model of the open-source system with its key processes, respectively. Possibilities for commercialization, paramount with proprietary software, are also described for the open-source business model. In a comparative organizational analysis in Section 7.5, these two distinct approaches are contrasted with each other. A discussion of the effects of open source on the larger system that constitutes the overall economy concludes the chapter.

7.2 The software industry

In the beginning of information technology, computers and machines were built for specific purposes, and for every new task that had to be performed, the wiring of the computer had to be changed. This was time-consuming and it eventually paid to build machines for more general purposes and specialize them through particular software programs that allowed the user to change the purpose and possibilities of the computer more easily than through rewiring the entire hardware. Initially, the development of software was generally undertaken by the firms that produced the hardware, like large mainframes and smaller computers, as an integral part of their product. The software industry came into being as a separate industry at the beginning of the 1980s, when more standardized, usually IBM-compatible hardware components were used, and when hardware manufacturers started to license the necessary software from independent developers.

The software industry today is a huge business with numerous companies of all sizes operating in it. It includes organizations engaged in providing expertise in the field of information technologies through writing, modifying, testing and supporting software to meet the needs of particular customers, and through planning and designing computer systems that integrate computer hardware, software and communication technologies. The industry's most important products include operating systems, general application or productivity suites, enterprise resource planning databases, and dedicated programs for specific firms or industries. For an overview of the software industry, see Siegele (2003) and West (2003, sec. 2).

The purpose of this section is to provide some background information on the programming of software. It also sheds some light on the phenomenon of open source and examines the distinct systems of private and collective innovation.

The economics and technology of software production

The economics of software production

The economics prevailing in the software industry are characterized by a cost structure skewed towards large upfront costs on the side of the developers, and implementation costs on the side of the users.[14] The first characteristic gives rise to economies of scale and scope in production. Developers have to invest significant amounts of money to design, code, test and maintain a program before they receive any revenue from the software, but once the program is developed, variable costs are negligible. Putting the compiled version on a server connected to the internet is often enough to distribute the software. While there have been some experiments with charging for software on a subscription basis, most software is still licensed for a particular version of the program with the necessity of renewing the licence for an upgraded version of the software.

The second characteristic, implementation costs on the side of the users, makes switching from one program to another difficult. Users often have to learn how to operate a particular program. The co-specialization of their knowledge towards the software leads to an effect of lock-in, and switching to a competing product becomes more difficult: another learning process would have to be incurred. Furthermore, switching costs for users are increased if considerable numbers of other users with whom frequent interaction is necessary have also adopted a particular software. Modifying files created with a certain software often demands the use of that particular software by other users as well. The results are network effects in the use of software.

Both characteristics – economies of scale and scope in production, and network effects in the usage of software – lead to a tendency for software programs to become standards. Such standardization has both merits and drawbacks. On the one hand, people using the same program can work together more easily on a document without bothering about converting it from one program to another, but on the other hand, such standardization can lead to a monopoly where one company dominates the market and charges a high price for a product of relatively low quality and further entrenches its position through a foreclosure strategy in related markets. The introductory example of the Netscape Navigator and the Internet Explorer with their, at different times, high market share has demonstrated the prevalence of standards in the software industry.

The technology of software production

Today's large software programs can easily contain several million source lines of code (SLOC).[15] And, as Brooks (1975, pp. 18–19) has observed, the costs of communication among programmers eventually outweigh any benefits from taking an increasing number of programmers on to a project. The necessity of having all of them working on a controlled version of the program increases complexity tremendously.[16] So how is the complexity inherent in a software program kept in check? The answer is through modularity in design, as has been described extensively by Baldwin and Clark (2000).[17] Unlike the early computers, which had complex and interdependent designs, today's software makes extensive use of distinct modules.

Example 7.1 Modularity was sacrificed by Netscape Communications in their Navigator browser. Ever more features were introduced over a short period to gain the upper hand in the browser war with Microsoft. Mingling the code, however, was not a good idea, as it grew ever larger, and the clarity of the design was impaired. This proved to be a considerable problem when the source code was opened in 1998 and contributions from the open-source community were solicited. Most parts of the code were therefore rewritten subsequently to make it consistent with the business model of open source.

Modularization to reduce complexity can be found everywhere. The separation of hardware and software in the information technology industry at the beginning of the 1980s is probably the most visible outcome of the decomposition of complex and interdependent systems. The use of standards in the form of Application Programming Interfaces (API) among operating systems and application software is a second example of how development is simplified. Standardized interfaces between different pieces of software allow for a modularization in software production. A third and important example is the rise of object-oriented programming in the late 1980s. In this programming paradigm, data or a particular functionality is packed into an object whose internal running is encapsulated and which works with other objects only over certain interfaces. Such objects represent previously codified knowledge that can easily be called upon when the need for it arises. Object-orientated programming thus allows for the reuse of existing code, thereby reducing the overall development time of a program.

Note that modularization is not only a feature of a software program but also of the process that leads to this product. Software production technology can be broken down into six distinct processes: the requirements have to be analysed; modules of the software have to be designed;

the code has to be written or reused; the code has to be tested for its functionality and quality; the program has to be built with the integration of the different modules; and the program has to be optimized. Designing software programs and the technology to produce them for modularity allows parallel developments which speed up the finishing of the project.[18]

Besides the option of modularizing both product and process in the software industry, managing complexity can also be simplified through other means. Enhanced possibilities for communication over the internet, especially dedicated project management tools such as the Concurrent Versions System[19] or the Bugzilla and Tinderbox tools developed by the Mozilla project, have all allowed the easier handling of the complexity inherent in software production. It is, along with modularization, especially these innovations in coping with complexity that have led to the prominence of open source, as argued below.

What is open-source software?

Definition of 'open source'

Different definitions exist, and the understanding of what in fact constitutes open source varies.[20] Open-source activities are promoted by two institutions. The Open Source Initiative (OSI) is a 'non-profit corporation dedicated to managing and promoting the Open Source Definition for the good of the community, specifically through the OSI Certified Open Source Software certification mark and program'.[21] To qualify as open source, software has to meet certain requirements. The Open Source Definition maintained by the OSI demands among other things that the redistribution is free and has to include the source code. Modifications and derived works based on the original open-source software must also be allowed.[22]

The Free Software Foundation (FSF) is the second major institution 'dedicated to promoting computer users' rights to use, study, copy, modify, and redistribute computer programs'.[23] The FSF is to a certain extent competing with the Open Source Initiative and has set up its own definition of 'free software' in contrast to 'open source' software. Freedom to use and modify software programs as well as access to the source code are requirements for software to qualify as free. The differences between free and open software are, however, quite small,[24] and are related more to ideology and philosophy than to substance. The Free Software Foundation is the main sponsor of the GNU/Linux operating system, and its founder, Richard Stallman, has co-authored the licences that most open-source programs use.

The General Public License

There are currently 58 different licences certified by the Open Source Initiative.[25] The most commonly used licence among the 105,081 OSS projects listed by sourceforge.net as at 20 August 2005 are the GNU General Public License (GPL) in 69 per cent of all projects, and the GNU Lesser General Public License (LGPL) in 11 per cent of all OSS projects under OSI-certified licences. Both licences are maintained by the Free Software Foundation. Other often used licences include the BSD and MIT Licenses as well as the Mozilla Public License (MPL).

The first two licences were set up by the Free Software Foundation, described previously. The intention of the GPL is 'to guarantee your freedom to share and change free software – to make sure the software is free for all its users'.[26] Free does not, however, refer to the price charged for the software, but rather to the unrestricted access to the source code. The difference between the GPL and the LGPL is its viral nature: every piece of software using any code released under the GPL must be distributed under these terms as well. The LGPL, in contrast, does not call for this necessity: a module or library released under this version of the licence, which is only executed by another software program without being modified, does not restrict the choice of licence for the other program. It is used for objects such as common runtime libraries. A more comprehensive discussion of the differences between commonly used open-source licences can be found in Lerner and Tirole (2005) or Kaisla (2001). See also O'Mahony (2003) for more information on the legal issues and possibilities to protect work 'in the commons'.

The GPL provides a legal framework that credibly commits programmers using previously written code to publish and release the derived product again under terms of open source. Original contributors to the code are hence reassured that code they have written and donated to the open source domain cannot be used in any commercial program for which they would have to pay a licence fee to use or modify it. The 'copyleft' provided by the GNU General Public License or similar OSI-certified licences is hence an important complementary element to retain the openness of the source code.

Paradigms of innovation

Two paradigms exist in economic theory explaining why innovative activity occurs. One is the pursuit of economic rents by an entrepreneur or a commercial company, and the other is based on collective action to overcome a market failure in the production of a public good. Both paradigms are described briefly in this section, with an emphasis on those aspects that are relevant for the understanding of the two organizational designs of proprietary software and open-source software.[27]

Private innovation

Generally, the pursuit of profit induces entrepreneurs or commercial firms to invest in innovative activities that will result in new products or a better process. Being the first to develop a new product allows the developer to benefit from economic rents from this monopoly position. If this powerful position is secured *ex post* for some time, it allows the recouping of the *ex-ante* costs of investing in innovative activities and thereby stimulates such investments. Both the individual innovator and society as a whole benefit from this arrangement.

Different means exist to secure a position of such an *ex-post* monopoly and help to keep copycats at bay. Legal institutions such as patents and copyrights provide barriers to entry in many industries. In the pharmaceutical industry, for example, the innovator is granted a patent by governments that rewards the innovative activity with a temporary monopoly on the particular drug. The same holds true for intellectual property embedded in software programs. The software companies retain the copyright of the program and license it to potential users. And software companies have an additional means to secure their intellectual property: they usually license to their customers only the binary version of the program. This version is meant to be executed on a computer and is only machine-readable. The binary is obtained through compilation of the source code, the set of instructions in a certain programming language that is easily readable and modifiable by those familiar with that programming language. Licensing only the binary and keeping the source code closed to customers and potential competitors allows software companies to secure their position, since a reverse engineering of the original source code from the binary version is next to impossible.

Collective innovation

The idea of collective innovation was first described by Olson (1967) in the context of the provision of public goods.[28] Collective action avoids the welfare loss associated with a monopoly, as is the case with private innovation. New insights are revealed freely to others, so they can build upon this knowledge for the benefit of all. The paradigm of collective innovation, however, also has its drawbacks. It suffers from a lack of incentives. Individuals are often disinclined to invest in research when the associated costs are too high, so waiting for someone else to innovate becomes attractive. Underinvestment in the provision of a public good is the result.

Collective innovation is feasible if the group of contributors is easy to survey, or if incentives can be provided selectively for some groups or individuals. As von Hippel and von Krogh (2003) have argued in their private-collective model, such calibration of incentives for different contributors to a public good can be achieved, and the proposition for open-source software with free access to source code and binary version becomes valid: '[C]ontributors to a public good can *inherently* obtain greater private benefits than free riders.'[29] Private benefits from using the software (for example, no associated implementation costs) are thus increased if some effort was spent on development.[30]

Additionally, any effort can be quite small if the total workload is distributed across many shoulders. Localization projects for open-source software provide excellent illustrations of this. The Hungarian version of OpenOffice, for example, was translated collectively, as *The Economist* (2003b) reports. More than a dozen people at the Technical University Budapest, and another hundred submitting their work over the internet, translated more than 21,000 text strings in just three days to build the Hungarian version of OpenOffice.

7.3 The system of proprietary software

The purpose of this section is a description of the traditional model of software production in commercial firms that keep access to the source code of their products restricted. The configuration of the different building blocks and organizational parameters in firms following this business model, such as Microsoft, Oracle or SAP, is illustrated briefly in an idealized and simplified way as a benchmark against which the system of open source can be analysed comparatively in Section 7.5. It is argued that the organizational design relying on proprietary source code is a consistent system in need of adaption to changes in the business environment that might threaten the appropriateness of the business model. For a description of the traditional business model from a computer science perspective, see Rothfuss (2002, pp. 61–71).

Organizational design of proprietary source firms

The organizational design of the traditional, proprietary software development model is based on commercial firms that operate along the lines described in conventional textbooks on economics and management. The pursuit of profit is high on the agenda of these firms. The software industry, as a relatively young industry, is characterized by companies in which the founders usually still play prominent roles as the biggest shareholders or, additionally, as executive managers. Incorporating allows entrepreneurs with an innovative idea to capitalize on their intellectual property. Incorporating also allows them to ask other constituencies to invest specifically in a co-specialized way. The shareholders finance the development costs of large software programs upfront, and programmers write the code, build and test the programs as employees who are paid in an incentive-compatible way. Both groups thus acquire a stake in the eventual success of the software program. By assigning the various constituencies their different roles in a company through this act of incorporation, it becomes possible to accelerate the development and to scale up the business built on the original innovation of the entrepreneur. This reinforces the strategy applied by many commercial software firms.

Strategy

The strategy of software firms rests on safeguarding the economic rents generated through their intellectual property and maximizing the part of the rents that accrues to their founder, his/her fellow shareholders, and key programmers. The intellectual property is protected by closing the source code, and commercialized by licensing the software only in its binary form to users. Adding to the source code and licensing such upgrade versions translates into future profits and makes any competitive advantage of such companies sustainable. Microsoft resembles this business model, with its occasional releases of new products and service packs for its Windows operating system or Office application, for which it charges its customers again.

Maximizing the profits based on the intellectual property embedded in the binary software is made easier through scaling up the company with the help of outside shareholders and the capital they provide. Being the first company in a market often characterized by winner-takes-all competition allows the firm to seize upon the economies of scale and scope in their segment of the software industry, and to benefit from network effects as more and more people start to use their program. This entrenches the firm in a powerful position and reinforces the possibility of extracting economic rents, to the advantage of its stakeholders. The strategy of software companies therefore often rests on innovation and the subsequent drive to establish the program as the standard software in that particular market segment.

Different means support this strategy. Subsidizing some users or early adopters allows the building of an established base which other users have to follow. These other users can then be charged for a complementary program. Such a strategy was adopted by Adobe, which gave its Acrobat Reader away free and then charged for its Acrobat PDF Writer. It could also be found with Netscape, as illustrated in the brief case study in the introduction to this chapter. For other means and the art of standards wars see Shapiro and Varian (1999).

External boundaries and internal structure

The decision about where to set the boundaries of the firm complements the strategy just described. One important configuration is the choice of where to locate the company. The need to control tightly access to the source code increases the payoff from centralizing the programmers in one location. A close geographical proximity of programmers in few development centres, such as that of Microsoft in Redmond or SAP in Walldorf, usually characterizes firms operating along the lines of the traditional business model.

Further possibilities exist to configure the organizational design of commercial software companies. Strategic alliances, for example, are a promising form to enhance the established base so important in any standards war. Firms of all sizes in software development, furthermore, cluster together in particular regions, like Silicon Valley in the USA or around Bangalore in India. This facilitates the transfer of talented programmers across the boundaries of the firm without imposing on them the necessity of moving location. Boundaries are therefore relatively permeable. What is, however, held tightly within the confines of the firm is the source code, as the basis for future profits.

The internal structure of commercial software companies is characterized by internal boundaries complementing the external ones. Internal barriers are erected for various purposes. A hierarchy allows the use of organizational parameters such as screening of programmers for more sophisticated tasks, or promotions as incentive devices. Clear assignments of tasks to programmers are possible with a hierarchy, and the information generated by continuous screening is used effectively. Co-ordination and centralized planning are facilitated. With internal boundaries, the power of different stakeholders – for example, of lower-rank employees – can be restricted. Information and knowledge, especially that embedded in the source code, can be classified. Restricting the access to the code in its human-readable form thus complements the strategic choice to exploit the innovation commercially.

Governance

Software firms can take on many organizational forms. Sole proprietorships and professional partnerships exist alongside huge and valuable corporations such as Microsoft or SAP. As indicated above, the stake-holding constituencies include the founding entrepreneurs, the share-holders, senior managers and key programmers. Customers often have to undertake co-specialized specific investments to implement the soft-ware as needed, or to learn how to operate it. As in any corporation, ownership rights are assigned to shareholders, although, through their usually significant shareholdings or their moral authority, the founders often still retain control. In the software industry, employees often hold large amounts of the share capital, especially since the use of stock options is often used as an incentive device in the internal structure of such an organizational design. Customers, however, usually lack special protection of their stake through a governance mechanism. Reliance on the exit mechanism provided by outside markets is rather crude. Too much value of co-specialized investment is often lost. This was shown when Oracle bid for Peoplesoft in 2003. Some customers, fearing a depreciation of their knowledge and the efficiency of internal processes designed around Peoplesoft's software, were sceptical towards the hostile takeover. Oracle was accused of simply trying to disrupt the business of Peoplesoft for strategic reasons.

Consistency and shortcomings

The cathedral

The organizational design of proprietary software is a consistent system with the important elements reinforcing each other. No small deviation in the configuration of a single element can increase efficiency. The systemic nature of the design of commercial software companies is acknowledged by Raymond (2000a). In his essay 'The Cathedral and the Bazaar', he likens the development of a complex program in a commercial soft-ware company to the building of a medieval cathedral: a well-known architect makes a blueprint of the building starting with the basic structures and ending with every detail and ornament of the cathedral. Sticking to that blueprint, the building work itself is done by people who are experts in their narrow domain and who have the necessary special-ized equipment to perform that particular task. The architect supervises and monitors progress, adjusting the grand blueprint whenever the need arises, although careful planning at the very beginning should make this unnecessary. It is more often the individual worker who has to find a solution to match the overall design requirements. The cathedral model is characterized by a strong role for the central planner who has the knowledge to generate the blueprint. Building or production takes time, since careful planning, co-ordination and supervision are necessary. The architect or leader of the project is the scarce resource and often the bottleneck in the process. Parallel work is almost ruled out.

The organizational design of commercial software companies follows the method of the building of cathedrals, according to Raymond (2000a). Important configurations in the system of proprietary software include a strong role for the central authority and a reliance on leadership and a formal hierarchy. The strong formal or moral authority of the founder reflects this. Such a strong leadership role increases the returns from following strategic demands to become the dominant program in the particular market segment. Careful management of the boundaries, external as well as internal, and tight control of access to the source code fits with the configuration of the other parameters since it increases the amount of rents that can be appropriated. This spills over positively into the incentives for the various constituencies to invest specifically into the development of new software programs and the maintenance of those already in existence. The relatively protected position, however, facilitates the appropriation of economic rents and can lead to complacency on the part of the entrenched quasi-monopolist. Innovative activity is impaired as a result, and it often takes a long time for the final product to reach its users. This makes the system vulnerable to sudden changes that might render the business model pursued inappropriate in the future.

Shortcomings of the traditional business model

Two shortcomings of the proprietary software system can be imagined. One concerns the appropriateness of the system in the light of external changes, and the other the efficiency of the wider economy of which commercial software firms are a part. Changes in the rugged landscape of competition occur and in particular the technological progress in information processing and information transfer has an impact on the appropriateness of the traditional business model of commercial software companies. Is the system of proprietary software coding still appropriate for an environment characterized by the internet with its possibilities of copying software easily and implementing it rapidly?[31] The internet has also fundamentally changed the possibilities of communication for people dispersed around the globe. New forms of co-operation have become possible. Automation in some parts of the software development chain, such as building and testing the program automatically overnight, further reduces the need for close geographical proximity among the different programmers.

The second shortcoming of the system of proprietary software is that it often fails to achieve efficiency in the larger organizational design of the overall economy. Network effects and standardization lead over time to monopolies. This reduces choice for customers and can make the incumbent quasi-monopolist reluctant to change, and possibly complacent if problems occur. Customization, for example, was not possible with the Windows operating system, and security holes caused by bugs in the programming are exploited by malicious hackers, leading to serious problems for many individual users and businesses. The strategy of bundling together different services, while it may enhance the functioning of the components and their interplay, at the same time erects barriers to entry and further entrenches the position of the monopolist. Regulation is in many industries the solution to counter the power of such a monopolist. In the software industry, some kind of *ad hoc* regulation through legal actions can be observed. Different lawsuits brought against Microsoft and various fines for uncompetitive behaviour levied on it by American judges and the European Commission are the result. This is, however, only a crude way to counter *ex post* the power of any monopolist. The sum of all economic rents – that is, including those that could be enjoyed by consumers or those lost due to the introduction of regulation – is not maximized. This organizational design often does not maximize the overall welfare.

7.4   The system of open-source software

The purpose of this section is an idealized description of the business model of software production in open-source projects. Common to such projects is the publication of software under licence that requires the revelation of the source code. In analogy to the previous section, the configuration of the different building blocks and organizational parameters in open-source software projects is illustrated. The change in the configuration of the publication of the source code from proprietary to open modus leads to changes in the configuration of other elements as well in order to keep the organizational system consistent. A distinct design emerges, with deviations in many organizational parameters compared to the proprietary business model. This design also constitutes an efficient business model. Recent changes in the business environment might even increase the appropriateness of this design, as will be argued in Section 7.5, where a more detailed comparative organizational analysis of both business models is undertaken.

Organizational design of open-source projects

Strategy

Open-source projects follow a fundamentally different approach to coding software than companies that keep the source code of their software proprietary. Rather than restricting access to the source code and prohibiting any modifications as a violation of copyright protection, a rapidly growing community of programmers actively encourage each other to build on ideas and codes generated by fellow programmers. The vision behind many open-source projects is to provide an easy solution to common problems without the necessity of 'reinventing the wheel' every time. Reciprocity within the community is an important pillar on which the strategies of such projects rest: the expectation of giving and receiving help from other members, if needed, is deeply embedded within the community.

Although well-known open-source programs such as Linux, Mozilla or Apache command several hundred or even a thousand programmers working on it, the number of developers in most open-source projects is relatively small. Often only one programmer develops and maintains the software project, as Krishnamurthy (2002) reports. He notes, however, that, with increasing maturity, a selection among open-source projects towards successful ones occurs, and the number of people working on these projects increases. This induces individual programmers to market their product actively in the community and to create a scaled-down version that nevertheless attracts other developers in the early stages. Frequent releases complement this strategy.

Once a project has succeeded in attracting more programmers, the success of the whole project is reinforced. Having many developers from a range of backgrounds using varied hardware offers a superb testing environment for finding flaws in the code and correcting the program to remove these bugs. Different versions of the same program, distinguished in the case of Linux by an even number for stable versions and an odd number for developments, often exist, so that users can self-select which one to use depending on their sophistication and inclination to co-develop the program.[32]

Without relying on large amounts of money to write many lines of code for a complex program, timeliness, functionality and simplicity are important from the very beginning. Modularity in the design of the program helps to achieve this and allows for parallel development, thereby positively reinforcing the speed with which the product is finished. Modularity also decreases the complexity and simplifies the management of the project.

Boundaries

The boundaries between different open-source projects, and often also between open-source projects and commercial firms, are blurred to a degree almost of non-existence. Open boundaries complement the strategic importance of an open source code. Many programmers work on several projects at the same time or shift from one project to another with ease. Programmers employed by commercial companies such as, for example, IBM or Nokia in the hardware industry, actively contribute to open-source projects as part of their job. Open-source projects are therefore clearly not confined, and any existing boundaries are highly permeable. Different projects easily combine into one, co-operate extensively or split into submodules that thus become viable open-source projects on their own. The latter example is best illustrated with the case of the Bugzilla component spun off from the Mozilla project. Splitting of projects, where a single software program develops in two or more distinct and competing directions, is also possible. Boundaries are hence often negligible and, applying the ideas of systems theory, would even be counter-productive in a consistent design of open source. The openness of the source code leaves nothing to protect from the outside. Erecting artificial barriers that make the crossing of resources across the boundary difficult would also run against the strategy of helping others and sharing information freely.

Internal structure

Many configurations in the internal structure support the strategy of open-source software development. A distinctly configured web of organizational elements characterizes the distribution of information and power of developers and users, provides incentives and helps to co-ordinate dispersed investment decisions.

Open source builds on superior availability of information. The knowledge embedded in the source code is accessible to all, and a culture of actively sharing knowledge prevails. Transparency is high.[33] Open source also rests on simple and effective communication of information over the internet. Knowledge becomes codified and accessible for every interested user through newsgroups or dedicated tools such as Bugzilla, which allows the tracking of any bugs and managing their removal from the code. And, of course, knowledge resides in the source code itself.

Information and knowledge are generally used in an incremental way and, apart from the initial version of the software put into open source, small improvements in the software program prevail. This complements the use of frequent releases of the program for strategic reasons. The use of knowledge is not restricted by the necessity to handle it sequentially since a modular production technology prevails. Disposing of rigid internal structures frees programmers to pursue work on the task that is the most beneficial in their opinion. Simultaneous and parallel work thus becomes the norm in open source. This accelerates the speed of development. The design of open source is furthermore enhanced by the deployment of a tournament style in the development process. An increase in the value of parallel work though complementarities in design also increases the benefits from relying on modularization, thereby positively reinforcing the other elements in the open-source system.

Communication in open source is accomplished with the aid of websites (for example, SourceForge or freshmeat), the use of mailing lists, newsgroups, instant messengers or dedicated software tools such as the aforementioned Bugzilla. Note that many open-source projects were initiated specifically to support the wider community through the development of such utility programs. Any outsourcing of these ancillary modules into separate projects helps to keep the focus on the original project and is consistent with the blurring of the boundaries. Modularization makes it easy to reuse the code, speeding up the development process and decreasing managerial complexity which again feeds back positively on the strategic importance of these configurations.

Power and incentives in the organizational design of open source are balanced in a congenial way and carefully adjusted to the information structure just described. The main pillar for assigning power and providing incentives is the peer review process. In this process, senior programmers or the founder of the project, who have an in-depth knowledge of a particular module and its interplay with other modules in the program, evaluate software code written by other programmers.[34] They also manage the different tasks that have to be undertaken in the project by steering other people into making the most effective contributions, given their particular abilities.

Example 7.2 In the Mozilla Suite, power is assigned to individual programmers by means of 'ownership' of certain modules, such as the handling of JPEG-images by the browser, for example. The staff of the Mozilla Foundation asks developers to manage such modules if they have qualified according to ten criteria. Among these criteria are a demonstrated expertise and past involvement with the code of the module. Other requirements include the ability to evaluate proposed code for this module and its likely impact on other parts of the architecture. Module owners should furthermore be open to different

Continued

proposals regardless of their origin. The owners of modules can draw on the help of their peers to evaluate code proposed to them. The peer group is also responsible for reviewing and approving code proposed by the module owner him/herself.[a]

---

[a]   See http://www.mozilla.org/hacking/module-ownership.html, accessed 3 June 2005, for the principles of module ownership; and http://www.mozilla.org/owners.html, accessed 3 June 2005, for a list of the various modules and their owners.

Taking part and being able to make such evaluations requires an intensive knowledge of the code, which is usually gained through many contributions. Power in open source is therefore acquired as a result of project-specific investments. The more code a particular programmer writes for a program, the higher his/her status in the peer review process. Advancing along a career path from the finding of bugs, the proposing of fixes or new code towards becoming a peer or finally a module owner also provides incentives.[35]

The peer review process is also consistent with some kind of hierarchy in the design of open source. A pyramid-like hierarchy among contributors seems to emerge naturally. Unlike hierarchies in traditional companies, however, the one in open source is a true meritocracy. The best programmers in terms of quantity and quality gain the reputation and the trust of their peers to direct the community and its future efforts in a certain direction. The system is self-organizing, and a selection of jobs by individuals according to their perception of existing capabilities and available tasks is the norm, strengthening the value of their local knowledge and circumventing the problem of quality uncertainty resulting from private information.

Although most of the incentives are set in the form of peer recognition or a deferred pay-off once the capabilities are public knowledge,[36] it should be mentioned that monetary incentives are used to a certain extent as well. The Mozilla Foundation, for example, awards a 'bug bounty' to everyone who reports a critical security bug in their programs. All who report such flaws receive US $500 and a T-shirt.[37] Monetary incentives for programmers employed by companies operating in the wider ecosystem of open source described below must also be mentioned.

Governance

In the organizational design of open source, shareholders do not exist. Large financial contributions are not necessary in the organizational design of open source. They would arguably even be counter-productive, making the whole system inconsistent and hence less efficient. Software production is a human-capital-intensive industry, and financial capital is needed mainly for the purpose of speeding up the development process to reach critical mass for strategic reasons, as described above. Open source substitutes human power for money. Employing a much larger workforce and using a technology resting on modularity that makes parallel work on a grand scale feasible allows open source to catch up with commercial companies and even to take the lead in the development of new products, as is the case with the Firefox browser described in the introduction to this chapter. The human capital embedded in software programs is donated to the community through small investments of time and effort by many different programmers.[38] And such donations are possible, since the roles of developer and user are combined. Economic rents are therefore consumed by those who created them in the first place.

The organizational form of a community or loose network is best suited to the demands in the configuration of other elements. Unlike other forms that restrict participation in the organization, open-source communities allow unrestricted access to their resources. Contact with peers as the 'senior management' of the project is possible, and welcome, whenever the strategic direction of the project is taken into account.[39]

Besides the governance mode of access, the possibility of exit is widely prevalent for all involved in the community. At the extreme, developers can 'fork' an open-source development project, effectively leaving a particular project and setting up a complementary, or sometimes competing, project. This allows them to add any critical components they need. Such a triggering of the exit option offers greater flexibility, and any user or developer can subsequently modify the program to meet his/her needs. The exit option coexists alongside the voice mode of governance, as described by Hirschman (1970). Those constituencies who want to acquire influence can do so easily and become peers. All that is necessary is specific investment into the project, thereby further strengthening the crucial relationship between incentives and power as described above. Such behaviour is immediately evident in the observation of the way that corporations in related industries (for example, hardware vendors such as IBM or software distributors such as Redhat or Novell) endorse particular open-source projects and support these through various means, either financially or by actively developing code for the project with their employees. As the next section will show, such profit-orientated companies play a crucial part in the wider ecosystem of open-source communities.

Consistency and the open-source ecosystem

The bazaar

The open-source system resembles a bazaar, as Raymond (2000a) explains in his metaphor of a cathedral and a bazaar for the two different systems of software production. In a bazaar, stands are built wherever there is enough room to set up shop by whoever wants to. There is no central authority that permits or directs individual merchants. Everyone is allowed to do whatever task s/he thinks is in his/her best interest. Network externalities are important. Such externalities make individual investments worth more if other people also invest in setting up their stand at the same place and at the same time to attract the greatest number of customers. A well-established bazaar thus attracts other merchants, thereby reinforcing its success. Centrally planned co-ordination, however, is not necessary. A bazaar organizes itself whenever the purpose and available wares are common knowledge. From a dynamic perspective, it is worthwhile noting that a bazaar is dissolved at the end of the day, to be set up from scratch again the next morning. This allows for rapid changes from one day to the next, unlike a building made of stone, such as a cathedral, which is erected for centuries rather than for just a few hours a day. While minor or major restorations occur in cathedrals, there is no possibility of changing the basic architecture. A bazaar, on the other hand, is not built to last. It is intended to be deconstructed quickly.[40] As such it is an efficient design if changes in the business landscape are frequent and unexpected.

The business model of open-source projects resembles a bazaar, according to Raymond (2000a). In open source, use of specific knowledge is made by giving people who hold this kind of information the power to decide. An organizational design evolves automatically over time and changes frequently subject to new local information. In such a system, leadership for co-ordination of dispersed decisions is necessary. If exercised for that purpose, it leads to successful open-source projects. Leadership and the exercise of power for the main purpose of the appropriation of economic rents, however, contradicts the configuration of other parameters in this design: the incremental nature of specific investments and the good exit opportunities in open source prohibit such a malign use of power. No merchant divested of the economic rent from his/her specific investments into a stand will return to the bazaar the next morning.[41]

No one exercises ownership of the open-source software program in the sense of excluding others from the right to use it under the General

Public Licence. Revenues from transferring or licensing this right, as is the case with commercial software, prove elusive. Economic rents need to be generated through small and incremental investments, and have to be appropriated through the use of the final product by its developers, who co-operate with each other. Through careful configurations of organizational parameters a system emerges in which incentives and power are both balanced, thus leading to an efficient design. The interdependence between different organizational parameters in the system of open source is illustrated in Figure 7.1.

We can hence conclude that the open-source system constitutes a consistent system. Any change in the configuration of a single element does not increase efficiency. A caveat has to be mentioned, however, that might mitigate the applicability of open source: getting the exact configuration of the organizational parameters right is a prerequisite for the functioning of the system. The design of open source therefore represents a peak with a steep incline in the rugged landscape of competition. Even small deviations or a balance of power skewed towards a particular constituency can easily destroy the system. The system of open source is hence less robust than the system in which private innovation is a key design parameter.

Ecosystem of open source

The organizational design of open-source projects described in an idealized way above does not exist in a vacuum. It is supplemented by a wider ecosystem consisting of various other institutions such as universities or commercial companies exploiting the products created in open source to make a profit. Their activities reinforce open-source projects by channelling additional resources such as necessary hardware, the sponsoring of conferences, or even employees, dedicated to the ongoing development of particular projects to the community. Numerous business models exist, different strategies are pursued, and many propositions to create additional value by supplementing open source through commercial companies can be discerned. A short and non-comprehensive classification follows. For additional examples, see Raymond (2000b) or Schiff (2002, table 1):

- One of the most common business models in the ecosystem of open source is the provision of supplementary services. Distributors of open-source software, such as Redhat for the Linux operating system, bundle different software programs or modules such as the Linux kernel, the Gnome and KDE desktop environments, the OpenOffice

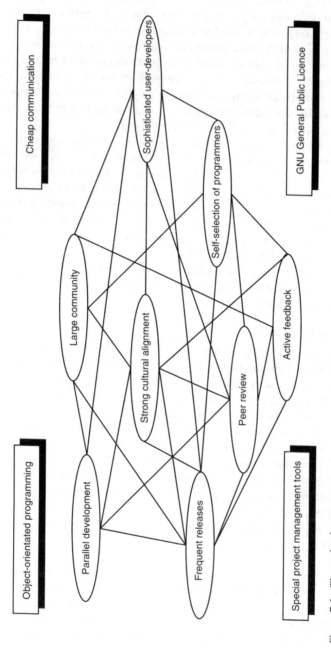

Figure 7.1 The web of open source

suite, the Firefox web browser and much more into different distributions in which the individual components work seamlessly together. While the distribution is still free for download from its website, Redhat charges for ancillary services such as complex installations and system administration, for the provision of continuous updates, for manuals and the training of users, or for consulting services related to its distribution. Redhat and other firms following such a business model generate economic rents from this value proposition and are profitable companies.

- Not only services supplement open-source software and the resulting system, products can also do so. The most prominent product to supplement software is traditionally the hardware called to life by the software. More established companies such as IBM enter the open-source domain to profit from complementarities between the two products. IBM is arguably the single most potent contributor to the community, with a budget of several billion US dollars related to open-source projects and a release of 500 patents into open source in January 2005.[42] The strategy to make a product cheaper, so that people are more likely to buy a related product that a company sells, is also applied by Sun Microsystems. Sun supports the development of the OpenOffice suite to encourage users to buy their computer hardware.[43]

- Another example of how the deployment of an organizational design based on open source benefits the wider ecosystem can be found in the area of standard-setting. Agreeing on an open, industry-wide standard is an act of collective innovation. To accommodate the needs of all industry participants, it is necessary to keep the profit motive subdued. This can be achieved through reliance on an organizational design following the layout of open source as described above. A blueprint for a business model along these lines, albeit no open-source project in the narrow sense, is provided by Symbian. Symbian is a consortium of the leading mobile handset makers such as Nokia, Sony Ericsson, Siemens and others.[44] By working together on a common operating system that makes the devices of different manufacturers compatible with each other, a sensible business proposition is involved and value generated. Users of mobile phones and the software running on them are also encouraged to participate in the development of the software, and more open-source projects evolve around Symbian.

- Many, if not most, open-source projects originate in academia. Universities are engaged in open source since it provides an ideal testing ground on which to train their students, and supports many research projects. The relatively weak incentives in universities to commercialize successful open-source projects in an institutionalized manner complement the key characteristic of a free and open source code. Universities offer an ideal breeding ground on which to develop complementary products or services that can be exploited by individuals. The 'ready access to venture capital'[45] that the proponents of open source have does not only positively feed back on their motivation but also allows them to scale-up their open-source product through a business model along the lines described here. As the wider ecosystem of open source thus grows, so does the success of the organizational design of open source.

7.5   Comparative organizational analysis

After the description of the two different organizational designs of proprietary software and open source in the previous sections, the evaluation of the two systems in a comparative organizational analysis remains to be undertaken to determine the systems' relative efficiency. This is the topic of this section. The configuration of organizational parameters in the two designs are contrasted with each other in a first step to determine whether one design is superior to the other. Then the interplay between the two systems and the effect on the efficiency of the larger design that constitutes the overall economy is discussed in a second step.

Comparison of the organizational designs

Synopsis of the two designs

Table 7.2 displays the differences in the configuration of important organizational design parameters for the two systems of software programming.

The different purposes underlying the two systems are reflected in the configuration of the parameters of strategy. A company operating along the lines of a business model resting on a proprietary source code is keen to restrict competition through the differentiation and complexity of its product in order to maximize economic rents for its stakeholders. Having invested to entrench its own position, a dissolution of the design does not occur unless the venture is grossly unsuccessful. The design of open source, on the other hand, rests on compatibility of different programs. Hence open standards and small modules prevail, and the resources employed in a specific project separate again once the

Table 7.2 Synopsis of the designs of open and proprietary sources

		Proprietary source	Open source
Strategy	Purpose	Create a proprietary program as standard	Create an ecosystem of compatible programs relying on open standards
	Product	Emphasis on differentiation and innovation	Emphasis on low-cost alternative
	Activities	Integration of different pieces to a single complex program	Reliance on modularity in design
	Duration	Going concern, designed to last	Designed for specific project
Boundaries	Setting of boundaries	Exclusiveness of resources	Programmers working on several projects simultaneously
	Permeability	Boundaries are difficult to cross	Blurred and open, sometimes no perceivable boundaries exist
	Interactions across boundaries	Alliances to create software standards	Whole ecosystem of symbiotic relationships
Internal structure	Use of information	Screening of resources and direction	Self-organization of resources through self-selection
	Power distribution	Power assigned through departments and hierarchy	Strong role of leadership, power contingent on specific investments
	Provision of incentives	Stock options as incentive device	Internal promotion and career concerns
	Co-ordination	*Ex-ante* planning and task assignment	CVS with approvement of leadership and rapid releases
Governance	Stakeholders	(Founding) entrepreneur, employees, shareholders	(Founding) programmers, users, distributors
	Mechanisms	Ownership of shareholders, employee share ownership plans	Access to peers, easy exit, acquisition of voice possible
	Organizational forms	Corporations, partnerships, sole proprietorship	Projects, communities, networks

project has achieved its (usually narrow) purpose. Dissolving an open-source project is simplified by highly permeable boundaries, and leaving is easy for programmers, who often work on several projects simultaneously. Moving between different projects advances their careers and status in the open source community, and also acts as an incentive device. In the design of proprietary software, boundaries are more restrictive to keep the source code secret and to protect the economic rents for the stakeholders of the company arising from the strategically entrenched positions.

In the internal structure of open-source projects, power and incentives are aligned almost automatically. Those constituencies investing specifically into the success of the overall project acquire generically the power to safeguard the economic rents resulting from their (usually small) investments. Power in proprietary software companies, on the other hand, is derived through the configuration of the various instruments of internal structure such as a superior position in the corporate hierarchy that facilitates co-ordination. Governance parameters such as the choice of the corporate form or the assignment of ownership rights to shareholders further skew the distribution of power. Obscuring the contribution of individual programmers to the software makes them less visible to the outside world and lowers their exit opportunities. In sharp contrast to this, the visibility of individual programmers is enhanced in open source, as argued by Lee *et al.* (2004) and is a key characteristic necessary for the functioning of the open-source system. Allowing developers and users to take advantage of the voice mechanism balances the power distribution in the communities and aligns it carefully with the necessary incentives for specific investments. Positions of power thus remain contestable over time.

Which design is more efficient?

The two organizational designs described in this chapter differ in many of their configurations. Although both idealized designs described above constitute consistent systems, one of them might be superior to the other, forming a global optimum in the rugged landscape of competition. To answer the question of which of the two organizational designs is relatively more efficient necessitates the definition of the dimensions along which efficiency can and should be measured. In the case of the production of software, suitable dimensions as well as the costs of production are, for example, the quality of the software, the speed of development or the availability of solutions to frequent or less frequent problems – all factors that influence the amount of economic rents generated by the organizational design. Additional factors can, of course, be imagined as well, but success is difficult to measure in most dimensions. Take the quality of a software program as an example. Not only the performance in terms of the execution of a given task is important, but usability also matters. The necessity of training users to operate a particular program, or the requirement to make the program compatible with other software through complex interfaces adds to the total cost of ownership, a concept commonly applied to measure the efficiency of a software program in financial terms. Economic rents, especially those accruing to users, are reduced in these cases. It is proprietary software that is often differentiated for strategic reasons, so that the amount of rents for particular constituencies of the organization is maximized disregarding economic rents for less powerful constituencies. This impairs the efficiency relative to a design in which power is more contingent on undertaking value-creating specific investments.

Another issue influencing the quality of the software is its security. In the case of web browsers and operating systems, this becomes obvious whenever another flaw in commonly used programs such as Microsoft Windows or Microsoft's Internet Explorer is exploited by malicious hackers. It is difficult to discern whether such security problems are a result of the production processes deployed in the traditional software model, or whether they result from the determination to have the greatest impact, in which case any malicious code is targeted against the prevailing software standard – that is, often proprietary products by companies such as Microsoft. Whatever the answer is to this question, the proponents of open source are probably correct in claiming that their products are at least better in terms of a quick removal of any flaws that are detected. Many programmers from diverse backgrounds yearn for a high-quality code that enhances their status and visibility in the community. Proponents of open source accuse proprietary software firms of achieving 'security through obscurity', implying that closed-source products remain secure because of the unavailability of the source code, but only as long as no one spots a weak point in it by chance.

The same argument of having a larger potential workforce slightly favours open source along the second and third dimensions mentioned above, the speed with which software can be developed, and the availability of solutions to common problems.

Example 7.3 The broader and more rapid development of open-source software can be illustrated by counting the different language versions in which the two dominating operating systems are available. Whereas Windows 2000 is available in twenty-four different languages and Windows XP offers a Multilingual User Interface Pack increasing this number to thirty-three,[a] KDE, one of the leading desktop developments for Linux, comes in as many as fifty languages.[b] The same holds true for office productivity suites: Microsoft Office is available in over twenty languages, whereas its main competitor in the open-source domain, OpenOffice, can be set up in forty-four different languages, with more under development. This pattern is topped by Mozilla, the open-source web browser, that at one time was available, in sixty-five languages.[c]

---

[a]   See http://www.microsoft.com/technet/prodtechnol/winxppro/evaluate/muiovw.mspx, accessed 8 June 2005.
[b]   See http://www.kde.org/announcements/announce-3.4.1.php, accessed 8 June 2005.
[c]   See *The Economist* (2003b).

Open source also beats proprietary software in terms of costs of licensing. The particular terms of the licence used create a distinct distribution of power between producer and consumer in the product market. Software that is available for free allows its users to enjoy an economic rent from its use.[46] For these reasons – that is, because of the prevalence of the profit motive that leads to rent-seeking behaviour – the organizational design of commercial software companies does usually not maximize the overall welfare. Only that share of economic rents that accrues to particular constituencies is taken into consideration in the proprietary software model when making decisions about value-creating investments. Efficiency is hence impaired in this business model, and the system of open source seems to be the superior organizational design.

Are mixed configurations possible?

Several companies adhering to the traditional, closed-source model of software production have reacted to the threat of competition from the open-source business model by adjusting their organizational design. Traditional software companies have begun to disclose selectively some part of their source code while retaining the copyright on it. Microsoft, for example, has started a Shared Source Initiative. With this initiative it reveals parts of the source code to governments, universities and some carefully chosen companies.[47]

But this strategy is not to be mistaken for open source. The software remains proprietary even if the source code is made available publicly. Control over the use of a software program, its distribution and its modification is retained under the Shared Source Initiative. It is not possible to split the software and release a modified version without restrictions. See also West (2003) for further examples of hybrid strategies, or Dinkelacker and Garg (2001) for a description of Hewlett-Packard's response to open source.

Can such a strategy succeed and increase efficiency relative to a pure open-source model? Several theoretical arguments and the anecdotal evidence in the case of the Shared Source Initiative speak against it. Applying the methodology of systems theory, it is clear why this is the case. Being open in production but retaining the final product proprietarily creates an imbalance in both the power distribution and the incentive structure. Closed-source systems are never able to emulate the incentive structure of open source. The incentives to undertake specific investments are out of balance if the balance of power to appropriate economic rents from the final product is skewed in favour of the constituency that holds the copyright on the software program. Other constituencies in such a setting are reluctant to invest their time and effort into helping with the development of the software. Changes in other organizational parameters would also be required: of particular importance will be changes in design to make the configuration of the individual contribution to a final product more transparent. This feature is, however, deliberately muted in firms. Having the best of both worlds is not going to work; it takes more than revealing the source code to obtain the benefits of open source. A strategic choice about the business model, such as the decision by Netscape Communications to release its Navigator web browser as an open source, has to be made.[48]

Efficient organizational design

The arguments above might lead to the temptation to disregard completely the traditional model of software development and to advocate a disclosure of the source code as a panacea. This, however, would be a little shortsighted. In analogy to the two case studies presented previously in the second part of this book, answering the question of which one of the two systems is actually best is no trivial task. One caveat concerns exogenous factors such as the rate of change. Another applies when considering the efficiency of the larger organizational design that constitutes the overall economy.

Change and innovation revisited

Bazaars are dismantled and rebuilt every day, while cathedrals built long ago have weathered many storms over the centuries. Bazaars are often built around cathedrals. The existence of a cathedral draws merchants from different regions and allows them to co-ordinate their actions. Cathedrals provide focal points. The architectural metaphor fits the organizational design well: like cathedrals, companies operating under the traditional business model with proprietary software have vested interests in resources and positions. They have erected rigid structures and often impermeable boundaries to protect these resources and positions, and the economic rents generated by them. Dissolution is not considered. The power distribution in companies can become skewed over time in favour of particular constituencies, thereby discouraging value-creating specific investments by other constituencies that lack an offsetting power. The configuration of the various organizational parameters applied by commercial companies thus ossifies as time goes by and handicaps them in dealing with disruptive changes.

The flexibility inherent in open source allows it to cope better with disruptive changes. Radical adjustments are facilitated as projects can easily be initiated or discarded. A high degree of change in the rugged landscape of competition therefore favours the open-source organizational design. Disruptive change happens (unless as a result of the idea of a single brilliant mind), mainly because of closely co-ordinated innovation. A system ensuring that no constituency can appropriate economic rents generated by specific investments of other constituencies encourages value creation. A thoroughly designed open-source system does this.

But recall that change and the desire to catch up with new products was one of the motivations behind the open-source system. If such change is absent and a crucial parameter has been altered in a configuration inconsistent with those of other elements, the whole system of open source can fall apart. As the software industry matures and the rate of change subsides, a model based on private innovation could become more appropriate again. Incentives to increase the share of economic rents through expropriation of rents from other constituencies are never muted. Even in open source, such behaviour remains rational for individual parties and, if at all possible, will occur. Although the open-source system is probably the higher mountain in the rugged landscape of competition, it is also the one with the steeper approaches. Small deviations from the optimal configuration of a few parameters are already enough to push the whole system over the edge into the abyss. As a high rate of change is an important parameter in the open-source configuration, the fragile open-source design is in danger when that rate is low. A general answer to the question of whether one system is better than the other is therefore not feasible.

Twin peaks and efficiency of the larger design

It is, instead, more likely that the interplay of an open-source with a closed-source system achieves maximum efficiency in the larger design of the overall economy than the dominance of one particular system. The coexistence of both business models keeps the power of incumbent software firms adhering to the proprietary model, and their strategic entrenchment in check. Companies operating under the traditional model of private innovation cannot exercise their power to the degree possible in a system in which open-source projects do not exist and other profit-orientated companies would not undertake the necessary investments to counter the power of a quasi-natural monopolist.

Open-source projects, on the other hand, would not exist if there were no competition from proprietary software corporations. Just as bazaars need cathedrals to build around, open source needs a functioning system containing commercial software companies. In this case it is, however, not the issue of keeping a monopoly position under control. If some constituency in open source uses its power as a way of appropriating rents from other parties, it is easy to split the project with an open-source code. The problem with a design in which only open-source communities prevail is that programmers in an idealized open-source system would lose the motivation to work for the commons. Free-riding on the efforts of others would be more widespread. With little competition there would be little focus in the projects, and the signalling rationale for able programmers would break down. Thus deprived of an important configuration, the design would become inconsistent and arguably would fall apart. Open source therefore needs closed-source companies to reinforce its merits, as is also argued by Lee *et al.* (2004).

From the point of view of maximizing the welfare in the system of the overall economy, the choice is then between an inefficient system with a skewed balance of power and one that would not live up to its theoretical promise. But for the task of optimizing the design of the overall economy, a third possibility exists. A coexistence and co-evolution of both systems of software production achieves efficiency in the overall economy. Competition between the two systems mitigates the potential weakness of each system on its own. Favouring either of these two idealized systems and switching between them over time allows the avoidance of the weaknesses that would prevail if settling on the steady state of applying only one system.[49]

The relative prevalence of the two distinct designs of software production determines the size of the commons area. If the commons domain is too large, no incentives to innovate exist because of the absence of a suitable appropriation regime. If it is too small, then incompatibilities between competing standards lead to inefficiencies in design. Balancing collective and private innovation thus appears to be the most efficient organizational design for the larger system of the overall economy. A rugged landscape of competition with two peaks – one representing the proprietary software system and the other the open-source system – is a suitable metaphor to describe the organizational design that would maximize the efficiency of the software industry in the overall economy.

Notes

1. See http://www.netscape.com/newsref/pr/newsrelease558.html, accessed 20 June 2005.
2. The name Mozilla was the codename used in the development of the original Netscape browser. It is a contraction of 'Mosaic killer' to clarify the intention in its development. The company mascot of Netscape, a Godzilla-like monster, was also called Mozilla. Furthermore, the name Mozilla is prevalent in the user agent string of many browsers that identifies the client software to the server and thereby allows it to bypass official standards.
3. See Raymond (2000a, p. 32).
4. The rendering engine is a piece of software responsible for the way that content and format information is displayed by the web browser or another program. It can be embedded in the overall software program or be a separate component, as is the case for the Gecko engine on which several web browsers are based.
5. For an extensive description of the history of Linux, see http://www.linux.org/info, accessed 3 June 2005.
6. See also increasing evidence for the success of other open-source software programs, such as Linux, provided by *The Economist* (2000, 2001b and 2002c).
7. See http://news.netcraft.com/archives/web_server_survey.html, accessed 22 June 2005.
8. See Section 2.2.
9. The most comprehensive collection of work related to open source is gathered by a team around Eric von Hippel, Georg von Krogh and Karim Lakhani on the website http://opensource.mit.edu. See also Schiff (2002) for a brief survey of different contributions.
10. Data on the motivation to work for open-source projects is provided in two surveys of open-source programmers, by Hars and Ou (2002) and Hertel *et al.* (2003).
11. See Zeitlyn (2003). See also Kuan (2002) for the role of intrinsic motivation to guarantee the quality of software.
12. See the original argument in Lerner and Tirole (2002), and the different models provided by Leppämäki and Mustonen (2003), Prüfer (2004) and Lee *et al.* (2004).
13. See, for example, the case studies of the Mozilla project by Reis and Fortes (2002); of the Linux project by Moon and Sproull (2000) and Dafermos

(2001); and of the Apache project by Franke and von Hippel (2003) and Mockus *et al.* (2000).

14. See also Schmidt and Schnitzer (2003) on the economics of software production and their implications for public policy.

15. Wheeler (2002) reports that the operating system Redhat 7.1 contains more than 30 million physical source lines of code. Later versions of Linux or other operating systems have surely further increased that number.

16. Communication is clearly important. Although it depends on the actual project, it is a sizeable part of a programmer's job. *The Economist* (2003a, p. 20) reports that a programmer spends on average only 30 per cent of his or her time coding while the rest of the time is taken up with discussions with the other members of the team.

17. See also the argument by Langlois (2002) on the relationship between complexity and modularity, which is based more in economics than computer science.

18. See Baldwin and Clark (2000, pp. 264–6) for the value of parallelism and experimentation in an unknown landscape. See also *The Economist* (2003a) for the different processes.

19. The Concurrent Versions System (CVS) is a source code collaboration tool. It allows the retrieval of previous versions of a file by storing the differences between various versions. CVS also helps to manage the code of a project when several people are working on it at the same time.

20. See Feller and Fitzgerald (2002) for a more comprehensive introduction to open source and its history.

21. See http://www.opensource.org, accessed 3 June 2005.

22. See http://www.opensource.org/docs/definition.php, accessed 3 June 2005, for all ten criteria.

23. See http://www.fsf.org, accessed 3 June 2005.

24. See http://www.gnu.org/philosophy/categories.html, accessed 3 June 2005.

25. See http://www.opensource.org/licenses/index.php, accessed 24 June 2005.

26. See http://www.opensource.org/licenses/gpl-license.php, accessed 24 June 2005.

27. See also von Hippel and von Krogh (2003), who propose a mixture of these two paradigms to produce a 'private-collective model' to explain the existence and functioning of open source.

28. For a case study of how such collective innovation can work, see Nuvolari (2004). He describes the improvements in mine pumping engines during the Industrial Revolution in Cornwall.

29. von Hippel (2005, p. 91; emphasis in the original).

30. See Henkel (2004), who provides brief case studies of commercial firms in the open-source domain.

31. Note that other industries, such as, for example, the music business, have also been affected by the internet and its possibilities for sharing digital content over peer-to-peer networks among strangers. Business models resting on a restriction of access to knowledge-based assets or copyright materials were threatened and a general discussion about intellectual property was instigated.

32. In this context see also Franke and von Hippel (2003) who illustrate the possibility of customizing any open-source software using the example of the Apache security software. This possibility increases the value of open source if demand is heterogeneous.

33. Not everything, however, is open and transparent in the open-source community. The Mozilla Foundation, for example, restricts access to critical security issues to deter the exploitation of such vulnerabilities until a patch is available for the bug.

34. See, in this context, also Iannacci (2003) for a more detailed description of the Linux managing model.

35. See also Osterloh *et al.* (2002a) for a description of how the peer review process reinforces rapid production.

36. See Lerner and Tirole (2002) or Lee *et al.* (2004).

37. See http://www.mozilla.org/projects/security/security-bugs-policy.html, accessed 30 June 2005.

38. See Franck and Jungwirth (2003) on the importance of the donation of software code in the governance of open source.

39. See von Krogh *et al.* (2003) for a case study of how developers join, specialize and contribute to the development of Freenet, a peer-to-peer file sharing network. See also Lakhani and von Hippel (2003) for an investigation of free user-to-user assistance.

40. Refer also to Sections 3.1 and 3.2 where the importance of deconstruction is discussed from a strategic perspective and a boundary view, respectively.

41. See also Demil and Lecocq (2006) on bazaar governance.

42. See IBM (2005, p. 16).

43. See http://www.sun.com/software/star/openoffice, accessed 28 July 2005. See also Henkel (2004) on the nexus of different firms as either users or sellers of a complement.

44. See http://www.symbian.com/about/ownership.html, accessed 28 July 2005.

45. Lerner and Tirole (2001, p. 822).

46. It should be noted that an economic rent can also be a result of network effects and the prevalence of a common standard. This usually favours proprietary software where such effects are considered explicitly in the strategy of closed-source companies.

47. For more detailed information on the Shared Source Initiative, see the Microsoft website – for example, http://www.microsoft.com/presspass/features/2004/mar04/03–19sharedsource.mspx, accessed 30 July 2005.

48. For a more recent example, see Morgan (2004) who proposes that Sun Microsystems releases its Java program into open source to capture its full potential, which is currently held back as a result of proprietary software companies fighting over the dominant standard.

49. See Nickerson and Zenger (2002) for this argument in the context of organizational design in general.

8
Conclusion

This book has been about organizational design. Of particular concern have been the two major themes of incentives and power in organizations. Both themes are influenced through numerous organizational instruments described in the course of this book. The design of the strategy and the internal structure, the boundaries and the governance determine the efficiency of the organization. The interplay between these building blocks, with their modules and elements, is of importance. Complementarities between these elements and modules make some sets of configurations superior to others in terms of efficiency. Complementarities between these elements and modules, while adding to the complexity of the design, generate returns from supermodularity that increase efficiency. Economic rents result from such consistently configured designs and are distributable among the constituencies of the organization.

An efficient organizational design is a system in which no small deviation in several elements nor a change in a single parameter leads to an enhancement of efficiency. Organizations designed for an exploitation of complementarities between these different elements constitute distinct business models. The success of these business models depends on the fit with the business environment. External factors, such as improvements in technology or changes in regulation, determine the appropriateness of an organizational system in the business environment. Changes in the rugged landscape of competition make adjustments in the organizational design necessary in order to restore efficiency through a rebalancing of power and incentives.

What will efficient organizations of the future look like? Whatever the answer, a thorough analysis of individual elements and a careful synthesis of these parameters to a consistent whole is the most appropriate methodology of dealing with a phenomenon as complex as the firm. Meaningful guidance for management decisions and sensible policy advice thus become possible. The first requirement, the analysis of individual elements, is far advanced in economics, but the second requirement – the synthesis of the individual elements into a consistent whole – is an area less well explored by economists. It is here where further research is most promising. Both routes – analysis as well as synthesis – are best supplemented by case studies. This allows one to see how theoretical predictions translate into practice.

Adjustments in the organizational system have occurred in many industries to cater for changes in the business environment. In the motor vehicle industry, for example, the craft system of the late nineteenth century yielded to a system of mass production, which was eventually replaced by the system of modern manufacturing. A design of decentralized power and incentives provided by markets thus yielded to a design in which power was more centralized, and more muted incentives were provided by different instruments within firms. Technological changes subsequently necessitated the replacement of these structures by the current one, in which power and incentives are balanced more subtly and boundaries have become more blurred and more permeable. Reconfigurations of several organizational parameters support these adjustments, and a deconstruction of formerly integrated firms has begun. This development can be spotted increasingly in many other industries as well.

The pharmaceutical industry provides such an example of disintegration and modularization. Smaller companies are set up to perform particular activities along the value chain. Each design has its own peculiar strategy, structure and governance, and focuses on a much narrower set of tasks. This allows a better balance of both incentives and power to be struck. The different activities along the value chain can be optimized independently in this modularized system of the industry. The most suitable organizational design can be chosen for each activity. Where financial capital matters most, such as production and distribution, a shareholder-controlled corporation achieves efficiency, while in research a business model along the lines of open source or academia fares better in stimulating the necessary specific investments and protecting the resulting economic rent.

A 'New Enterprise', to borrow the notion of Rajan and Zingales (2000a), thus emerges. In such a (more adequate) organizational design, several changes in the configuration of elements help to restore the balance of power between the different stakeholders in the organization and keep their incentives for value creation intact. The result from the balance in both power and incentives is a nexus of specific investments that maximizes the efficiency of the organizational design in many of today's companies, industries or other kinds of organization.

Just as technological innovation leads to progress, innovation in organizational design has to occur as well. Changes in the business environment demand adjustments in the business models and the configuration of the elements of organizational design to restore or to increase efficiency. This sometimes demands a radical and unconventional configuration in some parameters that, at first sight, looks surprising, as did the phenomenon of open source. The challenge is to take complementarities between the numerous elements of organizational design into consideration in order to achieve consistency in the whole system. Of particular importance is the balancing of incentives and power as a necessary condition for achieving efficiency in any organizational design.

Bibliography

Ackoff, R. L. (1989) 'From Data to Wisdom', *Journal of Applied Systems Analysis*, vol. 16, pp. 3–9.

Aer Lingus (2005) *Annual Report 2004* (Dublin: Aer Lingus).

Aghion, P. and J. Tirole (1995) 'Some Implications of Growth for Organizational Form and Ownership Structure', *European Economic Review*, vol. 39, no. 3/4, pp. 440–55.

Aghion, P. and J. Tirole (1997) 'Formal and real authority in organizations', *Journal of Political Economy*, vol. 105, no. 1, pp. 1–29.

Akerlof, G. A. (1970) 'The Market for "Lemons": Qualitative Uncertainty and the Market Mechanism', *Quarterly Journal of Economics*, vol. 84, no. 3, pp. 488–500.

Alchian, A. A. and H. Demsetz (1972) 'Production, Information Costs and Economic Organization', *American Economic Review*, vol. 62, no. 5, pp. 777–95.

Alchian, A. A. and S. Woodward (1987) 'Reflections on the Theory of the Firm', *Journal of Institutional and Theoretical Economics*, vol. 143, no. 1, pp. 110–36.

Alchian, A. A. and S. Woodward (1988) 'The Firm Is Dead; Long Live the Firm – A Review of Oliver E. Williamson's *The Economic Institutions of Capitalism*', *Journal of Economic Literature*, vol. 26, no. 1, pp. 65–79.

Allen, F. and D. Gale (2000a) *Comparing Financial Systems* (Cambridge, Mass.: MIT Press).

Allen, F. and D. Gale (2000b) 'Corporate Governance and Competition', in X. Vives (ed.), *Corporate Governance – Theoretical and Empirical Perspectives*, (Cambridge University Press), pp. 23–83.

Allen, F. and D. Gale (2002) 'A Comparative Theory of Corporate Governance', Wharton Financial Institutions Center, Working paper No. 03.27.

Allen, F. and P. D. Sherer (1995) 'The Design and Redesign of Organizational Form', in E. H. Bowman and B. M. Kogut (eds), *Redesigning the Firm* (Oxford University Press), pp. 183–96.

Allen, P. M. (1994) 'Evolutionary Complex Systems: Models of Technology Change', in L. Leydesdorff and P. van den Besselaar (eds), *Evolutionary Economics and Chaos Theory: New Directions in Technology Studies* (New York: St. Martin's Press), pp. 1–17.

Amable, B. (2003) *The Diversity of Modern Capitalism* (Oxford University Press).

Amit, R. and P. J. Shoemaker (1993) 'Strategic Assets and Organizational Rent', *Strategic Management Journal*, vol. 14, no. 1, pp. 33–46.

Anderson, E. (1985) 'The Salesperson as Outside Agent or Employee: A Transaction Cost Analysis', *Marketing Science*, vol. 4, no. 3, pp. 234–54.

Anderson, E., and D. Schmittlein (1984) 'Integration of the Sales Force: An Empirical Examination', *RAND Journal of Economics*, vol. 15, no. 3, pp. 385–95.

Anderson, P. (1999) 'Complexity Theory and Organization Science', *Organization Science*, vol. 10, no. 3, pp. 216–32.

Aoki, M. (1995) 'The Gains from Organizational Diversity: An Evolutionary Game Parable', in H. Siebert (ed.), *Trends in Business Organization: Do Participation and*

Cooperation increase Competitiveness? (Tübingen: J. C. B. Mohr (Paul Siebeck)), pp. 265–79.

Aoki, M. (2001) *Toward a Comparative Institutional Analysis* (Cambridge, Mass.: MIT Press).

Aoki, M. and H. Patrick (1994) *The Japanese Main Bank System: Its Relevance for Developing and Transforming Economies* (Oxford University Press).

Appelbaum, E., T. Bailey, P. Berg and A. L. Kalleberg (2000) *Manufacturing Advantage: Why High-Performance Work Systems Pay Off* (Ithaca, NY: Cornell University Press).

Argyris, C. (1998) 'Empowerment: The Emperor's New Clothes', *Harvard Business Review*, vol. 76, no. 3, pp. 98–105.

Arrow, K. J. (1962) 'Economic Welfare and the Allocation of Resources for Invention', in R. Nelson (ed.), *The Rate and Direction of Inventive Activity: Economic and Social Factors* (Princeton, NJ: Princeton University Press), pp. 609–25.

Arthur, W. B. (1996) 'Increasing Returns and the New World of Business', *Harvard Business Review*, vol. 74, no. 4, pp. 100–9.

Arthur, W. B., S. Durlauf and D. A. Lane (1997) 'Introduction: Process and Emergence in the Economy', in W. B. Arthur, S. Durlauf and D. A. Lane (eds), *The Economy as an Evolving Complex System II*, (Boston, Mass.: Addison-Wesley), pp. 1–14.

Aschhoff, G. and E. Henningsen (1996) *The German Cooperative System – Its History, Structure and Strength* (Frankfurt am Main: Fritz Knapp Verlag).

Athey, S. and J. Roberts (2001) 'Organizational Design: Decision Rights and Incentive Contracts', *American Economic Review*, vol. 91, No. 2, pp. 200–5.

Athey, S. and S. Stern (1998) 'An Empirical Framework for Testing Theories about Complementarity in Organizational Design', NBER Working Paper, no. 6600.

Auriol, E. and R. Renault (2001) 'Incentive Hierarchies', *Annales d'Économie et de Statistique*, no. 63/64, pp. 261–82.

Auriol, E., G. Friebel and L. Pechlivanos (2002) 'Career Concerns in Teams', *Journal of Labor Economics*, vol. 20, no. 1, pp. 289–307.

BAG Bankaktiengesellschaft (2001) *Konzernabschluß 2000* (Hamm: BAG Bankaktiengesellschaft).

Baker, G., R. Gibbons and K. J. Murphy (1999) 'Informal Authority in Organizations', *Journal of Law, Economics and Organization*, vol. 15, no. 1, pp. 56–73.

Baker, G., R. Gibbons and K. J. Murphy (2002) 'Relational Contracts and the Theory of the Firm', *Quarterly Journal of Economics*, vol. 117, no. 1, pp. 39–83.

Baker, G. and B. R. Holmström (1995) 'Internal Labor Markets: Too Many Theories, Too Few Facts', *American Economic Review*, vol. 85, no. 2, pp. 255–9.

Baker, G. P. (1992) 'Beatrice: A Study in the Creation and Destruction of Value', *Journal of Finance*, vol. 47, no. 3, pp. 1081–119.

Baldwin, C. Y. and K. B. Clark (2000) *Design Rules – The Power of Modularity*. (Cambridge, Mass.: MIT Press).

Bamberger, I. and T. Wrona (1996) 'Der Ressourcenansatz und seine Bedeutung für die Strategische Unternehmensführung', *Zeitschrift für Betriebswirtschaftliche Forschung*, vol. 48, no. 2, pp. 130–53.

Barney, J. B. (1991) 'Firm Resources and Sustained Competitive Advantage', *Journal of Management*, vol. 17, no. 1, pp. 99–120.

Barney, J. B. (1999) 'How a Firm's Capabilities Affect Boundary Decisions', *Sloan Management Review*, vol. 40, no. 3, pp. 137–45.

Baron, D. P. and D. Besanko (2001) 'Strategy, Organization and Incentives: Global Corporate Banking at Citibank', *Industrial and Corporate Change*, vol. 10, no. 1, pp. 1–36.

Baron, J. N. and D. M. Kreps (1999) *Strategic Human Resources – Frameworks for General Managers* (New York: John Wiley).

Bartlett, C. A. and S. Ghoshal (1995) 'Changing the Role of Top Management: Beyond Systems to People', *Harvard Business Review*, vol. 73, no. 3, pp. 132–42.

Bartlett, C. A. and S. Ghoshal (2000) *Text, Cases and Readings in Cross-Border Management*, 3rd edn. (Boston, Mass.: Mc-Graw-Hill).

Bebchuk, L. A. and M. J. Roe (2004) 'A Theory of Path Dependence in Corporate Ownership and Governance', in J. N. Gordon and M. J. Roe (eds), *Convergence and Persistence in Corporate Governance* (Cambridge University Press), pp. 69 –113.

Bebchuck, L., J. Fried and D. Walker (2002) 'Managerial Power and Rent Extraction in the Design of Executive Compensation', *University of Chicago Law Review*, vol. 69, no. 3, pp. 751–846.

Becht, M., P. Bolton and A. Röell (2003) 'Corporate Governance and Control', in G. Constantinides, M. Harris, and R. Stulz (eds), *Handbook of the Economics of Finance*, vol. 1A/Corporate Finance (Amsterdam: North-Holland), pp. 1–108.

Berle, A. A. and G. C. Means (1932) *The Modern Corporation and Private Property* (New York: Macmillan).

Bernheim, B. D. and M. D. Whinston (1998) 'Incomplete Contracts and Strategic Ambiguity', *American Economic Review*, vol. 88, no. 4, pp. 902–32.

Besanko, D., D. Dranove and M. Shanley (2000) *Economics of Strategy*, 2nd edn. (New York: John Wiley).

Bishop, M. (2004) 'Kings of Capitalism – A Survey of Private Equity', *The Economist*, vol. 373, no. 8403, pp. 1–16.

Black, J. A. and K. B. Boal (1994) 'Strategic Resources: Traits, Configurations and Paths to Sustainable Competitive Advantage', *Strategic Management Journal*, vol. 15(Special Issue), pp. 131–48.

Blair, M. M. (1995) *Ownership and Control: Rethinking Corporate Governance for the Twenty-first Century* (Washington, DC: Brookings Institution Press).

Blair, M. M. (1999) 'Firm-Specific Human Capital and Theories of the Firm', in M. M. Blair and M. J. Roe (eds), *Employees and Corporate Governance* (Washington, DC: Brookings Institution Press), pp. 58–90.

Blair, M. M. and T. A. Kochan (2000) *The New Relationship* (Washington, DC: Brookings Institution Press).

Bolton, P. and M. Dewatripont (1994) 'The Firm as a Communication Network', *Quarterly Journal of Economics*, vol. 109, no. 4, pp. 809–39.

Bolton, P. and M. Dewatripont (2005) *Contract Theory* (Cambridge, Mass.: MIT Press).

Bolton, P. and A. Rajan (2003) 'The Employment Relation and the Theory of the Firm: Arm's Length Contracting vs Authority', Princeton University Working paper.

Bolton, P. and D. S. Scharfstein (1998) 'Corporate Finance, the Theory of the Firm, and Organizations', *Journal of Economic Perspectives*, vol. 12, no. 4, pp. 95–114.

Boot, A. W. A. and A. V. Thakor (2003) 'The Economic Value of Flexibility When There is Disagreement', CEPR Discussion Paper No. 3709.

Brätland, J. (2003) 'Contestability: A New Theory of Natural Monopoly and a Vain Quest to Regulate Efficiency', Ludwig von Mises Institute Working Paper (Auburn, Alabama).

Bresser, R. K., M. A. Hitt, R. D. Nixon and D. Heuskel (2000) *Winning Strategies in a Deconstructing World* (Chichester: John Wiley).

Brickley, J. A., C. W. Smith and J. L. Zimmerman (1997a) 'Management Fads and Organizational Architecture', *Journal of Applied Corporate Finance*, vol. 10, no. 2, pp. 24–39.

Brickley, J. A., C. W. Smith and J. L. Zimmerman (1997b) *Managerial Economics and Organizational Architecture* (Chicago, Ill.: Irwin).

Brickley, J. A., C. W. Smith and J. L. Zimmerman (2003) 'Corporate Governance, Ethics and Organizational Architecture', *Journal of Applied Corporate Finance*, vol. 15, no. 3, pp. 34–45.

Brooks, F. P. (1975) *The Mythical Man-month and Other Essays on Software Engineering* (Chapel Hill, NC: Department of Computer Science, University of North Carolina).

Buckley, P. J. (1991) *New Directions in International Business: Research Priorities for the 1990s* (Aldershot: Edward Elgar).

Bundesverband der Deutschen Volks- und Raiffeisenbanken (2001) *Jahresbericht 2000* (Berlin/Bonn: Bundesverband der Deutschen Volks- und Raiffeisenbanken).

Bundesverband der Deutschen Volks- und Raiffeisenbanken (2002) *Jahresbericht 2001* (Berlin/Bonn: Bundesverband der Deutschen Volks- und Raiffeisenbanken).

Bundesverband der Deutschen Volks und Raiffeisenbanken (2003) *Jahresbericht 2002* (Berlin/Bonn: Bundesverband der Deutschen Volks- und Raiffeisenbanken).

Burrough, B. and J. Helyar (1990) *Barbarians at the Gate* (New York: HarperCollins).

Burton, R. M. and B. Obel (1984) *Designing Efficient Organizations: Modelling and Experimentation* (Amsterdam: North-Holland).

Bushnell, P. T. and A. D. Shepard (1995) 'The Economics of Modern Manufacturing: Comment', *American Economic Review*, vol. 85, no. 4, pp. 987–90.

Businessweek (2000) 'Heir Today, Gone Tomorrow', *Businessweek*, 3712, 214–17.

Cairncross, F. (2003) 'Tough at the Top – A Survey of Corporate Leadership', *The Economist*, vol. 369, no. 8347, pp. 1–24.

Campbell, A., M. Goold and M. Alexander (1995) 'Corporate Strategy: The Quest for Parenting Advantage', *Harvard Business Review*, vol. 73, no. 2, pp. 120–32.

Carson, I. (2004) 'Perpetual Motion – A Survey of the Car Industry', *The Economist*, vol. 372, no. 8391, pp. 1–16.

Casson, M. (1997) *Information and Organization: A New Perspective on the Theory of the Firm* (Oxford University Press).

Chacar, A. S. and R. W. Coff (2000) 'Deconstructing a Knowledge-based Advantage: Rent Generation, Rent Appropriation, and "Performance" in Investment Banking', in R. K. Bresser M. A. Hitt, R. D. Nixon and D. Heuskel (eds), *Winning Strategies in a Deconstructing World* (Chichester: John Wiley), pp. 245–65.

Chandler, A. D. (1962) *Strategy and Structure* (Cambridge, Mass.: MIT Press).

Chandler, A. D. (1990) *Scale and Scope – The Dynamics of Industrial Capitalism* (Cambridge, Mass.: Harvard University/Belknap Press).

Chemla, G. (2004) 'Takeovers and the Dynamics of Information Flows', *International Journal of Industrial Organization*, vol. 22, no. 4, pp. 575–90.

Chemla, G. (2005) 'Hold-up, Stakeholders and Takeover Threats', *Journal of Financial Intermediation*, vol. 14, no. 3, pp. 376–97.

Christensen, C. M. (1997) *The Innovator's Dilemma: When New Technologies Cause Great Firms to Fail* (Boston, Mass.: Harvard Business School Press).

Coase, R. H. (1937) 'The Nature of the Firm', *Economica*, vol. 4, no. 16, pp. 386–405.

Coase, R. H. (1993) 'The Nature of the Firm: Influence', in O. E. Williamson and S. G. Winter (eds), *The Nature of the Firm: Origins, Evolution, and Development* (Oxford University Press), pp. 61–74.

Cockburn, I., R. Henderson and S. Stern (1999) 'Balancing Incentives: The Tension between Basic and Applied Research', NBER Working Paper No. 6882.

Coff, R. W. (1999) 'When Competitive Advantage Doesn't Lead to Performance: The Resource-Based View and Stakeholder Bargaining Power', *Organization Science*, vol. 10, no. 2, pp. 119–33.

Cohen, W. M. and D. A. Levinthal (1990) 'Absorptive Capacity: A New Perspective on Learning and Innovation', *Administrative Science Quarterly*, vol. 35, no. 1, pp. 128–52.

Collis, D. J. and C. A. Montgomery (1995) 'Competing on Resources: Strategy in the 1990s', *Harvard Business Review*, vol. 73, no. 4, pp. 118–28.

Collis, D. J. and C. A. Montgomery (1997) *Corporate Strategy – Resources and the Scope of the Firm* (Chicago, Ill.: Irwin).

Collis, D. J. and C. A. Montgomery (1998) 'Creating Corporate Advantage', *Harvard Business Review*, vol. 76, no. 3, pp. 70–83.

Committee of European Securities Regulators and European Central Bank (2004) 'Standards for Securities Clearing and Settlement in the European Union', Report (Frankfurt: CESR and ECB).

Committee on Payment and Settlement Systems and International Organization of Securities Commissions (2001) 'Recommendations For Securities Settlement Systems', Report (Basel: CPSS and IOSCO).

Conner, K. R. and C. K. Prahalad (1996) 'A Resource-based Theory of the Firm: Knowledge versus Opportunism', *Organization Science*, vol. 7, no. 5, pp. 477–501.

Connolly, N. (2004) 'Aer Lingus Job Cuts Will Come at a Price', *The Sunday Business Post*, 1 August 2004.

Cruickshank, D. (2003) 'The Impact of the EU Financial Services Action Plan on the Regulation of the EU Securities Market', Speech at the 'Conference on the Impact of the EU Financial Services Action Plan on the Regulation of the EU Securities Market', 6 March 2003, Guildhall, London.

Cyert, R. and J. March (1963) *A Behavioral Theory of the Firm* (Englewood Cliffs, NJ: Prentice-Hall).

Dafermos, G. N. (2001) 'Management and Virtual Decentralized Networks: The Linux Project', *First Monday*, vol. 6, no. 11.

Dalle, J.-M. and N. Jullien (2001) 'Open-Source versus Proprietary Software', Mimeo.

d'Aveni, R. D. (1999) 'Strategic Supremacy through Disruption and Dominance', *Sloan Management Review*, vol. 40, no. 3, pp. 127–35.

David, P. A. (1985) 'Clio and the Economics of QWERTY', *American Economic Review*, vol. 75, no. 2, pp. 332–7.

Day, J. D. and J. C. Wendler (1998) 'The New Economics of Organization', *The McKinsey Quarterly*, vol. 15, no. 1, pp. 4–32.

de Bandt, O. and P. Hartmann (2000) 'Systemic Risk: A Survey', ECB Working Paper Series, no. 35.

de Meza, D. and B. Lockwood (1998) 'Does Asset Ownership Always Motivate Managers? Outside Options and the Property Rights Theory of the Firm', *Quarterly Journal of Economics*, vol. 113, no. 2, pp. 361–86.

Demil, B. and X. Lecocq (2006) 'Neither Market nor Hierarchy or Network: The Emergence of Bazaar Governance', *Organization Studies*, vol. 27, no. 10, pp. 1447–66.

Demsetz, H. (1993) 'The Theory of the Firm Revisited', in O. E. Williamson and S. G. Winter (eds), *The Nature of the Firm – Origins, Evolution, and Development* (Oxford University Press), pp. 159–78.

den Hond, F. (1996) *In Search of a Useful Theory of Environmental Strategy: A Case Study on the Recycling of End-of-Life Vehicles from the Capabilities Perspective*, Ph. D. thesis, Vrije Universiteit, Amsterdam.

Dessein, W. (2002) 'Authority and Communication in Organizations', *Review of Economic Studies*, vol. 69, no. 4, pp. 811–38.

Dessein, W. (2003) 'Hierarchies versus Committees', Mimeo, University of Chicago Graduate School.

Dessein, W., L. Garicano and R. Gertner (2005) 'Organizing for Synergies: Allocating Control to manage the Coordination – Incentives Tradeoff', University of Chicago Working paper.

Deutsche Bank (2001) *Results 2000 – Annual Report* (Frankfurt am Main: Deutsche Bank).

Deutsche Bank (2004) *Annual Review 2003* (Frankfurt am Main: Deutsche Bank).

Deutsche Börse Group (2005) 'The European Post-Trade Market – An Introduction', White paper (Frankfurt am Main: Deutsche Börse Group).

Deutsche Börse Group and Clearstream International (2002) 'Cross-Border Equity Trading, Clearing and Settlement in Europe', White paper (Frankfurt am Main: Deutsche Börse Group).

Deutsche Bundesbank (2004) 'Statistisches Beiheft zum Monatsbericht 1', *Bankenstatistik der Deutschen Bundesbank*, vol. 56, no. 6.

Dewatripont, M. and J. Tirole (1999) 'Advocates', *Journal of Political Economy*, vol. 107, no. 1, pp. 1–39.

Dewatripont, M., I. Jewitt and J. Tirole (1999a) 'The Economics of Career Concerns, Part I: Comparing Information Structures', *Review of Economic Studies*, vol. 66, no. 1, pp. 183–98.

Dewatripont, M., I. Jewitt and J. Tirole (1999b) 'The Economics of Career Concerns, Part II: Application to Missions and Accountability of Government Agencies', *Review of Economic Studies*, vol. 66, no. 1, pp. 199–217.

Dewatripont, M. and J. Tirole (2005) 'Modes of Communication', *Journal of Political Economy*, vol. 113, no. 6, pp. 1217–38.

Diamond, D. (1984) 'Financial intermediation and Delegated Monitoring', *Review of Economic Studies*, vol. 51, no. 3, pp. 393–414.

Dietl, H. M. and S. Royer (2003) 'Indirekte Netzwerkeffekte und Wertschöpfungsorganisation – Eine Untersuchung der zugrunde liegenden Effizienz- und Strategiedeterminanten am Beispiel der Videospielbranche', *Zeitschrift für Betriebswirtschaft*, vol. 73, no. 4, pp. 407–29.

Dinkelacker, J. and P. K. Garg (2001) 'Corporate Source: Applying Open Source Concepts to a Corporate Environment', Hewlett-Packard Position paper.

Domowitz, I. and B. Steil (1999) 'Automation, Trading Costs, and the Structure of the Securities Trading Industry', in R. E. Litan, and A. M. Santomero (eds), *Brookings-Wharton Papers on Financial Services: 1999* (Washington, DC: Brookings Institution Press), pp. 33–81.

Dow, G. K. (1993) 'Why Capital Hires Labor: A Bargaining Perspective', *American Economic Review*, vol. 83, no. 1, pp. 118–34.

Drucker, P. F. (1999) 'Knowledge Worker Productivity: The Biggest Challenge', *California Management Review*, vol. 41, no. 2, pp. 79–94.

Dunning, J. H. (1992) *Multinational Enterprises and the Global Economy* (Wokingham: Addison-Wesley).

Durlauf, S. N. (1998) 'What Should Policymakers Know About Economic Complexity?', *The Washington Quarterly*, vol. 21, no. 1, pp. 157–65.

Economides, N. (1993) 'Network Economics with Application to Finance', *Financial Markets, Institutions and Instruments*, vol. 2, no. 5, pp. 89–97.

Economides, N. (1996) 'The Economics of Networks', *International Journal of Industrial Organization*, vol. 14, no. 6, pp. 673–99.

Economist, The (2000) 'Open Sesame', *The Economist*, vol. 355, no. 8166, p. 78.

Economist, The (2001a) 'Japan Inc on the Treadmill', *The Economist*, vol. 359, no. 8225, pp. 73–4.

Economist, The (2001b) 'The Penguin Gets Serious', *The Economist*, vol. 358, no. 8206, p. 70.

Economist, The (2002a) 'Disney or Doesn't He?', *The Economist*, vol. 362, no. 8255, p. 68.

Economist, The (2002b) 'Face Value – The Great Swiss Hope', *The Economist*, vol. 363, no. 8273, p. 74.

Economist, The (2002c) 'Going Hybrid', *The Economist*, vol. 364, no. 8283, pp. 61–2.

Economist, The (2002d) 'Incredible Shrinking Plants', *The Economist*, vol. 362, no. 8261, pp. 75–8.

Economist, The (2002e) 'Struggling with a Supertanker', *The Economist*, vol. 362, no. 8259, pp. 56–7.

Economist, The (2003a) 'Building a Better Bug-trap', *The Economist Technology Quarterly*, vol. 367, no. 8329, pp. 18–20.

Economist, The (2003b) 'Open Source's Local Heroes', *The Economist Technology Quarterly*, vol. 369, no. 8353, pp. 3–5.

Economist, The (2003c) 'Plus ça change', *The Economist*, vol. 368, no. 8337, p. 59.

Economist, The (2005) 'Promises, ahem', *The Economist*, vol. 375, no. 8426, p. 74.

Ehrensberger, S., F. Opelt, H. Rubner, and A. Schmiedeberg (2000) 'Dealing with Deconstruction', in R. K. Bresser, M. A. Hitt, R. D. Nixon and D. Heuskel (eds), *Winning Strategies in a Deconstructing World* (Chichester: John Wiley), pp. 191–200.

Eisenhardt, K. M. (1999) 'Strategy as Strategic Decision Making', *Sloan Management Review*, vol. 40, no. 3, pp. 65–72.

Eisenhardt, K. M., and D. C. Galunic (2000) 'Coevolving – At Last, a Way to Make Synergies Work', *Harvard Business Review*, vol. 78, no. 1, pp. 91–101.

Eisenhardt, K. M., and D. N. Sull (2001) 'Strategy as Simple Rules', *Harvard Business Review*, vol. 79, no. 1, pp. 106–16.

Eliasson, G. (1996) 'Spillovers, Integrated Production and the Theory of the Firm', *Evolutionary Economics*, vol. 6, no. 2, pp. 125–40.

Enron (2001) *Annual Report 2000* (Houston; TX: Enron).

Erhardt, M. (2004) 'Network Effects, Standardization and Competitive Strategy: How Companies Influence the Emergence of Dominant Designs', *International Journal of Technology Management*, vol. 27, no. 2/3, pp. 272–94.

European Shadow Financial Regulatory Committee (2001) 'Re-plumbing European Securities Markets', Statement 12 (London: ESFRC).

Evans, P. and T. S. Wurster (2000) *Blown to Bits – How the New Economics of Information Transform Strategy* (Boston, Mass.: Harvard Business School Press).

Fama, E. F. and M. C. Jensen (1983a) 'Agency Problems and Residual Claims', *Journal of Law and Economics*, vol. 26, no. 2, pp. 327–49.

Fama, E. F. and M. C. Jensen (1983b) 'Separation of Ownership and Control', *Journal of Law and Economics*, vol. 26, no. 2, pp. 301–26.

Fast, N. (1975) *The Lincoln Electric Company*, Case Study 376–028 (Boston, Mass.: Harvard Business School).

Feller, J. and B. Fitzgerald (2002) *Understanding Open Source Software Development* (London: Addison-Wesley).

Foss, K. and N. J. Foss (1999) 'Understanding Ownership: Residual Rights of Control and Appropriable Control Rights', DRUID Working paper No. 99–4.

Foss, N. J. (1996a) 'Firms, Incomplete Contracts and Organizational Learning', *Human Systems Management*, vol. 15, no. 1, pp. 17–26.

Foss, N. J. (1996b) 'Knowledge-based Approaches to the Theory of the Firm: Some Critical Comments', *Organization Science*, vol. 7, no. 5, pp. 470–76.

Foss, N. J. (1997) 'Understanding Business Systems: An Essay on the Economics and Sociology of Economic Organization', Working Paper No. 97–6 Copenhagen Business School.

Foss, N. J. (1998) 'Firms and the Coordination of Knowledge: Some Austrian Insights', DRUID Working Paper No. 98–19.

Foss, N. J. (1999a) 'Research in the Strategic Theory of the Firm: "Isolationism" and "Integrationism" ', *Journal of Management Studies*, vol. 36, no. 6, pp. 725–55.

Foss, N. J. (1999b) 'Understanding Leadership: A Coordination Theory', DRUID Working Paper No. 99–3.

Foss, N. J. (1999c) 'The Use of Knowledge in Firms', *Journal of Institutional and Theoretical Economics*, vol. 155, no. 3, pp. 458–86.

Foss, N. J. (2001) 'The Boundary School', in T. Elfring and H. W. Volberda (eds), *Rethinking Strategy* (London: SAGE), pp. 97–115.

Foss, N. J. (2002) ' "Coase vs Hayek": Economic Organization and the Knowledge Economy', *International Journal of the Economics of Business*, vol. 9, no. 1, pp. 9–35.

Foss, N. J., H. Lando and S. Thomsen (2000) 'The Theory of the Firm', in B. Bouckaert and G. De Geest (eds), *Encyclopedia of Law and Economics*, Vol. III – The Regulation of Contracts (Cheltenham: Edward Elgar), pp. 631–58.

Franck, E. and C. Jungwirth (2003) 'Reconciling Rent-Seekers and Donators – The Governance Structure of Open Source', *Journal of Management and Governance*, vol. 7, no. 4, pp. 401–21.

Franke, N. and E. von Hippel (2003) 'Satisfying Heterogeneous User Needs via Innovation Toolkits: The Case of Apache Security Software', *Research Policy*, vol. 32, no. 7, pp. 1199–215.

Franks, J. and C. Mayer (1995) 'Ownership and Control', in H. Siebert (ed.), *Trends in Business Organization: Do Participation and Cooperation increase Competitiveness?*, (Tübingen: J. C. B. Mohr (Paul Siebeck)), pp. 171–95.

Galbraith, J. R. (1977) *Organization Design* (Reading: Addison-Wesley).

Gans, J. S. (2005) 'Markets for Ownership', *RAND Journal of Economics*, vol. 36, no. 2, pp. 433–55.

Garicano, L. (2000) 'Hierarchies and the Organization of Knowledge in Production', *Journal of Political Economy*, vol. 108, no. 5, pp. 874–04.

Garzarelli, G. (2003) 'Open Source Software and the Economics of Organization', in J. Birner and P. Garrouste (eds), *Markets, Information and Communication: Austrian Perspectives on the Internet Economy* (London: Routledge).

Gertner, R. (2002) 'Explaining Vertical Integration Practices', Working paper, University of Chicago.

Gerybadze, A. (1995) *Strategic Alliances and Process Redesign* (Berlin: Walter de Gruyter).

Ghoshal, S. and C. A. Bartlett (1995) 'Changing the Role of Top Management: Beyond Structure to Processes', *Harvard Business Review*, vol. 73, no. 1, pp. 86–96.

Ghoshal, S. and C. A. Bartlett (1997) *The Individualized Corporation – A Fundamentally New Approach to Management* (New York: Harper Business).

Ghoshal, S., C. A. Bartlett and P. Moran (1999) 'A New Manifesto for Management', *Sloan Management Review*, vol. 40, no. 3, pp. 9–20.

Ghoshal, S., P. Moran and L. Almeida-Costa (1995) 'The Essence of the Megacorporation: Shared Context, not Structural Hierarchy', *Journal of Institutional and Theoretical Economics*, vol. 151, no. 4, pp. 748–59.

Ghoshal, S., P. Moran and C. A. Bartlett (2001) 'Employment Security, Employability and Sustainable Competitive Advantage', in J. Gual and J. Ricart, (eds), *Strategy, Organization and the Changing Nature of Work* (Cheltenham: Edward Elgar), pp. 79–110.

Gibbons, R. (1998) 'Incentives in Organizations', *Journal of Economic Perspectives*, vol. 12, no. 4, pp. 115–32.

Gibbons, R. (2000) 'Why Organizations Are Such a Mess (and What an Economist Might Do About it)', Mimeo, MIT.

Gibbons, R. (2005) 'Four Formal(izable)Theories of the Firm', *Journal of Economic Behavior & Organization*, vol. 58, no. 2, pp. 200–45.

Giddy, I., A. Saunders and I. Walter (1996) 'Alternative Models for Clearance and Settlement: The Case of the Single European Capital Market', *Journal of Money, Credit and Banking*, vol. 28, no. 4, pp. 986–1000.

Giovannini Group (2001) 'Cross-border Clearing and Settlement Arrangements in the European Union', Report (Brussels: European Commission).

Giovannini Group (2003) 'Second Report on EU Clearing and Settlement Arrangements', Report (Brussels: European Commission).

Gittell, J. H. (1998) 'Designing Organizations for Coordination and Control', Working Paper No. 98–049, Harvard Business School.

Glassman, D. M. (1997) 'Contracting for Value: EVA and the Economics of Organization', *Journal of Applied Corporate Finance*, vol. 10, no. 2, pp. 110–23.

Goffee, R. and G. Jones (1996) 'What Holds the Modern Company Together?', *Harvard Business Review*, vol. 74, no. 6, pp. 133–48.

Goffee, R. and G. Jones (2001) 'Organizational Culture: A Sociological Perspective', in C. L. Cooper, S. Cartwright and P. C. Earley (eds), *The International Handbook of Organizational Culture and Climate* (New York: John Wiley), pp. 3–20.

Greifenstein, F. and M. Weiss (2004) 'Geschäftsmodelle am europäischen Luftverkehrsmarkt – eine Untersuchung der Kundenstrukturen von Low Cost Airlines und Full Service Carriern', *Tourismus Journal*, vol. 8, no. 1, pp. 5–25.

Greve, R. (2002) 'The German Cooperative Banking Group as a Strategic Network: Function and Performance', Working Paper No. 29, Institute of Co-operative System, Münster.

Grossman, S. J. and O. D. Hart (1986) 'The Costs and Benefits of Ownership: A Theory of Vertical and Lateral Integration', *Journal of Political Economy*, vol. 94, no. 4, pp. 691–719.

Gürtler, O. (2004) 'A Rationale for the Coexistence of Central and Decentral Marketing in Team Sports', GEABA Discussion paper No. 04–25.

Hackethal, A. (2000) *Banken, Unternehmensfinanzierung und Finanzsysteme.* (Frankfurt: Peter Lang).

Hackethal, A. and R. H. Schmidt (2000) 'Finanzsystem und Komplementarität', *Kredit und Kapital*, Special Issue (15), pp. 53–102.

Hackethal, A., R. H. Schmidt and M. Tyrell (2005) 'Banks and German Corporate Governance: On the Way to a Capital Market-Based System?', *Corporate Governance: An International Review*, vol. 13, no. 3, pp. 397–407.

Hagel, J. and M. Singer (1999) 'Unbundling the Corporation', *Harvard Business Review*, vol. 77, no. 2, pp. 133–141.

Hall, P. A. and D. Soskice (2001) *Varieties of Capitalism: The Institutional Foundations of Comparative Advantage* (Oxford University Press).

Hamel, G. (1996) 'Strategy as Revolution', *Harvard Business Review*, vol. 74, no. 4, pp. 69–82.

Hamel, G. (1999) 'Bringing Silicon Valley Inside', *Harvard Business Review*, Vol. 77, no. 5, pp. 70–84.

Hamel, G. and C. Prahalad (1989) 'Strategic Intent', *Harvard Business Review*, vol. 67, no. 3, pp. 63–76.

Hamel, G. and C. Prahalad (1996) 'Competing in the New Economy: Managing out of Bounds', *Strategic Management Journal*, vol. 17, no. 3, pp. 237–42.

Hansen, M. T., N. Nohria and T. Tierney (1999) 'What's Your Strategy for Managing Knowledge?', *Harvard Business Review*, vol. 77, no. 2, pp. 106–16.

Hansmann, H. (1988) 'Ownership of the Firm', *Journal of Law, Economics and Organization*, vol. 4, no. 2, pp. 267–304.

Hansmann, H. (1996) *The Ownership of Enterprise* (Cambridge: Belknap Press).

Harris, L. E. (1991) *Liquidity, Trading Rules, and Electronic Trading Systems* (New York: New York University Salomon Center).

Hars, A. and S. Ou (2002) 'Working for Free? Motivations for Participating in Open-Source Projects', *International Journal of Electronic Commerce*, vol. 6, no. 3, pp. 25–39.

Hart, O. D. (1990) 'Is "Bounded Rationality" an Important Element of a Theory of Institutions?', *Journal of Institutional and Theoretical Economics*, vol. 146, no. 4, pp. 696–702.

Hart, O. D. (1995) *Firms, Contracts, and Financial Structure*, Clarendon Lectures in Economics (Oxford University Press).

Hart, O. D. (2001) 'Financial Contracting', *Journal of Economic Literature*, vol. 39, no. 4, pp. 1079–100.

Hart, O. D. and B. R. Holmström (2002) 'A Theory of Firm Scope', MIT Department of Economics Working Paper No. 02–42.

Hart, O. D. and J. Moore (1990) 'Property Rights and the Nature of the Firm', *Journal of Political Economy*, vol. 98, no. 6, pp. 1119–58.

Hart, O. D. and J. Moore (1996) 'The Governance of Exchanges: Members' Cooperatives versus Outside Ownership', *Oxford Review of Economic Policy*, vol. 12, no. 4, pp. 53–69.

Hasan, I. and M. Malkamäki (2001) 'Are Expansions Cost Effective for Stock Exchanges? A Global Perspective', *Journal of Banking and Finance*, vol. 25, no. 12, pp. 2339–66.

Hasan, I. and H. Schmiedel (2003) 'Do Networks in the Stock Exchange Industry Pay Off? European Evidence', Discussion Papers No. 03–02, Bank of Finland.

Hastings, D. F. (1999) 'Lincoln Electric's Harsh Lessons from International Expansion', *Harvard Business Review*, vol. 77, no. 3, pp. 162–78.

Hayek, F. A. (1945) 'The Use of Knowledge in Society', *American Economic Review*, vol. 35, no. 4, pp. 519–30.

Heinrich, R. P. (2002) *Complementarities in Corporate Governance* (Berlin: Springer Verlag).

Helper, S., J. P. MacDuffie and C. Sabel (1998) 'The Boundaries of the Firm as a Design Problem', Columbia University Law School Conference on the Boundaries of the Firm, Proceedings.

Henkel, J. (2004) 'Open Source Software from Commercial Firms – Tools, Complements and Collective Invention', *Zeitschrift für Betriebswirtschaft*, vol. 74, no. EH 4/04, pp. 1–24.

Hennart, J.-F. (1988) 'A Transaction Cost Theory of Equity Joint Ventures', *Strategic Management Journal*, vol. 9, no. 4, pp. 361–74.

Hermalin, B. E. (1998) 'Toward an Economic Theory of Leadership: Leading by Example', *American Economic Review*, vol. 88, no. 5, pp. 1188–206.

Hermalin, B. E. (2001) 'Economics and Corporate Culture', in C. L. Cooper, S. Cartwright and P. C. Earley (eds), *The International Handbook of Organizational Culture and Climate* (New York: John Wiley), pp. 217–62.

Hertel, G., S. Niedner and S. Herrmann (2003) 'Motivation of Software Developers in Open Source Projects: An Internet-based Survey of Contributors to the Linux Kernel', *Research Policy*, vol. 32, no. 7, pp. 1159–77.

Higl, M. and P. Welzel (2004) 'Intra-Firm Coordination and Horizontal Mergers', GEABA Discussion Paper No. 04–23.

Hill, C. W. L. (1996) 'The Organizational Advantage: The Firm as an Engine for the Discovery of Knowledge', Mimeo, University of Washington.

Hirschman, A. O. (1970) *Exit, Voice, and Loyalty – Responses to Decline in Firms, Organizations, and States* (Cambridge, Mass.: Harvard University Press).

Holmström, B. R. (1979) 'Moral Hazard and Observability', *Bell Journal of Economics*, vol. 10, no. 1, pp. 74–91.

Holmström, B. R. (1982) 'Moral Hazard in Teams', *Bell Journal of Economics*, vol. 13, no. 2, pp. 324–40.

Holmström, B. R. (1999a) 'The Economics of Corporate Governance', Third Louise and Göran Ehrnrooth Lectures, Swedish School of Economics, Helsinki.

Holmström, B. R. (1999b) 'The Firm as a Subeconomy', *Journal of Law, Economics and Organization*, vol. 15, no. 1, pp. 74–102.

Holmström, B. R. (1999c) 'Managerial Incentive Problems: A Dynamic Perspective', *Review of Economic Studies*, vol. 66, no. 1, pp. 169–82.

Holmström, B. R. and S. N. Kaplan (2003) 'The State of U.S. Corporate Governance: What's Right and What's Wrong?', *Journal of Applied Corporate Finance*, vol. 15, no. 3, pp. 8–20.

Holmström, B. R. and P. Milgrom (1991) 'Multi-task Principal–Agent Analyses: Incentive Contracts, Asset Ownership, and Job Design', *Journal of Law, Economics and Organization*, vol. 7 (Special issue), pp. 24–52.

Holmström, B. R. and P. Milgrom (1994) 'The Firm as an Incentive System', *American Economic Review*, vol. 84, no. 4, pp. 972–91.

Holmström, B. R. and J. Roberts (1998) 'The Boundaries of the Firm Revisited', *Journal of Economic Perspectives*, vol. 12, no. 4, pp. 73–94.

Holmström, B. R. and J. Tirole (1989) 'The Theory of the Firm', in R. Schmalensee and R. D. Willig (eds), *Handbook of Industrial Organization*, Vol. 1, (Amsterdam: North-Holland), pp. 61–133.

Holthausen, C. and J. Tapking (2004) 'Raising Rival's Costs in the Securities Settlement Industry', ECB Working Paper Series, No. 376.

Iannacci, F. (2003) 'The Linux Managing Model', *First Monday*, vol. 8, no. 12.

IBM (2005) *Annual Report 2004* (Armonk; NY: IBM).

Jensen, M. (1986) 'Agency Costs of Free Cash Flow, Corporate Finance, and Takeovers', *American Economic Review*, vol. 76, no. 2, pp. 323–9.

Jensen, M. C. and W. H. Meckling (1976) 'Theory of the Firm: Managerial Behavior, Agency Costs and Ownership Structure', *Journal of Financial Economics*, vol. 3, no. 4, pp. 305–60.

Jensen, M. C. and W. H. Meckling (1991) 'Specific and General Knowledge, and Organizational Structure', in L. Werin and H. Wijkander (eds), *Main Currents in Contract Economics* (Oxford: Blackwell), pp. 251–74.

Jensen, M. C. and W. H. Meckling (1999) 'Specific Knowledge and Divisional Performance Measurement', *Journal of Applied Corporate Finance*, vol. 12, no. 2, pp. 8–17.

John, K. and S. Kedia (2003) 'Institutions, Markets and Growth: A Theory of Comparative Corporate Governance', Mimeo, Stern School of Business at Rutgers University.

John, K. and S. Kedia (2005) 'Design of Corporate Governance: Role of Ownership Structure, Takeovers, Bank Debt and Large Shareholder Monitoring', Working paper.

Johnson, J. P. (2002) 'Open Source Software: Private Provision of a Public Good', *Journal of Economics & Management Strategy*, vol. 11, no. 4, pp. 637–62.

Kahn, C. M., J. McAndrews and W. Roberds (2003) 'Settlement Risk under Gross and Net Settlement', *Journal of Money, Credit and Banking*, vol. 35, no. 4, 591–608.

Kaisla, J. (2001) 'Constitutional Dynamics of the Open Source Software Development', Working paper, Copenhagen Business School.

Kanter, R. M. (1989) 'The New Managerial Work', *Harvard Business Review*, vol. 67, no. 6, pp. 85–92.

Kauko, K. (2005) 'Interlinking Securities Settlement Systems: A Strategic Commitment', ECB Working Paper Series No. 427.

Kay, N. M. (1997) *Pattern in Corporate Evolution* (Oxford University Press).

Kirzner, I. M. (1987) 'Austrian School of Economics', in J. Eatwell, M. Milgate and P. Newman (eds), *New Palgrave: A Dictionary of Economics* Vol. 1, (New York: Stockton Press), pp. 145–51.

Klein, B. (1980) 'Transaction Cost Determinants of "Unfair" Contractual Arrangements', *American Economic Review*, vol. 70, no. 2, pp. 356–62.

Klein, B., R. G. Crawford and A. A. Alchian (1978) 'Vertical Integration, Appropriable Rents, and the Competitive Contracting Process', *Journal of Law and Economics*, vol. 21, no. 2, pp. 297–326.

Klein, B. and K. M. Murphy (1997) 'Vertical Integration as a Self-enforcing Contractual Arrangement', *American Economic Review*, vol. 87, no. 2, pp. 415–20.

Koeppl, T. V. and C. Monnet (2004) 'Guess What: It's the Settlements!', ECB Working Paper Series No. 375.

Kogut, B. and U. Zander (1996) 'What Firms Do? Coordination, Identity, and Learning', *Organization Science*, vol. 7, no. 5, pp. 502–18.

Krahnen, J. P. and R. H. Schmidt (1994) *Development Finance as Institution Building* (Boulder, Col.: Westview Press).

Krahnen, J. P. and R. H. Schmidt (2004) *The German Financial System* (Oxford University Press).

Krahnen, J. P., R. H. Schmidt and E. Terberger (1985) 'Der ökonomische Wert von Flexibilität und Bindung', in W. Ballwieser and K.-H. Berger (eds), *Information und Wirtschaftlichkeit* (Wiesbaden: Gabler), pp. 253–85.

Kreps, D. M. (1990) 'Corporate Culture and Economic Theory', in J. E. Alt and K. A. Shepsle (eds), *Perspectives on Positive Politcal Economy* (Cambridge University Press), pp. 90–143.

Krishnamurthy, S. (2002) 'Cave or Community? An Empirical Examination of 100 Mature Open Source Projects', *First Monday*, vol. 7, no. 6.

Kuan, J. (2002) 'Open Source Software as Lead User's Make or Buy Decision: A Study of Open and Closed Source Quality', Mimeo, Stanford Institute for Economic Policy Research.

Laffont, J.-J. and J. Tirole (1993) *A Theory of Incentives in Procurement and Regulation* (Cambridge, Mass.: MIT Press).

Laffont, J.-J. and J. Tirole (2001) *Competition in Telecommunications* (Cambridge, Mass.: MIT Press).

Lakhani, K. and E. von Hippel (2003) 'How Open Source Software Works: "Free" User-to-user Assistance', *Research Policy*, vol. 32, no. 6, pp. 923–43.

Lamfalussy, A. (2001) 'Final Report of the Committee of Wise Men on the Regulation of European Securities Markets', Report (Brussels: European Commission).

Lane, D. and R. Maxfield (1997) 'Foresight, Complexity and Strategy', in W. B. Arthur, S. Durlauf and D. A. Lane (eds), *The Economy as an Evolving Complex System II* (Boston, Mass.: Addison-Wesley), pp. 169–98.

Langlois, R. N. (2002) 'Modularity in Technology and Organization', *Journal of Economic Behavior and Organization*, vol. 49, no. 1, pp. 19–37.

Langlois, R. N. (2003) 'The Vanishing Hand: The Changing Dynamics of Industrial Capitalism', *Industrial and Corporate Change*, vol. 12, no. 2, pp. 351–85.

Lannoo, K. and M. Levin (2001) 'The Securities Settlement Industry in the EU – Structure, Costs and the Way Forward', Research Report, CEPS.

Laux, C. and U. Walz (2004) 'Tying, Entry, and Competition in Investment Banking', Working paper, University of Frankfurt.

Lee, S., N. Moisa and M. Weiss (2004) 'Conditions for Open Source as a Signalling Device', WP Series Finance and Accounting, University Frankfurt, No. 102.

Leijonhufvud, A. (1986) 'Capitalism and the Factory System', in R. N. Langlois (ed.), *Economics as a Process: Essays in the New Institutional Economics* (Cambridge University Press), pp. 203–23.

Leppämäki, M. and M. Mustonen (2003) 'Spence Revisited – Signalling with Externality: The Case of Open Source Programming', Discussion Paper No. 558, University of Helsinki.

Lerner, J. and J. Tirole (2001) 'The Open Source Movement: Key Research Questions', *European Economic Review*, vol. 45, no. 4–6, pp. 819–26.

Lerner, J. and J. Tirole (2002) 'Some Simple Economics of Open Source', *Journal of Industrial Economics*, vol. 50, no. 2, pp. 197–234.

Lerner, J. and J. Tirole (2005) 'The Scope of Open Source Licensing', *Journal of Law, Economics and Organization*, vol. 21, no. 1, pp. 20–56.

Levin, J. and L. Rayo (2003) 'Control Rights and Relational Contracts', Mimeo Stanford University and University of Chicago.

Levin, J. and S. Tadelis (2005) 'Profit Sharing and the Role of Professional Partnerships', *Quarterly Journal of Economics*, vol. 120, no. 1, pp. 131–72.

Levinthal, D. A. and M. Warglien (1999) 'Landscape Design: Designing for Local Action in Complex Worlds', *Organization Science*, vol. 10, no. 3, pp. 342–57.

Liebeskind, J. P. (1996) 'Knowledge, Strategy, and the Theory of the Firm', *Strategic Management Journal*, 17(Special Issue), pp. 93–107.

Lippman, S. A. and R. P. Rumelt (1982) 'Uncertain Imitability: An Analysis of Interfirm Differences in Efficiency Under Competition', *Bell Journal of Economics*, vol. 13, no. 2, pp. 418–38.

Malkamäki, M. (1999) 'Are There Economies of Scale in Stock Exchange Activities?', Discussion Paper No. 4, Bank of Finland.

Markides, C. C. (1999) 'A Dynamic View of Strategy', *Sloan Management Review*, vol. 40, no. 3, pp. 55–63.

Markides, C. C. and P. J. Williamson (1994) 'Related Diversification, Core Competences and Corporate Performance', *Strategic Management Journal*, 15(Special Issue), pp. 149–65.

Massmann, J. (2003) *Nonprofits: Analyse, Entwicklung und Rechtspolitik* (Frankfurt am Main: Peter Lang).

Massmann, J. and R. H. Schmidt (1999) 'Zur strategischen Implementierung des Shareholder-Value-Ansatzes', *Wirtschaftspolitische Blätter*, vol. 46, no. 6, pp. 554–64.

McKelvey, B. (1999) 'Avoiding Complexity Catastrophe in Coevolutionary Pockets: Strategies for Rugged Landscapes', *Organization Science*, vol. 10, no. 3, pp. 294–321.

Milgrom, P. (1988) 'Employment Contracts, Influence Activities, and Efficient Organizational Design', *Journal of Political Economy*, vol. 96, no. 1, pp. 42–60.

Milgrom, P. and J. Roberts (1990a) 'Bargaining Costs, Influence Costs and the Organization of Economic Activity', in J. E. Alt and K. A. Shepsle (eds), *Perspectives on Positive Political Economy* (Cambridge University Press), pp. 57–89.

Milgrom, P. and J. Roberts (1990b) 'The Economics of Modern Manufacturing: Technology, Strategy and Organization', *American Economic Review*, vol. 80, no. 3, pp. 511–28.

Milgrom, P. and J. Roberts (1992) *Economics, Organization and Management* (Englewood Cliffs, NJ: Prentice-Hall International).

Milgrom, P. and J. Roberts (1995a) 'Complementarities and Fit: Strategy, Structure and Organizational Change in Manufacturing', *Journal of Accounting and Economics*, vol. 19, no. 2/3, pp. 179–208.

Milgrom, P. and J. Roberts (1995b) 'Continuous Adjustment and Fundamental Change in Business Strategy and Organization', in H. Siebert (ed.), *Trends in Business Organization: Do Participation and Cooperation increase Competitiveness?* (Tübingen: J. C. B. Mohr (Paul Siebeck)), pp. 231–58.

Milgrom, P. and J. Roberts (1995c) 'The Economics of Modern Manufacturing: Reply', *American Economic Review*, vol. 85, no. 4, pp. 997–9.

Miller, M. H. (1994) 'Is American Corporate Governance Fatally Flawed?', *Journal of Applied Corporate Finance*, vol. 6, no. 4, pp. 32–9.

Milne, A. (2002) 'Competition and the Rationalisation of European Securities Clearing and Settlement', Working paper, City University Business School, London.

Mintzberg, H. and L. van der Heyden (1999) 'Organigraphs: Drawing How Companies Really Work', *Harvard Business Review*, vol. 77, no. 5, pp. 87–94.

Mockus, A., R. T. Fielding, and J. Herbsleb (2000) 'A Case Study of Open Source Software Development: The Apache Server', ICSE Proceedings, pp. 263–72.

Moon, J. Y. and L. Sproull (2000) 'Essence of Distributed Work: The Case of the Linux Kernel', *First Monday*, vol. 5, no. 11.

Moran, P. and S. Ghoshal (1996) 'Value Creation by Firms', in J. Keys and L. Dosier (eds), *Academy of Management Best Paper Proceedings* (Statesboro, Ca.: Academy of Management), pp. 41–5.

Morel, B. and R. Ramanujam (1999) 'Through the Looking Glass of Complexity: The Dynamics of Organization as Adaptive and Evolving Systems', *Organization Science*, vol. 10, no. 3, pp. 278–93.

Morgan, T. P. (2004) 'Why Sun and Microsoft Should Merge Java and .NET', *The Four Hundred*, vol. 13, no. 27.

Mustonen, M. (2003) 'Copyleft – the Economics of Linux and Other Open Source Software', *Information Economics and Policy*, vol. 15, no. 1, pp. 99–121.

Nalebuff, B. J. and J. E. Stiglitz (1983) 'Prizes and Incentives: Towards a General Theory of Compensation and Competition', *Bell Journal of Economics*, vol. 14, no. 1, pp. 21–43.

Nelson, R. R. (1994) 'Economic Growth via the Coevolution of Technology and Institutions', in L. Leydesdorff and P. van den Besselaar (eds), *Evolutionary Economics and Chaos Theory: New Directions in Technology Studies* (New York: St. Martin's Press), pp. 21–32.

Nickerson, J. A. and T. R. Zenger (2002) 'Being Efficiently Fickle: A Dynamic Theory of Organizational Choice', *Organization Science*, vol. 13, no. 5, pp. 547–66.

North, D. C. (1990) *Institutions, Institutional Change and Economic Performance* (Cambridge University Press).

Novaes, W. and L. Zingales (2004) 'Bureaucracy as a Mechanism to Generate Information', *RAND Journal of Economics*, vol. 35, no. 2, pp. 245–59.

Nuvolari, A. (2004) 'Collective Invention during the British Industrial Revolution: The Case of the Cornish Pumping Engine', *Cambridge Journal of Economics*, vol. 28, no. 3, pp. 347–63.

Olsen, T. E. and G. Torsvik (2000) 'Discretion and Incentives in Organizations', *Journal of Labor Economics*, vol. 18, no. 3, pp. 377–404.

Olson, M. (1967) *The Logic of Collective Action* (Boston, Mass.: Harvard University Press).

O'Mahony, S. (2003) 'Guarding the Commons: How Community Managed Software Projects Protect Their Work', *Research Policy*, vol. 32, no. 7, pp. 1179–98.

Ortega, J. (2003) 'Power in the Firm and Managerial Career Concerns', *Journal of Economics and Management Strategy*, vol. 12, no. 1, pp. 1–29.

Osterloh, M., S. Rota and B. Kuster (2002a) 'Open Source Software Production: Climbing on the Shoulders of Giants', Working paper, University of Zurich.

Osterloh, M., S. Rota and B. Kuster (2002b) 'Trust and Commerce in Open Source – a Contradiction?', in O. Petrovic, M. Ksela, M. Fallenböck and C. Kittl (eds), *Trust in the Network Economy* (Vienna: Springer Verlag), pp. 129–41.

Patel, N. (2006) *Organization and Systems Design: Theory of Deferred Action.* (Basingstoke: Palgrave Macmillan).

Penrose, E. (1959) *The Theory of the Growth of the Firm* (Oxford University Press).

Peteraf, M. A. (1993) 'The Cornerstones of Competitive Advantage: A Resource-Based View', *Strategic Management Journal*, vol. 14, no. 3, pp. 179–91.

Pfeffer, J. (1992) *Managing with Power* (Boston, Mass.: Harvard Business School Press).

Pixar (2005) *Annual Report 2004* (Emeryville, Calif.: Pixar).

Pleister, C. (2001) *Genossenschaften zwischen Idee und Markt* (Frankfurt am Main: Campus).

Polanyi, M. (1966) *The Tacit Dimension* (New York: Doubleday).

Porter, M. E. (1980) *Competitive Strategy: Techniques for Analyzing Industries and Competitors* (New York: Free Press).

Porter, M. E. (1985) *Competitive Advantage: Creating and Sustaining Superior Performance* (New York: Free Press).

Porter, M. E. (1986) *Competition in Global Industries* (Boston, Mass.: Harvard Business School Press).

Porter, M. E. (1992) 'Capital Disadvantage: America's failing Capital Investment System', *Harvard Business Review*, vol. 70, no. 5, pp. 65–82.

Porter, M. E. (1994) 'Toward a Dynamic Theory of Strategy', in R. P. Rumelt, D. E. Schendel and D. J. Teece (eds), *Fundamental Issues in Strategy: A Research Agenda* (Boston, Mass.: Harvard Business School Press), pp. 423–62.

Porter, M. E. (1996) 'What Is Strategy?', *Harvard Business Review*, vol. 74, no. 6, pp. 60–78.

Porter, M. E. (1998) 'Clusters and the New Economics of Competition', *Harvard Business Review*, vol. 76, no. 6, pp. 77–90.

Porter, M. E. (2001) 'Now Is the Time to Rediscover Strategy', *European Business Forum*, vol. 8, pp. 20–1.

Prahalad, C. K. (1994) 'Corporate Governance or Corporate Value Added? Rethinking the Primacy of Shareholder Value', *Journal of Applied Corporate Finance*, vol. 6, no. 4, pp. 40–50.

Prahalad, C. K. and G. Hamel (1990) 'The Core Competence of the Corporation', *Harvard Business Review*, vol. 68, no. 3, pp. 79–91.

Prahalad, C. K. and G. Hamel (1994a) *Competing for the Future* (Boston, Mass.: Harvard Business School Press).

Prahalad, C. K. and G. Hamel (1994b) 'Strategy as a Field of Study: Why Search for a New Paradigm?', *Strategic Management Journal*, 15(Special Issue), pp. 5–16.

Prahalad, C. K. and J. P. Oosterveld (1999) 'Transforming Internal Governance: The Challenge for Multinationals', *Sloan Management Review*, vol. 40, no. 3, pp. 31–9.

Prahalad, C. K. and V. Ramaswamy (2000) 'Co-opting Customer Competence', *Harvard Business Review*, vol. 78, no. 1, pp. 79–87.

Prendergast, C. (1993) 'The Role of Promotion in Inducing Specific Human Capital Acquisition', *Quarterly Journal of Economics*, vol. 108, no. 2, pp. 523–34.

Prüfer, J. (2004) 'Why Do Developers and Firms Contribute to the Production of Open Source Software?', Working paper, University of Frankfurt.

Rajan, R. G. and J. Wulf (2006) 'The Flattening Firm; Evidence from Panel Data on the Changing Nature of Corporate Hierarchies', *Review of Economics and Statistics*, vol. 88, no. 4, pp. 759–73.

Rajan, R. G. and L. Zingales (1996) 'The Tyranny of the Inefficient: An Enquiry into the Adverse Consequences of Power Struggles', Working paper, University of Chicago.

Rajan, R. G. and L. Zingales (1998) 'Power in a Theory of the Firm', *Quarterly Journal of Economics*, vol. 113, no. 2, pp. 387–432.

Rajan, R. G. and L. Zingales (2000a) 'The Governance of the New Enterprise', in X. Vives (ed.), *Corporate Governance – Theoretical and Empirical Perspectives* (Cambridge University Press), pp. 201–26.

Rajan, R. G. and L. Zingales (2000b) 'The Tyranny of Inequality', *Journal of Public Economics*, vol. 76, no. 3, pp. 521–58.

Rajan, R. G. and L. Zingales (2001a) 'The Firm as a Dedicated Hierarchy: A Theory of the Origins and Growth of Firms', *Quarterly Journal of Economics*, vol. 116, no. 3, pp. 805–51.

Rajan, R. G. and L. Zingales (2001b) 'The Influence of the Financial Revolution on the Nature of Firms', *American Economic Review*, vol. 91, no. 2, pp. 206–11.

Rajan, R. G. and L. Zingales (2003) *Saving Capitalism from the Capitalists – Unleashing the Power of Financial Markets to Create Wealth and Spread Opportunity*, (New York: Crown Business).

Rappaport, A. (1999) 'New Thinking on How to Link Executive Pay with Performance', *Harvard Business Review*, vol. 77, no. 2, pp. 91–101.

Raymond, E. S. (2000a) 'The Cathedral and the Bazaar'; accessed at: http://www.catb.org/~esr/writings/cathedral-bazaar.

Raymond, E. S. (2000b) 'The Magic Cauldron'; accessed at: http:// www.catb.org/~esr/writings/magic-cauldron/.

Reis, C. R. and R. P. de M. Fortes (2002) 'An Overview of the Software Engineering Process and Tools in the Mozilla Project', in C. Gacek, and A. Budi (eds), *Proceedings of the Open Source Software Development Workshop* (Newcastle: University of Newcastle upon Tyne), pp. 155–75.

Rey, P. and J. Tirole (2000) 'Loyalty and Investment in Cooperatives', IDEI Working Paper No. 123, University of Toulouse.

Rey, P. and J. Tirole (2001) 'Financing and Access in Cooperatives', Mimeo, University of Toulouse.

Rifkin, J. (2000) 'Is Ownership an Outmoded Concept?', *Los Angeles Times*, 10 April 2000, p. 7.

Roberts, J. (2004) *The Modern Firm – Organizational Design for Performance and Growth* (Oxford University Press).

Roberts, J. and E. van den Steen (2000) 'Shareholder Interests, Human Capital Investment and Corporate Governance', Stanford GSB Research Paper No. 1631.

Rochet, J.-C. and J. Tirole (2003) 'Platform Competition in Two-Sided Markets', *Journal of the European Economic Association*, vol. 1, no. 4, pp. 990–1029.

Roider, A. (2006) 'Delegation of Authority as an Optimal (In) Complete Contract', *Journal of Institutional and Theoretical Economics*, vol. 162, no. 3, pp. 391–411.

Romme, A. G. L. (2003) 'Making a Difference: Organization as Design', *Organization Science*, vol. 14, no. 5, pp. 558–73.

Rotemberg, J. J. and G. Saloner (1995) 'Overt Interfunctional Conflict (and Its Reduction through Business Strategy)', *RAND Journal of Economics*, vol. 26, no. 4, 630–53.

Rotemberg, J. J. and G. Saloner (2000) 'Visionaries, Managers and Strategic Direction', *RAND Journal of Economics*, vol. 31, no. 4, pp. 693–716.

Rothfuss, G. J. (2002) *A Framework for Open Source Projects*, Masters degree thesis, University of Zurich.

Rugman, A. M., D. J. Lecraw, and L. D. Booth (1985) *International Business – Firm and Environment* (New York: McGraw-Hill).

Ryle, G. (1946) 'Knowing How and Knowing That', *Proceedings of the Aristotelian Society*, vol. 46, pp. 1–16.

Salanié, B. (1997) *The Economics of Contracts – A Primer* (Cambridge, Mass.: MIT Press).

Schelling, T. C. (1956) 'An Essay on Bargaining', *American Economic Review*, vol. 46, no. 3, pp. 281–306.

Schiff, A. (2002) 'The Economics of Open Source Software: A Survey of the Early Literature', *Review of Network Economics*, vol. 1, no. 1, pp. 66–74.

Schmidt, K. M. and M. Schnitzer (2003) 'Public Subsidies for Open Source? Some Economic Policy Issues of the Software Market', *Harvard Journal of Law & Technology*, vol. 16, no. 2, pp. 473–505.

Schmidt, R. H. (1995) 'Die Grenzen der (Theorie der) multinationalen Unternehmung', in R. Bühner, K. D. Haase and J. Wilhelm (eds), *Die Dimensionierung des Unternehmens* (Stuttgart: Schäffer-Poeschel), pp. 73–95.

Schmidt, R. H. (1997) 'Corporate Governance – The Role of other Constituencies', in A. Pezard, and J. Thiveaud (eds), *Corporate Governance: Les Perspectives Internationales* (Paris: Montchréstien), pp. 61–74.

Schmidt, R. H. and G. Spindler (2002) 'Path Dependence, Corporate Governance and Complementarity', *International Finance*, vol. 5, no. 3, pp. 311–33.

Schmidt, R. H. and M. Weiss (2003) 'Shareholder vs. Stakeholder: Ökonomische Fragestellungen', in P. Hommelhoff, K. J. Hopt and A. von Werder (eds), *Handbuch Corporate Governance* (Cologne: Verlag Dr Otto Schmidt), pp. 107–27.

Schmidt, R. H., A. Hackethal and M. Tyrell (2002) 'The Convergence of Financial Systems in Europe', *Schmalenbach Business Review*, Special issue(1), pp. 7–53.

Schmiedel, H., M. Malkamäki, and J. Tarkka (2006) 'Economies of Scale and Technological Development in Securities Depository and Settlement Systems', *Journal of Banking and Finance*, vol. 30, no. 6, pp. 1783–1806.

Schumpeter, J. A. (1934) *The Theory of Economic Development: An Inquiry into Profits, Capital, Credit, Interest and the Business Cycle* (Cambridge, Mass.: Harvard University Press).

Seifert, W. (2003) 'On Europe plc and America Inc.', *The Finance Foundation Review*, no. 2, pp. 75–82.

Serifsoy, B. and M. Weiss (2003) 'Efficient Systems for the Securities Transaction Industry – A Framework for the European Union', WP Series Finance and Accounting, University of Frankfurt, no. 120.

Serifsoy, B. and M. Weiss (2007) 'Settling for Efficiency: A Framework for the European Securities Transaction Industry', *Journal of Banking and Finance*, vol. 31, forthcoming.

Shapiro, C. and J. E. Stiglitz (1984) 'Equilibrium Unemployment as a Worker Discipline Device', *American Economic Review*, vol. 74, no. 3, pp. 433–44.

Shapiro, C. and H. R. Varian (1999) *Information Rules*. (Boston, Mass.: Harvard Business School Press).

Shleifer, A. and L. H. Summers (1988) 'Breach of Trust in Hostile Takeovers', in A. J. Auerbach (ed.), *Corporate Takeovers: Causes and Consequences*. (Chicago, Ill.: University of Chicago Press), pp. 33–56.

Shleifer, A. and R. Vishny (1997) 'A Survey of Corporate Governance', *Journal of Finance*, vol. 52, no. 2, pp. 737–83.

Siegele, L. (2002) 'How About Now? – A Survey of the Real-time Economy', *The Economist*, vol. 362, no. 8258, pp. 1–20.

Siegele, L. (2003) 'Coming of Age – A Survey of the IT Industry', *The Economist*, vol. 367, no. 8323, pp. 1–28.

Simon, H. A. (1961) *Administrative Behavior*, 2nd edn (New York: Macmillan).

Simon, H. A. (1962) 'The Architecture of Complexity', *Proceedings of the American Philosophical Society*, vol. 106, no. 6, pp. 467–82.

Smith, A. ([1776] 1937) *An Inquiry Into the Nature and Causes of the Wealth of Nations*, Cannan edn (New York: Modern Library).

Solectron (2004) *Annual Report 2004* (Milpitas, Calif: Solectron).

Spence, M. (1973) 'Job Market Signaling', *Quarterly Journal of Economics*, vol. 87, no. 3, pp. 355–74.

Stalk, G., P. Evans and L. E. Shulman (1992) 'Competing on Capabilities: The New Rules of Corporate Strategy', *Harvard Business Review*, vol. 70, no. 2, pp. 57–69.

Stein, J. C. (2002) 'Information Production and Capital Allocation: Decentralized versus Hierarchical Firms', *Journal of Finance*, vol. 57, no. 5, pp. 1891–1921.

Stein, J. C. (2003) 'Agency, Information and Corporate Investment', in G. Constantinides, M. Harris and R. Stulz (eds), *Handbook of the Economics of Finance*, Vol. 1A: Corporate Finance (Amsterdam: North-Holland), pp. 109–63.

Sterman, J. D. and J. Wittenberg (1999) 'Path Dependence, Competition, and Succession in the Dynamics of Scientific Revolution', *Organization Science*, vol. 10, no. 3, pp. 322–41.

Stiglitz, J. E. (2002) 'Information and the Change in the Paradigm in Economics', *American Economic Review*, vol. 92, no. 3, pp. 460–501.

Tapking, J. and J. Yang (2004) 'Horizontal and Vertical Integration in Securities Trading and Settlement', ECB Working Paper Series No. 387.

Teece, D. J. (1986) 'Firm Boundaries, Technological Innovation and Strategic Management', in L. Thomas (ed.), *Economics of Strategic Planning* (Lexington, Md.: Lexington Books), pp. 187–99.

Teece, D. J., G. Pisano and A. Shuen (1997) 'Dynamic Capabilities and Strategic Management', *Strategic Management Journal*, vol. 18, no. 7, pp. 509–33.

Theurl, T. and T. Kring (2002) 'Governance Strukturen im genossenschaftlichen Finanzverbund: Anforderungen und Konsequenzen ihrer Ausgestaltung', Working paper No. 27. Institute of Co-operative System, Münster.

Tirole, J. (1988a) 'The Multicontract Organization', *The Canadian Journal of Economics*, vol. 21, no. 3, pp. 459–66.

Tirole, J. (1988b) *The Theory of Industrial Organization* (Cambridge, Mass.: MIT Press).

Tirole, J. (2001) 'Corporate Governance', *Econometrica*, vol. 69, no. 1, pp. 1–35.

Topkis, D. M. (1995) 'The Economics of Modern Manufacturing: Comment', *American Economic Review*, vol. 85, no. 4, pp. 991–96.

Topkis, D. M. (1998) *Supermodularity and Complementarity* (Princeton, NJ: Princeton University Press).

Tushman, M. and P. Anderson (1986) 'Technological Discontinuities and Organizational Environments', *Administrative Sciences Quarterly*, vol. 31, no. 3, pp. 439–65.

Tyrell, M. (2003) *Kapitalmärkte und Banken – Formen der Informationsverarbeitung als konstitutives Merkmal* (Wiesbaden: Deutscher Universitätsverlag).

van Cauwenberge, S. (2003) 'New Structure for Clearing and Settlement Systems in the EU', *Financial Stability Review*, pp. 83–103.

van Cayseele, P. (2004) 'Competition and the Organisation of the Clearing and Settlement Industry', Discussion paper No. 04–13, Catholic University, Leuven.

van Wegberg, M. and P. Berends (2000) 'Competing Communities of Users and Developers of Computer Software: Competition between Open Source Software and Commercial Software', University of Maastricht.

von Hippel, E. (2005) *Democratizing Innovation* (Cambridge, Mass.: MIT Press).

von Hippel, E. and G. von Krogh (2003) 'Open Source Software and the "Private-Collective" Innovation Model: Issues for Organization Science', *Organization Science*, vol. 14, no. 2, pp. 209–23.

von Krogh, G., S. Spaeth and K. R. Lakhani (2003) 'Community, Joining, and Specialization in Open Source Software Innovation: A Case Study', *Research Policy*, vol. 32, no. 7, pp. 1217–41.

Weber, M. (1922) *Wirtschaft und Gesellschaft* (Tübingen: Mohr Siebeck).

Weiss, M. (2005) 'Organizational Design in the Banking Industry – A Comparative Institutional Analysis of the German Cooperative Banking Group', in T. Theurl and E. C. Meyer (eds), *Strategies for Cooperation* (Aachen: Shaker Verlag), pp. 441–63.

Weitzel, T., S. V. Martin and W. König (2003) 'Straight Through Processing auf XML-Basis im Wertpapiergeschäft', *Wirtschaftsinformatik*, vol. 45, no. 4, pp. 409–20.

Wernerfelt, B. (1984) 'A Resource-based View of the Firm', *Strategic Management Journal*, vol. 5, no. 2, pp. 171–80.

Wernerfelt, B. (1997) 'On the Nature and Scope of the Firm: An Adjustment-Cost Theory', *Journal of Business*, vol. 70, no. 4, pp. 489–514.

West, J. (2003) 'How Open Is Open Enough? Melding Proprietary and Open Source Platform Strategies', *Research Policy*, vol. 32, no. 7, pp. 1259–85.

Wheeler, D. A. (2002) 'More Than a Gigabuck: Estimating GNU/Linux's Size', Mimeo.

Whinston, M. D. (2003) 'On the Transaction Cost Determinants of Vertical Integration', *Journal of Law, Economics and Organization*, vol. 19, no. 1, pp. 1–23.

Williamson, O. E. (1984) 'The Economics of Governance: Framework and Implications', *Journal of Institutional and Theoretical Economics*, vol. 140, no. 1, pp. 195–223.

Williamson, O. E. (1985) *The Economic Institutions of Capitalism* (New York: Free Press).

Williamson, O. E. (1999) 'Strategy Research: Governance and Competence Perspective', *Strategic Management Journal*, vol. 20, no. 12, pp. 1087–108.

Womack, J. P., D. T. Jones and D. Roos (1990) *The Machine that Changed the World.* (New York: Rawson Associates).

Wruck, K. H. and M. C. Jensen (1994) 'Science, Specific Knowledge and Total QualityManagement', *Journal of Accounting and Economics*, vol. 18, no. 3, pp. 247–87.

Zack, M. H. (1999a) 'Developing a Knowledge Strategy', *California Management Review*, vol. 41, no. 3, pp. 125–45.

Zack, M. H. (1999b) 'Managing Codified Knowledge', *Sloan Management Review*, vol. 40, no. 4, pp. 45–58.

Zeitlyn, D. (2003) 'Gift Economies in the Development of Open Source Software: Anthropological Reflections', *Research Policy*, vol. 32, no. 7, pp. 1287–91.

Zingales, L. (1998) 'Corporate Governance', in P. Newman (ed.), *The New Palgrave Dictionary of Economics and the Law* (New York: Macmillan), pp. 497–503.

Zingales, L. (2000) 'In Search of New Foundations', *Journal of Finance*, vol. 55, no. 4, pp. 1623–53.

Index

ABB, 52, 117
academia, 52, 133, 139, 281
Accenture, 159
access, 123, 149–50, 170, 269, 277
accounting standards, 51
Ackermann, J., 240, 244, 252
adaptability, 247–8
adaptive change, 182
adjustment
  continuous, 182–7
  radical, 187–91
Adobe, 269
adverse selection, 25, 49, 110
advocates, 115
Aer Lingus, 190
agency problem, 134, 245
agency setting, 119–20
agency theory, 25–7, 66–6
airline industry, 46–7
Akerlof, G.A., 25
alliances, 100–1, 251
ambiguity, 41, 45, 146
  causal, 73, 89, 187
  of cause and effect, 168
American Airlines, 188
Amnesty International, 145
analysis, 8, 37
Andreesen, M., 254
AOL, 254
Apache, 257, 273
appropriability, 83
asset-specificity, 23
asymmetric information, 105, 109,
  234
Austrian School of Economics, 31–3, 54

Bankers Trust, 235, 239
bargaining power, 77, 83, 96,
  142, 149
Barnevik, P., 117
barriers to market entry, 78
bazaar, 278–9, 287

BCG (Boston Consulting Group)
  matrix, 129
Beatrice, 62
benchmarking, 86, 248, 250
best practice, 176, 248
big leap, 45, 190–1, 250
Body Shop, 117
boundaries
  setting of, 90–5, 150
  within organizations, 112
bounded rationality, 27, 68
brand name, 78
Bugzilla, 264, 274
bureaucracy, 113, 154, 156
business model
  characteristic of, 177–8
  definition of, 175–7
  discovery of, 57
  in open source, 279
  inappropriate, 187, 271
BVR (Bundesverband der Volks- und
  Raiffeisenbanken), 240, 245, 248

capabilities, 80–1
capital budgeting, 129
career concerns, 124–5
career path, 170, 239, 242, 249, 276
cathedral, 270–1, 287
central bank, 208
central counterparty, 205
Central Intelligence Agency, 75
centralization of power, 107
CESR (Committee of European
  Securities Regulators), 200
Chandler, A.D., 18
change, 287–8
  adaptive, 182
  disruptive, 187, 288
choice, 176
Chrysler, 54
Cisco Systems, 97
Citibank, 104

Clearnet, 232
cluster, 87, 101–3, 171, 269
co-determination, 153, 243
co-operative banking group, 233,
    235–6, 240–6
co-operatives, 154–5, 217, 233
co-ordination, 30–1, 107, 127–33,
    170, 191
  and leadership, 117
  in open source, 278
co-specialization, 49, 84, 262
coalition, 138–9, 148
Coase, R.H., 8, 21
codifiable knowledge, 106
collective innovation, 266–7
commitment, 169, 186–7
communication
  and leadership, 117
  network, 31
communities, 156, 173, 260, 277
comparative organizational analysis,
    9–10
  in German banking industry, 246–51
  in securities transaction industry,
    224–30
competence perspective, 33, 80–1
competitive advantage, 81, 115
competitive fragmentation, 220–2
complementarity, 38–40, 150, 165,
    218, 237
  between building blocks, 167–74
  effects of, 174–5
complexity, 69, 166, 263
Concurrent Versions System, 264
configuration
  and co-ordination, 49
  of elements, 40, 174
consistency, 40–2, 174
constituency, definition of, 139
consulting, 84
contagion, 208
contestability, 206
contestable monopolies, 222–4, 227
continuous adjustment, 182–7
contracts
  complete, 27, 64, 119
  enforceable, 146
  implicit, 132
  incomplete, 27–8, 64, 132, 170

  long-term, 21
  relational, 30, 121, 133, 171
  self-enforcing, 24
copyleft, 265
copyright, 266
core competencies, 80–1, 96
corporate culture, 249
corporate governance, 47–8, 134
corporation, 152–3
CPSS (Committee on Payment and
    Settlement Systems), 200
craft system, 20
creative destruction, 54, 73, 82, 179–80
credible commitment, 116
Crédit Suisse, 240
Crest, 211
culture
  communal, 133
  fragmented, 133
custodian, 198
CVS (Concurrent Versions System),
    283, 291

decentralization, 116
decision control, 115
decision management, 114–15
decision rights, 106
deconstruction, 86–8, 96–8, 172, 185,
    242, 278
demutualization, 215
departments, 112, 128–30, 169
deregulation, 57–8
Deutsche Börse, 198, 210
Deutsche Bank, 233–5, 238–40, 243–4,
    246–51
disintermediation, 79, 98–9
Disney, 184
disruptive change, 187, 215, 288
dissolution, 183–4, 278, 282
divisions, 128–30, 169
DTCC (Depository Trust & Clearing
    Corporation), 198, 218
dynamic efficiency, 179, 185,
    202–3
DZ Bank, 240–1, 246

eBay, 55
eclectic paradigm, 13
eclecticism, 10–11

economic rents
  and exit option, 146
  and innovation, 54
  and market positions, 76–7
  and ownership, 137
  and power, 83–4
  and resources, 81–2
  and specific investments, 22–3
  and strategy, 73
  definition of, 48–9
  distribution of, 118
  expropriation of, 114
  from supermodularity, 112
  in Austrian economics, 32
  in networks, 59
  measurement of, 50
Economic Value Added (EVA), 85–6
economies of scale, 42, 56, 87, 205, 258, 262
economies of scope, 56, 88, 205–6, 258, 262
ecosystem of open source, 279–82
efficiency
  definition of, 49–50
  dynamic, 179, 202–3
  static, 178, 202
  systemic, 203
efficiency wage, 120
Elance, 55
elements, in systems, 37–8
employability, 123–4, 147, 170, 239
employees, 141–2
empowerment, 116, 169, 172, 239
Enron, 52, 58, 194
entry barrier, 122, 208
equal compensation principle, 34
Ericsson, 97
ESFRC (European Shadow Financial Regulatory Committee), 200
Euroclear, 232
Euronext, 232
European Central Bank, 209, 231
European Commission, 199–200, 209, 272
European Union, 190, 197
exit, 64, 277
exit option, 146–8, 170, 173, 277

feedback, 42–3, 259
financial system, 61–3
Finanzverbund, 241, 251
Firefox, 256, 277, 281
firms, 94–5, 107, 134
Fisher Body, 23–4
five forces framework, 76
flexibility, 184–5, 247–8
focal point, 61, 76, 102, 116, 132, 288
Ford, 193
Ford, H., 46
foreclosure strategy, 94, 210, 212, 216, 262
foresight horizon, 45
forking, 274
franchising, 24, 100
free software, 264
Free Software Foundation (FSF), 264
free-riding, 22, 25, 121, 259, 289
freshmeat, 275
full-service carriers, 54, 190
fundamental transformation, 23, 49

Gecko engine, 256
General Electric, 122, 124
General Motors, 23–4, 54, 96, 128, 193
General Public License, 257, 265
Giovannini Group, 200, 209
Gnome, 279
governance system, 63, 150–1
government ownership, 154
GPL (General Public License), 257, 265

Hayek, F.A., 107
heterarchy, 247
Hewlett-Packard, 97, 287
hierarchy, 31, 112, 131–2, 169, 247, 269
high-commitment work system, 194
high-powered incentives, 126, 211
hill-walking, 43
hold-up, 23, 49, 58, 79, 94, 101, 152
Home Depot, 122
human capital, 25, 67, 81, 84, 114, 122–3
  at Deutsche Bank, 239
  general, 142
  specific, 142, 149, 169
hybrids, 100–1

IBM, 42, 97, 261, 274, 277, 281
IKEA, 117
Immelt, J., 122
inalienability of human capital, 25, 29
inappropriateness of design, 187–9
incentive schemes, 125
incentives, 214
  and creative destruction, 179
  and ownership, 138
  and power, 66
  balance of, 33–5, 67, 92, 125–7
  for innovation, 32
  for investment, 79, 83, 114, 172
  high-powered, 173
  implicit, 124
  in open source, 275
incomplete contract theory, 27–30,
  65, 91
inconsistencies in design, 182–3
increasing returns, 49
industrial organization, 76
industrialization, 5, 18
influence costs, 109, 115, 132, 148
information
  and boundaries, 173
  and leadership, 117
  and strategy, 169
  and theory of the firm, 91–2
  as public good, 32
  asymmetric, 25–6, 65
  garbling of, 125
  innovations in, 55
  inside, 61, 149
  of intermediaries, 98
  outside, 61
  private, 25
  processing, 131
  transfer of, 106, 108–9
  types of, 105–6
inimitability, 82
innovation, 54, 287–8
  collective, 266–7
  private, 266
insider control system, 145, 169
intellectual property, 268
interfaces, 38
internal capital market, 91, 94, 129,
  170, 173
internal labour market, 94, 121–3,
  170, 188, 239, 242

Internet Explorer, 42, 255
investment banking, 84
investment incentives, 93, 102
Investment Services Directive, 209
investments
  co-specialized, 60
  specific, 28, 65, 118, 234, 276
IOSCO (International Organization
  of Securities Commissions),
  200

JavaScript, 255
job design, 34, 127
job rotation, 129, 169
joint ventures, 100

KDE, 279, 286
KKR (Kohlberg Kravis Roberts & Co.),
  62, 191
knowledge
  and economic rents, 84
  and human capital, 67
  and network effects, 43
  and power, 106–8
  and strategy, 169
  and theory of the firm, 30–3
  as resource, 81
  codifiable, 92–3
  codified, 263, 274
  dispersed, 116, 129
  embedded, 260
  local, 66, 107, 276
  tacit, 67, 116
  types of, 105–6
knowledge management, 108
knowledge worker, 143, 153

Lamfalussy, A., 199
lattice theory, 38
leadership, 76, 116–18, 168, 191, 244,
  247, 271, 278
leading by sacrifice, 117
licensing, 100
Lincoln Electric, 176, 186
Linux, 257, 273, 279
local knowledge, 107, 115, 241
London Clearing House, 211
London Stock Exchange, 198,
  211
low-cost airlines, 47, 177, 190

low-powered incentives, 125
Luddites, 5

macro-efficiency, 50
management, 142–3
Manchester United, 175
market failure, 181
market for corporate control, 147
market segmentation, 78, 130–1
market share, 51
marketing, 78
markets, 94–5, 107, 134, 139
mass production, 177
   system of, 19, 20, 46, 128, 140
Matsushita, 60
McKinsey, 159
McNerney, J., 122
meritocracy, 276
micro-motives, 50
Microsoft, 42, 60, 144, 255, 267, 285,
   286
mission statement, 74–5
modern manufacturing, 46, 177
modularity
   in software, 263, 273
   in systems, 37–8
modularization, 79, 97, 185, 263
monitoring, 26
monopolistic advantage, 54
monopoly in the software industry,
   262
moral hazard, 26, 110, 124, 207
Morgan Grenfell, 235, 239
Mosaic browser, 254–5
Motorola, 97
Mozilla
   browser, 256, 286
   Foundation, 256
   project, 255, 273–5
   Public License, 257, 265
multi-tasking, 125, 133, 146
mutual, 214

Nardelli, R., 122
natural monopoly, 56–7, 180, 201,
   202, 214
NCSA (National Center for
   Supercomputing Applications),
   254
NEC, 97

Netscape, 42, 254–6
Netscape Navigator, 254, 263
network, 101–3, 156, 171, 203
network effects, 42, 204–5, 258, 262,
   268
network externalities, 59–61, 156,
   202, 278
New York Stock Exchange, 215
Nike, 88
Nintendo, 60
Nokia, 185, 274, 281
non-profit organization, 155–6, 214
Novell, 277

Open Source Definition, 264
Open Source Initiative, 264
open standard, 211–13
OpenOffice, 267, 279, 286
Oracle, 267, 270
organizational culture, 132–3, 168
OSI (Open Source Initiative), 264
outside option, 77, 83, 123, 147, 155,
   242
   for human capital, 147
outsourcing, 95–6, 150, 209, 242
overinvestment, 220
ownership, 28, 64, 91, 120, 126, 134,
   136–7, 152
   and incentives, 34
   coalition, 138–9
   exclusive, 137–8
   in securities transaction industry,
      214–15
   mutual, 214
   of open source, 278

parallel development, 273
partnerships, 153–4
patent, 266
path dependencies, 42–3, 82, 85,
   182
pay for performance, 34, 174
peer review, 275
Penrose, E., 80
Peoplesoft, 270
performance measurement, 109–10,
   129, 133, 249
permeability, 100, 113, 129, 171, 173,
   274, 284
persistence, 48, 189

Philips, 60
piece-rates, 126
Pixar, 184
Porsche, 96
positions, 73, 89, 111, 171
  on markets, 76–7, 168, 174
power
  and creative destruction, 179–80
  and economic rents, 83–4
  and governance, 169
  and information, 106–8
  and internal structure, 169
  and ownership, 138
  and specific investments, 63–4
  balance of, 66–7, 75, 79, 114–15
  bargaining, 77
  centralization of, 107, 115–16
  collective, 113
  decentralization of, 115–16, 169
  distribution of, 112–14, 182
  formal, 116, 143, 245
  from incomplete contracts, 28
  generic, 149
  in open source, 275
  ossification of, 182
  real, 116, 143
  sources of, 111–12
price mechanism, 107
private benefits, 93
  of control, 47
private firms, 152
private innovation, 266
profit, 51
project management, 183
promotion, 122, 269
property rights, 27, 120, 134
proprietary standard, 211–13
public good, 266
punishment, 119
purpose of organizations, 74–6

quasi-rents, 23

radical adjustment, 187–91
Raiffeisen, F.W., 235
Raiffeisenbank, 241
reciprocity, 273
Redhat, 277, 279

redundancy, 10–11
regulated monopoly, 218–20
regulation, 78, 102, 181, 202, 208–9, 272
rent-sharing, 119–20
rent-seeking, 47, 113–14, 148, 151, 173, 226, 286
reputation, 52, 132, 156, 183, 245, 276
residual control rights, 28
resources, 73, 80–1, 89, 111, 171
  and theory of the firm, 31
  creation of, 82–3
  specific, 122
returns from supermodularity, 73, 88–9, 132, 145, 167, 174, 186
reverse engineering, 9
rewards, 119, 124, 133, 169
risk management, 207, 220
risk-sharing, 26
RJR Nabisco, 2, 191
rugged landscapes, 43–5

Saab, 96
sales agents, 35
SAP, 267
Schulze-Delitzsch, H., 235
Schumpeter, J.A., 54
screening, 25, 269
securities transaction value chain, 204, 212
segment reporting, 129
self-enforcement, 30
self-regulation, 209, 221, 223
self-selection, 239, 260, 273
seniority, 122
seniority pay, 32, 185
Shared Source Initiative, 286
shareholders, 140–1
Siemens, 281
signalling, 25, 289
signalling device, 259
Silicon Valley, 87
silo, 210–1
small steps, 45, 189–90, 250
sociability, 133
Solectron, 97
solidarity, 133
Sony, 60, 97
Sony Ericsson, 281

SourceForge, 265
Southwestern Airlines, 188
span of control, 116
specific information, 242
specific investments, 22–3, 66, 103,
    111, 123, 132, 136, 270
specific knowledge, 116
specificity, 49
Spyglass, 255
stakeholder, 136, 172, 189
Stallman, R., 264
standardization, 219
standards, 43, 102, 269
    in software, 262
    industry-wide, 156, 281
    open, 59, 211–13
    proprietary, 60, 186, 207, 211–13
    setting of, 58–61
static efficiency, 178, 202
Stern Stewart, 85
stock options, 120, 249
straight-through processing, 207, 210,
    219, 226
strategic alliances, 100, 269
strategy
    and leadership, 118
    definition of, 72–4
    of foreclosure, 94, 212
subadditivity, 56
Sun Microsystems, 281
sunk costs, 23, 47, 140
superadditivity, 39
supermodularity, 38–40, 166, 218, 237
sustainable competitive advantage,
    73, 120, 140
switching costs, 43
Symbian, 281
synthesis, 8, 38, 165
systemic crisis, 204
systemic efficiency, 203
systemic risk, 206–7
systems perspective, 168
systems theory, 7–9, 36–45, 260

tacit knowledge, 85, 106, 131
team production, 21–2, 120–1
3M, 122
throughput, 18–19
Thunderbird, 256
Tinderbox, 264
Total Quality Management, 158
tournament, 122, 275
Toyota, 46, 54, 177, 237
transaction cost theory, 22–5, 67, 91
transaction costs, 21
transparency, 123
travel agents, 98

unbundling, 58, 86, 97
underinvestment, 23, 49, 64, 114,
    123, 212, 267
unions, 142
United Airlines, 194
US Airways, 188

Valmet, 96
value
    definition of, 48–50
    measurement of, 50–3, 85
value chain, 57, 86–8, 95–7, 172,
    242
    securities transaction, 204, 212
vertical integration, 23, 57, 64, 78, 97,
    174, 207, 210–11, 216, 223
virtual company, 88
visibility, 123, 284
vision, 117
vision statement, 74
voice, 148–9, 172, 174, 245, 277
Volksbank, 241
VR Kreditwerk, 243

Welch, J., 122
Williamson, O.E., 22
Windows, 42, 144, 255, 272, 286

Yamaha, 60